Sexual Abuse, *Shonda* and
Concealment in Orthodox
Jewish Communities

Sexual Abuse, *Shonda* and Concealment in Orthodox Jewish Communities

MICHAEL LESHER

Foreword by Dane S. Claussen

McFarland & Company, Inc., Publishers
Jefferson, North Carolina

LIBRARY OF CONGRESS CATALOG ONLINE DATA

Lesher, Michael.
    Sexual abuse, shonda and concealment in Orthodox Jewish
communities / Michael Lesher ; foreword by Dane S. Claussen.
        p.   cm.
    Includes bibliographical references and index.

    ISBN 978-0-7864-7125-6 (softcover : acid free paper) ∞
    ISBN 978-1-4766-1597-4 (ebook)

    1. Child sexual abuse—United States.   2. Sexually abused children—
United States   3. Orthodox Judaism—United States.   4. Conspiracies—United States.   I. Title.
HQ72.U53L47 2014
362.76088'296832—dc23   2014019604

BRITISH LIBRARY CATALOGUING DATA ARE AVAILABLE

Cover image © Ingram Publishing/Thinkstock

Printed in the United States of America

McFarland & Company, Inc., Publishers
  Box 611, Jefferson, North Carolina 28640
  www.mcfarlandpub.com

To my children, Shmuel and Chava Esther:
May you contribute to a wiser and better world.

Table of Contents

Shonda is a Yiddish word meaning "shame" or "scandal." As used by traditional Jews, it can refer to a shameful act or to the public exposure of scandalous information, especially if the publicity will reach non–Jews. The word is often used to "explain" why some truths are best kept hidden; it follows that the way a community reacts to *shonda* may itself be a *shonda*.

Foreword

by Dane S. Claussen

As is known by many and amply detailed in this book, the Orthodox Jewish community tries to handle internally all kinds of matters that not only should, but must be, handled by police, district attorneys and the civil and criminal courts. As writer and lawyer Michael Lesher shows, this isn't just because secret religious courts are not objective, nor because they make bad decisions, nor because they do not have the necessary expertise, but because—in addition to all of these reasons—they do not have jurisdiction. One of the more bizarre, relatively recent developments in U.S. law is the now frequent assumption, indulged even by many lawyers, judges and law professors who should know better, that separation of church and state means that religious organizations (and individuals, such as priests and rabbis) are above criminal law—in other words, that criminal laws that apply to everyone else, all the time, somehow don't apply to Jewish communities and the Catholic Church. (I also note the similar arrogance of U.S. universities that cannot even make a false First Amendment claim, but deal with on-campus rapes via a student committee holding a kangaroo court.)

That is a public policy problem involving Orthodox Jews (plus the Catholic Church and universities) that must concern all Americans. Another kind of problem arises from the way Orthodox Jews make decisions about their own public relations. I don't use the term "public relations" to trivialize the very serious criminal issues, psychological damage and other matters addressed in this book. And it is certain that decisions made by Orthodox Jewish leaders to cover up child rape and fondling, to evade police, bully district attorneys, stonewall the news media and ignore the general public are, on a case-by-case basis, made partially or entirely with the goal (however misguided) of keeping individuals from going to prison, or at least from going to trial. But one does not have to read very far into this book to confirm that the covering up, the bullying and the stonewalling, and more, are also done to preserve the reputation and image of the entire Orthodox Jewish community, both internally and externally.

The public image of Orthodox Jews benefits from both the First Amendment principles of separation of church and state and freedom of religion, and the historical fact of small, new and/or controversial U.S. religious groups seeking (and often achieving) a substantial level of separateness from the general population. All Jews also benefit from Americans' particularly salient sentiment that Jews have been among history's most persecuted minorities, and most Americans' resulting assumption that Jews, of all people, would not victimize anyone else. (Obviously, to many people, the Palestinian situation is a contrary example, even if conceptually or geographically remote for the usually inwardly-focused American public). As Michael Lesher shows here, U.S. Orthodox Jewish leaders worry a lot about the reputation and image of their community; in fact, they worry to an extent some might think bizarre, even fearing that a negative public image of U.S. Jews could ultimately result in their persecution, not unlike how Jews have been persecuted in other countries. (In their defense, to give only one mild example, we should not forget, as most Americans have, that Ivy League universities had quotas for Jewish students— maximum, not minimum, numbers—as recently as fifty years ago.)

Whatever one thinks is a realistic worst-case scenario for American Jews (the most likely one being the assimilation of the Jewish population as Jews increasingly marry non–Jews and leave the faith), it should still be clear— even if Orthodox Jewish leaders don't see it—that a public relations strategy consisting entirely of covering up, stonewalling, bullying, and evading or ignoring prosecutors, police and the public, is doomed to fail.

The recent history of the Catholic Church is instructive. Numerous journalists had learned of various sexual abuse allegations around the country long before the *Boston Globe*'s bombshell reporting in 2002, which generally opened the floodgates of Catholic Church sex abuse coverage. Why didn't mainstream U.S. news media cover the allegations more thoroughly, more often, and much sooner? Overall, it was because responsible U.S. news media don't want to publish "he said-she said" coverage (or, in this case, mostly "he said-he said") in the absence of arrests or lawsuits. Journalists are safer from libel suits when they can quote documents such as police reports and court filings; besides, responsible journalists don't want to publish or broadcast what they think of as mere "gossip" or "rumor." (These standard rationales ignore the point that children very rarely fabricate sexual abuse allegations and when they do, it's often because adults are coaching the children and fabricating claims themselves; for the worst relatively recent examples, see Dorothy Rabinowitz's 2004 book, *No Crueler Tyrannies: Accusation, False Witness, and Other Terrors of Our Times*.) Perhaps Orthodox Jewish leaders learned the lesson that no arrests and no lawsuits mean no (or, at best, little) media coverage. But they need to learn the related lesson: the arrests and lawsuits come sooner or later, and lack of them is no guarantee of avoiding media coverage in the meantime, as already has happened to Orthodox Jewish communities in and around New York City.

This, too, could have been predicted from the unfolding of the Catholic clergy sex-abuse scandal. Even where the majority of the population is Catholic (and where most local journalists are also Catholic, as was the case in Newfoundland when the Mount Cashel Orphanage sex scandal erupted in 1989) even the most reluctant journalists—facing probable public criticism for reporting stories that they cannot ignore—will eventually cover a story that is difficult and unpleasant to cover. (See Ian A.G. Barrie's chapter, "A Broken Trust: Canadian Priests, Brothers, Pedophilia, and the Media," in my 2002 book, *Sex, Religion, Media*.) And while U.S. journalists may err on the side of doubt when covering the Jewish community, for reasons already mentioned, it hardly needs to be said that Orthodox Jews do not compose a substantial percentage of either journalists or the general public in greater New York City (or anywhere else outside Israel).

The experience of the Catholic Church abuse stories (as well as Watergate, and the Clinton-Lewinsky scandal, and many others) is also instructive in another way. When crimes that have been covered up are eventually exposed, public and media outrage is greater—usually much greater—than would have been the case without the cover-up. In fact, the saying, "It's not the crime, it's the cover-up," has been used so often in recent years that even the most reclusive Orthodox Jewish leader should have heard it by now.

The ideal practice in public relations for many years now, starting with Chicago deaths due to cyanide-laced Tylenol in 1982, has been to manage crises by dealing with them head-on, quickly, openly, with a combination of sincere apology and proactive steps. Tylenol's maker, Johnson & Johnson, did this extremely well, as did Coca-Cola during its crisis in 1999. Richard Nixon, Bill Clinton, and the perpetrators and enablers in every political, business or religious scandal that comes to mind, did not. As I write this, in March 2014, the headline on a current Religion News Service article is, "Pope Francis criticized for defensive comments on abuse scandal." That is a lesson for anyone willing to listen. This book by Michael Lesher tells us why that lesson, as well as the reminder that the prosecution of horrible crimes cannot be delegated by public officials to religious organizations, are so urgent.

Dane S. Claussen is a visiting professor at the School of International Journalism, Shanghai International Studies University (China), the editor of *Sex, Religion, Media* (2002), and the former executive director of the American Civil Liberties Union of Nevada and former professor and faculty chair, School of Communication, Point Park University (Pittsburgh).

Introduction

It isn't every day you're accused of being a traitor to your people, so I remember the date pretty clearly: August 7, 2011.

That was the day a particularly toxic email reached my inbox—its author a rabbi from Kew Garden Hills, New York, who assured me that a column I'd published in the *New York Post* a week earlier was "one of the most treacherous acts ... of modern times."

Language like that might sound over the top to most people. But the rabbi was just getting started. Though he disclaimed any intent to discuss "the details of the case," he didn't hesitate to accuse me of "trashing out fellow Jews" in a "diatribe" aimed, in his view, at every last one of my coreligionists in the Orthodox Jewish community. After pointedly asking, "Why couldn't you keep your comments to yourself?" he pronounced my writing "shameful" as well as "treacherous," and wound up with a warning that were he to elaborate further, "I am afraid I will say things I may regret sending in an email."

What had I done to arouse the rabbi's wrath?

In a word, I had told the truth.

Now, I realize that sounds like too pat and too narrow an answer to completely explain what had happened. Yet it perfectly conveys the nub of the matter. Here is the whole story: I had written a column[1]—by no means my first—in which I complained about cover-ups of child sex abuse within traditional Jewish communities. In the column, among other things, I accused leading members of a Brooklyn Hasidic sect of systematically derailing one serious case of alleged child abuse by lobbying the Brooklyn District Attorney's Office with highly questionable "evidence" until the charges were dropped.[2] I pointed out that Rabbi Shmuel Kamenetsky, "one of America's most influential Orthodox authorities," had recently insisted that anyone wishing to report child sexual abuse allegedly committed by a Jew must go first to a rabbi, who would then decide whether or not the complainant could speak to police—even though, in many cases, such a procedure could lead to a flagrant violation of state law.[3] In fact (I showed), Rabbi Kamenetsky's position, bad as it was, was

5

only a weak echo of the pronouncement in a Yiddish-language newspaper printed in New York in June 2000, signed by dozens of rabbis, explicitly calling for the murder of anyone who "informs" on a Jew to secular authorities. And on top of all this—as my column stressed—those same "secular authorities," instead of punishing Jewish organizations that were devoted to protecting accused child abusers, acknowledged their political influence by rewarding them with public funds and special treatment.

Now all that is pretty strong stuff, to be sure, but the rabbi who attacked me didn't deny a word of it—as he said, he wasn't interested in "the details of the case." Nor did he deny my credentials, as a lawyer, an Orthodox Jew, and a writer with considerable experience in cases of child sex abuse, to make the claims I did. His problem with my column was that I had written it at all.

In other words, for this all too typical Orthodox spokesman, the real evil—the thing that stirred his righteous anger—was not that Orthodox Jewish communities tolerate, even protect, abusers of children; the evil lay in the possibility that the general public might learn the facts. Writing like mine could help people to find out the truth about our communities, warts and all. *Ergo*, it was criminal—and so was I.

As a matter of fact, the general public doesn't need me to inform it about sex abuse by prominent figures in Orthodox Jewish communities. Feature-length articles like Robert Kolker's "On the Rabbi's Knee" in *New York Magazine*, as far back as 2006, vividly illustrated what Kolker called Orthodox Jews' "Catholic-priest problem."[4] When Brooklyn District Attorney Charles J. Hynes announced in April 2009 that his office would henceforth cooperate with prominent Orthodox Jewish institutions in the hope of encouraging more victims of sex abuse in that community to report those crimes to secular authorities, he was clearly, if indirectly, acknowledging the same thing.[5] In fact, as this book was being written, a Hasidic therapist and rabbi named Nechemya Weberman was sentenced to 103 years in prison for repeated acts of sexual abuse of a minor, after a much-publicized trial during which seven of the culprit's coreligionists were charged with bribery and intimidation of the victim.[6] That case led the Brooklyn D.A. to publicly denounce "some in [the victim's Jewish community]" for trying "to kill her soul"; he also (correctly) accused many Orthodox Jews of having "intimidated and forced" other sex abuse victims "into silence ... by scare tactics that support the abuser and discard the victim."[7] All this, by now, is obviously a matter of record.

So the implied question of personal responsibility on my part is moot. It's also trivial. No gangs of hooligans are poised on the fringes of Jewish neighborhoods, just waiting for a newspaper column about child abuse as their cue to start the next pogrom. That simply isn't the world we live in, though the anachronistic guilt trip about what "they" will do if "we" give them an "excuse" still comes all too easily to Jewish lips.

Rather, it seems to me, the only real question involved is one that balances moral against social priorities. The Kew Garden Hills rabbi knows as well as I do that an end to sex abuse cover-ups in Orthodox Jewish communities will mean a reordering of the communities' political assumptions, their hierarchical social arrangements and the silence these have imposed on abuse victims. What distinguishes me from the rabbi and those like him really turns, I think, on our respective evaluations of such a prospect. In their eyes, the goal of protecting abused children (by ending the cover-ups) just isn't important enough to be worth disturbing the community's status quo. The rabbi didn't exactly write that, of course, but his criticisms amount to a muddled paraphrase of it.

There is surely no need to stress that I disagree with that sort of thinking. But it does seem worthwhile, in light of the criticism and my response to it, of which more presently, to underline the purpose and goals of the book you are now reading. For what I perceive as information crying out to be disseminated is by no means obvious to the general public. And those who share my knowledge of the broader problems in religious communities like mine do not often share my determination to expose the truth.

So let me be clear. This book is not meant simply to inform readers about the occurrence of sexual abuse in Jewish communities. Other books have already traversed that crucial ground. *Tempest in the Temple: Jewish Communities & Child Sex Scandals*, edited by Amy Neustein, appeared under the prestigious Brandeis University imprint in 2009, and a cluster of other books has joined it over the last few years. Even if these books did not exist, nothing could prevent any curious reader from scouring newspaper archives and reading all about the criminal prosecutions of Orthodox Jews like Rabbis Baruch Lanner, Nechemya Weberman and Israel Weingarten for sex-related offenses against children. While it may once have been taboo even to acknowledge that sexual abuse occurs in traditional Jewish communities, that children are often victims, and that rabbis or lay leaders may be the perpetrators of such crimes, that taboo is not in effect today.

This book's focus, as its title suggests, is different: not on cases of sexual abuse *per se* but on the dismal history of how far too many of those cases have been assiduously concealed both from the public and from the police; how influential rabbis and community leaders have sided with the alleged abusers against their victims; how victims and witnesses of sex abuse have been pressured, even threatened, not to turn to secular law enforcement for help; how autonomous Jewish "patrols," displacing the role of official police in some large and heavily religious Jewish neighborhoods, have played an inglorious part in the history of cover-ups; how Jewish media (with some commendable exceptions) have tended to minimize the problem; how some Jewish communities have even succeeded in manipulating law enforcement officials to protect suspected abusers. This book is an attempt to anatomize these phenomena and to identify the people, institutions and organizations that have made them possible.

Nor do I think it sufficient to lay out the facts of individual histories of abuse and concealment. Even "naming names" will not accomplish the goal this book aims at—though I do intend to be as explicit as the provable facts enable me to be. Instead, I seek to analyze just how and why these things have happened, and why these abuse cover-ups have yet to awaken the outrage of Orthodox Jewish communities generally—even though most of the victims of child exploitation within Orthodox communities are, of course, Orthodox Jewish children, and even though those children are inevitably re-victimized when denied the basic compensations of criminal justice. I also want to suggest ways in which these communities can reform themselves in order to make such cover-ups less likely in the future—and why I think this is vitally important for all of us.

Because such a book would not be necessary if someone else had already written one, a preliminary word is in order about the paucity of published writing on this topic. Considering the frequency and severity of the organized cover-ups this book addresses, it may seem hard to fathom how the subject has escaped detailed analysis so far—especially in light of the Catholic clergy abuse scandal that has rocked the Church since at least 2002. Yet it is no exaggeration to say that sex abuse cover-ups in traditional Jewish communities have hardly been explored in print, apart from the occasional (if sensational) newspaper or magazine article. Until now, nearly all of the published work on sex crimes in Jewish communities has focused on the crimes themselves. *Tempest in the Temple*, a book I've already mentioned, represented a critically important first step toward investigating Jewish sex abuse scandals when it appeared in 2009. But only one chapter of that book (a chapter I co-authored with Dr. Amy Neustein) addressed the problem of sex abuse cover-ups. Apart from *Tempest*, the only analysis I know of in the relevant scholarly literature that addressed this phenomenon was published that same year, as a single chapter in a book dealing broadly with "clergy sexual abuse"—again, an article written by Dr. Neustein and myself.[8]

Why the issue has received relatively scant attention will be addressed later. For the moment, by way of suggesting the dimensions of the problem, I think it is important to stress two related facts: first, that the fledgling scholarship on sex abuse among Orthodox Jews has so far treaded gingerly around those features of the community's culture that tend to promote cover-ups; second, that spokesmen for Orthodoxy are still vociferous in their denial that anything is wrong in the first place. Again, this is not to say that Orthodox rabbis and lay leaders are denying the existence of child sex abuse among their coreligionists. They used to do that, but today the route their denial takes is more insidious, as well as deeply (if unconsciously) revealing. Instead of refusing to acknowledge the occurrence of sex abuse or—the only really honest alternative—candidly announcing that in their view abused children are an acceptable price to pay for the communities' ingrained policy of avoiding secular law enforcement, Orthodox leaders try to dodge the issue by miscasting it. They maintain that any writing that exposes unpleasant facts about Jewish communities must be a product of Jew-hatred. And so, whenever a specimen appears, they respond with indignant protestations of their own victim status. This approach functions to cover their retreat from the facts. It also deepens and widens the terms of the cover-ups they claim to be guiltless of.

Consider, for instance, what happened to Ben Hirsch, president of Survivors for Justice, an organization devoted to advocacy on behalf of Jewish victims of sexual abuse. Months after my column in the *New York Post*, he published his own in the same venue, decrying the toxic effect on sex abuse victims of combining a publicity-averse and politically powerful Brooklyn rabbinate with a compliant District Attorney. Hirsch wrote that influential Orthodox communities were receiving "special treatment" from the criminal justice system that included "passive to weak-willed" handling of sex abuse cases; he added that "the strictly Orthodox rabbinic leadership's conduct" had descended "to levels so deplorable that they begin to tarnish the credibility and reputations of the communities they're employed to serve."[9]

As the material presented in this book shows, Hirsch's analysis was, alas, perfectly accurate. And Rabbi Avi Shafran, an official spokesman for the prominent Orthodox organization Agudath Israel of America, did not actually attempt to disprove any of Hirsch's claims when he denounced the column in an Orthodox magazine a week later. Instead, he conjured demons from the Jewish past:

> [A] recent opinion piece ... called Jews "a small minority of the population ... granted special privileges"...whose "behavior violates the law and infringes on the rights of others." Wielding "considerable political clout"...they represent "a dangerous trend that has been allowed to fester and grow for decades." Jews ... deny "the civil rights of [crime] victims."...Moreover, the piece reports, Jews represent "a demographic tidal wave" and threaten to become "dominant" in the United States.... Oh, my mistake! It wasn't "Jews" to whom the writer, an "activist" named Ben Hirsch, was referring, but rather "strictly Orthodox Jews."

Having garbed the unsuspecting victim's advocate in an SS uniform (Orthodox Jews "fester" and "grow," "threaten to become dominant," enjoy "special privileges," use "clout" to harm the innocent, etc.), Rabbi Shafran could ignore the cautionary message of Hirsch's column: after all, Shafran assured his readers, Hirsch was a "hater" and a "bigot" who "offers the public a hodgepodge of sinister insinuations, half-truths, and outright lies about Jews."[10]

Mind you, Shafran is something of an equal-opportunity trash-talker: in the very same issue of the same magazine, he equated Egyptian Islamic parties with the Nazis and encouraged a nuclear attack against Iran.[11] So I am less concerned with the viciousness of his prose than with its underlying logic. The point to be stressed is two-fold: first, that Shafran's position, which presumably reflects that of the major Orthodox organization he writes for, rules out telling the truth about sex abuse because such truths are "bad for the Jews"; second, that it effectively excludes abuse victims from the Jewish community.

The latter is a particularly interesting feature of Shafran's choice of rhetorical tropes. Behind the lurid *ad hominem* thrusts, Shafran was quite clearly saying that exposing sex abuse cover-ups is not only evil—and therefore unacceptable, even if every word written about them is true—but an attack on "*the Jews.*" But since the arguments he anathematized were obviously offered in *support* of at least some Jews—that is, of sexually abused Jewish children— Shafran's cries of anti–Semitism could only mean that while the abusers and their rabbinic protectors belong among "the Jews," the victims do not: the guilty are part of the religious community, and deserve its sympathy and support; victims are by definition outside it and must be regarded as its enemies.[12]

I have examined this particular polemic in a little detail because it helps to illustrate why my analysis of abuse cover-ups in Orthodox communities must have a wide scope—extending beyond the details of who did what, to a consideration of more abstract features of contemporary Orthodox Jewish culture. As long as rabbinic leaders (and their epigones) are still prepared to regard abuse victims as threats to the community in ways the perpetrators are not—prepared, in fact, to dismiss them as *strangers* to the community by virtue of being victims—no account of sex abuse cover-ups in Orthodox Jewish communities can be complete if it ignores the religious and sociological roots of the hostility the victims arouse. This is why, although this book is not an exposition of Jewish theology nor an examination of Jewish history, I do attempt to identify those aspects of contemporary Orthodoxy that affect its reaction to the challenges posed by sex abuse.

Of course, the book is built first of all from facts, beginning with the outlines of child sex abuse cases in Orthodox communities for which documented narratives are available. In the first two chapters I divide these narratives into two groups—those that have involved something like a just resolution or at least a truthful public summary, and those that have not—in order to juxtapose the similarities and differences between them. That leads to a third chapter in which I analyze the way these stories have been reported—or not—in popular media, and a fourth dealing with community responses to these reports, including the all too prevalent "backlash" against the victims and those who defend them.

The book's second section turns to an analysis of Orthodox community leadership, and how and why this leadership has consistently failed to take up a position in defense of sexually abused children—how, in fact, it has generally done the opposite. I attempt to detail the connections between influential rabbis and other important figures within the Orthodox community, and how the efforts of these key "players" have coalesced on several levels—theological, political, practical—to make it harder for sex abuse victims to press their claims inside or outside the community, while all the time claiming outwardly to be sympathetic to victims' needs. To make this point clearer, I analyze what has happened to Orthodox Jews who publicly expose cases of sex abuse, juxtaposing these narratives against the experiences of Orthodox Jews caught in sexual or even criminal scandals. I show that the consequences of being an accuser are generally more serious than those of being caught in flagrant misconduct, sexual or financial.

How then do Orthodox communities institutionally manage sex abuse accusations? I address this crucial question in two separate chapters. One describes the unique institution of the religious Jewish court or *beth din*, which wields important power within traditional Jewish communities, and to which all too many victims are pressured to take their complaints. These courts, staffed entirely by Orthodox rabbis and governed by rules partly derived from the Talmud and partly cobbled together by the rabbinic judges themselves, lack both the powers and the expertise needed to prosecute sex abuse cases. Yet they exert devastatingly effective power over victims, since they can—and often do—order them to recant their accusations to avoid secular law enforcement, a practice that, as I will show, is not always in keeping with local law, but has never been denounced by the most powerful or prominent Orthodox rabbis. The next chapter discusses another uniquely Orthodox Jewish phenomenon: the development of strictly Jewish "patrols" whereby Orthodox authorities have taken over many of the duties and powers of the police, encouraging victims of crimes within Orthodox communities to contact a Jewish constabulary instead of the secular authorities. In heavily Orthodox Brooklyn these patrols have grown so powerful that some of them receive public funding, yet they operate as private police forces devoted to protecting a specific segment of the population, with agendas that often include suppressing sex abuse allegations.

The third part of the book discusses the religious and cultural factors that have helped to bring about these problems. I argue that it would be deeply unfair, and untrue, to say that Jewish tradition necessarily protects abusers of children. But it would also be untrue to deny that Jewish law, culture and theology have been conscripted for this purpose in a number of ways that, if not corrected, will continue to plague the innocent. Finally, I suggest ways in which traditional Jewish communities can do more to protect potential victims from abuse, and to develop better ways to face the murky questions of sexuality, authority and religious priorities that lie behind the surface of sex abuse cover-ups.

This last point is a complex one, but it cannot be passed over. Sexual abuse is a terrible evil in itself, but the toleration of abusive sexuality and the strategies that aim at concealing or rationalizing it are also symptoms of a culture gone dangerously wrong. Until we understand why so many deeply religious people, convinced of their own righteousness, choose protecting the guilty over defending the innocent, preferring hypocrisy or silence to truth-telling, we will not be able to build a safer environment for the next generation of children. And there is no reason to believe that this is a problem for Orthodox Jews alone. The Kew Garden Hills rabbi who accused me of "treachery" attacked me in religious terms, but he inadvertently slipped me a ray of light when he linked my column about the evil of sex abuse cover-ups to a United Nations fact-finding mission's report on atrocities in Gaza, co-authored by Richard Goldstone. The rabbi condemned that report, along with my writing, as a species of "informing"—but against whom? The targets of the so-called Goldstone Report were not Orthodox Jews but members of Israel's armed forces who had attacked civilians as part of an effort to maintain Israel's military occupation and blockade of Gaza. Bracketing my work with Goldstone's writing suggested that the rabbi's fears ran much deeper than a critique of sex abuse by one of his coreligionists.

And that insight gave me, in turn, the clue I needed to answer him without either defensiveness or anger. After all, how could I be his enemy if, besides me, he felt threatened by the entire defenseless population of Gaza precisely because it had suffered the assault of one of the world's most powerful armies? For that matter, why see me as an enemy at all? Logically I should be a friend. Not only am I an Orthodox Jew, I am one who turned to religion as an adult, deliberately choosing the life of Orthodoxy to the more secular faith in which I was raised. To an Orthodox rabbi I ought to represent a living vindication of his creed. If in fact this rabbi and I were in conflict, it could only be because I believed in his religion's principles more deeply than he did; faced with the reality of sex abuse cover-ups, I saw Judaism in terms of moral demands, while he saw it in terms of communal defensiveness and chauvinism. I tend to think that kind of conflict is relevant to people of every creed and every affiliation, just as how one takes sides in the conflict is relevant to anyone who has to choose between victims and perpetrators.

So, in reply to the rabbi, I took the trouble to say what to me seemed obvious. Referring to the crimes alleged in the U.N. mission's account of the Gaza violence, I laid my faith on the line. "[T]o criticize the [Goldstone] report without refuting its contents," I wrote,

> is necessarily to defend those crimes. And, by the same token, to take me to task for telling the truth, which is clearly the gist of what your email says, is to endorse lying. It is also to defend child molestation, domestic abuse, spousal rape, etc., etc.—all the things the lying has been done to protect. One simply can't have it any other way.
>
> Perhaps this isn't the position you meant to take... But if that's the case, then I would urge you to reconsider ... your assessment of your role in the community and the nature of its contemporary crisis. At the risk of preaching, may I suggest that what our community needs now is not unconditional cheerleading (which inevitably means support for its wrongs) but some moral leadership that can distinguish between what's good for the tribe and what brings humankind a little closer to God?

I never received an answer from the rabbi. In all likelihood I never will. But writing this book is, among other things, an act of faith on my part—call it the concrete expression of a belief—that I will yet have some sort of answer from those who, like me, see religion as a way to strengthen the innocent, and perhaps also as an aid to giving some of the world's ugliest crimes against the most defenseless victims their true names. Many such people certainly exist, and the fate of much more than Orthodox Judaism depends on them. May they find something in these pages that will help point the way to a better future.

PART I

Coverage and Cover-Ups

Dear Family,

You have all turned your backs and walked away from me. My father, my mother, and eleven siblings. All gone....

What is the terrible crime I committed that warranted the loss of my entire family? What could cause parents to abandon a child? Siblings to abandon a sister? And a community to collectively turn its back in silence?

I committed a terrible crime.

My unforgivable crime is that I spoke the truth about my childhood.[1]

1

Some You (May) Know About

...and if we turn to the passage a hundred thousand times in succession ... Francesca will speak her words, never repeating them mechanically, but saying them as though each time were the first time with such living and sudden passion that Dante every time will turn faint.
—Luigi Pirandello[1]

In December 2000, a special commission of the National Conference of Synagogue Youth (NCSY) published a scathing report on the conduct of its officials and those of its parent organization—the Union of Orthodox Jewish Congregations of America (commonly known as the "Orthodox Union" or OU)—for their failure to protect students from a sexually abusive teacher, Rabbi Baruch Lanner.[2] According to the report—issued even before Lanner's criminal conviction in 2002 for the sexual abuse of two female students[3]—the rabbi had been molesting, sexually harassing and assaulting some of his teenaged pupils for decades, while officials at one of the United States' largest and most prestigious Orthodox Jewish organizations[4] had either ignored or actively suppressed a series of credible accusations against him. In fact, as more students complained of his abusive conduct, the Orthodox Union had actually promoted Rabbi Lanner, so that his contact with impressionable young people and his influence over them had increased.[5]

This public indictment of officials of an Orthodox Jewish organization for a cover-up of a rabbi's sexually abusive conduct was as extraordinary for its rarity as for its candor. The fact is, the report would almost certainly never have been commissioned at all, let alone published, had not a Jewish periodical, the *New York Jewish Week*, broken a traditional taboo of Jewish journalism and printed a searing article detailing the accusations against Lanner months before the "official" investigation began. Entitled "Stolen Innocence," the article described the reports of "scores" of women who, as teenagers, had been sexually abused, harassed or propositioned by Lanner while he was supposedly training them in the values of traditional Judaism.[6]

The rare defiance of precedent registered by "Stolen Innocence" was not without its cost. For his temerity, the article's author was promptly vituperated from every segment of the Orthodox rabbinate.[7] Not a single Orthodox rabbi defended the *Jewish Week* in print for exposing Lanner's misconduct; only one, Yosef Blau, offered any public criticism of the decades-long cover-up of the allegations against the rabbi. (Rabbi Blau's honorable stance was, unfortunately, late in coming: eleven years earlier he had participated in a rabbinic court that had ended up protecting Lanner.)[8] Little changed even after Lanner's criminal conviction. One Orthodox rabbi I encountered in a New York subway around that time assured me that the *Jewish Week's* article had "hurt a lot of people" (he didn't say who), and emphatically denied that its author, Gary Rosenblatt, could possibly be Orthodox himself. (He is.)

In fact—and as the pages that follow will show, all of this was tragically typical—the rabbi's strictures against the *Jewish Week* were not only unfounded, they turned reality completely on its head. It was not Lanner's exposure but the long conspiracy of silence preceding it that had "hurt a lot of people."[9] Rosenblatt's critics would have been more honest had they attacked "Stolen Innocence" as an exceptional breach of the ordinary code of silence about sexual abuse among Orthodox Jews. Sadly, the only really unusual thing about the Lanner case is that the perpetrator was punished in the end.

And he almost wasn't, at that.

In 1989, a panel of Orthodox rabbis had heard extensive testimony about Lanner's abusive conduct, including an account of an alleged attack with a kitchen knife on one young man, and many reports of sexually inappropriate behavior. After an 18-hour session, these rabbis concluded that "Lanner had kneed boys in the groin, used 'salty' language, and engaged in 'crude talk [with female students] with sexual overtones.'"[10] But instead of censuring him publicly, the rabbinic panel not only officially cleared Lanner—while keeping to itself all the evidence it had collected—but even ordered one of Lanner's accusers, Elie Hiller, to publicly apologize to the rabbi. After that episode, Lanner's students were understandably reluctant to make their accusations public. All the same, reports of Lanner's sexual harassment, physical attacks, and sexual relationships with vulnerable teenaged students continued to reach officials of NCSY and OU. The officials routinely brushed them aside. Only when prompted by the unprecedented candor of the *Jewish Week*—and, it should be noted, after several influential Orthodox rabbis, having learned about the story before it appeared, failed to convince the newspaper to suppress it[11]—did the OU finally change tack and convene a commission to examine the evidence against Lanner.

What emerged from this belated report dramatically underscored the injustice of the long years of silence. The evidence, once it could no longer be shoved under the rug, admitted of only one interpretation. Not only did the facts indict Lanner, they illuminated a prolonged cover-up by the rabbis and lay officials supposedly responsible for supervising him.

Consider, first, the blatancy of Lanner's abusive behavior throughout a thirty-year career. The NCSY commission could not claim that the allegations against the rabbi were new; on the contrary, it acknowledged that complaints about Lanner had been piling up for many years.[12] Nor could the commission depict the rabbi as a con artist who had skillfully deceived his superiors with a pious façade. Its report noted, instead, that Rabbi Lanner

> denies many, *but not all*, of the allegations of physical sexual abuse in the "Stolen Innocence" article [which detailed his extensive sexual abuse of "scores" of teenagers]; *[he] is silent on the many [similar] allegations* the Commission received that were not contained in that article. Although in some cases Lanner claimed, either contemporaneously or in his Submission to the Commission, that these actions were consensual, most of the witnesses told the Commission that Lanner's advances were unwelcome and that they were scared or confused and eventually attempted to rebuff or avoid him. In any event, the Commission believes that the combination of the age of the girls involved—*as young as fourteen in one instance*— and the position of authority that Lanner held over them, meant that there could not have been meaningful "consent" to Lanner's conduct. Moreover, regardless of any alleged "consent," *Lanner's conduct amounted to a gross and flagrant* violation of *halachic* rules [that is, standards based on Jewish law], *making him unfit to serve as a role model within a religious-youth organization.*[13]

Collectively, these statements paint an astonishing picture of a man who had been trusted for decades, by one of the United States' most important Orthodox rabbinic organizations, with the spiritual education of impressionable teenagers. Publicly accused of sexually abusing his young female students, Rabbi Lanner doesn't bother to deny some of the most sensational allegations against him, admitting by his silence that he repeatedly abused students. Against some of the other charges, his "denial" doesn't even amount to a refutation: his only defense is the patently meaningless claim that these girls—as young as fourteen—"consented" to sexual relations with a married Orthodox rabbi. On top of that, despite clearly admitting to at least a partial range of abusive and illicit sexual conduct, there is not a word of remorse to be found anywhere in Lanner's written response to the charges against him. There isn't even an acknowledgment that anything he did could have harmed his vulnerable students or that any of it was inconsistent with his role as teacher, as clergyman, as spiritual director. If this was Lanner's attitude *after* he was publicly accused—his career obviously on the line—how can anyone suppose that he diligently concealed his illicit conduct during the years his superiors were demonstrably paying little or no attention? (In fact, even one of Lanner's long-time defenders admitted that, among his supervisors, "the perception was that he was cruising close to the boundary" well before the public accusations surfaced; the same man even ventured that Lanner was not "squeaky clean"—an undeniable assessment, however understated.[14])

With Lanner's more or less flagrant misconduct in mind, let us now examine the specific evidence against the rabbi's supervisors—who, of course, were also Orthodox rabbis entrusted with the care of children. The commission's report leaves no room for any claim of ignorance on their part. Reports of Lanner's mistreatment of students had been passed on to officials at NCSY and the Orthodox Union as far back as the 1970s. As early as 1977, according to the commission's findings, NCSY knew of at least three teenaged students with whom Rabbi Lanner had had full-fledged sexual relationships. Indeed, the commission stressed that even to the extent particular officials may not have been "directly aware of some of the most serious elements" of Lanner's abuse, they "were aware of his overtly inappropriate behaviors and frequently abusive personality traits," and "[t]his knowledge alone should have led them to take effective action against Lanner at any one of many points in his career."

But they didn't. Instead, Lanner was allowed to continue teaching for more than twenty years after these revelations, leading the commission to conclude that "by their inaction, members of the OU and NCSY leadership ... enabled him to continue his abusive behavior."[15]

So far the Lanner case closely parallels other stories of child sex abuse in Orthodox communities, except for the fact that the cover-up ultimately disintegrated. But the portrait is not quite finished. No rabbinic cover-up would be complete without the imposition of silence on those most likely to speak out. In this respect, too, the Lanner case is depressingly typical. In its public conclusions, the NCSY commission conceded that "the profound misjudgments made by some in the OU and NCSY leadership in their handling of Lanner resulted in part from a culture prevalent within the OU and NCSY," and stressed that an important aspect of this "culture" was to discourage complaints against the rabbi:

> [T]he many witnesses who spoke to the Commission ... indicated that the OU and NCSY failed to foster an environment in which students and advisors felt free to report misconduct without suffering retribution and failed to have in place appropriate reporting mechanisms and processes. There was a widespread perception that complaints would be disregarded or that the person making the complaint would be subjected to scorn and even banishment from NCSY.[16]

Other critics were still more blunt. "The pattern of protecting Baruch [Lanner] rather than his victims" went back fully twenty-five years, Rabbi Blau told the *Jewish Week*, and reflected "a broader inability within the Orthodox community to acknowledge improper behavior by rabbis."[17]

Unfortunately, that is the exact truth. And still more unfortunately, it is just the beginning.

The long cover-up that enabled Lanner to abuse his students for decades with virtual impunity was anything but an isolated occurrence. Since 1995, when I first engaged with this issue, the evidence of the systematic suppression of child sex abuse charges among Orthodox Jews has, if anything, grown clearer and grimmer. Let me be clear from the outset: the question to be addressed is not whether Orthodox Jewish communities breed more or less child sex abuse than other communities; nor is the question whether Orthodox rabbis are more abusive than, say, Catholic priests. I cannot answer questions like these, and even if I could, I am not at all sure what the answers would signify. What most concerns me—as an Orthodox Jew, as a human being—is the way my religious community handles accusations of child sex abuse when they do appear. Over the years, in case after case, what ought to be a straightforward matter of justice has dissolved in a palimpsest of denial, evasion and double standards, the specifics changing over time but too often tending in the same direction. Charges are ignored or suppressed; victims are blamed; perpetrators, especially rabbis, are shielded from credible accusations on the flimsiest of excuses.

Perhaps the quickest way to gauge the seriousness of the problem is to see how much of this applies even to the *good* cases—that is, cases like those of Baruch Lanner, in which the perpetrator was ultimately punished, at least to some degree. Let us quickly summarize the disturbing background to that unusually successful outcome. First, although he ultimately paid a penalty, Lanner appears to have committed acts of abuse long before entering the justice system. Second, the accusations against him suggest that he abused far more children than the official charges against him—for abusing two female students—reflect. Third, early efforts to publicize concerns about Lanner were unsuccessful; in fact, those attempts were rebuffed or driven underground. And were it not for the unusually strong intervention of a Jewish newspaper, they probably would have stayed that way. As we will see, the Lanner case was typical in all these respects.

* * *

One unqualified benefit of the Lanner case was that it finally brought child sex abuse committed by Orthodox Jewish men into the open. Until recently, the traditional rabbinate never examined its attitudes toward child sex abuse charges, let alone its handling of them, because it refused altogether to acknowledge that such crimes ever occurred in Jewish communities. The conventional view has been candidly expressed by Rabbi Dr. Elliot Dorff, who, despite his experience as a board member of Jewish Family Service of Los

Angeles, admitted that as late as 1993, he believed that "child sex abuse simply does not happen among Jews."[18]

It is only fair to recall that little or no published writing on the problem existed at that date. I myself put out my first accounts of Orthodox child sex abuse cover-ups in 1996[19]; and when I was researching those articles, it was still possible for a prominent Orthodox rabbi—Morris Shmidman, head of the Council of Jewish Organizations of Borough Park—to claim that he had "never heard of such a case" among Orthodox Jews. (As I will show in the next chapter, Rabbi Shmidman was not telling the truth; in fact, he had personal experience in a sex abuse cover-up, though it had not yet been publicly reported. Later, after his organization was mired in "one of the ugliest non-profit corruption scandals of the decade"[20] and he himself was accused by a close associate of having, along with others, "stole[n] or misappropriated hundreds of thousands of dollars from COJO' and two affiliated organizations,"[21] Rabbi Shmidman drifted quietly out of sight until his death in 2004.)[22] Against such a background, ignorance of the problem among Orthodox Jews might be judged excusable.

But what could have been forgivable then, or just barely, is out of the question today. The year 2007—seven years after the Lanner story surfaced—saw the publication of "the first study to document prevalence of sexual abuse in a Jewish population," whose sobering findings suggested that "prevalence rates of sexual abuse in [the Orthodox Jewish] community parallel the rates of abuse in the larger society."[23] In 2009, Brandeis University Press published *Tempest in the Temple: Jewish Communities & Child Sex Scandals* as part of its prestigious series on American Jewish History, Culture and Life.[24] Besides considerable information about the extent of sex abuse among Orthodox Jews, *Tempest* contained a detailed analysis of how several Orthodox rabbis had suppressed credible charges of child sex abuse by a Hasidic rabbi—with the complicity of the Brooklyn District Attorney's office, no less.[25] The following year, under the pseudonym "Eishes Chayil," an author who later identified herself as an Orthodox Jewish woman published a novel entitled *Hush*,[26] which describes a young Hasidic girl's victimization by sexual abuse, and how a campaign of silence eventually drives her to suicide. The book generated something of a stir among Orthodox readers, of which I will have more to say in Chapter 4.

These books did not emerge in a vacuum. In the wake of the Lanner case, communal silence had already begun to crack under the pressure of new communications technology. In the preface to *Tempest in the Temple*, Dr. Jeremy Rosen, himself an unconventional Orthodox rabbi, could already write of "a dishonorable tradition of rabbinic authorities failing to take objective, immediate, and forthright stands on sexual issues."[27] That such a "dishonorable tradition" could even be identified had much to do with the way Orthodox Jewish victims of sex abuse, for the first time, were beginning to find and communicate with one another by means of the Internet.[28] Orthodox rabbis might frown, but Orthodox Jews with complaints gravitated more and more to muckraking Internet blogs specifically devoted to misconduct in their communities. One of those blogs, "Unorthodox-Jew,"[29] was largely responsible in 2006 for the discussion in a major news magazine of a child sex abuse case that arose at an Orthodox school, or *yeshiva*—a first for the issue.[30]

The blogger behind "Unorthodox-Jew"—who for years identified himself only as "UOJ," though now he publicly uses his real name, Paul Mendlowitz—started his blog primarily to criticize misconduct in Orthodox Jewish *yeshivos*. Soon, however, he received so much information about child sex abuse in Orthodox religious circles that he began to focus his blog on that subject. In particular, he publicized sex abuse complaints against Rabbi Yehuda Kolko, who had taught in Orthodox schools for over three decades. That many of his former students accused Kolko of sex abuse was bad enough. But the alleged victims, and UOJ, alleged that Kolko had been protected by the head of his *yeshiva*, Rabbi Lipa Margulies, and by powerful Orthodox rabbis Margulies had assembled in order to intimidate victims over the years. Inspired by UOJ, and by the communication between alleged victims his blog made possible, several men who alleged having been abused by Kolko as children filed a multi-million dollar lawsuit against the school, and other defendants, alleging that the rabbis had knowingly harbored a child molester. The whole story then landed in *New York Magazine*,[31] thus shattering another precedent as a frank discussion of Orthodox sex abuse appeared prominently in mainstream rather than Jewish media.

Kolko eventually pleaded guilty to two counts of child endangerment and received three years' probation. This weak *denouement* to literally decades of allegations against the rabbi was sharply criticized by families of some of his more recent alleged victims. Reportedly, Brooklyn prosecutors actually pressured at least one of those families not to allow the child victim to testify.[32] Notwithstanding the newly aroused publicity around the issue, the Kolko case—no less than the Lanner story, itself a breakthrough for the issue of child sex abuse in popular Jewish discourse—thus ended less with a bang than with a whimper.

Which leads me to stress how the pattern established in the Lanner case applies to Rabbi Kolko's story as well: after more than thirty years of accusations, Rabbi Kolko was finally charged, but only for a fraction of the abuse his accusers alleged; the charges followed decades of silence, during which he is alleged to have abused more boys; and he was protected at every step by other Orthodox rabbis.

And that was another of the *good* cases.

*　*　*

Let us now examine one still more recent. On a cold Saturday morning in January 2007, Rabbi Ron Yitzchok Eisenman astonished his Passaic, New Jersey, congregation by announcing that a young man named Stefan Colmer, who had moved into the Passaic Jewish community the previous summer, was suspected of having sexually abused several boys in Brooklyn.

Other rabbis in Passaic reportedly made similar announcements that day, but since I regularly attend Rabbi Eisenman's synagogue—though I wasn't there on that particular day—it was his declaration I learned about first; and since Rabbi Eisenman opened his synagogue later that month to a community-wide discussion of child sex abuse issues, prompted by the shock waves released by the earlier statements, it seems only natural to focus on his role in publicizing the Colmer story.

That he made such an announcement at all was the first surprise. As far as I know, this was the first time an alleged sex abuser was publicly named from an Orthodox Jewish pulpit in Passaic. I later found out that the public form of the announcement was spurred by urgent demands from a handful of community members who had learned about Colmer's record. But the fact remains that their pleas were heeded. A year or two earlier, they might not have been. (*New York Magazine*'s groundbreaking exposé on Rabbi Kolko and Orthodox child sex abuse cover-ups generally had appeared just half a year before the announcement about Colmer, generating considerable comment among Orthodox Jews; in what would soon prove a predictable pattern, mainstream publicity, as well as local pressure, was probably decisive in nudging the rabbis into action.) The public announcement was doubly remarkable because Colmer had not yet been formally charged. I would eventually learn that Colmer, then thirty years old, had a history of alleged sex abuse stretching back twelve years, and that his most recent alleged victims numbered as many as a dozen. But at the time, his criminal record was spotless.

The same could not be said for the record of Orthodox rabbis and institutions whose paths Colmer had already crossed. That was the crucial point missing from all the public statements on that Saturday morning, as it would be missing from the large meeting held later that month—at Rabbi Eisenman's synagogue—to discuss child sex abuse issues in general. Officials from Ohel Children's Home and Family Services, a large and politically powerful Orthodox-run institution based in Brooklyn, made their appearances at that meeting; one was its Executive Director, David Mandel. But Mandel, "a total gentleman and pleasure to work with" according to Rabbi Eisenman, never mentioned the darker side of Colmer's story he must already have known: that Colmer had been forced, years earlier, to participate in a sex offenders' program run by Ohel; and, still more important, that Colmer had dropped out of the program without completing treatment, while Ohel had done nothing afterward to monitor his actions or to warn the *yeshiva* Colmer settled next to of the risk he posed to the children studying there.[33] Ohel, at least indirectly, was therefore responsible for the fact that Colmer was allegedly able to chat up boys at the *yeshiva*, invite them to his house on various pretexts, and, once there, to sexually abuse them.[34] Mandel presumably knew all this. His audience didn't.

So, although Passaic's rabbis certainly deserve credit for the public announcements—first about Colmer, then about the danger of child sex abuse in general—the apparent openness of the discussion about Colmer's case concealed a cover-up in its history. Those of us who attended did not know at the time that Ohel had "treated" Colmer, along with other Orthodox Jewish sex offenders, in a program it opened in 1997 (allegedly at the request of the District Attorney) "to address the fact that religious pedophiles were rarely prosecuted for their crimes" because "most Orthodox victims and their families [were] reluctant to report abuse to the authorities out of fear of intimidation and ostracism." We did not know that when Colmer entered the program—probably in 2001 or 2002—Ohel, despite knowing that Colmer was a pedophile, made no stipulations to its treatment program providing for follow-up in the event he did not successfully complete treatment. Still less did we know that when Colmer did, in fact, drop out of the program, Ohel did absolutely nothing to protect potential victims: it did not contact the state's child abuse authorities (not even to ask for guidance); it made no attempt to follow Colmer's movements or actions; and its officers did not approach officials of the *yeshiva* where he allegedly did most of his hunting to see if his conduct warranted concern. (Had they done so, they would likely have learned of two boys who had reported being abused by Colmer to a school administrator—a discovery that could have saved future victims.)[35] And few knew—though I did, because I had personally taken the trouble to find out—that Ohel's official rabbinic advisor, Dovid Cohen, had already urged Passaic residents to "stay quiet" about Colmer while keeping their own children at a safe distance from him.

Remember: Ohel's sex offenders' program was established for dangerous Orthodox Jewish pedophiles, ostensibly to protect the community in lieu of criminal prosecution. Yet Ohel's record in the Colmer case revealed the program as an open door for repeat offenders; indeed, it called into question the *bona fides* of the agency's entire approach to the issue. But this critical information went unmentioned at the public meeting where Ohel's top executive officer (whose annual salary exceeds $300,000)[36] appeared as an authority on child sex abuse. "Pleasure to work with," indeed.

Just as we didn't know about the secret buried in the Colmer story's past, the Passaic audience didn't know about an attempted end-run of the scandal that lurked in the story's near future. Among the comments made at that public meeting, one that stands out sharply in my memory came from the meeting's sponsor, Rabbi Eisenman, when he stressed that the event had "the support of all fifteen shuls of our neighborhood," along with their rabbis. This was indeed an unusual show of unanimity. And that very fact underscores the gravity of the questionable events that followed.

Less than a month after the first public announcement about Colmer's alleged abuse, the fugitive once again decamped. Shortly after that, Rabbi Eisenman—the same man who had promised at the public meeting that the days of silence were over for Orthodox child abusers—conveyed an extraordinary message to his congregants, first in synagogue, then via email.

"Three weeks ago," he began, "I stood at this same pulpit and informed you of the possible danger to our children which existed in our vicinity." He went on: "Without going into details and without compromising anyone's privacy, I am happy to declare that the resolution of the specific issue seems at hand and the neutralization of the issue has already taken place."

Since Rabbi Eisenman did not specify *how* the "neutralization of the issue" had "already taken place," most of his audience probably assumed Colmer had been arrested. But Colmer had only shifted locations; it was not even known in Passaic where he had gone. Colmer was still at large, and still—on the strength of Rabbi Eisenman's own prior statements—dangerous to children, particularly if those children lacked the benefit of a public declaration about Colmer in *their* neighborhoods.

Besides being significantly (if unintentionally) misleading, the rabbi's comforting declaration was flawed by a couple of important omissions. First, it said nothing about encouraging Colmer's victims to go to police so that the perpetrator could be charged and, with luck, prevented from harming others. (Given the information available by then, this should have been possible; I and other activists were soon able to reach out to some of the victims' families.) Second, the statement contained not a word about locating Colmer in the hope that his new neighbors, wherever they were, could be warned against him. No doubt unwittingly, Rabbi Eisenman's message therefore conveyed the impression that an Orthodox community's only responsibility in dealing with an abuser of children is to move him out of town. The likelihood that he will go on abusing children in other communities—to say nothing of justice for his victims—seems, in such a formulation, to be a matter of indifference.[37]

In fact, something very similar to that approach was already the operative policy of at least a portion of the local Orthodox community. Although Rabbi Eisenman insisted that "I have received much encouragement and support about the public stand I took ... from the general community," I soon learned that some of Passaic's wealthier Orthodox Jews, including at least one prominent rabbi, had raised money for the purpose of buying Colmer's house in order to ease him quietly out of the neighborhood.[38] That this would have amounted to protecting Passaic's children at the expense of children some-where else—rather like dealing with the discovery of a batch of poison by dumping the stuff in the next town's well—does not seem to have occurred to these leading Orthodox citizens.

As it turned out, Colmer did not drift quietly over the horizon. But not because of the rabbis of Brooklyn, where he had left behind a trail of ignored victims, nor those of Passaic, where the great majority sought only Colmer's relocation. It happened largely because of a chain of other events. To name some of the more significant: the allegations against Colmer were publicized via Internet blogs; I happened to discover Colmer's whereabouts; the families of two of the victims decided to turn to the Brooklyn police, despite rabbinic discouragement of many of those involved; and, finally, the pressure that I and others were able to keep on the authorities helped to ensure Colmer's arrest in Israel, his extradition from there, and his criminal prosecution in New York.[39]

Once again, though, the success was only partial. As with Rabbi Kolko, a suddenly-announced plea deal eliminated most of the charges against Colmer and drastically reduced the jail time he faced. Particularly offensive to many abuse victims was the statement of the presiding judge, in accepting the lenient plea deal, that Colmer "was being treated for his sexual problems"—a flagrant untruth, and one that prosecutors should not have let pass. But did.

When these facts were reported, I told the *Jewish Week* that "child sex abuse victims in the Orthodox community are still fighting every element of the system to get justice.... Few rabbis will support them when they come for-ward; they're attacked by other Orthodox Jews; the Brooklyn D.A. is in no rush to prosecute the offenders; an agency like Ohel will look the other way..." Lonnie Soury, spokesman for a new Orthodox Jewish advocacy group called Survivors for Justice, agreed that the Colmer case revealed

> the ongoing failure of the Brooklyn Orthodox community and its institutions to protect its children because they are instead focused on protecting their own rep-utations and the reputations of the pedophiles. The fact that there are at least 10 more victims who seem to have been discouraged from coming forward ... high-lights the severity of this problem."[40]

Which pretty much says it all.

As of this writing, Colmer has been released from prison, without ever being charged with most of the sexual abuse he is alleged to have committed. The Orthodox Jewish sources who helped me locate Colmer, thus ensuring his arrest, were eventually instructed by "a prominent American *rav* [rabbi]" not to communicate with me or with the *Jewish Week*, which pursued the story.[41] One brighter note is that Passaic's Rabbi Eisenman continues to speak out vigorously about child sex abuse, and to stress that perpetators should be promptly reported to police, whoever they are.

As for me, I certainly don't regret the scores of hours I devoted to the cause of seeking justice for Colmer's victims. But I cannot say that my efforts, or those of many others who fought for the same goal, were repaid with the right result, considering the number of victims who remained silent, the overly lenient plea deal, and—perhaps worst of all—the fact that, to the best of my knowledge, Colmer has never admitted his guilt, let alone undertaken any sort of genuine rehabilitation. This leads me to fear that one day soon, some of the rabbis sympathetic to Colmer may find him an out-of-the-way Orthodox community, whitewash his record for the locals, and install him among unsuspecting people where he can begin the cycle of abuse all over again. One never knows.

A final note: Orthodox community members often discourage the reporting of child abuse on the grounds that the abuser's wife and children will face hardship in the event he goes to prison. That touching concern for the family of an abuser does not seem to have prevented Orthodox rabbis from giving glowing testimonials about Colmer—after he dropped out of Ohel's offenders program—to the young woman who married him, and bore him children, before he fled to Israel. In fact, worry for his family members does not seem to have moved any rabbinic consciences even after Colmer's conviction and prison sentence. None of the rabbis who praised Colmer as a worthy marriage prospect has ever apologized to these additional victims of crimes for which, by any moral standard, those rabbis bear at least partial responsibility.[42]

* * *

These are not the only stories that illustrate the themes developed in this chapter, but additional examples only serve to reinforce the same patterns. Even when the Orthodox Jewish child abuser faces some sort of justice, it is almost always incomplete justice, to say nothing of justice delayed. Most disturbing of all, the "good" cases underline the courage—and sometimes luck— needed by sex abuse victims to overwhelm rabbinic efforts at concealing their tormentors' crimes before the guilty can be penalized at all.[43]

Consider the case of Rabbi Israel Weingarten. In 2009 Rabbi Weingarten, a Satmar Hasid, went on trial in a federal court after one of his daughters, then in her twenties and no longer a member of the sect, accused him of sexually abusing her over a seven-year period beginning when she was barely ten years old. The facts were widely reported in New York City newspapers as the trial proceeded: the young victim testified that throughout her tormented childhood her father would, from time to time, move the family from one Hasidic community to another—sometimes to Brooklyn, sometimes Antwerp, sometimes Israel—while he continued abusing her physically and sexually, with increasing violence, in every locale. This pattern of movement made his rapes a federal crime under a law according to which the transportation of a woman or girl to or from the United States, for illicit sexual purposes, is itself a felony.

Weingarten was sentenced to thirty years in prison after a bizarre jury trial during which he insisted at the last minute on representing himself, a maneuver that gave him the opportunity to cross-examine his daughter personally. Not surprisingly, the young woman found the process "cruel ... like being molested again." "He thought he still had power over me," she added after the trial—doubtless the exact effect Weingarten had hoped to induce.[44]

But the crueler question, ignored in the otherwise sensational coverage the trial received in the tabloid press, was the late date of the trial itself. Why was Weingarten only charged in 2008, and then only in *federal* court? For the sex abuse allegations against him incorporated many serious crimes under New York law, and they were not new: when his wife sought a divorce from him in 2001, charges that he had mistreated the children—with acts including rapes and beatings—were at the core of her case. But Weingarten never faced justice in a state court. In fact, until his victim's resolve carried her to U.S. prosecutors in 2008, Weingarten had consistently been the winner, not the loser, in legal proceedings.

By the time Rabbi Weingarten's wife gained the courage to escape from her marriage, she was well aware that her eldest daughter, at least, had been made Weingarten's "sex slave," to borrow the language later used by federal Judge John Gleeson.[45] But in keeping with Orthodox Jewish tradition, she had agreed to accept the authority of a rabbinic court, a panel of Orthodox rabbis, over the fate of her family as the marriage dissolved. I will have more to say in Chapter 7 about the general role of rabbinic courts or *batei din* (their traditional Hebrew name) in suppressing charges of child sex abuse; here, it is enough to record that the results were disastrous for the Weingarten family. After hearing graphic testimony from Rabbi Weingarten's chief victim, and from her mother, the rabbis not only ignored Weingarten's felonies but actually turned the sexual abuse question on its head. Instead of protecting Weingarten's three daughters—all of whom, their mother argued, either had been or were in danger of being abused—the rabbis ordered all six of the minor children into the sole custody of their father. Seven years later, as Weingarten was finally sentenced, Judge Gleeson would agree with the prosecution that the rabbi had not only used physical violence to silence his victim, but had deployed his influence in the Hasidic community to cause the girl's truth-telling, and her mother's attempts to protect her, to be used against the innocent, making "pariahs" of them both.[46]

That was not all. When the rabbis turned a deaf ear to the reports of Weingarten's conduct—a reign of terror that included "extended rapes, beatings, psychological torture"[47]—the desperate mother had taken her concerns to secular authorities in two New York counties where the family had been living most recently. Yet those officials accepted Weingarten's—and the rabbinic judges'—version of reality, ignoring the victim's pleas and dismissing the whole range of her mother's reports of maltreatment and abuse. Ultimately a Rockland County civil court confirmed the rabbis' custody ruling, leaving all of the young children at their father's mercy.[48] Once again, an Orthodox rabbi who sexually abused children was convicted and punished in the end—but only many years too late, only for abusing one child (despite credible evidence that all three girls were abused), and only after the victim, along with her mother and the one sibling who supported her, endured the torment of being calumniated, and doubly punished (in rabbinic and in secular court) for having told the truth.

Why was Weingarten's cover-up so successful for so long, even after child abuse authorities came into the picture? It is not easy today to assess how reasonable the actions of New York caseworkers, and a family court judge, might have seemed at the time. The record of those proceedings is sealed, as is customary in such cases; the Child Protective Services record is confidential; and we do know that Rabbi Weingarten deluged the local court and CPS with shameless testimonials from "teachers, family and friends, students, colleagues and leaders from the Satmar community." But we also know that Weingarten vainly tried the same trick in federal court, where he offered 103 pages of more or less identical drivel—in which one is particularly depressed to find the young rape victim's school "director," two of her teachers and a former fellow student all denouncing her as "a constant liar" and "actress" who used "crocodile tears to stir the emotions of her listeners."[49] Since Weingarten's blame-the-victim theatrics fell flat as soon as he had to face his young accuser before an impartial jury, it is not clear why they had worked so well to deflect the investigation of putative professionals in the area of child sex abuse. (In fact, Judge Gleeson found the statements offered in his defense by Weingarten's other grown children so inauthentic as to suggest that they were made under Weingarten's "domination and manipulation.")[50]

But whether secular officials were successfully duped, or whether they went along with the rabbis of a powerful voting bloc—a possibility that cannot be ruled out—the central blame for the cover-up must rest with the leaders of Rabbi Weingarten's Orthodox Jewish community. Rabbis, teachers, school official and rabbinic judges had ample evidence of Rabbi Weingarten's abusive behavior, and of the massive deceit he used without hesitation to blame his victim and to conceal his crimes. As a matter of fact, Judge Gleeson, noting that "the [Hasidic] community has embraced the defendant apparently," also stressed that "anybody who watched this trial—who actually came to the trial and watched the evidence would know that the defendant was a vicious predator, victimizing his daughter over a period of many years." Note the judge's conviction that *anybody* who watched the trial would *know* the abuse at issue in the case. That was even true of Weingarten's "defense," which consisted mostly of his personal cross-examination of his daughter, ex-wife and elder son, a blatant display of his determination, as the judge put it,

> to own them once again, to get inside their heads...I had seen fear in courtrooms before but I have never seen anything like what I saw in this case...Anyone present could feel [the victim]'s fear of her father. It filled the courtroom.... [T]he defendant's obvious effort to climb back into their heads failed, and courtroom observers could actually watch them coming to that realization.[51]

Again, Weingarten was "obvious," not subtle; inspired "fear," not doubts; publicly tried not to defend himself but to "own" his former victim. A unanimous jury saw all of this clearly. So did a judge. Is it plausible that Orthodox rabbis who observed at least as much of Weingarten's behavior as these relative latecomers to the case could not do the same? By this standard, the rabbis' defense of the abuser and defamation of his victim—actions consistent with rabbinic behavior in the other cases we have examined here—was far worse than merely negligent.

And once more, let me emphasize that even this was only part of the story. The evidence suggested that Weingarten had done more than the acts for which he was sentenced. Beyond that, it was clear that something could have been done to check Weingarten's abuse long before he was brought to justice, if only members of the Orthodox Jewish community had not bent all their efforts to protect the rapist and to manipulate and deceive the secular authorities charged with protecting his children. Judge Gleeson wondered aloud during sentencing "where this community was for the defendant's daughter."[52] The truth, of course, is that the community and its rabbis were firmly on the side of the daughter's abuser. And just how egregious a case they were covering up could be inferred even from the testimony Weingarten presented from two of his daughters, each one claiming in revolting detail that his ex-wife, not the rabbi, was the real child molester. (He even tried to bring three minor children into court to testify to his ex-wife's alleged "physical abuse.")[53] Yet there was not a murmur of protest from the local rabbis as Weingarten and his young soldiers defamed the innocent—not even at the blood-chilling callousness with which one of the victim's brothers reviled her at the end of the trial: "I didn't look at her. She's not even human."[54] If this is the kind of conduct Orthodox rabbis are prepared to defend, even when privy to overwhelming evidence of a rabbi's long-standing child abuse years before the case goes public, who can doubt their pernicious role in child sex abuse cases generally?

And, of course, not every case has an ending as "happy" as this one.

*   *   *

This chapter's epigraph comes from Luigi Pirandello, and its relevance to the contents may require a word of explanation. Referring to Dante's famous description of Francesca da Rimini in hell, as she narrates the circumstances of her murder and damnation, Pirandello reminds us that no matter how often we read the passage it will always be new: "Francesca will speak her words, never repeating them mechanically, but saying them as though each time were the first time with such living and sudden passion that Dante every time will turn faint."

Pirandello is exploring the paradoxical relation between the timelessness of art, or of any recorded narrative, and the spontaneous, combustible human passions such a fixed history must contain. In writing down the record of these cases, and those that follow, I know I have committed the victims' suffering to a medium in which it is vulnerable to the staleness of documentation and the wasting effects of time. That is inevitable, I suppose—particularly since I am also using these cases as material for analysis.

But I want to stress that no matter how well we come to understand the patterns of the injustices I am trying to record, we should never forget that each story is irreducibly human, and therefore that each story never ages, never dulls, is never reconciled to its facts. Each sex abuse victim I meet confirms Pirandello's teaching. The stories they tell are familiar, repetitious—in some ways they resemble one single story told over and over. But there is nothing mechanical about any of them; nor is there any excuse for mechanical listening, no matter how many times the act is repeated.

I am not so arrogant as to imagine that in writing this book I am acting as other people's voices. They have a right to their own. But I do feel the obligation to make some small redress for the imposed silence that has been a particularly ugly part of their long victimization. Though they are members of a highly verbal and historically conscious culture, Orthodox Jewish victims of sex abuse have been denied the affirmation of their own experience.

Even the relative "justice" dispensed in the cases discussed above has never really addressed that specific evil. "The system failed us," one survivor, now an adult, told me—not only because "nobody [was] there to protect us," but because "no one really even wanted to hear it." He once wrote an account of his experience and gave the narrative to one of America's leading Orthodox rabbis, who told him what he had written should not be circulated because "people will think there's too much hate in it."

So now I ask: in light of what has been written so far, in the face of what can no longer be denied and whose trauma kills in silence, mightn't it be better for religious communities to face the honest anger of an abuse victim than to be deprived of the truth?

2

The Ones That Got Away

The greatest triumphs of propaganda have been accomplished, not by
doing something, but by refraining from doing. Great is truth, but
still greater, from a practical point of view, is silence about truth.
                                        —Aldous Huxley[1]

It was a murky, drizzly morning in the summer of 2006. Lawns and gardens outside the urban grip of New York City had been in bloom for months, but the judicial hub of north Brooklyn, where I was walking, looked like a scene from a black-and-white movie; I could almost imagine that the low, steely clouds overhead had rubbed away whatever color might otherwise have been visible between the Borough Hall subway stop and my destination, which was the District Attorney's office at 350 Jay Street.

Not that there would have been much visual relief in any case. The Brooklyn District Attorney's office is a study in urban stolidity: upright, featureless, combining massive panes of plexiglass with polished steel beams. It stands, a bit oddly, on a recessed lot next to a Marriott hotel, the sprawl of which runs so far along the street that it nearly cuts off the view of the office to casual passersby—almost as if its builders were ashamed of it.

I was going to the D.A.'s office that morning in the hope of reopening the twenty-one year old child sex abuse case against Rabbi Avrohom Mondrowitz, a fugitive living openly in Israel despite an indictment involving five separate children and listing thirteen counts of first-degree child abuse and first-degree sodomy. Next to murder, that is the blackest sort of ink in the New York Penal Code, but I knew perfectly well that if there was one case in New York's history that Charles J. Hynes—Brooklyn's District Attorney since 1990—would prefer to forget, it was Mondrowitz.

The Mondrowitz case stood for everything the Orthodox Jewish community wanted to keep out of public view. The indictment alleged that Mondrowitz, a prominent member of the Ger Hasidic sect, had cut an ugly swath of child sex abuse through Brooklyn over a period of years in the early 1980s. In fact, that was only a fraction of the story: police believe that

33

Mondrowitz abused as many as hundreds of boys during that time, nearly all of them from the rabbi's own Orthodox Jewish community. Worse, rabbinic leadership had apparently hushed up the case for years, before several non–Jewish victims broke the silence by reporting Mondrowitz to police. Rabbi Mondrowitz, who had been an administrator of a school for troubled youth, had even run a psychology practice for children out of a basement office of his Borough Park house years after allegations of sex abuse surfaced against him, while the local rabbis kept mum about what they had heard. Worst of all, at least partly due to Orthodox pressure, Mondrowitz had never been punished: when charges were finally pressed in December 1984, the rabbi fled the country for Israel, where he remains to this day, never having been tried for the horrific offenses for which he was indicted in absentia in February 1985.

If publicity about Mondrowitz wouldn't be good for the Orthodox leadership in Brooklyn, it wouldn't be any better for Charles Hynes; he largely owed his election in 1989, and his tenure in office ever since, to the political clout of the Orthodox Brooklyn rabbinate. Hynes was Brooklyn's first D.A. to boast a "Jewish Advisory Council," made up almost entirely of Orthodox rabbis and lay leaders. Through that council Hynes had certainly learned (if he had ever doubted) that Orthodox rabbis did not want the Mondrowitz case pursued—and, according to all available evidence, the D.A. had heeded their wishes. So to tell the story of Rabbi Mondrowitz was to expose the way Orthodox leadership had buried heinous crimes against children committed by Orthodox Jews, and how it had used a compliant District Attorney as part of the cover-up. No wonder that for well over a decade Hynes had been trying to make the Mondrowitz case go away.

And no wonder that the eight years during which I had been trying to stop him from ignoring it—partly through patient research, and partly through impatient appeals to various reporters—had proved one of my more quixotic efforts.[2]

Still, on that summer day in 2006 there seemed to be one bit of hope. Over the previous eight years, I had been pursuing Mondrowitz alone. Now, at last, there was someone I could speak for: an Orthodox Jew who was prepared to swear that twenty years earlier, as a boy, he had been one of Mondrowitz's victims.

Finding him had not been easy. In fact, I really hadn't found him at all; he had found me. In May 2006, *New York Magazine* ran an article by Robert Kolker about child sex abuse in Orthodox communities.[3] I had spoken at length to Kolker while he was researching the story: we met in Manhattan and I shared some of my files with him, including the steadily-accumulating stack of paper, mostly copies of records obtained from years of requests and appeals under the Freedom of Information Act, about the Mondrowitz case. Kolker had used some of the information (though without naming me) and his article had prominently referred to Rabbi Mondrowitz—not only his alleged history of serial sex abuse, but the fact that he got away unscathed when he fled to Israel.

Mordechai—as I'll call him—was electrified by Kolker's article. For years, he had imagined that he was Mondrowitz's only victim. He had never told anyone, not even his parents, about the abuse he'd suffered in Mondrowitz's basement office as a nine-year-old, supposedly receiving "therapy" from a man who claimed he was a psychologist—though in fact Mondrowitz had no professional credentials at all. And if he *had* told someone, who would have taken the boy's word that a respected rabbi could have done such things? Even when Mordechai remembered every terrifying detail of what had happened, the memory sucked him into a captive solitude: he and his secret had only each other for company.

But Kolker's article had changed all that by describing the sheer scale of Mondrowitz's alleged offenses. And when Mordechai searched Mondrowitz's name on the Internet, he found another name linked to it: mine. Three years earlier, I had been credited in *Newsday* with revealing a part of the cover-up by the D.A.'s office: a memorandum from the Justice Department proving that in September 1993 Charles Hynes had asked the federal government to abandon all efforts to extradite Mondrowitz so long as he remained in Israel. That gave the lie to the office's continuing protestations that it was doing all it could to bring Mondrowitz to justice, and that "we don't know anything about the State Department closing its file."[4]

So Mordechai had asked me if there was anything we could do to revitalize the case against Mondrowitz, who was still living openly in a Jerusalem neighborhood. And I had answered that maybe, if we used cases like Mordechai's to get the Mondrowitz story into the press, and used the publicity to pressure the District Attorney into renewing efforts to extradite Mondrowitz, we still might see justice. That was our errand on that summer morning in 2006.

After being made to wait forty-five minutes downstairs, the two of us finally rode up an elevator and walked together into a prosecutor's office—I as a lawyer, Mordechai, my client, as a crime victim who wanted to add his evidence to the case against Mondrowitz. Yet the two young prosecutors, both from the Sex Crimes Bureau, showed little interest in what we had to say—amazingly enough, since the D.A. still claimed to be committed to bringing Mondrowitz to trial. They refused to take an official statement from Mordechai and, as he spoke, jotted down only a handful of notes. When they said anything, it was to point out that the statute of limitations had run on any charges that might be based on what Mondrowitz had done to Mordechai in the 1980s. We knew that, I said, but we wanted to place the office on notice that Mordechai was available as a witness, a live source who could back up the victims who *had* come forward if and when the case came to trial. We also wanted to express our strong interest in having the D.A. resume his predecessor's efforts to see Mondrowitz returned to Brooklyn. The prosecutors had little to say to that. Their supervisor, they insisted in response to a question from me, was not in the office that day. They were referring to the head of the Sex Crimes Bureau, Rhonnie Jaus. I asked that she call me when she returned. She never did.

Mordechai, always taciturn, seemed mildly disappointed as we left the office. I was aghast. Here was a new witness in one of the worst sex abuse cases in New York's history, and the prosecutors responsible for it didn't even want to talk to him.[5]

Maybe I shouldn't have been so shocked. After all, it wasn't the first time such a thing had happened. And it would not be the last.

*   *   *

Because I have written elsewhere about it, I do not want to rehearse all the details of the tragically mishandled Mondrowitz case. For the purpose of this book—which is to describe how child sex abuse cases in the Orthodox Jewish community have been ignored or suppressed—I want to focus on the astonishing extent of the official cover-up I encountered, and what it reveals about the people and institutions involved.

First, the rabbis. From alleged victims' personal accounts, I have no doubt at all that prominent rabbis knew of credible claims of Mondrowitz's child abuse years before he was reported to police—and did nothing about it. Brooklyn police, including (former) detectives Patricia Kehoe and Sal Catalfumo, believe that Mondrowitz's victims may have numbered in the hundreds, the overwhelming majority of them Orthodox Jewish boys; after Mondrowitz's flight, scores of these alleged victims reportedly told their stories to the detectives.[6] Even apart from the off-the-record statements made to me, it would be very hard to believe that none of these children's parents ever spoke to a rabbi while Mondrowitz was still in Brooklyn. Yet not a single report reached secular authorities until after Mondrowitz was safely out of the country.

Actually, evidence of the rabbinate's contribution to the Mondrowitz cover-up has been publicly confirmed. In 2011, the on-line Jewish magazine *Tablet* published a long retrospective article on the case, in which an Orthodox school principal described learning that three of his students had reported being molested by Mondrowitz. The principal, who didn't want to be named, said he had "called a meeting with the leaders of Agudath Israel, the leading ultra–Orthodox organization in America.... [T]he Agudath representatives were horrified by the finding [that Mondrowitz had sexually abused children], *but they did not go to the police.*" More, the principal was certain that his report was not the Orthodox leadership's first information about Mondrowitz's abuse. "If I were a betting man," he said, "I would bet 100 percent that there were people who knew about it."

Rabbi Yosef Blau, whose activism against Orthodox child sexual abuse dates from the collapse of the Lanner cover-up, has correctly described the belated intervention of the Agudath Israel rabbis as "whitewashing." "Yes, they didn't want him abusing kids," he told *Tablet*, "but did they really do anything? ... [D]id they tell people to cooperate [with police]?" Blau accused the U.S. rabbinic leadership of being "afraid" to engage secular justice officials, while considering Mondrowitz's flight to Israel "enough" of a solution—a charge that rings especially true in light of the rabbis' parallel performance in the Colmer case.[7]

Add to all this the grim reality that not one Orthodox Jewish child, not even one of those who ultimately met with police after Mondrowitz fled the country, ever went before a grand jury. That sort of unanimity couldn't have happened by accident. I will have more to say in later chapters about the long history of rabbinic hostility toward the secular justice system. In this case, it is enough to note that deterring Jewish victims from addressing a grand jury would have served a dual purpose: by curtailing testimony, the rabbinate could limit the scope of Mondrowitz's indictment, and thus the institutional pressure behind pursuing him in Israel; by setting an example of silence, the rabbis would also render the story easier to suppress among the Orthodox rank and file. And even granting the benefit of every possible doubt, I cannot imagine such steps being taken with the welfare of the alleged victims in mind. The primary consequence of discouraging testimony was quite different and perfectly predictable: to protect the rabbis who, for so long, had shielded the accused abuser.

Next, consider the institutions. During his years in Brooklyn, Mondrowitz was one of the top administrators of an Orthodox Jewish school for children with educational handicaps. As in the Lanner case, Mondrowitz's alleged misconduct there was far too flagrant to have been a secret. One of the school's former students has described how, at the age of eleven, he was pressured by Mondrowitz to bring other children into his office or to his home in Borough Park, where the boy saw Mondrowitz fondle "dozens" of them. "I used to bring kids to his house," he told a reporter in 2007. "He'd grab kids in front of me, in his office."[8]

When one considers the sheer number of witnesses implied in this account—and remember, this comes from just one alleged victim out of many—

it is hard to believe that no one at the school ever noticed conduct so egregious, much of which allegedly occurred within the school's precincts. What is more, all sources agree that Mondrowitz abruptly severed his relationship with the school at some time around 1982 or 1983, when he opened an office for "therapy" in the basement of his own home. All the information I have strongly suggests what common sense would dictate in any event: namely, that Mondrowitz only stopped working at the school because he was warned to stay away from children, and that his new, private office practice was a way to evade whatever restrictions the authorities—the Jewish authorities, that is—had unofficially placed on him by that time. It would be nearly two years, and heaven knows how many more alleged victims, before anyone reported him to police.

Mondrowitz also worked with Ohel Children's Home and Family Services, the same agency that would turn Stefan Colmer loose in Brooklyn over fifteen years later. Ohel dealt with Colmer as a known "offender," though the latter had not been criminally charged; in Mondrowitz's case Ohel served as a source of young foster children, whom it referred to Mondrowitz for "therapy." Apart from the fact that Mondrowitz's credentials as a psychologist were entirely falsified, and that a reasonable inquiry by Ohel would almost certainly have revealed the fraud,[9] there is evidence that the agency got reports of Mondrowitz's abuse from some of the children they sent to him, which Ohel "swept under the rug," in the words of detective Catalfumo. David Mandel, Ohel's executive director, laughed off that charge in 1999. But more evidence came my way when one of Mondrowitz's alleged victims told me he had actually known one of those Ohel foster children who had reported being abused by Mondrowitz—to no avail.[10] All this implicates Ohel at least indirectly in a sex abuse cover-up, though it has never acknowledged any wrongdoing in this or any similar case.

Now consider the role of officials of the secular justice system acting under the influence of Brooklyn's Orthodox leadership. It is no secret that Brooklyn D.A. Charles J. Hynes, whose "Jewish Advisory Council" guided him on all issues affecting the Jewish community, courted the rabbis' favor even before he was elected in 1989.[11] Similarly, it is no secret that the Orthodox members of the council did not want Avrohom Mondrowitz prosecuted.[12] (And still don't: one of the former members, Rabbi Herbert Bomzer, said in an interview aired as recently as October 2006 that Mondrowitz should not be extradited from Israel.)[13] Since Mondrowitz was already living in Jerusalem when Hynes took office, it wasn't hard for the rabbis to get their wish. All that was needed was for Hynes to quietly drop efforts his predecessor, Elizabeth Holtzman, had set in motion to have Mondrowitz returned for trial—and that is exactly what he did, though the news was hidden from the public until I uncovered it years later.[14]

2. The Ones That Got Away

Yet Hynes wasn't the only official who yielded to rabbinic pressure in the Mondrowitz case. As early as October 1986, the U.S. State Department was complaining that the Israeli government was giving Mondrowitz "special treatment" by extending his visitor's visa in spite of the pending charges in New York and an open request for Mondrowitz's deportation—a request opposed in Israel, as the American ambassador noted dryly in a cable the following May, "by those whose interests lie in areas other than his guilt or innocence." I have since learned that Mondrowitz's "special treatment" went even farther than that. After specifically refusing to grant him citizenship in 1987, the Israeli government nonetheless issued Mondrowitz an Israeli passport on December 9, 1999, thus immunizing him from any future attempt at deportation.[15] In Israel as in Brooklyn, the Orthodox rabbinate ultimately got what it wanted.

The same pattern continued with infuriating predictability even when Hynes, bowing to escalating public pressure, finally renewed the extradition request some time in 2007. The official two-step never changed. When the case generated publicity,[16] government employees did what they had to do: the U.S. formally called for extradition in October 2007; the Israeli government arrested Mondrowitz, and initiated legal proceedings to return him to Brooklyn, the following month.[17] But once media attention flagged, so did any real progress in the case. Yes, Mondrowitz was denied bail and, yes, a local court initially upheld the Justice Ministry's extradition order.[18] But everything changed at the crucial moment when the case came before Israel's Supreme Court.

"I have never heard of such a thing in all my life," exclaimed the presiding judge, Ayala Procaccia, during oral argument—referring to the fact that Mondrowitz's alleged crimes had occurred over twenty years before the date of his requested extradition. Of course there were reasons for the delay, not least of which was the consistent pressure exerted by Orthodox leadership in two separate countries to shield Mondrowitz from prosecution. Procaccia never mentioned that, however; for her, all the difficulties involved in bringing together District Attorney, U.S. officials and Israel's Justice Ministry for concerted action on the case meant only a hardship to *Mondrowitz*. An internal memo of the Brooklyn D.A.'s office would later describe Procaccia's strident questions about "the timely prosecution of the charges" as "an unexpected challenge"—which they certainly should have been, if the law had anything to do with the matter.[19]

But apparently the law didn't. Years earlier, Procaccia had joined a ruling that upheld her government's destruction of houses owned by the families of suspected Palestinian terrorists,[20] making Israel one of only two countries in the world—the other was Saddam Hussein's Iraq—in which house demolition was a legal form of collective punishment.[21] But when it came to Mondrowitz,

indicted child rapist though he was, Procaccia and the other judges were trans-
formed into champions of the rights of the accused. No previous case on record
in either the United States or Israel has ever seen extradition denied on the
grounds that the two governments took too long to revise their treaty so as to
facilitate the extradition of a fugitive on charges that, despite the passage of
time, were still viable in the country where the crimes were allegedly committed.[22] But that was precisely the line taken by Justice Procaccia in Mondrowitz's
defense. In effect, she penalized Brooklyn prosecutors—and, more importantly, Mondrowitz's victims—for the slow pace of Israel's Foreign Ministry
and the U.S. State Department in negotiating a new extradition treaty. A summary prepared by Israeli prosecutors for the Brooklyn D.A. described Procaccia's reasoning this way:

> It's hard to attribute to the U.S. and to the U.S. authorities that they were "prevented
> from acting" which tolls the statutes of limitations period, when the ability, power
> and authority to remove the barrier by worthy amendment of the treaty was in
> their hands and their hands alone. Let's hypothesize for ourselves that the treaty
> countries would have decided to amend the treaty after 50 years from the date of
> the filing of the indictment against the appellant, then could it be argued that the
> SOL period was tolled for fifty years ... and that it would be possible to extradite
> an elderly man half a century later?[23]

There *are* rare cases in which the inexcusable delay of the *prosecutors* can cost
them the right to claim the indefinite suspension of the statute of limitations.
But no one has ever blamed prosecutors for the delicacies of international
negotiation over the terms of an extradition treaty—something over which
prosecutors have no control, since such bi-national dealing is the work of
diplomats. Besides, according to all relevant precedents, amended extradition
treaties do not amount to *ex post facto* laws[24]; so why should Justice Procaccia
worry about the extradition of "an elderly man" long after his crimes were
allegedly committed? After all, penal laws in both countries allowed for such
a prosecution; it was Mondrowitz's own decision to evade justice that gave
him so many years of freedom. Should his victims be made to pay for *that*?[25]

* * *

Having read this far, you may well be awaiting my pronouncement on
the reason for all this official fumbling and avoidance. Alas, I cannot claim to
know what influenced the Israeli judges behind the scenes—just as I do not
know why, after oral argument, they took more than a full year to announce
their decision. Was it mere coincidence that Procaccia and the other judges
ordered the freeing of this indicted felon—the rabbi *Ha'aretz*'s weekly magazine called "the predator from Brooklyn"[26]—just two days after a massive
earthquake struck Haiti, while international news media were chock-full of

stories about the heroic role played by Israeli crews in rescue efforts there?[27] Was it coincidence that Israeli prosecutors, after a conference call with Justice Department officials and the Brooklyn D.A.'s office, decided not to challenge the panel's ruling, even though Israeli law allowed them to seek a review by the entire Supreme Court?[28]

I cannot say. But I do know things that put a rather bitter sheen on these questions. I know that just weeks after Mondrowitz's arrest, and almost certainly at the prompting of the Brooklyn D.A., a federal prosecutor named Harvey Bartle IV called me to demand that I surrender to the FBI my only copy of evidence that Mondrowitz had illegally obtained hard-core child pornography while in Israel (thus disproving the claim made to me by a prominent Orthodox rabbi that Mondrowitz was under close watch in Israel and had committed no crimes involving children). The timing of Bartle's demand was particularly striking because I had notified federal officials of the evidence I had more than nine months earlier—and back then, no one had expressed the slightest interest. Only when the Mondrowitz story was in the newspapers did the Justice Department suddenly act to take useful evidence out of my hands; Bartle even threatened me with a criminal charge if I didn't comply. It was years before Bartle and the FBI returned the evidence to me—a computer disk containing stored images, now scrubbed of any actual child porn.[29] By the time I got it back, Israeli prosecutors had decided not to charge Mondrowitz for violating Israeli law that criminalizes the possession of child pornography, even though the discovery of child pornography in his apartment had been affirmed in open court.[30]

So I know that government officers supposedly working for justice have at least appeared to be pursuing Mondrowitz's interests instead. And I also know, from the proven facts of this case and others,[31] the truly exceptional power of the Orthodox Jewish community to stifle sex abuse reports—not only internally but with the support of secular officials. Over two thousand years ago, Cicero complained about the political influence of Roman Jews: "You know how numerous that crowd is, how great is its unanimity, and of what weight it is in the popular assemblies."[32] Maybe he exaggerated. But how different is Cicero's criticism from that of one of Mondrowitz's alleged victims who said "there are probably more kids harmed in this community than any other because everything is placed under the rug"?[33] Or that of another alleged victim who predicted to me that the District Attorney would never bring Mondrowitz to justice because he "is listening to people in the community who never want this to see the light of day.... There are a lot of them—and they vote"?[34] Keeping such cases "under the rug" requires exactly the sort of coordinated political effort at which Orthodox leadership excels. It is obvious, after all, that Orthodox Jews constitute a formidable voting bloc in places like

Brooklyn and Israel; it is just as obvious that, wielding such influence, the rabbinate's power can easily be brought to bear on public officials to accomplish its ends. We know such power was applied to the Brooklyn District Attorney, and we can reasonably assume it secured for Rabbi Mondrowitz both the D.A.'s astonishing quiescence in the case (at least until 2007), and the "special treatment" given Mondrowitz by the Israeli government. Whatever remains obscure about the story's *denouement*, isn't it perfectly clear that the rabbinate got what it wanted—and equally clear who paid the price for the outcome?

*　*　*

Let anyone who doubts such an analysis try to explain away the massive cover-up that attended the case of Dr. Amy Neustein, which began less than two years after Mondrowitz skedaddled from Brooklyn. "One of the most tragic and highly publicized cases on record," according to investigative reporter Karen Winner in a book published in 1996,[35] the Neustein case also presents a breathtaking catalogue of cover-up tactics by Orthodox rabbis, institutions and prominent lay officials.

It is impossible today, given a flawed investigation and the subsequent passage of time, to say with certainty whether or not Dr. Neustein's five-year-old daughter, Sherry, was sexually abused by her father, Dr. Ozzie Orbach, in 1986. (As I will discuss later, after a massive propaganda campaign and some sixteen years after the termination of all contact with her mother, Sherry—then 24—declared for the first time that she had not been abused.) However, there can be no doubt about the credible evidence of abuse at the time the case was before Brooklyn child welfare officials. "Over a three-year period, various individuals, including Sherry's grandmother, a foster mother, a nurse, and the child herself made and backed up complaints of the father's sexual abuse," as Winner summarized the facts.[36] An eyewitness, the child's grandmother, observed and reported an incident of alleged sexual abuse by Orbach, Neustein's ex-husband, in May 1986, while he was visiting the five-year-old child. Sherry later confirmed the alleged abuse to Dr. Anne Meltzer, one of New York State's leading authorities on child sexual abuse, who wrote after a clinical interview that she had "strong reason to believe that Sherry had been sexually abused on more than one occasion by her father." Sherry gave a similar account of her father's actions to an investigating caseworker; he acknowledged under oath that the girl's symptoms were consistent with sexual abuse.[37]

With what result? According to Dr. Neustein's parents, a politically prominent Brooklyn rabbi told them even before any evidence had been taken in the case that Sherry would be removed from her mother's home, and that Dr. Neustein would be deemed "insane" because she had dared to accuse her ex-husband, an Orthodox Jew, of sexual abuse. And on October 21, 1986, that's just what happened—by means of a court order that according to Jeremiah McKenna, former chief counsel to the New York Senate's Select Committee on Crime and Correction, "violated the Constitution, our state statutes, decisions of our highest court, and decency."[38] Remember, this was fourteen years before the Orthodox rabbinate was forced to admit that sex abuse can actually happen in Orthodox Jewish communities. And according to McKenna, the rabbinate had close ties to Brooklyn's child welfare agency at the time, the Brooklyn Society for the Prevention of Cruelty to Children, which was specifically "known for assisting divorced Orthodox Jewish fathers in custody proceedings."[39]

The record of the Neustein case leaves little room for doubt that the purpose of such assistance was not just to favor fathers over mothers[40]; it also served the crucial rabbinic policy of squelching public accusations against allegedly abusive Orthodox men. When, in 1996, I met Sherry's grandmother Shirley Neustein—a generous, graying, maternal woman who, by all accounts, was very close to her granddaughter—she told me, her voice halting with unquenched outrage, how an aging rabbi had assured her ten years earlier that "[it was better] Sherry should die than that the non–Jewish world should hear about such things among Jews."[41]

That was only the beginning. Rabbi Morris Shmidman, executive director of the Council of Jewish Organization of Borough Park, reportedly told Dr. Neustein's parents that she was a "mental case." Then, according to McKenna, Shmidman actually arranged a meeting between McKenna's boss, State Senator Christopher Mega, and representatives of the BSPCC to explain "why the court was right" in punishing mother and child for the sex abuse allegations, their shared goal clearly being to ensure that Mega's committee and other state legislators would not investigate. Meanwhile, community activist Thaddeus Owens confirmed that Orthodox rabbis would actually prefer Sherry's death to an open report of sex abuse by an Orthodox Jew: since Dr. Neustein was now a "self-hating Jew," they told him, her daughter's death "would only be justice." Orthodox Jews who knew better were intimidated into silence. "The others are afraid," a rare rabbinic supporter of Dr. Neustein told me, after asking for anonymity. "The opposition frightened them." Chief among the "opposition" he named was Ohel Children's Home. That agency's role in the awful Mondrowitz case had not yet been publicly revealed, but here too it would play a crucial part in demonizing the accuser (Dr. Neustein) and protecting her daughter's alleged molester.[42]

Ohel had good reason to be so interested in damning the messenger. The true story of the case impugned not only the agency's good faith, but even its compliance with New York law. A year after Sherry's removal from her home, one of her foster parents reported to the agency yet another suspected incident of abuse by her father; but there is no record that Ohel ever made the legally-required call to the state hotline, nor has Ohel ever explained that lapse.[43] Even earlier—in fact, less than a month after the agency first got control over Sherry in the fall of 1986—"an official from the Ohel foster care agency ... threatened Neustein with the termination of her parental rights and [admitted] to having talked to Ohel's attorney about putting the child up for adoption"—though the agency had no legal right to do any such thing.[44]

And Ohel wasn't acting alone. State Senator David Paterson (later governor of New York) held two separate legislative hearings into the official misconduct in the Neustein case, concluding before long that "the handling of this case may be linked to powerful players within Brooklyn's Orthodox Jewish community." For the record, he complained publicly of "an intensely ferocious effort made by judges, social services and law-guardian agencies, rabbis, and elected officials to protect the father from an investigation."[45] Orthodox Assemblyman Dov Hikind was part of that "intensely ferocious effort." Though Hikind would later claim to be an activist on behalf of sexually abused children in Orthodox Jewish neighborhoods,[46] he played the opposite role in the Neustein case, in which he gave Paterson a "stern warning" not to interfere with the system protecting the accused molester. "The assemblyman," according to Paterson, "insisted that Dr. Orbach is innocent of sexual abuse." Orbach's own rabbi told the *Village Voice* in 1996 that Hikind's attempted interference was "probably" prompted by Ohel. Small wonder: according to Dr. Neustein, a social worker for Ohel told little Sherry to her face that she had been removed from her mother's home because "you lied about your father" when she reported being abused by him. Nor is it surprising to read McKenna's judgment on the case: for trying to protect her daughter from alleged sexual abuse, he wrote, Amy Neustein was "the victim of a criminal conspiracy."[47]

The Neustein case was my personal initiation into the shadow-world of Orthodox sex abuse cover-ups, and it was an unpleasantly revealing one. From the time I started researching the story around the end of 1995 until the fruits of my labor appeared in print in October and November 1996—first a longish article for the *Village Voice* co-written with Adam Fifield, then a column the next month in the *Jewish Week*—I found it hard to believe that the reckless, often scurrilous personal attacks mounted by Orthodox sources against Dr. Neustein really dealt with the same facts I was gleaning from the documentary record and personal interviews.

Dr. Neustein, Orthodox sources repeatedly insisted, was mentally ill. Yet they couldn't point to a psychiatric diagnosis against this obviously competent woman, who had received her Ph.D. in sociolinguistics at age 23, had published articles in the *Judges' Journal* and the *Investigative Reporters and Editors Jour-*

nal, and even before her legal travails had lectured widely on conversation analysis (her academic specialty), giving talks to such organizations as the New York State Trial Lawyer's Association and a guest lecture at Columbia University's Graduate School of Journalism.[48]

Her daughter hated her, my co-writer and I were told. Yes, there was evidence that Sherry had started to show anxiety around her mother *after* a Brooklyn Family Court judge (notorious throughout his career for his hostility to women)[49] forced the girl into her father's custody. But the record was clear that before being subjected to well-timed pressure from Orbach and his relatives,[50] Sherry repeatedly expressed her desire to return to her mother's home. The expert evaluator picked by Sherry's law guardian confirmed this in a written report[51]; even Judge Leon Deutsch, who ordered Sherry into Orbach's sole custody in 1988, and the following year severed all contact between Sherry and her mother, admitted that nearly eight months after her removal from Dr. Neustein, Sherry told him personally that she disliked her father and wanted to live with her mother.[52]

Sherry was driven to illness by her mother's conduct, the Orthodox sources claimed. It is certainly true that Sherry developed severe anorexia nervosa after being transferred into her father's custody; in fact, she may well have been at death's door when her mother—*not* her father, though the latter was an M.D.—took her to a hospital for emergency treatment in March 1989. Several doctors have testified that Dr. Neustein's action likely saved Sherry's life; one called Sherry "by far the worst case of emaciation I have ever seen."[53] But to blame Sherry's grave psychosomatic illness on Dr. Neustein is to ignore, among many other things, the fact that Sherry's symptoms began shortly after being placed with her father and recurred—costing the twelve-year-old girl eleven pounds—some three years *after* Dr. Neustein and her parents had been barred from all contact with the young girl. (This was Dr. Neustein's punishment for having taken Sherry to the hospital without Orbach's permission; why her parents were included in the penalty is unclear.)[54] By contrast, apart from having "all the symptomatology that she was sexually abused," according to the BSPCC's own attorney, Sherry by all accounts was perfectly healthy when she was removed from her mother's home in October 1986.[55]

Arguably the strongest evidence that Sherry's father, not her mother, was responsible for her frightening decline came from eight-year-old Sherry herself. While bedridden at Brooklyn's Brookdale Hospital in the spring of 1989, still hooked up to intravenous feeding tubes, she was overheard by a nurse telling her father, "You got me into this. If you don't get me out of here, I'm going to tell everything." The nurse duly recorded Sherry's statement, which in turn was reported to child welfare officials—though this crucial evidence was concealed by New York's Human Resources Administration until an honest employee, Rosalie Harman, testified about it at a legislative hearing in Albany in January 1993.[56]

But facts seemed to mean little against the rumors about Dr. Neustein assiduously circulated in the Orthodox community. When my *Village Voice* article appeared, I got a telephone call from a woman who identified herself as an Orthodox Jewish journalist. After asking me whether the contents of the article had been dictated by Dr. Neustein (a peculiar question from a "journalist"), she assured me that she had personal knowledge that Dr. Neustein had "serious emotional problems." Her evidence turned out to be that Ozzie Orbach's supporters had told her so.

A whole new cover-up effort unrolled in 2005, when Dr. Neustein and I, having become collaborators, were about to publish a book on the failings of the American family court system in cases involving alleged child abuse by a father—a subject on which Dr. Neustein is the leading expert and in which I too, as a writer and lawyer, had acquired considerable experience. When one Jewish newspaper mentioned the forthcoming book, and also traced Dr. Neustein's personal experience of a sex abuse charge suppressed in her Orthodox Jewish community,[57] influential Jewish organizations put two and two together and swung into action. In rapid succession, Dr. Neustein and I were pressured by representatives of the (Orthodox) National Council of Young Israel and the nondenominational Jewish Community Relations Council to either drop the book entirely or to purge it of references to the Neustein case.[58]

When that failed, the cover-up crowd launched its *pièce de résistance*: a column apparently written by Sherry herself, then 24 years old, for the *Jewish Press*, an Orthodox weekly, in May 2005.[59] Sherry, who had never before agreed to comment on the case, claimed that her goal in writing was to "counter deceptive reporting." But like all the Orthodox propaganda that preceded it, the column contained little but personal attacks on Amy Neustein, a woman the author admitted not having laid eyes on in sixteen years. Insisting that Dr. Neustein had only fought for Sherry's safety as a way to gain "fame," the column featured, for instance, an arch *tableau* that captured Dr. Neustein "softly stroking her hair with an antique silver brush as she gazed at herself in her bedroom mirror and wondered out loud whether she was pretty enough to be famous." Since Sherry described herself as five years old at the time, this over-the-top image of her mother hardly bolstered her credibility as a witness ("antique silver brush"?). But it certainly suggested malice in the stories she must have absorbed about her mother while in her father's custody, and which (as I had already found) were favorites of the Orthodox rumor mill almost from the moment Dr. Neustein broke the taboo on reporting suspected child sexual abuse.

On provable details, nearly everything in the column—entitled "Silent

No Longer"—was inaccurate. Apart from grossly inflating the incidence of "false allegations" of sex abuse "in court cases,"[60] the column claimed that Sherry had "rarely" seen her mother since "long before the legal battles began." But no one involved in the lengthy Family Court trial ever claimed there had been any significant separation between Sherry and her mother before she was judicially ordered from her mother's home at age six. The column's writer maintained that Dr. Neustein "used to tape record me and pose me for pictures to gain material for her next media performance." But I can find no evidence of Dr. Neustein ever using a tape recording of Sherry in any of her television or radio appearances, and the few pictures she took of her daughter after the girl's removal are quite ordinary—with the sole exception of a snapshot of a severely emaciated (but clearly un-posed) Sherry shortly before Dr. Neustein took her for much-needed emergency treatment. Blaming Dr. Neustein for that one is rather like blaming the Allies, instead of the Nazis, for photographs of concentration camp survivors. The irony is enriched by the fact that secretly made tape recordings of Sherry *have* been distributed to media—but by Orbach and his supporters, not by Dr. Neustein. Adam Fifield and I got one from Orbach as part of an amateur press kit when we researched the story in 1996.

The most puzzling feature of "Silent No Longer" was the recollection the writer claimed to have—"as if it were yesterday"—of the circumstances of the sex abuse allegations she herself made as a child to psychologists and child welfare officials. According to the column, her mother had carefully instructed Sherry ("for hours") to accuse her father of sexually abusing her, detail by detail, as they sat together "on the plastic covered couch in my grandmother's country home.... She then instructed me to repeat the story word for word until she was satisfied with my rendition. At the time, my father had indicated he would be filing for custody. My mother warned that if I did not tell these lies to the judge, I would be taken from my grandmother." Why a mother who had supposedly abandoned her daughter long before this would have been so determined to retain custody, and why the abandoned five-year-old would have so readily obeyed her in this revolting campaign, is not clear; but the bigger problem is the arrangement of particulars. Sherry's grandmother testified that she saw Orbach molesting Sherry in May 1986 in the Ellenville, New York, country home Sherry described in her column. The next month, the Neusteins left for Seattle, where Dr. Neustein underwent reconstructive surgery on her left foot. As far as anyone can make out from the record, Sherry never went back to the Ellenville house; court records show that she and Dr. Neustein were living at their year-round home in Brooklyn when Orbach, without warning, filed for custody in August.[61] Two months later Sherry was removed from her mother's home by court order, never to return.

Now Sherry was emphatic in recalling that she had been coached to accuse her father of abuse "on the plastic covered couch"[62] in the Ellenville summer house, and equally emphatic that the coaching was motivated by the filing, or threatened filing, of her father's custody papers. But this is chronologically impossible, because *Sherry was never in Ellenville at any time the Neusteins were aware of a custody challenge from Orbach.* In fact, Orbach's supporters have insisted, in material sent to me several years after "Silent No Longer" appeared, that the whole abuse charge was fabricated after the Neusteins received Orbach's legal papers.[63] But since by all accounts that didn't happen until August, the only place Sherry could possibly have been coached, as she described it, was Brooklyn, not Ellenville—which means that everything she claimed to remember about the Ellenville setting simply cannot be true. Of course, anyone recalling childhood incidents at a distance of eighteen years is bound to have uncertainties and blind spots. The trouble is that Sherry claimed not to have any doubts; she said she retained each sense memory of the crucial incident—furniture, setting, location, words—"vividly" and "as if it were yesterday," yet the memories she related had to be fictitious. That would make sense only if Sherry had been "coached" by someone opposed to Dr. Neustein, not by Dr. Neustein herself.

An even bigger problem with the account was that it failed to explain why Sherry kept up the lying, if it was lying, for so long. In an email she sent to me and my publisher shortly after her column was printed, Sherry—or whoever was writing the message—insisted that she had disclosed her mother's coaching to her law guardian and to the therapist assigned to her by Ohel. That claim is very hard to credit. The therapist, Zipporah Friedman, testified against Dr. Neustein in Family Court over a year after Sherry had been removed from her mother.[64] Ohel, Friedman's employer, was unremittingly hostile to Dr. Neustein throughout the case, as was Legal Aid Society, which served as Sherry's law guardian. Friedman, Ohel and the Legal Aid lawyers would have jumped at the chance to reveal Sherry's accusation that her mother had fabricated the abuse charges and made Sherry lie to support them. Yet there's not the slightest record of them conveying any such thing to Family Court during nearly three years of contentious litigation; nor have they ever made such a statement to the press in all the years this case has been publicized. They certainly would not have held their peace if Sherry had told them what she says she did.

Another glaring problem is that Sherry did *not* make a claim of having been coached to any of the mental health professionals (at least five) who interviewed her during the litigation. Dr. Arthur Green, whose evaluation was hostile to Dr. Neustein (he had been hand-picked by Judge Deutsch), interviewed Sherry on several occasions well after she was removed from her mother's home, yet she never recanted her sex abuse charges to him.[65] And, as already noted, Dr. Anne Meltzer, the only actual child sex abuse expert who interviewed Sherry (and whose testing of Sherry included anatomically correct dolls, among other things), stated her "strong reason to believe" the abuse actually occurred. Like Dr. Green's, Meltzer's interview with Sherry happened after the girl was taken from Dr. Neustein's custody, when she was presumably speaking without constraint. Under these conditions, why would Sherry maintain her abuse allegations to the experts, while simultaneously denying them to others—who, mysteriously, never reported her recantation?

All in all, it seems most likely that the adult Sherry was misled about her own history; that, with desperate cynicism, the same people who had tried to stifle discussion of her case persuaded her to accept a fictitious past in order to discredit her own childhood disclosures against her father. That Sherry eventually succumbed to the effort (assuming that is what happened) is tragic but not terribly surprising. In fact, such acts are readily explained by child abuse expert Alice Miller, who has written: "Since the fact of abuse must be repressed for the sake of survival, all knowledge that would threaten to undo this repression must be warded off by every possible means."[66] As for Dr. Neustein—specifically praised by Professor Maureen Hannah, in a chapter of a forthcoming book, as one of "a minuscule number of Orthodox women who have gone eyeball to eyeball against the hierarchy of the local Orthodox Jewish community" and become "a champion of women throughout the U.S." (*Domestic Violence, Abuse and Child Custody: Legal Strategies and Policy Issues*, Volume 2, which Professor Hannah is editing together with attorney Barry Goldstein)—she has expressed no doubts about the source or purpose of the cover-up. As she told Professor Hannah, "[T]his is what happens to anyone who speaks out against a collectivity of wrongdoers." The only real questions are, (1) who has been brainwashing whom?—and, (2) are Orthodox spokesmen attacking discussion of the Neustein case in order to protect Sherry Orbach, or is their real goal the exact opposite: to further victimize her, and through her, to intimidate today's young Orthodox victims of sex abuse cover-ups so that they never speak up in the first place?

* * *

After a guided tour of cases like Mondrowitz and Neustein, what is there to add about the history of Orthodox Jewish sex abuse cover-ups that could shock an attentive reader? Given Ohel's role in the Colmer, Mondrowitz and Neustein cases, one can hardly be surprised by the *New York Post's* 1999 revelation about two boys in an Ohel group home who reported being repeatedly raped by a counselor (once at knifepoint) while the agency ignored their pleas for protection.[67] Similarly, it was business as usual when sex abuse allegations surfaced in 1990 against the Hasidic operator of a Brooklyn day care center, and accusing parents told of Orthodox clergymen who had shunted them to a politically influential rabbi, who then discouraged them from testifying. "[T]hey [the rabbis] have an 'in' with the District Attorney's office and hold weight as to whether a case is pressed or not," a friend of one of those parents complained to the *New York Jewish Week*. "They want this one shoved under the carpet." That case never even reached a grand jury.[68]

I should not leave you with the impression that you have only my reporting to rely on for the scale and persistence of such sex abuse cover-ups among my coreligionists. Even the staid *New York Times* has acknowledged the extent of rabbinic control over child sex abuse prosecutions in the Orthodox redoubts of Brooklyn. In May 2012, the Gray Lady reported that Rabbi Chaim David Zwiebel, one of the top officials of the rabbinic organization Agudath Israel of America, had personally informed Brooklyn D.A. Charles Hynes the previous fall that his organization "was instructing adherent Jews that they could report allegations of child sexual abuse to district attorneys or the police only if a rabbi first determined that the suspicions were credible," a position that represented "a blunt challenge to Mr. Hynes's authority." "But the district attorney 'expressed no opposition or objection,'" according to Rabbi Zwiebel.

Rabbi Yosef Blau attended a Hanukkah party Hynes gave the following December. In a room crowded with bearded, black-suited rabbis from Agudath Israel—including Zwiebel, who was actually made keynote speaker at the party despite his scofflaw position on abuse reporting—Blau was one of the few people with any record of advocacy for abuse victims. "Basically, I looked around the room," Blau told the *Times*, "and the message that I got is: You are in bed with all the fixers in Brooklyn.... Nothing is going to change, because these people, the message they got is: These are the ones that count."

Plus ça change... In April 2009, D.A. Hynes had announced the launch of a program supposedly meant to encourage reporting of child sex abuse by Orthodox Jews. Called "Kol Tzedek" (the "voice of justice," in Hebrew), the new program was a partnership between the D.A.'s office and, of all institutions, Ohel Children's Home and Family Services. To no one's surprise, the main consequence of the Kol Tzedek partnership was a new policy—unique in New York—according to which Hynes' office stopped announcing the name of any Orthodox Jew charged with sex abuse, even after conviction. "I think that's [not naming suspects] where the rabbis put a little pressure on him," admitted Rabbi Shea Hecht (an informal adviser and the son of one of Hynes' original Jewish Advisory Council members). Hynes claimed that the policy was necessary because of the danger that giving out the perpetrators' names would indirectly identify victims, frightening them off when their testimony was vital. But former prosecutors "said the policy seemed to make little sense," according to the *Times*. "The idea is that the more information you give out, the more likely it is that victims might come forward with complaints," one stressed, calling Hynes' protection of perpetrators' identity "illogical, and almost perverse."[69] Which it is—except when viewed as part of the Orthodox community's campaign of concealment and denial. Under pressure, rabbinic leadership will tolerate some prosecutions for child sex abuse under some conditions. But the rabbis still want to control the circumstances under which a prosecution can take place, and to minimize the public consequences when a charge actually moves ahead in the secular courts. That's what the "voice of justice" says—at any rate, when the rabbis write the script.

* * *

To illustrate what these rabbinic imperatives really mean for abuse victims, let us consider, finally, two recent and wrenching cases—one in an ultra–Orthodox enclave in the West Bank, the other in Brooklyn.

Early in 2013, news sources in Israel began to report that a five-year-old girl had been sexually assaulted on her way to a preschool in ultra–Orthodox Modi'in Illit, a Jewish West Bank settlement. "Police suspect that some people have information about the incident," reported the Israeli newspaper *Israel Hayom*, "but have been pressured by rabbis to keep it under wraps."

"Pressured" is right: a few days after a preschool superintendent confirmed to police that she had treated the rape victim—even though the woman refused to elaborate, insisting, "I vowed not to say anything"—she suddenly reversed herself and insisted publicly that she had made up the story, hoping "to help the many children who had experienced sexual assault but did not get the treatment they need." In a final swerve of poetic injustice, police are now considering whether to charge *her* with a crime.[70] As for me, I am waiting—with little optimism—for Orthodox public opinion to muster some show of support for the alleged victim (to say nothing of the "many" others mentioned by the superintendent), and some defiance of the rabbinic cover-up pressure that is presumably being applied to those in the know.

So much for the Middle East. Are abused Orthodox Jewish children any better off in the United States, in the heart of New York City? Not according to Joel Engelman, who says he was first abused by an older boy while he was a student at an elementary-school level *yeshiva* in Williamsburg, Brooklyn. His Hasidic parents did not go to the police, but they did alert the school's principal, Avrohom Reichman. The older boy's abusive behavior stopped. But almost at once, Engelman, then eight years old, was summoned to Rabbi Reichman's office.

"I remember him telling me, 'Close the door behind you,' and he motioned for me to get on his lap," Engelman later recalled. Reluctantly he did as he was told, and the normally stern Rabbi Reichman unbent a little, asking him questions about how he liked school, how his day was going. "This started becoming a pattern of him calling me into the office, telling me to get on his lap, starting to swivel the chair ... and he would sort of caress me, my shoulders, and then every now and then, his hands would sort of find themselves a little lower on my body and sometimes on my genitals." This went on about twice a week, says Engelman, for two months.[71]

According to Joel's mother, Pearl Engelman, the school briefly removed Rabbi Reichman when the family complained years later, while continuing to deny any wrongdoing on his part. Then, when Joel turned 23, too old to file charges under the state's statute of limitations, Reichman suddenly returned to teaching.[72]

Janet Heimlich, author of *Breaking Their Will: Shedding Light on Religious Child Maltreatment*, tried without success to get a comment from Rabbi Reichman or his school about Engelman's accusations; all they would say was that they don't share information with "the media." But Engelman—a soft-spoken young man who is now a rock drummer—says that when, as a young adult, he confronted school officials about his abuse, they repeatedly put him off, claiming that rabbis would "deal" with Reichman. That went on until the day after the statute of limitations had run on any abuse claims he might make to police.

Then, he says, the rabbis' tone turned harsh: "There's nothing you can do," they told him. "If you put up a fight, we're a lot stronger than you.... And that was their response: 'We decided that he's not so harmful. Go fly a kite.'"[73]

3

Child Sex Abuse as News

"Truth, which is one of the few really great and precious things in life, cannot be bought. Man receives it as a gift, like love or beauty. But a newspaper is a commodity, which is bought and sold.... To see history as an accumulation of events is meaningless. What matters is the significance of the events. But we shall not discover that in the newspapers...."

—Franz Kafka[1]

"I was as uninformed and naïve about child sexual abuse [in the 1990s] as virtually everyone else," wrote Rabbi Dr. Elliot Dorff in comments from which I quoted in Chapter 1. "It was completely off the radar screen."[2]

"Off the radar screen"? Even twenty years ago, Rabbi Dorff was far better situated than most Jewish clergymen to know about the extent and severity of child sexual abuse in traditional Jewish communities. As a former president of Jewish Family Services of Los Angeles, he had access to plenty of information about domestic abuse issues.[3] And he was a man of sufficiently wide learning to connect what he knew about hidden troubles in Jewish family life with wider patterns of sexual misconduct. How could someone like Dorff have been so "naïve" as not to know that if child sexual abuse was not being discussed among Orthodox Jews, this was only because the subject was taboo? Couldn't he have deduced, from what he knew, that something was amiss?

Yet what seems astonishing at first blush is actually not too difficult to understand. Even Dorff could know little of what was really happening to victims of child sex abuse—or what was being done to suppress the truth about their plight—apart from what he could read in the press. And as of the late 1990s, that amounted to virtually nothing.

Oh, here and there one might encounter a relevant piece of information: a snippet in the *New York Times* in December 1984 mentioning the flight of Rabbi Avrohom Mondrowitz, wanted on charges of first-degree child abuse and sodomy[4]; a column inveighing against the atrocious mishandling of the evidence of child abuse in the Neustein case.[5] But that was about all. Rabbi

53

Irving "Yitz" Greenberg, a well known but mostly marginal figure in American Orthodoxy, was the first to mention the subject of child sex abuse in print from within the Orthodox clergy (as far as I know), but even he did not pick up the theme until 1990, though when he did it was in sharp language: "Spiritual leaders who ignore or even cover up the presence of sexual abuse, Jewish media that continue the conspiracy of silence by acting as if this does not happen ... bring upon themselves the judgment that the Torah places on the accessory and the bystander."[6] Note that Greenberg pointedly included "Jewish media" in the "conspiracy of silence" about sex abuse. He was correct: even the few and exceptional glimpses of the issue that surfaced during the 1980s and 1990s attracted little attention in popular media, let alone the Jewish media.

There is more coverage today, certainly, but how adequately it probes the real nature of the problem is another question. True, most of the Orthodox Jews I know seem to think the subject has received more than enough attention already: they assume that Jewish publications (except for those directly controlled by Orthodox publishers) and mainstream media have been straining at the bit to print anything that can embarrass the Orthodox community. In particular, Orthodox Jews tend to assume that newspapers delight in trapping Orthodox men, especially rabbis, in sex scandals whenever and however they can. I no longer bother to count my coreligionists who assure me that nothing could possibly be easier than to interest the *Times* or the *Jewish Week* in stories about bearded Hasidim molesting young children.

Reality tells a different tale. I would be surprised if any unprejudiced reader or viewer, perusing the current reporting on child sex abuse, could discern an aggressive preference for the "anti–Orthodox" story. But an unprejudiced Orthodox reader may be hard to find. Well aware of the sensitivity of Jewish media to the reactions of Orthodox subscribers—a sensitivity shared, more or less, by secular publications in areas with large Orthodox communities—rabbinic publicists stoke grievances among their coreligionists, tirelessly indicting the mainstream press for "bias" against the Orthodox.[7] Within the intended audience it's an argument they can hardly lose, because it rests on assumption rather than fact. (Orthodox Jews believe that they are the prime targets of anti–Semitism, and that less traditional Jews resent them for being "too Jewish.") And to the extent the rabbis succeed in stirring hostile reactions to press coverage, they achieve their objective: pressure on the media for less searching reporting of the community, which in turn plays its part in inhibiting that coverage.

The first point to grasp, then, is that criticism of press coverage by the Orthodox leadership is meaningless as an index of the unfairness or thoroughness of that coverage, because the criticism's real purpose is political rather than corrective. A glance at the timing and substance of what the Orthodox critics write is usually enough to expose its tendentious underpinnings. This criticism cannot be explained away as a defensive reaction to hostile coverage of sex scandals, as often alleged[8]; preemptive attacks on the press were being launched by Orthodox spokesmen well before such scandals became a public issue. In 1994, six years ahead of the Lanner story, Sheldon Rudoff—a one-time president of the Orthodox Union who also played a key role in the scandal-ridden Conference on Material Claims Against Germany[9]—raged in the *Jewish Journal* about the secular media's putative anti–Orthodox bigotry, his chief exhibit being a column by the liberal Jewish editor Michael Lerner in the *New York Times* that compared ultra–Orthodox West Bank settlers to Palestinian terrorists.[10] Rudoff's choice of evidence is instructive. Many of the well-documented acts of the Orthodox settlers against indigenous Palestinians—beatings, crop burnings, destruction of mosques and greenhouses, systematic vandalism, armed raids on schoolchildren, to say nothing of car bombings, murders, etc.[11]—are in fact classical examples of terrorism. To denounce Lerner's juxtaposition of Jewish and Arab terrorist violence as a "smear of the Orthodox community," as Rudoff did, is necessarily to adopt the (unstated) premise that Orthodox Jews cannot be judged by the same standards as other people. I will have more to say about this sort of exceptionalism in later chapters. For now, it is enough to observe the irony of railing at the press for a putative double standard against Orthodox Jews, while all the time relying on one's own double standard to make the case. The point is central: it's not the media that single out the Orthodox for special treatment, it's the Orthodox demanding special treatment and crying foul when they don't get it.

Anyone who doubts that need only observe how Orthodox animosity toward the mainstream press runs just as high in the rare case in which the conventional relations of the two are inverted. Recently, the rabbis and residents of Nachlaot, a small Jerusalem neighborhood, publicly declared that their community had been preyed upon by several child molesters.[12] After testifying before a legislative committee to what they decried as lackluster police work in pursuit of the alleged culprits, some of them actually blamed the press for giving the accusations *less* attention than they deserved:

A.L., a neighborhood resident whose child was a victim of abuse, said as he left the hall in pain: "Because we are talking about a haredi neighborhood in Jerusalem, the media has not come to investigate and to protect us. We saw how the media acted in the case of the "Corrido brothers" [a pair of pedophiles living in Haifa]. We have no way to protect our children even within our buildings. Most of the families are living hand-to-mouth, yet we still came out to struggle. But we have the feeling that nothing will help us."[13]

The same secular press accused of anti-religious *Schadenfreude* for its coverage of Orthodox sex abuse cases was here attacked for *underreporting* exactly the kind of story it's supposed to love. Why? Because this time the local Orthodox rabbis wanted the case publicized—and according to them, the press will even choke down its appetite for religious scandal if that means frustrating the Orthodox. Given such assumptions among Orthodox Jews, the media can never win. Which means that the rabbis who seek to pressure the media away from the stories they *don't* want publicized can never really lose.[14]

In fact, Orthodox Jews have had little cause to complain of unfair treatment in recent media coverage. If anything, the press underplays stories unflattering to the Orthodox community. For one thing, major Jewish publications (the ones most likely to approach such stories) are heavily influenced by Orthodox opinion. "We don't want to look like we're piling on the Orthodox," one Jewish newspaper editor told me when rejecting a column I proposed; another said proudly, "We position ourselves at the political center of any issue so we don't alienate any part of the community more than necessary." These editorial postures are not absolutes, and good reporting has managed to thread the obstacles on important occasions—Hella Winston's work in the *New York Jewish Week* is an honorable example. But even the best of such reporting runs up against resistance before it can reach the public, as I will show a bit later.

Even the secular media tend to tread gingerly around Orthodox Jewish opinion—particularly where a taboo subject like child sex abuse is concerned. The mere reporting of such crimes prompts accusations of anti–Semitism, which (as the accusers well know) strike a sensitive chord with media bigwigs. When ABC's *Nightline* reported the outrageous abuse case of Rabbi Avrohom Mondrowitz in October 2006, no mention was made of the Orthodox Jews who had heckled the film crew that visited Mondrowitz's former neighborhood, demanding to know why ABC was "attacking" the rabbi. Not only that: the entire piece, though filmed in the late summer, was held up for airing until after the Jewish High Holy Days, because ABC executives felt it would be "in bad taste" to show the extent of the Orthodox community's complicity in shielding an accused child rapist while Jews were celebrating their most solemn religious festivals. One can only wonder whether similar sensitivity would have applied to reporting about, say, crimes committed by fundamentalist Muslims.[15]

Against this background it comes as no surprise that press coverage has only recently, and so far incompletely, addressed the underlying reasons for the relative impunity of child abusers who prey on Orthodox Jewish children. With some important exceptions, media treatment has minimized both the extent of the problem and the socio-political patterns within the community that militate against justice for the victims, thus perpetuating a vicious cycle of abuse and re-victimization. For reasons I will discuss, Jewish media have been particularly slow to break out of this fog, but the mainstream press has not been a great deal better. Individual cases are reported, yes, but the impression left behind is of isolated and lurid crimes committed by a few depraved people; the social conditions that set the stage for those crimes, that ensure that they will be repeated, the politics that undermines even the integrity of the secular justice system in order to protect the guilty—all these are given short shrift. And despite the increased coverage of the topic in recent years, the key defects remain largely the same.

*   *   *

The first species of media misfire, and still the most common, is avoidance. Take the case of Solomon Hafner. A young Hasidic rabbi and private tutor, Hafner was charged with 96 counts of child sexual abuse for allegedly tugging and twisting the genitals of a hearing-impaired boy he was supposed to be teaching in an isolated Brooklyn building known, on Saturdays, as the Voydislaver Shul [Synagogue].[16] Hafner's arrest was reported by television news in New York. Yet not a single Jewish newspaper picked up the story, even after Amy Neustein and I discovered—and reported to the editor in chief of the *New York Jewish Week*—that a rabbinic court had quietly "cleared" Hafner while a grand jury was still taking evidence in the case. Not even this obvious attempt by Orthodox rabbis to influence the criminal justice system—an effort that ultimately succeeded—made the story newsworthy in the eyes of the Jewish media.[17] (A particularly poignant irony was that the *Jewish Week*'s editor, Gary Rosenblatt, would break the silence about Rabbi Baruch Lanner's history of abuse a few months later. Even then, however, his paper would not touch the Hafner case.) One short article in one New York tabloid mentioned that rabbinic interference might undermine Hafner's criminal prosecution,[18] but this was never followed up after the Hafner charges actually *were* dropped.

In fact, for all the effort that went into illuminating the rabbinic upending of the Hafner prosecution—on the basis of trumped-up "evidence" offered by a panel of Orthodox rabbis who first tried to silence the victim and then, when that failed, lobbied the Brooklyn D.A. into dropping all charges—Dr. Neustein and I found it even harder to publicize our findings. At first we put the facts into an article we were under contract to write for *New York Magazine*. I even accompanied *New York*'s photographer for the story to Borough Park, helping her as she snapped the pictures that were supposed to accompany our piece: the locked, empty, forbiddingly quiet building in which the boy was allegedly abused, week after week, where the only windows were far too high above ground to see through (though the rabbis claimed, falsely, that the building was always full of people and that the scene of the boy's tutoring sessions was clearly visible from the street)[19]; the huge synagogue that served as a central place of worship for the Bobov sect of Hasidim, and where, on the holiday of Purim, when the rabbis' victory over the justice system was announced, some three thousand pious Jews broke out in song to mock the alleged victim's family.[20] But shortly after the pictures were taken, the magazine's top editor pulled the plug on our story.

The Associated Press did mention the Hafner case in a well-written article on the role of rabbinic courts in child abuse cases in 2002[21]; but that story was picked up by only a handful of newspapers, and remains available on-line via just one small publication called *Worldwide Religious News*.[22] Another six years were to pass before Dr. Neustein and I could publish our own analysis of the Hafner cover-up in print—not in a popular magazine but in an academic journal.[23]

And that was the secular press. Jewish media all but unanimously turned its back on the story. To date, the only Jewish publication that was interested in the first (and, as far as I know, still the only) detailed account of a rabbinic conspiracy to derail an active child sex abuse prosecution was the small-scale *Jewish Voice and Opinion*.[24] Every mainstream Jewish newspaper avoided it. No major secular newspaper would touch the story either, even with extensive evidence of the cover-up readily available in our articles.

When, in addition to the journal articles, Dr. Neustein and I published an account of the Hafner story as part of *Tempest in the Temple* in 2009, one limited-circulation New York paper, the *Brooklyn Eagle*, did report it. But even the *Eagle* went out of its way to minimize the story's impact. The headline called the entire book "strange" (though the article never explained what was "strange" about it) and failed to mention numerous facts fatal to the rabbis' version of events and blindly accepted by prosecutors.[25] The reporter quoted the D.A.'s Sex Crimes Bureau Chief Rhonnie Jaus as saying that our account of the cover-up was "untrue," and that Brooklyn prosecutors had "conducted a long and thorough investigation of the victim's claims"—a brazen falsehood in light of what the witnesses told us. Far from challenging the office, however, the *Eagle* was prepared to quote some unnamed "employees" who accused my co-author of "a grudge against ... the Brooklyn D.A.'s office" because "in 1986, she filed for custody of her 6-year-old daughter, accusing her husband of molesting her."[26] Needless to say, the D.A.'s office is not involved in child custody litigation[27]; the idea that our detailed reporting of the Hafner case turned on a child-custody issue from more than twenty years earlier is, well, the sort of camouflage only a cover-up artist would try on. (Of course, the Neustein case did involve a gross miscarriage of justice, as discussed in the previous chapter, but that is beside the point.)

Since Dr. Neustein and I have told the story elsewhere in detail, I will not revisit the entire narrative here. But to emphasize the significance of the Jewish and mainstream media silence about the facts, let me reiterate the gist of what we reported—and it is worth remembering that none of it has ever been refuted since we finally managed to publish the story.[28] A major case of child sexual abuse against a Hasidic rabbi was dropped by the Brooklyn District Attorney at the urging of a group of Orthodox rabbis—a five-member panel headed by David Feinstein, one of the best-known Orthodox rabbis in the United States—though the rabbis presented, at most, only highly unreliable hearsay evidence of Hafner's innocence. The rabbis insisted that Hafner could not have abused the boy as charged, because the two were never out of sight of others: "There are twenty, thirty in and out [of the synagogue where the tutoring took place] daily," and there were "big, huge half-wall windows ... open to the street." Each of the factual claims contained in this statement was demonstrably false.

The rabbis also impugned both the psychological stability and the character of the alleged child victim, saying, for instance, that "because he's hearing impaired ... he always wants to get attention." These claims, too, were utterly unsupported by any evidence. Finally, and perhaps most damning, our reporting showed how the handling of the case reflected lively cooperation between the Orthodox rabbinate and the Brooklyn District Attorney. Their collaboration went so far that prosecutors asked the rabbis not to publish their "verdict" in the case before the D.A. announced his own dropping of the charges, because "they didn't want it to look like they bent under pressure."[29] In fact, the statements of the rabbis themselves fell short of a denial that they had superseded the official justice system so far as the Hafner case was concerned. Although Rabbi Chaim Rottenberg, one of the rabbinic judges, questioned whether he and his colleagues were "powerful enough to pressure the D.A. and the police to drop the charges" when the AP's reporter quizzed him about it in 2002,[30] he sang a different tune four years later, boasting that the rabbis had made all the difference: "If we didn't convince the D.A., then why did Hynes drop the case so suddenly?"[31]

Bear in mind that this cover-up didn't happen in the Russian Pale; all this took place in New York City in the last year of the twentieth century. And it was carried out, not just by prominent rabbis, but by the highest officers of local secular law enforcement acting at the rabbis' behest. Was such a conspiracy to protect a credibly accused child abuser, in one of the world's largest and most modern cities, really unworthy of mainstream press coverage?

The media's avoidance of stories like the Hafner cover-up is mostly self-chosen. But even when a press outlet does seem prepared to delve into Orthodox sex abuse, a well-timed intimidation campaign can checkmate the effort. Consider the case of a young Orthodox woman who offered to talk publicly about her own alleged abuse under the pseudonym "Hadassah." She had been a foster child under the supervision of the notorious Ohel Children's Home, which knew of her allegation that she and her brother had both been sexually mistreated in foster care. Just hours before a scheduled live broadcast on a popular television show, "Hadassah was called into [Ohel's] offices for an emergency meeting at which a prominent rabbi, along with two staff members, was present." Nobody knows what was said at that meeting, but the young woman "arrived at the studio visibly shaken, and sat mutely throughout an hour-long broadcast." There her story ended, as far as the public was concerned. Nor do Orthodox rabbis spare the reporters themselves. The personal secretary of former *New York Post* columnist Ray Kerrison has recalled that when Kerrison wrote about the notorious cover-up of the facts in the Neustein case, "rabbis would call up in a rage."[32]

Their "rage" presumably arose from their failure to stifle the story altogether. Martin Burger, relative of an Ohel officer,[33] has boasted of being "successful in killing a few stories" about the Neustein case, including one by the Associated Press and another for local New York television. Whether or not this was true (some of Burger's other public claims were plainly inaccurate),[34] prominent Jewish officials both inside and outside the Orthodox community have made well-documented efforts to silence public discussion of the case. Steven Mostofsky, lay president of the National Council of Young Israel—a sizable Orthodox organization—threatened to sue the one Jewish newspaper that mentioned a forthcoming book by me and Dr. Neustein on the American family court system,[35] after guessing from the newspaper's coverage that our book might refer to the suppression of credible evidence that an Orthodox Jew had molested his daughter. (When asked what was inaccurate in the article, Mostofsky declined to specify.)

At the same time, Martin Samson, a lawyer who frequently represented Mostofsky's organization, wrote the paper an angry eighteen-page letter about the same article, and though he claimed not to be writing on behalf of Young Israel or Mostofsky, the client he did name was Leon Deutsch, who had been the Family Court judge in the Neustein case (where Mostofsky had served as his law clerk). David Pollock, assistant director of the Jewish Community Relations Council, based in New York City, demanded to speak with me about the book and, before our telephone conversation had ended, threatened to "see [me] in court" because I wouldn't allow him and Deutsch to review the manuscript before publication—for what exact purpose, he wouldn't say. He never did sue, but our publisher was treated to a string of bellicose emails and letters, including one from attorney Samson, seeking to thwart publication or at least to limit in advance the book's discussion of the Neustein case.[36] One such communication referred to me as "corrupt" and an "egregious liar"; the comments about Dr. Neustein were even worse. (Ironically, the book never even names Sherry or her father, and apart from a brief reference in the introduction, never connects any case described in the book with one of the authors.) Fortunately for us, our publisher was not impressed, and in the end agreed to only one minor clarification regarding a detail about Judge Deutsch's retirement—nothing about any of the cases we described in the book.[37] But anyone who has experienced such a campaign first-hand will readily grasp why threats and intimidation have dissuaded many a wavering editor from publishing on so controversial a topic.

Jeremiah McKenna, former chief counsel to the New York State Senate Committee on Crime and Correction, who had focused on the Neustein case when he investigated the mistreatment of women in the courts, called the bullying tactics Jewish officials deployed against the story "proof of a continuing conspiracy to conceal the truth of what happened in this case."[38] Those tactics also illustrated the real relation between the Orthodox Jewish community and the press. Far from being victims of exaggerated reporting of child sex abuse, Orthodox Jews, more often than not, are able to control the kind of reporting the issue receives. What was unusual about this particular tussle was that the publication and the reporter in question—the *Jewish Voice and Opinion* and its publisher, Susan Rosenbluth—followed the lead of a different drummer and did not give in to pressure. Rosenbluth's willingness to resist the threats and propaganda aimed at stifling a story of alleged sex abuse in the Orthodox community represented an honorable exception—not, unfortunately, the rule.

* * *

The examples of press failure I have described so far involve stories that got short-changed in both Jewish *and* secular media. But these branches of the press are not equivalent in this respect. Between the two, Jewish media still lag behind. In September 1999, a New York tabloid revealed that two foster children in a group home run by Ohel Children's Home and Family Services—New York's largest Orthodox-run child care organization—reported having been repeatedly raped by one of Ohel's counselors, while agency officials ignored the assaults. Dr. Neustein and I knew of at least two other cases in which Ohel had failed to make legally required reports of suspected abuse, so we submitted a jointly written column to the *New York Jewish Week* outlining the boys' charges. Gary Rosenblatt, the newspaper's editor, refused to print the column after meeting with Ohel representatives—though he never gave us a reason why.[39]

Part of the problem besetting coverage of such cases doubtless stems from the anomalous way Jewish journalists—Rosenblatt among them—view their own profession. In an interview with blogger Luke Ford, Rosenblatt reportedly opined that "a Jewish journalist works with two competing mandates":

> The first commandment for journalists is to probe, explore and uncover and all the things people expect when they pick up their daily paper. On the other hand, one of the commandments in the organized Jewish community is the opposite, to cover-up and create a unified front, and not present any negative impression to the outside world. The Yiddish expression, *shandze fer* [sic] *de goyim* (scandal for the goyim). You're always walking that tightrope—doing the job of a journalist and being a responsible part of the Jewish community.[40]

Rosenblatt's eminence in Jewish journalism over a period spanning several decades gives particular resonance to his admission of following "competing mandates." In fact, his career exemplifies the effect of trying to reconcile irreconcilables. Though he bristles at suggestions that, after breaking the Lanner story, he backed away from exposing other abusive Orthodox rabbis, Rosenblatt demonstrably treads on eggshells where powerful interests in the Jewish community are involved—as they undoubtedly are when a prominent rabbi is accused of child abuse. To give one example from an unrelated issue: after Rosenblatt published a column that accurately named fat-cat Jewish businessman Lawrence Tisch as an owner of Lorillard Tobacco Company, Tisch—who is also a heavy contributor to Jewish causes, including the *Jewish Week*'s sponsor organization—obtained a written apology in which the editor confessed that "I can never be too attuned to people's feelings," and promised the nicotine merchant "to be more diligent in the future" about writing things that might embarrass his family.[41] Even before he issued that craven *mea culpa*, Rosenblatt's paper was apparently at pains to appease Tisch: an anti-smoking ad that named Tisch among "five of America's richest drug pushers," accepted for publication by the *Washington Post*, was turned down at the *Jewish Week*.[42]

What holds for Rosenblatt's "competing mandates" on other topics may also apply to reporting about child sex abuse in Orthodox communities, as specifically alleged by a blogger who has closely followed the issue:

> Although he [Rosenblatt] was very kind and professional with victims of Rabbis Lanner and [Mattis] Weinberg, there is a lack of attention or courtesy that he has displayed in other situations where there were desperate vulnerable people who thought he would help. My concern is that if he has journalistic standards in this area of reporting that differ from the mainstream media be upfront. I have noted in the past that [if] the standards he applies to abuse stories were applied in the general media, there would be no catholic church abuse scandal.[43]

Rosenblatt denies that he or his newspaper has ever deliberately slighted abuse victims; he told me, "We can't cover every case," which is doubtless true. Still, my own experience with Jewish media has all too often confirmed the blogger's accusations of inconsistency and timidity. The column I published in the *Jewish Week* on the Neustein cover-up was my tenth for the paper in about a year, but it was also my last. Having broached the subject of child sex abuse, I instantly became *persona non grata* with the editors, and it was ten years before my status changed appreciably. As for the Neustein story, the *Jewish Week* never once reported it *as news*; in fact, no Jewish newspaper ever reported the Neustein cover-up, though the story grabbed the attention of New York newspapers and *USA Today*, appeared on television news and received lengthy treatment on National Public Radio.[44] My experience was no different with several on-line Jewish news outlets: none of them wanted stories about the suppression of child sex abuse reports.

In 1997 I drafted a complete article for the *Jewish Week*, with Rosenblatt's express agreement, about a young, divorced mother in the Lubavitch Hasidic community of Brooklyn who believed her five-year-old son was being physically and sexually abused during visits with her ex-husband. I documented in detail how an Orthodox Jewish social worker (once again, connected with Ohel) had persuaded the Brooklyn D.A.'s office to have the child removed from his mother's home on the strength of trumped-up charges that she was mentally ill and "homicidal." I also reported that the Orthodox Jewish lawyer representing the young boy backed these charges against his mother, though the report of the court-appointed psychologist did not. Finally, I noted that Orthodox community politics, as well as the ingrained rabbinic resistance to admitting the reality of child abuse in its ranks, could well have played a part in the conduct of these key actors, since the boy's father was related to a powerful rabbinic family within the Lubavitch Hasidic sect. No one at the paper gainsaid the facts I reported or criticized my writing. But the story never ran.

*   *   *

Since then there have been some encouraging signs, but coverage of the issue remains far from complete—often in very troubling ways. I should begin with the good news. Around 2008, the *New York Jewish Week* began to feature the reporting of Hella Winston, who in her book *Unchosen*[45] had narrated the stories of formerly Orthodox Jews, some of whom who had been sexually abused as children. Her articles on sex abuse in Orthodox communities signaled, and contributed to, a sea change for the newspaper's handling of such stories. Child abuse allegations that might once have been ignored now received detailed reporting. Not only that, Winston's articles (and sometimes those of other reporters for Jewish media, notably Larry Cohler-Esses of the *Jewish Week*, and Anthony Weiss and Nathaniel Popper for the *Jewish Daily Forward*) started to move behind the surface of the scandalous facts. For example, when Popper reported the growing pressure on Brooklyn D.A. Charles Hynes to seek Mondrowitz's extradition, he specifically noted accusations that

"Hynes' silence may have been due to pressure from the Orthodox community, which [anti-abuse activists in the Orthodox community] claim has historically been reluctant to see alleged sex offenders prosecuted." And he went a step further by asking one of the original members of Hynes' Jewish Advisory Council for his current position on the Mondrowitz case, which turned out to be "leave it alone"—essentially confirming complaints I had started making years earlier.[46]

Winston similarly broke fresh ground. One of her early articles—co-written with Cohler-Esses—stressed facts that suggested Hynes and Orthodox leadership had colluded to spare Rabbi Yehuda Kolko a more serious sex abuse charge, with prosecutors urging the victims' families to accept a weak plea deal, "resurrect[ing] questions in some quarters about Hynes' competence or his political will in pursuing allegations of wrongdoing involving prominent institutions and individuals in Brooklyn's politically powerful Orthodox community." Not only that, the article suggested that the District Attorney had concealed his actual motives for soft-pedaling the case: a source at the D.A.'s office claimed that the victims did not want to testify, but this was sharply disputed by people close to the victims themselves; according to the father of one of them, "My son was ready to go to trial, and we feel he would have done an excellent job," and it was the prosecutors who didn't want the boy to testify.[47] The Jewish media's new seriousness about reporting these facts doubtless prodded the secular press into following suit, with the *New York Times* finally entering the fray in 2012.[48]

But this new willingness to challenge taboos of the Jewish media still had its limits. When Stefan Colmer went on trial in 2009 for sexually abusing two minors, I shared with Winston what I had learned about Ohel's having allowed him to leave an agency-run program for sex offenders without successfully completing treatment, and then keeping mum about it during the very period he was abusing boys. At least one other source confirmed my account. Winston and her editors agreed that these facts were highly newsworthy, and they were slated for inclusion in coverage of Colmer's trial. At the last minute, however, I learned that the newspaper's lawyer—an Orthodox Jew—was obstinately opposed to printing this part of the piece on the grounds that Ohel had not actually violated a New York statute. He continued to insist on changes, over the reporter's—and an editor's—strenuous objections, even after I volunteered to have all of the relevant facts quoted in my name as my personal opinion.

Ultimately the *Jewish Week* did report on Ohel's sorry performance in the case, and all in all the facts were correctly stated—much to Winston's credit, especially considering the opposition she had encountered. But the article was larded with disclaimers in Ohel's defense. "Because Colmer was never reported to the police and thus came to the agency ... without a mandate from the court ... Ohel was not required to report him to the authorities for non-compliance" when he dropped out of Ohel's sex offenders' program, the piece declared. But this evaded the central issue. Whether Ohel had broken reporting statutes had never been the question: alerting Jewish schools near where Colmer lived in Brooklyn—including the *yeshiva* from which he allegedly lured victims to his home—that the young man chatting up boys in the study hall was an uncured pedophile might, in this case, have made all the difference to the future victims. Similarly, the article volunteered not only that "no one interviewed for this story suggested that Ohel did anything illegal," but that "laws about confidentiality that govern the doctor-patient relationship limit what a psychologist can divulge about his patient." That defense only begged the question why Ohel didn't stipulate with its patients—all of whom in this particular program were deemed sex offenders—that they waived such confidentiality in the event they dropped out against their therapists' instructions. Finally, the article offered the rationalization that "[Colmer's] name did not appear on any public registries designed to alert the public to those who might pose a danger to children." But Ohel didn't need to see Colmer's name on a public registry to know the danger he posed: he had been their *patient*, for heaven's sake, and he was treated there precisely as a sex offender. If Ohel didn't consider that reason enough to worry about what he might do as an uncured dropout, that fact alone called into question its competence to offer such a program, suggesting that the whole arrangement existed merely to give Orthodox child molesters a way to end-run the law.[49] Yet this crucial issue—one that went to the heart of the complicity of Orthodox institutions in covering up sex abuse allegations—was dodged in the *Jewish Week*'s coverage.

At least Ohel's behavior in that case was *reported*. Not even that much happened when Ohel's own publicists produced direct evidence that the agency's putative partnership with the Brooklyn D.A. to bring more Orthodox sex abuse cases to the police was, in fact, a sham. In June 2009, Ohel released a promotional newsletter[50] that boasted about the "Kol Tzedek" program launched a few months earlier. According to a press release from D.A. Charles Hynes on April 1 of that year, the partnership with Ohel was "a new outreach program aimed at helping sex-crime victims in Brooklyn's Orthodox Jewish Communities report abuse." "Because of the insular nature of Orthodox Jewish communities," Hynes was quoted as saying, "many victims are reluctant to report crimes to secular authorities. This program will go a long way to address those impediments." The D.A.'s press release concluded that "victims who call the Project Kol Tzedek hotline" would speak to "a prosecutor from the Sex Crimes Bureau" and would "be encouraged to come forward with allegations of abuse."

Ohel's own description of the same venture gave the lie to the pretense that the Orthodox-run agency was going to help turn over Orthodox child molesters to the police. In Ohel's description of the joint program—which in every other respect tracked the language of the D.A.'s press release, and even included a photo of Hynes announcing the launch—not a single word referred to reporting child sex abuse to police or prosecutors; every mention of this central issue in Hynes' press release was carefully excised from Ohel's version. According to Ohel, and directly contrary to what the press had been told, the vaunted Kol Tzedek program was not about reporting Orthodox sex abuse to police. A victim who called the hotline would be connected only to the *agency*, and would *not* speak to a prosecutor (as the D.A. had specified); nor, as far as anyone could tell from its description, would the agency encourage a victim or witness to report abuse to secular authorities, though that is precisely what the D.A. had promised. To date, no one in the press has found these facts to be newsworthy.

Here, I think, we encounter an important barrier limiting coverage of Orthodox child sex abuse. It is much easier to get the facts of a specific case into the press than to obtain reporting of institutional patterns and policies, even when those policies are clearly needed to *explain* the facts. Ohel's failure to protect Colmer's potential victims was covered; its policy toward sex abuse reporting in general has received much less attention, even as the mainstream press blandly continues to describe Kol Tzedek as a program intended to bring Orthodox abuse cases to secular authorities.

This point deserves emphasis. If news coverage is to inform public discourse about child sex abuse among the Orthodox, the reporting must at least address the connections between individual cases, exposing sex abuse as a community problem that demands to be solved. Yet this is precisely where the press has been least satisfactory. One recent analysis of 260 articles in the general media dealing with child sexual abuse concluded that such articles "rarely addressed solutions." "When prevention was referenced," the authors noted, "it was either as a small-scale program for individual parents [of abused children] or described in terms of vague cultural shifts rather than concrete policies or programs." Particularly important for our purposes is the authors' theory about *why* small-scale approaches were more likely to be discussed in print than bolder "policies or programs": "Because they [the former] do not confront challenging political issues surrounding CSA [child sex abuse]."[51] That is exactly the point. It is one thing to record the reality of child sex abuse. It is quite another to challenge the politics of the institutions that protect the abusers.

Equally convenient for the guardians of a corrupt status quo is the "episodic" way child sex abuse is generally narrated in news reports. This means more than a flattening of the dimensions of a news story. According to the authors of the study just cited, such reporting "has important consequences":

> Because potential solutions to CSA are not usually covered, episodic criminal justice stories help reinforce the idea that CSA "just happens," or is a problem too big and complicated to address.... In the absence of news stories that include policy solutions or other ways to prevent the problem, CSA may seem insurmountable and overwhelming, making parents feel anxious and powerless to address it.[52]

Note that this approach—still the norm in press coverage of sex abuse cases—could scarcely have been better designed to give Orthodox Jewish leadership what it wants. Doubtless the rabbis would have preferred that such stories never reach the press at all. But if they do, so long as the incidents look like aberrations that "just happen," or the facts appear too complicated to untangle, or the problem just too big for the overwhelmed reader to confront, the propagandists' work is done. After all, what is really needed is a systematic challenge to the institutions that are normalizing these crimes. But that will not happen until the reporters drag the institutions and their paladins into the spotlight, revealing what is being suppressed and exposing the superstructure of deceit and intimidation that makes the suppression possible.

This point underscores the political impact of such journalistic omissions: leaving out facts that could challenge powerful institutions tacitly supports the status quo. I'm afraid it is no accident that the most prominently circulated column touching on the facts of the Neustein case, for instance, is an antifeminist apologetic by Wendy McElroy that begins by vaguely gesturing at "misconduct or incompetence on the part of New York's child protection services and family courts in New York," then brushes off the facts as "too complicated and protracted to address," and finally dismisses the whole business because "debate continues to surround the case"—though her column discloses no "debate" whatsoever.[53] Mainstream media (including the *Fox News* web site) have given plenty of exposure to McElroy's column, while ignoring the vastly more informed account of the same case in the *Village Voice*. What is a reader of such "coverage" to believe about the Neustein cover-up? That child welfare professionals can make mistakes (big surprise); that the average reader can't be expected to understand the facts (so why bother?); and that no conclusions can be reached because someone, somewhere, is still "debating" the case. From reading such "treatment," no one would ever really know anything about the massive cover-up, involving prominent rabbis, political officials and a major foster care institution, that was still unfolding around the Neustein case at the very moment McElroy's column was published. *Caveat lector.*

*   *   *

As we have seen, part of the problem with the coverage of child sex abuse stories stems from structural patterns common to much of the media. And these, in turn, involve prejudices about the very nature of the subject—prejudices much wider than the Orthodox Jewish community. It is hardly an exaggeration to say that ignoring cruelty toward children, or minimizing its importance, represents something of a social norm. Two examples will suffice to illustrate my point. David Ben-Gurion retains his image as a liberal and a humanist (at least among Jews) despite having publicly proclaimed during World War II that he would prefer the annihilation of half of Germany's Jewish children to their relocation anywhere but in Palestine, where they were to add to the raw material of the Zionist project.[54] More recently, "father's rights" groups have unabashedly argued that young children of divorce who fear or dislike their fathers are not entitled to financial support; it's clear that the leaders of these groups aren't afraid that this position will hurt them politically.[55] Both avowals—one by a famous Jewish figure, the other by prominent social advocates—are openly cruel in their attitude toward children, but the cruelty in both is seldom remarked. And what people don't notice isn't likely to be reported in the press.

Sentimentality is no substitute for honest attention. Maybe the *frisson* of shock and outrage that always greets the most gruesome child abuse stories serves to deflect our collective gaze from realities far too close for comfort. Alice Miller, a truly revolutionary voice in psychology, notes that many of her own readers "reacted with horror to the excerpts from the child-rearing manuals I included in *For Your Own Good*, even though these works have never been kept secret but probably even formed the nucleus of our parents' or grandparents' libraries."[56] Jewish fundamentalists have no monopoly on what Miller calls the "poisonous pedagogy" that rationalizes all sorts of abusive treatment of children. While researching this book, I had a rather unnerving experience when I looked over one of my old religious school textbooks—still on my shelves—one of whose authors was the prominent liberal writer Meyer Levin. I was astonished to find that this book, published when I was four years old, clearly if somewhat tentatively approves of spanking "very young children" for being "naughty."[57] Even liberal Jews in 1962 were prepared to endorse violence against children as a form of education. And of course they did this under a long shadow of history, the effects of which can be discerned in traditional Jewish writing as well: one need only mention, from the Orthodox law codes, the narrowly seasonal warning issued to teachers against striking young students—"even with a strap"—during the three-week interval between the fast of the 17th of Tammuz and that of the 9th of Ab.[58] The same texts are silent concerning whether teachers are permitted to use physical violence against children during the rest of the year.

But this brings us back to the particular responsibility of the Jewish press for the coverage—or non-coverage—of the scourge of child sex abuse among one of its most significant populations. The Jewish media's protection of the Orthodox community from accurate reporting is not an oversight; nor can it be attributed wholly to patterns of inattention that plague the press in general. Its complicity in what Rabbi Irving Greenberg, over two decades ago, called "a conspiracy of silence" will persist as long as Jewish professionals are trained to exclude truth-telling from the traditional canon of Jewish "values," a phenomenon candidly admitted by the Orthodox reporter Alan Borsuk in 1997:

> Journalism's cardinal tenet of laying out the facts and letting the chips fall where they may is definitely in conflict with Jewish tradition's strong emphasis on not saying things that unnecessarily harm others, even if they are true.... The neutral or accepting position that the news media take on a lot of social and lifestyle issues is very different from the strong stand Orthodox Judaism takes on many of the same issues.[59]

This analysis closely resembles Gary Rosenblatt's confession of following "competing mandates" in his reporting of Jewish community issues. But notice the disingenuous assumptions that line Borsuk's argument. First, it is far from true that secular media are indifferent to the effects of the stories they run. One need only consider how American news organizations suppressed the truth about the criminal invasion of Iraq in 2003 on "patriotic" grounds (a failure that was widely reported after the fact) to realize that Borsuk is asserting a specious distinction; the choice is not between the religious and the conscienceless, but between journalism that is honest and journalism that is unprincipled. Second, Borsuk's claim that "Jewish tradition" discourages truth-telling—at least, where the facts could "unnecessarily harm others"—should give anyone pause. If Borsuk were correct, "Jewish tradition" would be at loggerheads not only with journalism but with science, teaching, politics and the practice of law, any of which can involve asserting inconvenient truths.

Finally, and very significantly, Borsuk elides the distinction between editorializing and reporting when he declares that Orthodoxy cannot be squared with "neutral" coverage of "lifestyle issues." (He may have in mind a religiously contentious issue like gay marriage.) Again, if Borsuk were correct, the problem would be much larger than he acknowledges. A gay man, for instance, would presumably be incapable of reporting on factual issues relevant to gay men on the grounds that he personally takes a "strong stand" on them. Or does Borsuk mean that Orthodoxy requires reporters to evade or distort the truth in order to indoctrinate the "right" beliefs in their readers? If so, the problem Borsuk complains of lies less with the "position" of the news media with respect to "social and lifestyle issues," and much more with a dishonest approach to facts fostered by Orthodoxy.

Ominously enough, precisely this latter version of the "Jewish" approach to journalism enjoys a widening impact on the press as traditional Jewish observance spreads through the professional classes. Consider the Orthodox anchorwoman of a metropolitan New York television station who, when confronted in 1987 with Dr. Neustein's personal account of "an alleged sex abuse cover-up at an Orthodox Jewish-run foster care agency"—that is, Ohel—urged Dr. Neustein "not to publicize the alleged scandal." After all, that sort of thing wouldn't be good for the Jews. Several years later, the Orthodox anchorwoman left that station; only then did its reporters air the story, which, as a feature piece, won the segment producers an Emmy.[60] This anecdote is far more than a bit of media gossip. The nub of the matter is the shuffling of news priorities by a woman supposedly in the business of sharing information with a viewing public. Perhaps she regretted her choice afterwards—but if she did, she has never said so.[61]

And this problem has only sharpened with time. When *New York Magazine* first printed the abuse allegations against Rabbi Yehuda Kolko in 2006—after some of his former students sued him and his *yeshiva* for sexual assaults allegedly spanning a period of years[62]—Agudath Israel spokesman Rabbi Avi Shafran weirdly attacked the article as "lurid," as if the author were at fault because the facts were unpleasant to read. Whether the article was accurate was apparently unimportant to Shafran.[63]

But of course, the reader may suppose, *the magazine's editors weren't swayed by propaganda that transparent.* Maybe not. But in the eight years since Kolker's article appeared, *New York* has touched on child sex abuse among Orthodox Jews exactly once, and then only in a brief piece on how documents I obtained under Freedom of Information laws proved the Brooklyn D.A. had been lying about his office's role in obtaining a change in the U.S.-Israel extradition treaty as part of the Mondrowitz case.[64] A useful nugget of information, yes; but one that only throws into sharper relief the same magazine's failure to investigate the patterns of official dysfunction that lone article implied. A freelance journalist who *was* interested in writing about these patterns for *New York* informed me that, according to the magazine's editors, the story was already played out and didn't call for any further publicity.

* * *

It is often said, truthfully enough, that Orthodox leadership wants to stifle press coverage of child sex abuse in order to protect the community's public image. But there are other motives as well, chief among them the inverse relation between rabbinic power and the spread of accurate information among the Orthodox rank and file. Journalism about child sex abuse undermines rabbinic authority in several ways. First, it calls attention to children's rights and needs, thus undermining a hierarchy in which children have few recognized grievances against adults who exploit them. Second, it punctures the elaborate fiction of the infallibility of rabbinic scholars, according to which a man steeped in the Talmud could not possibly be guilty of an abusive act.

Finally, and perhaps most importantly, it attacks the rabbinic monopoly on the terms—and therefore the control—of legitimate or illegitimate sexuality. Daniel Boyarin has carefully dissected this idea in its most common application, the exclusion of women from Talmudic study, and his comments are relevant here:

> I theorize that the exclusion of women from the study of Torah [specifically, the area of Jewish study connected with law-making and regulation] subtended the rabbinic Jewish gender hierarchy in two closely related ways, via the construction of a "fraternity" and via the production of a social system within which a group of men (the Rabbis) held power over the actual practices and pleasures of female bodies.

Boyarin pointedly applies this principle to the medieval Jewish discourse on wife-beating—still the basis of contemporary Orthodox rabbinic opinion—showing that even the "liberal" rabbis who condemned domestic violence (as opposed to Maimonides and other authorities, who specifically licensed it) did so in terms that "demonstrate how that condemnation served as a technology for the control of women by men."[65]

What is true of gender politics is equally true of the control of children by adults: the rabbis insist on the exclusive power to determine what is and what is not acceptable, and will not tolerate competing claims advanced or even implied in the general media. Recently an Orthodox Jewish lawyer in Israel, Rivka Schwartz, offered her own ideas about the prevalence of child sex abuse among the ultra–Orthodox:

> My theory is that many ultra–Orthodox commit these acts because they are unaware that a specific act is a crime and because [of] a lack of awareness of the punishments associated with these crimes.... In the ultra–Orthodox community, the media doesn't report [such crimes]. There's no newspaper or other place to hear about what happened....[66]

Schwartz is obviously thinking of sexual abuse other than genital penetration, as was a rabbi sympathetic to abuse victims who repeated, as a belittling response typical of his community, "Someone messed around with a friend of mine, and he got over it. Why can't [others]?"[67] I am not convinced that ignorance alone can explain the extent of such abuse. After all, many of the victims of Orthodox Jewish perpetrators I know *were* penetrated, and their abusers showed no more remorse than the others, though even the most conservative reading of traditional Jewish law unequivocally prohibited what they did. But the implication behind Schwartz's comments—that such ignorance is deliberately enforced through the absence of newspaper reporting—rings like gold. I do not mean that the rabbis want their followers to abuse children. But their insistence on monopolizing the discourse about sexuality, including abusive sexuality, to the exclusion of all objective information from any non-rabbinic source, ultimately has the identical effect.

Which is why, even as some Orthodox publications are being pried out of the closet on abuse issues, almost every step forward is followed by two steps back. In June 2012, a supplement to the Orthodox *Ami Magazine* featured an interview with an Orthodox social worker who stressed that "we've come so far in our community in terms of being open to talking about [domestic abuse]," whereas "fifteen to 20 years ago, it was taboo to even mention abuse."[68] All perfectly true. Yet the publisher of the same *Ami Magazine* had denounced me less than two months earlier as "a longtime agitator against the Orthodox community," precisely because my writing and legal work had played some part in making that change possible.[69]

"Thought would destroy their paradise," wrote Thomas Gray in his lugubrious *Ode*. He was describing schoolboys, whose callow ignorance was sure to collapse under the pressure of the future slowly gathering on their horizon. But Orthodox Judaism is already some fifteen centuries old. In all those years, we must have learned how to think a few thoughts for ourselves, including the simple realization that our rabbis don't know everything. Isn't it time we started reading our newspapers like grownups?

4

Backlash Strategies,
Past and Present

Self-righteousness is not religion. To attack the first is not to assail the
last.... The world may not like to see these ideas disseevered, for it has
been accustomed to blend them; finding it convenient to make external show pass for sterling worth—to let white-washed walls vouch for
clean shrines. It may hate him who dares to scrutinize and expose ...
but hate as it will, it is indebted to him.
—Charlotte Brontë[1]

The same year the story of Rabbi Baruch Lanner's abuse finally surfaced
in Jewish media, an Israeli Jew named Shaiya Brizel published an angry memoir, *The Silence of the Ultra-Orthodox*. The book describes an Orthodox
upbringing during which Brizel was sexually abused by his father, a rabbi and
teacher who, according to the author, also abused many of his students. Brizel
went back to his father's school before his book appeared and confronted the
rabbi in charge. "You are right that we covered up for him," the aging rabbi
admitted. But there was no apology—only a plea that Brizel not publish his
book. "Shaiya, these things happened a long time ago," said the rabbi. "Your
father is old and can no longer sin."[2]

Neatly encapsulated in this account is the germ of a rhetorical strategy
by which victims of abuse become, in effect, the aggressors—note it well. The
key is that the perpetrator's point of view is taken as normative, while the victim's experience is only a threat to be fended off. What matters to the old rabbi
in Brizel's story—who has already admitted his role in protecting the child
molester—is the perspective of the abuser, who in this case "can no longer
sin"; the victim figures in the rabbi's calculations only to the extent that he
"threatens" to tell the inopportune truth. The rabbi does not ask Brizel
whether what he suffered as a child is moot in *his* eyes. Doubtless it isn't, and
doubtless it wouldn't be for almost anyone victimized as he was: "The consequences of sexual abuse ... impair the development of the self and of an

autonomous personality," cautions Alice Miller, who also emphasizes that at least some of the enduring "consequences" result from a history of denial, precisely what the rabbi demands of Brizel. "An unacknowledged trauma," Miller writes, "is like a wound that never heals over and may start to bleed again at any time."[3] But we don't really need the great psychotherapist's wisdom to puncture the fallacy in the rabbi's argument. We can simply observe a glaring double standard. Have Orthodox Jews stopped talking about the Nazi holocaust because the killers and tormentors of those days are old now, removed from political power, and "can no longer sin"?

Backlash against victims is nothing new. What needs to be emphasized is that the backlash continues in Orthodox Jewish communities, albeit by somewhat altered means. As information about child sex abuse has spread too widely to be either ignored or denied, Orthodox Jewish leaders have shifted away from their first line of denial—blank insistence that such things never happen—only to fall back on other strategies for accomplishing similar ends.

I have noted already that, as late as the 1990s, Orthodox Jewish authorities usually denied altogether that religious Jews abused children, let alone that cases of child sex abuse were being suppressed or ignored. That line of defense collapsed as names like Lanner, Kolko and Mondrowitz irrevocably entered the popular discourse. "Because of the Lanner case the Orthodox Union has undergone almost two years now of deep introspection and examination of our policies and procedures," its executive vice president, Rabbi Tzvi Hersh Weinreb, told the Associated Press in 2002. The Orthodox Union, one of the largest Orthodox organizations in the United States, had also, according to Rabbi Weinreb, "implemented standards for all staff members who work with youth and [had] set up extensive training sessions."[4] By 2010, the Rabbinical Council of America, another influential organization of American Orthodox rabbis, had adopted an official resolution entitled "Condemning and Combating Child Abuse." According to the resolution, the rabbis formally acknowledged that sexual and physical abuse of children in Orthodox Jewish communities were realities; that some Orthodox rabbis had been indicted or convicted for acts of child abuse or endangerment; and that such abuse caused great harm to victims.[5]

This book is being written years after the issuance of those lofty declarations by prominent rabbinic associations. Has the Orthodox leadership's attitude toward sex abuse cases really improved, now that the victims' plight has received so much attention in popular media that the rabbinate has been forced to confess it?

My own recent experience in the Mondrowitz case—one of the worst cases of serial child sex abuse in New York State history—unfortunately suggests the opposite: rabbinic suppression of sex abuse cases seems only to have grown more hypocritical. In 2006, when I was campaigning for the reopening of the Mondrowitz extradition and badly needed to reach as many of his alleged victims as possible, I learned of a way that dozens of them could be given my name, and the reasons I was seeking them out, through a source who had records of the statements they had made to him shortly after Mondrowitz fled the United States. To access this information I needed only the approval of one of two prominent rabbis, both of whom are routinely numbered among America's most influential Orthodox authorities. Despite several telephone conversations, and although one of the two rabbis expressed sympathy for abuse victims when we talked, I never got the needed say-so. In fact, at one point this "leader" even questioned how it would help Mondrowitz's alleged victims to see him brought to justice. (And yet the same rabbi has publicly declaimed that the exposure of children to Internet porn is a "tragedy"[6]; one might have thought he would show at least as much concern over the effects of being sodomized by a rabbi.)

My experience was no better in the case of Stefan Colmer. In 2009, as Colmer's trial approached, Jewish media began to show an interest in the tragic results of the *laissez-faire* policy of the Orthodox-run Ohel agency, which had knowingly allowed a pedophile to leave its treatment program uncured and had made no effort to protect future victims. Two Orthodox sources with important information—at my request—consulted their local rabbi about sharing what they knew with the *New York Jewish Week*. Their rabbi referred them to "a prominent American *rav* [rabbi]." Soon afterward, I was told that the "prominent" rabbi had forbidden them not only to communicate with the *Jewish Week*, but also to work with me. The *Jewish Week* was "anti–Orthodox," I was given to understand; heaven knows what sort of epithet I had earned. Some "progress."

True, Mondrowitz and Colmer both faced jail time if convicted—but even a perversely excessive concern for the welfare of alleged abusers cannot explain the rabbinate's continuing fondness for cover-ups where criminal penalties are not in question. Recall that in 2006, spurred by Internet blogs, serious evidence began to circulate through Orthodox institutions, and the press, that prominent *yeshivos* had knowingly suppressed repeated reports of child sexual abuse by certain rabbis—Yehuda Kolko and Avrohom Mondrowitz were only the most prominently named suspects. This allegation did not threaten anyone with incarceration, but it did challenge the integrity of some of Orthodox Judaism's highly valued educational institutions.

What was the rabbinate's response? Nothing at all was done to investigate the affected schools. The issue was tackled, instead, in the most topsy-turvy fashion imaginable. Agudath Israel of America, perhaps the most powerful Orthodox organization in the United States, devoted the bulk of a session at its national convention that same year to warning its members not to read the Internet blogs containing the cover-up accusations. The event even featured a fiery speech by famed Rabbi Mattisyahu Salomon, who said that yes, Orthodox rabbis do "sweep it [child sexual abuse] under the carpet sometimes"—but that the public should *respect* them for so doing, since their motive was "to protect human dignity."[7] Nor did Agudath Israel revise its position when, only a few weeks after this bizarre address, Rabbi Kolko was arrested on charges of child sex abuse in Brooklyn—after some thirty years' worth of accusations from former students, and after his example was made a *cause célèbre* by the very blogs denounced by Salomon and the other rabbinic heavyweights at the convention.[8]

An isolated instance? Alas, no. The same thing happened the following year, when the *Baltimore Jewish Times* published an article describing decades of sexual abuse allegedly perpetrated by an Orthodox rabbi.[9] The ink on the offending issue was hardly dry when Rabbi Moshe Heinemann, one of Baltimore's most influential Orthodox authorities, reportedly banned the newspaper to all local Orthodox Jews—no doubt *his* way of "protecting human dignity." And this despite the fact that he had just signed an open letter, along with dozens of other Baltimore rabbis, insisting that charges of child sexual abuse in the Orthodox community would no longer be hidden, but conveyed to secular authorities![10]

Obviously the Orthodox rabbinate's recent actions, whatever its words, reveal little real improvement where child sex abuse is concerned. But what about the words themselves? While denial of the problem in general may be crumbling, I have not heard a specific apology from any Orthodox rabbi for a past sex abuse cover-up since Rabbis Yosef Blau and Mordechai Willig (to their great credit) apologized more than twelve years ago about their protection of Rabbi Lanner. If anything, most of the Orthodox rabbinate seems to have been circling the wagons of denial during that period—a phenomenon notable on both the "right" and the "left" wings in contemporary Orthodoxy.

I will give a couple of typical examples of what I mean. In the spring of 2012, Jerusalem was host to an enormous funeral for the revered ultra–Orthodox Rabbi Chaim Pinchas Scheinberg. Extravagant praise for the departed rabbi poured in from every corner of the Orthodox Jewish world, reverberating even in secular publications as far away as the United Kingdom, where he was lauded for "outstanding scholarship" and "great spirituality."[11] Missing from all of these encomiums, however, was any reference to Scheinberg's vigorous defense of Rabbi Kolko (since convicted of endangering the welfare of minors), a position he publicly reaffirmed in a letter dated nine days *after* a detailed exposé on Kolko's abusive history appeared in *New York Magazine* in 2006.[12] Nor has this part of Scheinberg's record been mentioned anywhere in the press since his death. The whole shabby story, and the role played in it by leading figures like Rabbi Scheinberg—obviously a point of departure for any genuine reform in the Orthodox community's treatment of child sex abuse—has been scrubbed from history, as far as the rabbinate is concerned. Not one official of any Orthodox rabbinic organization, so far as I am aware, has ever addressed Scheinberg's mishandling of the Kolko allegations at any time since the cover-up unraveled six years before Scheinberg's death.

The same pattern of denial, of whitewashing rabbinic history, can be seen in what the Orthodox rabbinate releases for general consumption. Consider the case of a book of religious teachings issued in 2009, and in a second edition in 2011, by ArtScroll, probably the most influential of all English-language Orthodox Jewish publishers. Note that this book was first printed several years after child sexual abuse among Orthodox Jews was—according to all Orthodox spokesmen—frankly acknowledged as a reality and as a reprehensible crime. Yet the book commences with an expression of gratitude to Rabbi Mattisyahu Salomon[13]—the same Rabbi Salomon who boasted in 2006 that Orthodox rabbis sweep child abuse under the carpet "to protect human dignity." Would the book's rabbi-editors have praised a Holocaust denier who argued that the facts about the Nazi genocide should be suppressed in order to protect "German dignity?"

That isn't all. The same book contains a glowing reference to a eulogy delivered by Rabbi Mordechai Elon for an Israeli soldier killed during a botched military rescue attempt in 1994. The reference is retained in the 2011 edition.[14] What makes this astounding is that by February 2010, Elon—a leading light of the "modern" wing of Orthodoxy in Israel—had been publicly identified by an Orthodox investigatory panel as a sexual abuser of some of his students. (The respected Rabbi Aharon Lichtenstein, one of the investigators, also accused a relative of Elon of threatening to kill him—that is, Rabbi Lichtenstein—a threat apparently never disowned by Rabbi Elon himself.)[15]

It's hard to believe the ArtScroll editors didn't know about this (the facts were widely publicized), and they could scarcely have overlooked the reference to Elon's sermon when completing the new edition, *after* the damning information about Elon was released. The book prominently quotes the rabbi as part of a dramatic story—exactly the sort of passage that would be hard to miss even in a casual review of the text. What is more, against the background of the child abuse accusations, the choice of imagery quoted from the rabbi's eulogy seems positively eerie: "Sometimes [a father] had to say 'no' though the child might not understand why, so our Father in Heaven heard our prayers, and though we don't understand why, His answer was 'no.'"[16] (One wonders what Elon's alleged victims thought of those words when, reading them in awestruck press accounts of the soldier's funeral, they recalled how *they* had pleaded with the rabbi, the agent of God, to spare them, and how *he* had answered "no.")

The most credible conclusion is that the Orthodox rabbis who edited this book simply didn't care about the facts—not about Salomon's praise for abuse cover-ups, not about the incongruity of showcasing a sermon by a credibly accused child molester—just as those who heaped praise on Scheinberg didn't care that he too, by defending the perpetrator, had added to the abuse of Kolko's alleged victims. If they thought about child sex abuse at all, the editors doubtless dismissed it as a vague, pesky complication to the unchallengeable sanctity of the rabbis they wanted to praise, those caryatids of tradition whose solid figures anchored the editors' frame of reference. *They* were real; next to them, abuse victims were not—particularly if acknowledging their reality might impair the perfection of the rabbis' image. I will have more to say, in later chapters, about the roots of this sort of thinking in a theology that uses images of child abuse in defense of the faith. But I first want to stress how such rationalizations serve as a potent form of denial, and therefore an ideological accessory to crimes against children, even if the form they take today is more refined than the old-fashioned "it can't happen here" variety. Surely if the Orthodox rabbinate can overlook the roles played in child sex abuse cases by some of the loftiest figures in its pantheon, on the "right" and on the "left," then it hasn't really come to grips with the greater part of the problem.

And denial springs eternal—whatever protestations the rabbinate may have offered to the contrary. Time after time, what happened to Shaiya Brizel happens again: rabbis accept without question the perspective of the abuser, so that *he* is the victim of slander (when first accused), the captive awaiting redemption (after confinement); the victims are at best challengers of the community's tranquility, at worst outright criminals. When Rabbi Nechemya Weberman was accused and later convicted of repeatedly raping a minor, the rabbis of his Satmar community launched a fundraising campaign to pay his legal bills, simultaneously plastering shopping malls with posters depicting his victim as a missile aimed at the heart of the community.[17] The year before, many leading rabbis in the heavily Orthodox enclave of Monsey, New York, had made a pilgrimage to the prison cell of Rabbi Israel Weingarten, who had been convicted of raping his young daughter over a period of nearly seven years. The rabbis carried with them a signed declaration that Weingarten was innocent, exhorting the faithful to raise money for the "redemption of the captive."[18]

Lest anyone still hope to find more circumspection at the highest levels of the rabbinate, consider the sorry record of Tel Aviv's Rabbi Chaim Kanievsky, famed not only in his own right, but as the son of one of Orthodoxy's most brilliant Talmudic scholars since World War II and the son-in-law of the single most revered Israeli ultra–Orthodox authority, Rabbi Yosef Shalom Elyashiv. In 2007, Rabbi Kanievsky reportedly discouraged taking any action against then accused (now convicted) child molester Stefan Colmer.[19] And a few years later, Rabbi Kanievsky actually signed a petition, along with his famous father-in-law, defending Rabbi Elior Chen when that wanted criminal—eventually sentenced to 24 years in prison for extreme acts of child abuse—was in the process of being extradited from Brazil for trial in Israel. The statement endorsed by Kanievsky insisted on Chen's innocence and demanded that readers actively support him. Somehow Kanievsky had managed to miss a few reported details about the tortures Chen inflicted on eight children, "which included beatings with clubs and hammers, kicks to the head, severe shaking, burning, being handcuffed and stuffed in a suitcase, food and sleep deprivation," as the judge concluded when pronouncing sentence. One of the child victims was left in a permanent coma.[20] Even after a public outcry about the petition, Kanievsky confirmed that he had signed in support of Chen because "my rabbis sign[ed] it."[21]

Can this story get worse? Unfortunately, yes. It seems Kanievsky's moral turpitude is tinged with another familiar rabbinic sin: hypocrisy. When not protecting Orthodox child abusers or savage criminals, Kanievsky is known for his ardent preaching against women's "immodest dress" and the use of the Internet; the latter, he claims, is a sin one must die rather than commit.[22] An awfully stern moral stand, one might think, from a man who offers up party-line patronage for a brute Bill Sykes might have shunned.

*   *   *

So far I have examined the outward mechanics of Orthodoxy's sex abuse denial. Now I want to deal a bit more specifically with the sort of reasoning the Orthodox rabbinate has employed to carry on the business. Remember, to justify stifling public reports of child sex abuse, the apologists for silence must invert the roles of perpetrator and victim: the threat to expose the abuser must be seen, by extension, as an indictment of the religious community to which he belongs, while the abuser himself, who offers no such "threat," is numbered among the innocent. But it is no small feat to present abused children as a moral danger to the community, while at the same time emphasizing—as the rabbinate now does—how baneful is the reality of child sex abuse, and how deeply committed the rabbis are to preventing its spread.

How, then, is abuse to be denied when it cannot be passed over in silence? To summarize the relevant strategies, I will first examine the leadership's reaction to one of the earliest public accusations of a large-scale rabbinic sex abuse cover-up to surface in popular media since the Lanner case. Next I will explore how rabbinic attitudes have been handed down to the larger Orthodox Jewish public, and how the terms of their discourse are affecting discussion of the issue within the community. Finally, I will examine the way rabbinic leadership has struck back at the primary medium of dissent—namely the Internet blogs in which Orthodox Jews, under the protective cloak of anonymity, have been able to evade communal strictures against speaking out on taboo topics such as child abuse.

In June 2009, two newspaper articles appeared in Israel—one in *Ha'aretz* and the other in the *Jerusalem Post*[23]—detailing allegations by a number of parents in the ultra–Orthodox enclave of Ramat Beit Shemesh. These parents charged that their children had been sexually abused by certain local teachers, and that the rabbis—instead of acting to protect their children and other potential victims—were pressuring the alleged victims to drop the matter.

The parents' accounts were damning. A mother complained that the rabbis in her community often "turn a blind eye" to child sex abuse. Not only that; when she reported her own child's abuse (with "proof," according to *Ha'aretz*), the rabbis "called me a liar and said that this kind of thing does not happen here." Another parent, whose abuse allegation was supported by professional evaluators, spoke of "a combination of denial, protecting your good name and not involving the secular world" that characterized the rabbinic leadership. In fact, he told the reporter that "his family was threatened and pressured by community leaders not to pursue the matter with the police," and even the abused child was "ostracized by most former classmates" because of the public report.

Rare as such stories have been in mainstream media, this one—appearing in two major Israeli newspapers at once, and both available in English—was obviously too big for the Orthodox establishment to ignore. Nor did it. But despite the nine years of "deep introspection and examination" that had supposedly overtaken the rabbinate in the wake of the Lanner case, Orthodoxy's reaction was anything but sympathetic. Instead, the leadership turned to Rabbi Jonathan Rosenblum—a prolific author of columns defending ultra–Orthodox rabbinic policies—to put the unruly critics of Ramat Beit Shemesh's rabbis in their place.

Rosenblum has experience in cover-ups. When a fifty-year-old Orthodox Jewish grandmother reported to him how four ultra–Orthodox men beat her up on a bus she was riding after praying at the Western Wall—because she refused their demand to move to the back—Rosenblum chided her for "going to the media."[24] Small wonder, then, that Rosenblum's column on the Ramat Beit Shemesh allegations turned out to be a sustained piece of special pleading, using every possible sleight of hand to shift the burden of blame from the alleged child abusers to the victims.[25]

Ignoring the details of the abuse reports, Rosenblum first insisted that the allegations could not be true, simply because so many of the parents involved weren't born into Orthodoxy. He developed this peculiar argument as follows: (1) the newly–Orthodox Jews who moved to Ramat Beit Shemesh (presumably seeking a deeply religious lifestyle) were too savvy, thanks to their gritty backgrounds, to "tolerate" rabbis who were "passive in the face of such [sexual] abuse"; and, therefore, (2) no such rabbis could possibly exist there. Riding this roller-coaster of invidious assumptions, Rosenblum went on to indict the concerned parents as liars: since they were, after all, accusing their rabbis of covering up sex abuse, and since they were, on Rosenblum's assumptions, the sort of people who wouldn't tolerate such conduct in the first place, it followed that their accusations were incredible *ipso facto*.[26] Note how this logical trick appears to concede the reality of child sex abuse only to turn it on its head: Orthodox Jews who care about protecting their children from sex abuse can't be believed when they ... try to protect their children from sex abuse. Got it?

Just as parents who believed their children were abused could never be right, Ramat Beit Shemesh's Orthodox rabbis could never be wrong. Rosenblum lauded the town's rabbis as "young, worldly and energetic." But what did those vigorous young rabbis actually do in a case of alleged abuse? What did they look for? Whom did they consult? Rosenblum was silent on those points, and equally uncommunicative on the most important question of all: did the rabbis encourage their congregants to report abuse to police without first seeking rabbinic permission? If they didn't, then for all Rosenblum's cheerleading, we only know that the rabbis *might* support reporting a given case to police, *assuming* that they themselves were persuaded of the sufficiency of the evidence. But of course Rosenblum has given us no idea how, in their view, that standard is to be satisfied. In fact, his lazy generalizing suggested that the rabbis never do resort to the authorities, since in the only cases of alleged abuse he referred to in his column, he applauded the rabbis because "problematic individuals or families were forced to leave the neighborhood." By implication this means that even those "problematic individuals" were not reported to police. If so, when was *any* case reported?

Careless as he was about the key issues, Rosenblum showed his true colors just as clearly when he zeroed in on those few in Ramat Beit Shemesh who had openly supported the criticism aimed at the rabbis (although, revealingly, he never even attempted to refute their complaints). "It is true," Rosenblum wrote caustically, "that the rabbis do not think a teacher should be automatically fired the first time any student complains of untoward behavior, and he and his family stigmatized for life." No one quoted in the press asked for any such thing, but that didn't save the victims from Rosenblum's venom any more than it stopped his favorite rabbis from slandering the accusers in the first place. (Note, too, Rosenblum's gesture of concern for the "family" of the accused, even while sniping at family members of the alleged abuse victims.)

The most amazing part of Rosenblum's column was what it conceded. The gravamen of the public charge, remember, was that the local rabbis had blocked victims from using the secular justice system. Having trashed the critics for daring to make such claims, Rosenblum went on to admit the truth of what they said, while actually transforming rabbinic guilt into a *point d'honneur*. The rabbis did suppress sex abuse reports, said Rosenblum, but they did it *for the victims' own good*. The relevant passage is so bizarre as to merit exact quotation:

> The rabbis' preference for working behind the scenes derives not from a desire to sweep problems under the rug, but from a considered philosophy about what is best for victims, their families and the community. The knowledge that incidents will be publicized can keep victims or their parents from coming forward. In addition, publicity can lead to hysteria in which parents become convinced that their children are at great risk in school. (In fact, more abuse takes place within families or involves older children as perpetrators.)

Let us ignore, for the moment, Rosenblum's self-contradictory notion that letting victims come forward somehow deters other victims from doing the same thing. Let us also forget that he was more concerned with the mere possibility of unwarranted future accusations—"hysteria"—than with the real and present danger facing allegedly abused children and other young students of the same alleged perpetrators. We are still left with a breathtaking euphemism—"working behind the scenes"—for what the critics actually described: rabbis calling accusing parents "liars," rabbis forbidding any contact between parents and police, rabbis punishing the alleged victims of abuse instead of the teachers they accused. *That* is what Rosenblum, as spokesman for the Orthodox rabbinate, was necessarily lauding as the rabbis' "considered philosophy." Rabbis know best; the justice system is not for Orthodox Jews; victims are to be seen and not heard. Sound familiar?

"To allay their sense of guilt," wrote Aldous Huxley, "the bullies and the sadists provide themselves with creditable excuses for their favorite sport," rationalizing "brutality toward children," for instance, as "obedience to the Word of God."[27] Refining its techniques for concealing child sex abuse, the Orthodox rabbinate (through Rosenblum) seems to be following a similar path. Abuse cover-ups, always a means of re-victimizing the young targets of violence, must now be rationalized as a measure taken "for their own good"— as well as a way of serving God, who apparently frowns on Orthodox Jews suffering the legal consequences of their actions.

There is another precedent for Rosenblum's logic, but it is no more encouraging than Huxley's. American Catholic bishops, faced with overwhelming evidence that the Church had covered up child sex abuse by priests, recently were forced to the position that "they had not known any better in previous decades," but that "the problem was solved" once they had acknowledged it.[28] Of course, that self-serving pablum didn't fool anyone. Anyone, that is, but Jonathan Rosenblum, for whom it is enough that Orthodox rabbis are prepared to recognize child sex abuse as an unfortunate reality—in the past—so that now, when "worldly and energetic" rabbis have made that sole admission, the matter is closed and anyone who dares to speak out is a troublemaker whose real agenda is a quarrel with rabbinic wisdom. Once again, cover-ups are good; the rabbis have everything under control; complaining victims must be silenced; the outside world must know nothing of the Orthodox community's faults. Only the verbal window dressing seems to be new.

* * *

Although Rosenblum published his column in the *Jerusalem Post*, where the first of the news articles on Ramat Beit Shemesh appeared, nearly all of his writing on this and similar subjects has been aimed at the Orthodox community.[29] I do not think this is an accident; the rabbinate's first priority is to control the discourse among Orthodox Jews, and spokesmen for the rabbinate have generally picked their audiences accordingly. That leads to the question: How effective are the rabbinate's new lines of denial in controlling discussion about child sex abuse within the Orthodox community itself?

The publication of Judy Brown's novel *Hush* in 2010—at first under the pseudonym Eishes Chayil—offered a convenient test for the application of the rabbinate's recent strategies. After all, *Hush* was a most unusual and provocative book: aimed at young adults, it unflinchingly told the story of a sex abuse cover-up and its tragic effects within a Hasidic community very much like the author's own. And it was seen and read by at least some Orthodox Jews.

At first, predictably, the community's reaction was silence. As the book gained more and more favorable attention, however, a response could not be avoided. Rabbi Tzvi Hersh Weinreb, executive vice president of the Orthodox Union, subtly set the tone in a somewhat belated review, first offering the author grudging praise because she did *not* "claim that incest is rampant, or even prevalent, in the close-knit [Orthodox] community," then cautioning that, despite this, "some find" her narrative "to be 'airing dirty laundry in public.'" Rabbi Weinreb tended to side with the latter: he found "troublesome" the book's implication—he called it a "claim"—"that the community denies, even to itself, that such abuse even exists." He also complained about "the author's portrayal of the females in her life," who appear to be "empty-headed materialists and narrow-minded gossips who are obsessed with surface appearances, shidduchim [marriages] and clothing." Now *there's* a twist: the Orthodox Jewish woman breaking silence about child sex abuse turns out to be ... a misogynist![30]

Although Weinreb's comments were cautious, his multi-pronged critique—faint praise, denial of the scope of the problem, hints that the critic is neither accurate nor fair-minded—could easily be deployed with greater ferocity, as it was probably meant to be. By the time Orthodox readers were commenting openly on the book, the counterattack was already in full swing, as evidenced by an uninhibitedly nasty on-line review posted in November 2011. After describing herself as "an advocate of open discussion as a tool to fight the sexual abuse of children" (Rosenblum had cloaked himself in a similar testimonial), the Orthodox reviewer sneered that *Hush* amounted to "deliberate falsification in order to sell more films/books." Her proof? Well, in telling its story of suppressing the truth about sex abuse, the novel paints an unflattering portrait of Brown's Hasidic community, which *must* be false because it amounts to an attack on God and his faithful: "Someone obviously on the inside, someone who clearly knows better, has decided to badmouth our entire society, our way of life and the Torah itself for the sake of sensationalism." Note how the novel's admitted truth-telling about abuse somehow degenerates to mere "sensationalism" when set against what really matters—namely the Orthodox community's reputation. To make matters worse, Brown had dared to name herself after publication, thus "accusing and hurting [her] family and (former) friends." As with Rabbi Rosenblum's treatment of the abuse allegations in Ramat Beit Shemesh, the moral reversal here is complete: those whose "closed-minded and cruel" actions—the reviewer's words—caused the tragedy in *Hush* have become the real victims, as far as Orthodox Jews are supposed to believe. Their denial of the understanding and honesty an abused child needed to survive no longer matters; what matters is that their reputation for piety might be impaired.[31]

Other Orthodox readers posted similar comments. One claimed that only a "prejudice" reader who delighted in an "attack on the hasidic communities" could "make an assumption that at least some of [what the book portrays] is fact."[32] Since only a Jew-hater could make that "assumption," it followed that the book's portrayal of an abuse cover-up was false *ipso facto*. Another poster insisted that writing about child sex abuse cover-ups "DOES NOT JUSTIFY" what the poster called the book's "underlying tone ... of condescension."[33] Again, the priorities were clear: one may describe how a religious community protects a criminal and facilitates a child's abuse, ending in her death, but not if that description is less than flattering to the community. The poster did not vouchsafe any advice as to how such a description could ever escape her opprobrium, doubtless because no alternative was actually desired.

Perhaps the most vicious counterpoint—though a coincidental one—came from Rabbi Avi Shafran, official spokesman for Agudath Israel of America. Brown revealed her identity as the author of *Hush* in an on-line column shortly after—and largely because—an eight-year-old Hasidic boy, Leiby Kletzky, was found murdered in Brooklyn's Borough Park, and all Orthodox minds seemed fleetingly attuned to questions of child abuse.[34] Days earlier, Shafran had published an article in the Orthodox *Ami Magazine*—which then appeared on-line the very day after Brown's did—in which he fulminated against "some Jews in the polluted realm of Blogistan" who "sought to exploit the death of an innocent child, amazingly, to promote their rabid anti-rabbi agenda."[35] You might think the timing of Brown's dramatic disclosure would have troubled a rabbi who had just smeared everyone concerned about abused Jewish children as "rabid" rabbi-haters and exploiters of the dead. Apparently it didn't, though; Shafran never retracted or qualified what he had written. Nor did he hesitate to add hypocrisy to libel: he registered no objection when his own rabbinic organization hijacked young Kletzky's murder to the tune of $1 million in New York state funds to install security cameras in Orthodox Brooklyn neighborhoods, which Agudath Israel, despite its "long history of shielding the Jewish community from police," would "oversee."[36] I wish I could report an eruption of Orthodox community outrage at Shafran's selective silence, but none was forthcoming. "Exploitation," in this sort of moral universe, is evil when it means honesty for victims of child sex abuse; when it augments the rabbinate's bottom line, it's all for the glory of God.

* * *

Now let us turn to the Orthodox rabbinate's reaction to the primary medium for recent dissent, including criticism of rabbis who have covered up sex crimes. The Internet, with its twin promises of anonymity and instant connection, has opened a new chapter in public discourse among Orthodox Jews, because it allows—really for the first time—far-flung conversations that rabbis cannot directly control and whose participants, as long as they remain unidentified, cannot be threatened with sanctions for criticizing Orthodox leadership. Like it or not, the rabbinate soon found it was powerless to stop that kind of discourse.[37] So it had to develop new strategies for discouraging it.

The innovations weren't long in appearing. In the last month of 2007—the same year public pressure, expressed largely through Internet blogs, resulted in the arrests in Israel of accused serial child molesters Stefan Colmer and Avrohom Mondrowitz—Orthodox leaders mounted hysterical attacks on "Blogistan," as Shafran derisively dubbed the venues of Internet discussion. In prominent articles appearing within weeks of one another, rabbinic publicists insisted that blogs were a "spreading plague" that deserved "zero tolerance."

The thrust of their arguments left no doubt about the focus of concern: what was "deadly" about "Orthodox Jewry's plunge into the quicksand of the 'blogosphere'" was that the writers "criticize and heap scorn on our *gedolei Torah* [leading rabbis] and *manhigei Yisroel* [accepted Orthodox authority figures]."[38]

As with other statements we have examined from representatives of the rabbinate, the challenge to rabbinic power—not the safety of children—was the clergy's biggest problem when it came to Internet discourse. Its spokesmen's articles bristled with pejoratives but were conspicuously silent about the content of the criticism found on the blogs, much of which, of course, had to do with the rabbis' protection of child predators. Rather, the new tide of dissent served mainly as a pretext for avowals of the absolute power rabbis ought to have. For instance, Rabbi Shafran, never one to mince words, insisted that Orthodox rabbis are above questions of truth or justice, no matter how accurately they are being criticized: "Truth may be 'an absolute defense' in American libel law, but not in Jewish law ... the evil of such speech [criticism of rabbis] is inherent, not a function of falsehood."[39]

Thus, Shafran did not accuse the rabbis' critics of lying; he denounced them for having the temerity to discuss their religion outside the parameters of rabbinic control. ("The evil of such speech is inherent.") The *Jewish Observer*, Agudath Israel's house organ, likewise lamented that "most of those blogs [discussing Jewish issues] were full of critiques or absolute *lashon hara* [critical speech] about the revered *tzaddikim* [righteous rabbis]" and that "many are written and visited by religious Jews."[40] Again, this lament did *not* claim that the "critiques" were *false*. By implication that didn't matter: Orthodox rabbis, like Hegel's "great men of history," were assumed to be above the moral constraints that govern their communities. In a separate article, Rabbi Asher Meir underscored the same point by stressing that leading rabbis cannot be treated like other mortals, not even by the Orthodox Jews they purportedly serve:

> While we are commanded to judge every member of our people favorably, this mitzvah [religious commandment] applies with greater force to Torah scholars and leaders. So information which might be considered damning to an ordinary person may justify a more charitable interpretation to these individuals.

To me, there is something really terrifying in this casually enunciated double standard. In its context—and remember, all this was written about Internet blogs discussing child abuse and rabbinic cover-ups—it means that an abused child, who is merely "an ordinary person," is automatically less credible than a "Torah scholar," so that even if his or her criminal accusation is supported by "damning" evidence, the pious Jew must support the accused abuser, and his rabbinic protectors, over the victim. And this, not because we disbelieve the child or are convinced by the rabbis, but simply because of the latter's superior religious stature. According to Meir, Orthodox rabbis are raised so far above the demands of justice that they can seldom be judged at all. Even when guilty, they enjoy a special immunity from their victims' charges since, he says, "[t]he damage done [by an accusation] ... is greater when leaders are scorned."[41] So the fact that an accusation against a rabbi, especially a prominent one, may cause the target to be "scorned" tells decisively against it—even if it is true. Political power trumps justice.

What clearly worried the rabbis' spokesmen most was not just that the truth was being *told* on blogs—it was being *believed*. "Perhaps even more disturbing" than Orthodox Jews daring to print information critical of rabbis, according to Shafran, was "the apparent gullibility of so many visitors to those blogs, who ... seem ready to swallow any accusation or character assassination, as long as the charges are sufficiently salacious or forcefully asserted."[42] Of course, no one in his or her right mind would believe everything found on the Internet, but for that very reason it is hard to credit Shafran's ostensive concern about the "gullibility" of readers. The real problem was the spread of justified complaints, not the occasional dupe falling for a specious one. And Shafran's choice of words—"salacious," "accusation," "forcefully asserted"—in this crucial passage brought him as close as he ever came to admitting what all the discussion was really about: for as he well knew, accusations that Orthodox rabbis had both committed and covered up sex crimes for decades were being proved, beyond any reasonable doubt, at the very moment his column appeared.

In fact, Shafran himself, in a followup to his "Blogistan" column several years later, could not deny that blog discussion might have raised awareness of "the scope and tragedy of [child] abuse," a fact that, by that time, even his superiors at Agudath Israel had been forced to acknowledge. In Shafran's eyes, though, this only added to the evil of public truth-telling by Orthodox Jews. The fact that their criticisms forced an issue of such moment into public scrutiny illustrated, for Shafran, the critics' "unbridled and unhidden contempt" for rabbis and proved that "[i]t is not the welfare of the Jewish people they seek, but rather ... to attack and undermine true Jewish authority."[43] The choice of words was revealing: for Shafran, fighting child abuse did not protect "the Jewish people," evidently because the only people who really matter are those who represent "Jewish authority" (which must never be undermined), that is, rabbis. Protecting *them*—not ridding the community of dangerous predators—enhances "the welfare of the Jewish people."

Other officials of Shafran's organization have affirmed the same hierarchy of values, deploring the exposure of criminal cover-ups even as they admit the critics' accuracy. Thus the *New York Times* reported:

> David Zwiebel, executive vice president of Agudath Israel ... acknowledged that dissidents had surfaced a troubling issue [that is, child sexual abuse]. But, he asked, is it "worth the cost?" "At the very least," he added, "it's rechilus, lashon hara, and bittul zman." Translated this means malicious gossip, evil tongue, and waste of time, all prohibited by the Torah.[44]

For one not trained in doublethink, it can be difficult to keep the real subject in focus while reading such a passage. Let us be clear: the point is not whether blog discussions contain a good deal of nonsense, gossip, slander, *ad hominem* attacks, and so forth. Of course they do. The point is Zwiebel's blanket assumption that the persiflage in this discourse weighs against the value of exposing criminal conspiracies, something that, by Zwiebel's own admission, could hardly have been accomplished anywhere but on the Internet. Let us leave to one side the fact that, in the absence of rabbinic censorship, Orthodox Jews probably would not have taken their complaints to blogs in the first place. The bigger problem is that if we take seriously Zwiebel's assumption about the "cost" of Internet truth-telling, we cannot simultaneously credit his opening premise, namely that child sex abuse is a "troubling issue." If it is, why is exposing it a "waste of time?" If child abuse cover-ups are unacceptable, why is denouncing them "malicious gossip?" And why is Zwiebel's only unequivocal, unconditional denunciation—"prohibited by the Torah"—aimed not at protecting child abusers but at blog discussions devoted to exposing them? Putting Zwiebel's words into practice could only mean curtailing the one forum for public discussion that has forced the rabbinate to admit that the problem exists. It isn't hard to imagine the consequences for rabbinic candor if that forum were shut down.

It is worth stressing here that even the rabbis' admission that their critics are telling the truth about child sex abuse does represent a change of position. In the past, the same spokesmen were willing to throw truth to the winds in the face of public criticism. Shafran, for instance, denounced a 1996 report in the *New York Daily News* about the revival of the use of concubines among contemporary ultra–Orthodox Jews. The story was meticulously documented. The reporter, Susan Forrest, met and talked with several of the concubines; she even collected voice mail messages left by numerous Orthodox customers on the service's answering machine. (There were also messages from some of the customers' angry wives.) But Shafran called the story "unsubstantiated" and whined, in a column printed in the Jewish magazine *Moment*, that articles like Forrest's proved it was "open season" on Orthodox Jews in the secular media.[45] That Shafran, years later, could at least tacitly concede the systematic cover-ups alleged in popular media represents a significant retrenchment.

But as I have tried to show, that shift in position owes less to rabbinic reform than to public pressure, which the rabbis, for all their posturing, are doing their best to deflect. Surely real reform would look considerably different from this. To begin with, Orthodox rabbis could publicly address cases like that of Mordechai Jungreis, who reported to police that a member of his Hasidic community had sexually abused his mentally disabled son. Jungreis quickly found himself ostracized by other Hasidim, including "the mother of a child in a wheelchair" who said that "the same man had molested her son, and she 'did not report this crime, so why did [Jungreis] have to?'"[46] Here complicity has actually become a virtue, a badge of honor to be waved at the victim who dares to seek the same justice spurned by other victims. This is the sort of theological evil the rabbinate is perfectly positioned to correct—if it really wants to change the culture of denial and cover-ups.

Similarly, the rabbis could speak out against the perverse ideal of "forgiveness" too often used to bully Orthodox abuse victims into joining the silence that protects their abusers. One target of such bullying, the mother of two sexually abused boys, one of whom later killed himself, sadly emailed me that she was resigned to the idea that the world holds no justice for children like hers: "only [God]," she wrote, "could be judge and jury" over her children's abuser. No doubt she heard this from the rabbis who warned her not to report their abuse in the first place. Isn't it time the rabbinate atoned for such sins by teaching a more humane ethic? Honesty alone demands it. The nostrum that only God metes out justice to criminals is still peddled to abuse victims. But the same rabbis who tell that tale take a different line when faced with other grievances—those that, unlike the complaints of children, work in tandem with religious power politics. Rabbi Meir Soloveichik, for instance, in an essay widely circulated among Orthodox Jews, has insisted that there must be no "forgiveness" for Palestinians who resist Israeli occupation: "When we are facing those who seek nothing but our destruction, our hate reminds us who we are dealing with. When hate is appropriate, then it is not only virtuous, but essential for Jewish well-being."[47] Setting aside the rabbi's distortion of the Israel-Palestine conflict and his blindness toward the legitimate causes of resistance, isn't it rank hypocrisy for the same rabbis who endorse "hate" in one context to demand that victims of child sexual abuse forgive and forget? Why is it "virtuous" to hate Palestinians, whose chief crime appears to be that they are Palestinian, but wrong to seek just retribution against the victimizers of children? The only way to make sense of this double standard is to note, again, the arrangement of priorities: by implication, children are expendable to "Jewish well-being"; Palestinian land isn't. No one who thought of children first as human beings, rather than as shares of human stock the community leadership may bargain with as it sees fit, could fail to see an irony as ghastly as that. If Orthodox rabbis really want reform, how about some public teaching along those lines?

"There is no nice way of saying it," said Pearl Engelman, mother of an alleged sex abuse victim whose attacker is still teaching Hasidic children in Williamsburg, New York. "Our community protects molesters. Other than that, we are wonderful."[48] Of course, Ms. Engelman's tone was sardonic, but the comment deserves more than passing attention, because far too many Orthodox Jews—including many who claim to be advocates for victimized children—do inflect child abuse cover-ups as something genuinely exceptional, an aberration in an otherwise moral society. But is it reasonable to suppose that a community that has no qualms about protecting child rapists is really a moral one? Why should protecting child molesters be dismissed as an exception? Isn't it much more probably symptomatic of a larger pattern of evil? If it is, the Orthodox rabbinate's grudging, partial, and often hypocritical reforms so far do not even amount to an honest beginning.

*   *   *

I should not leave this part of my analysis without stressing the horrible effects of the rabbinic denial I have been examining. In a recent journal article, Steven Resnicoff, a professor at DePaul University's College of Law, pulls no punches about the appalling results of the sexual abuse of children in Orthodox Jewish communities:

> The consequences of this abuse can be devastating. Numerous studies indicate that the likelihood of suicide and attempted suicide are dramatically greater for those who were sexually abused as children than for those who were not. Indeed, psychologists deeply involved in the Orthodox Jewish community have called for more action to combat child sexual abuse because of the "unconscionable number of suicides of children who have been sex abuse victims." ... In addition to an increased propensity for actual or attempted suicide, child sexual abuse victims suffer a panoply of other extremely physically and emotionally traumatic, dangerous, and life-altering consequences. These short-term and long-term consequences include nightmares, flashbacks, fear, anxiety, panic-attacks, depression, social withdrawal, anger, hostility, mistrust, poor self esteem, inclination toward substance abuse, eating disorders, inappropriate sexual behavior, criminality, difficulty in developing and maintaining close social relationships, and a greater risk of sexually transmitted diseases, including HIV infection.[49]

It need hardly be added that the pain is doubled when the abuse is overtly linked with religious authority, whether through the perpetrator or his enablers: "Those harmed within a religious institution—especially if abused by religious authorities—suffer trauma, shame, and guilt in a way that is different from the emotional, social, and physical injury of all abuse victims," as one expert writes.[50]

Suicides, violence, crime, depression, panic, drug addiction, deadly disease, shame—that's a short summary of the hell the Orthodox rabbinate has fueled with decades of denial. Yet the rabbis, as I have shown, do not want to purge this evil; they want to minimize it, to fend off its implications as much as possible. They want to tear off the scarlet letter without really acknowledging, let alone correcting, the nature of their complicity.

Am I being too harsh? Not according to those who should know best. Judy Brown, author of *Hush*, grew up in a Hasidic family and wrote her novel to exorcise her own traumatic experience of witnessing her best friend being sexually abused when both girls were children. After Rabbi Nechemya Weberman was found guilty of repeatedly abusing a young girl sent to him for "therapy," Brown framed an eloquent public appraisal of today's Orthodox community "reforms." First she summarized the conventional wisdom of "those in the ultra–Orthodox community" who

> say that much has changed, that there is more awareness than before. They say that many schools have taken on the issue, bringing in experts and educating teachers about the symptoms and dangers of abuse; so why don't the survivors just shut up already? Why do they still demand attention and embarrass the community in the media? What more do they want?

Then she gave the answer:

> This is a community that wants to leave sin, so long as it can do so without expressing regret. It is willing to change the future, so long as we allow it to forget the past, so long as we don't ask it to account for its actions. It wants change, it really does, but the change is conditional: change on its own terms, change it can take credit for without ever looking back, change that is another form of denial.[51]

Still think I'm being too harsh? Then listen to the words of a survivor whose abuser, an Orthodox rabbi, is still at large. He told me he feels less anger toward his attacker than toward the Orthodox community that followed rabbinic guidance in protecting the man. While a bullet in one's flesh "does the damage," he said, it's obviously the one who fires the gun who deserves the greatest blame.

And then he said what the Orthodox rabbinate cannot bring itself to admit, just as it will not accept Charlotte Brontë's reminder that the "whitewashed walls" of an unexamined religious public do not "vouch for clean shrines" within: "The abuser is the bullet. He does the damage. But the *community*—all the people who let him get close to you, who don't stop him when the damage starts, who don't listen when you tell them ... *they're* the ones who pull the trigger."

PART II

Who Guards the Guardians?

We hold the broken truth, the one we experienced firsthand when our rabbis, teachers, and leaders ripped their own lie piece by piece, life by life, in front of our eyes, and then intimidated, threatened, brutalized and suppressed any victim or witness who dared speak out, warning that they would destroy us and our broken truth if we did not accept their lie....

The Internet is terrifying to the rabbanim perhaps because of porn, perhaps because it exposes youth to foreign ideas, but even more importantly, because it enables open dialogue and an honesty they cannot afford if they are to survive as a community, the community they insist they are; pure, innocent, and above their own frailties. And if a few children must be sacrificed for this wholesome lie, then so be it. It is better than any broken truth.

—Judy Brown, "The Importance of
Internet Asifa," May 20, 2012

5

Abuse of Power, Orthodox Style

You cannot expect a group of landlords to enforce laws which reduce rent.

—Benjamin Spock and Mitchell Zimmerman[1]

Do the names Rafael Valis and Malka Sitner ring any bells?

Probably they don't; few people remember the tragic stories of these two Israeli children. Yet for a time, both of them figured in news that stretched far out of Israel, far beyond the enclaves of the ultra–Orthodox, merging briefly into the general bustle of international media. The names belonged to two very young people—babies, in fact—who died needless deaths not many years ago, and whose stories, for reasons I will try to explain, ought to be better known.

Neither Rafael Valis nor Malka Sitner was sexually abused; their place in this book is not among the grim roll call of Orthodox Jewish children who have been molested, only to have the facts of their cases suppressed, ignored or misrepresented. Yet both of them were born into Orthodox Jewish families—where they died soon afterward—and the very obscurity of their names, in death as in life, reflects the cruel paradox of their victimization.

Their short lives were ushered out with a hullabaloo in the Orthodox Jewish press, a fact unsurprising in itself, for the reporters had plenty to write about: following these children's deaths, Orthodox Jews rioted in the streets, set fires, destroyed property, attacked police, issued frantic rabbinic edicts, and made angry claims of mistreatment while threatening still more violence. But here is the paradox and the cruelty: absolutely none of this fury was exercised on behalf of the two dead children. On the contrary. All of it served the interests of those who caused their deaths. And it was encouraged by Orthodox Jewish leadership.

If Orthodox rabbis really mean to protect children from sexual abuse (as they keep telling us), if the cover-ups and stifling of reports I have been describing are really aberrational, then how do we explain the rabbinate's position in *other* controversies that pit children's welfare against other rabbinic values? Why do children consistently lose out to almost any other consideration?

As long as that question remains unanswered, I think we are forced to the despondent conclusion of Orthodox writer Judy Brown, quoted at the beginning of this section of the book—namely that rabbinic concealment of child sex abuse is not an aberration at all. It is part and parcel of the "wholesome lie" with which the community protects its self-image. The community's pious façade, Brown has written, is sacrosanct; the rabbinate will protect it even if that means "a few children must be sacrificed."[2] I wish I could prove her wrong.

* * *

Let us begin with the case of Rafael Valis. Having lived only three months, Rafael died in Jerusalem in April 2006 from injuries that resulted from the severe beatings administered by his Hasidic father, Yisrael Valis, himself just nineteen years old. Valis, who was eventually convicted of manslaughter,[3] had not only hurled the baby against a wall—because he was crying—but had repeatedly bitten and punched the infant since its birth. According to Jerusalem police, the father "did not accept" little Rafael, "due to a defect in the child's neck muscles."[4]

Rabbinic leadership promptly sprang to the father's side. Even though Valis had admitted to beating the baby—an admission he later retracted—Rabbis Yosef Shalom Elyashiv and Chaim Kanievsky issued a public decree declaring him innocent, much as they would do a few years later for the brutal child abuser Rabbi Elior Chen. Armed with such rabbinic support, "extremist elements in the haredi [ultra–Orthodox] community ... threatened to riot and to 'make Jerusalem burn'" unless the father was set free. The "extremists" were as good as their word. Violent protests spread rapidly through Orthodox Jerusalem neighborhoods, causing tens of thousands of dollars' worth of property damage and leading to tense negotiations between rabbis and civic authorities to forestall further rioting.[5]

The evidence against Valis was undeniably strong; what is more, the judge who sentenced him noted that Valis had "expressed no remorse for his actions whatsoever."[6] Nevertheless, all discourse under rabbinic control presented Valis as a victim of injustice and anti–Orthodox bigotry. Orthodox publicist Sarah Shapiro compared a cartoon about the case on a "secular" Internet news site to "something from *Der Stuermer*."[7] Meanwhile, leading rabbis, while silent about the fate of the dead child, called the charges against his father—a "good, quiet and disciplined" young man, according to ultra–Orthodox politician Meir Porush[8]—a "blood libel."[9] In keeping with an all too familiar pattern, the child's death was apparently less offensive to Orthodox leadership than the stain it threatened to place on the community's image.

The next such "sacrifice"—to use Judy Brown's word—was not long in coming. Malka Sitner, an infant aged a few months, died quietly one Sunday morning in May—about a month after Rafael Valis—following a week during which she suffered from a high fever that her parents, according to police, refused to treat with the antibiotic prescribed by the girl's doctor. News reports duly informed the public that the parents—American immigrants to Israel— were vegans who believed in "natural medicine" and preferred a homeopathic treatment to a life-saving drug.

If that choice caused their daughter's death, as police maintained at the time, the sincerity of the parents' belief alone would not have protected them from legal consequences; they might well have been charged with negligent homicide. But the Sitners were Hasidic Jews, a fact that made their personal beliefs a matter of politics, since in Israel (as in Brooklyn) the right-wing Orthodox—or *haredim*, as they are more commonly called in Israel—form a powerful voting bloc. Most ultra–Orthodox Jews are not vegans, but they do generally oppose autopsies—as ordered in the Sitner case—on religious grounds. They are also suspicious of Israel's secular government, to them an alien and sometimes threatening force. Such, at least, were the reasons given publicly for the sudden eruption of *haredi* violence and obstructionism on the heels of the announcement of a coroner's inquest into Malka Sitner's death, an inquest that might have paved the way for an indictment of her parents.

Rioting started before an investigation could even begin. Out of nowhere, a crowd of more than a thousand ultra–Orthodox Jews converged on the Ashdod cemetery where the girl's tiny corpse was temporarily housed; in minutes, the mob was trying to invade its buildings in an effort to prevent what they called a "desecration" of the body. While some of the pious pelted policemen with stones and empty bottles, shouting epithets, others destroyed cemetery property. Still others broke inside the private room where bodies are stored, pried open the heavy refrigerator door with a crowbar and spirited away little Malka's remains.

"One young guy stood at the entrance of the women's bathroom, like he was guarding the women's privacy," boasted Yoel Greuss, an ultra–Orthodox veteran of many such corpse-stealings, years after the riot. "Inside there were a few men.... [One of them] climbed up the wall, broke the window and climbed down into the next room where the refrigerator was. He broke open the refrigerator door, took out the little girl's body, pushed it through the window down to the guys on the other side, and they ran out of the bathroom with it." A getaway car containing the corpse then managed to beat the police out of Ashdod, Greuss added proudly, because "God protects us."[10]

No trace of the girl's body has ever been found.

By the lights of Greuss and his fellow *haredim*, this ghoulish escapade was a double victory: not only did they prevent an autopsy—which, according to their reading of some traditional Jewish texts, causes pain to the soul of the departed—the rioters also paralyzed the inquiry into Malka's death, saving her parents from a possible criminal charge for letting her die.

"They've won," admitted Yehuda Hiss, Israel's chief coroner at the time— and there could be no doubt that little Malka Sitner was not among the victors.[11]

But were the grave-robbers merely fanatics, unrepresentative of Orthodox Jews in general? And if so, was the same true of the most belligerent supporters of Yisrael Valis after his son's killing? Most Orthodox spokesmen would later characterize both groups in exactly that way. Still, after ugly eruptions like those in the Valis and Sitner cases, which shocked much of the Israeli public, one might have expected to hear at least a few rabbinic voices raised against the use of mob violence to subvert investigations into young children's deaths.

Yet nothing of the sort ever happened. In fact, rabbinic sympathies continued to incline to the killers. Months after Valis confessed to the brutal abuse of his infant son, several leading Orthodox rabbis, with bevies of *yeshiva* students at their heels, were still making pilgrimages to Valis' apartment—where he was held under house arrest awaiting trial—to join him for daily prayers. Meanwhile, a prominent Orthodox rabbi in Ashdod, asked by police to request his community's assistance in locating Malka Sitner's burial place, angrily refused. On the contrary, he declared, anyone who brought information to the police would be an "informer" and subject to the most extreme penalties. After all, the police were persecuting the Orthodox; they were no better than Nazis.[12] And when an Israeli reporter visited the sect from which Malka's body-snatchers apparently issued, in Jerusalem's cluttered and deeply Orthodox Meah Shearim neighborhood, and was pointedly told that if he didn't leave at once on his own "we'll use other ways,"[13] rabbinic leadership was silent about that too—even after this thuggish threat was widely publicized.

Altogether, the ultra–Orthodox press offered scarcely a word of criticism for any of these criminal acts. Its publicists didn't even pause to express concern for the dead children or for others whose lives might be jeopardized by repeat performances of the Valis or Sitner riots. Instead, the Orthodox writers focused their ire on Larry Derfner, the journalist who covered the two stories for the right-wing *Jerusalem Post*. While admitting that neither Derfner nor his paper could be called "an inveterate chareidi-baiter," Rabbi Jonathan Rosenblum (whose column was typical) nevertheless freely retrofitted the facts of both cases into a fairy tale of the misunderstood Orthodox and the Big Bad Press.

Rosenblum found no fault at all with Orthodox leadership, even when faced with some embarrassing questions. For instance: Had the rabbis demanded the return of Malka Sitner's body for medical tests into the cause of her death, as reasonable people would have done? No, Rosenblum couldn't say they had—he even admitted that "thwarting the police" had given "folk hero status" to ultra–Orthodox Jews in similar situations. And didn't those same Orthodox rabbis actually order their flocks to *support* the father accused and later convicted of beating little Rafael Valis to death? Didn't they insist that every Orthodox Jew help fund Valis' legal defense? Well, yes, admitted Rosenblum; but that was only "an act of self-defense for hundreds of thousands who will inevitably find themselves tarred by the act of any member of the community."[14] As for the rabbis' winking at the Sitner body-snatching, Rosenblum weirdly blamed the *police*, on the grounds that they had treated the girl's death as suspicious in the first place.[15]

You almost have to admire the pathological beauty of this web of *non sequiturs*. According to Rosenblum, police have no business investigating a possible crime if the suspects are Orthodox Jews. As for the Orthodox Jews themselves, they *have* to protect coreligionists who kill their children, because, if those criminals were to face the justice they deserve, all other Orthodox Jews would run the risk of being identified with child-killers. A less daring mind than Rosenblum's might suggest that the best way to prevent such identification would be not to support the child abusers to begin with, at least not with violent demonstrations and rabbinic fiats. Similarly, most people would probably conclude that the quickest way the Sitners and their supporters could have allayed the authorities' suspicions would have been to cooperate with their investigation, instead of making off with the evidence and hurling bottles at police officers who tried to protect it. But an approach that reasonable wasn't open to an apologist for the rabbis. After all, Israel's single most respected ultra–Orthodox rabbinic leader had already accused the police of a "blood libel" for arresting Rafael Valis' accused killer and—along with two other rabbis—had even threatened a new round of violence if the man wasn't released.[16] In Rosenblum's world, therefore, supporting the accused murderer was a categorical imperative.

And the right of little children not to be bashed to death, not to be negligently allowed to die? Anyone interested in those questions would have to look elsewhere. For all his air of pious concern, Rosenblum didn't even discuss them.

He did manage to misrepresent the facts, insisting, for instance, that Rafael Valis' body showed no marks from his father's teeth, despite police reports to the contrary[17]—not to mention the father's own admission during questioning that he had slapped and violently shaken the baby the very night it was hospitalized.[18] I should add that Rosenblum, a graduate of Yale Law

School, was clever enough not to mention the rabbis' stated reason for continuing to insist on the father's innocence, as quoted in the *Jerusalem Post*: "Valis' wife was still supporting him ... if he had indeed killed his son, she would not be at his side still."[19] Maybe Rosenblum, unlike the venerable rabbis, had learned the words "denial" and "wishful thinking." Or maybe he could grasp the absurdity of enjoining an entire community to support a man because he is innocent, then proving the man's innocence from the fact that one community member—namely his wife—supported him. In any event, the important thing for Rosenblum was that Derfner, whose reporting of this appalling case was admittedly accurate, was still guilty of "a particularly nasty attack on the chareidi community" because he had depicted Orthodox Jews as "marching in lockstep conformity to orders from above."[20] Gosh, what fair-minded person could ever have suggested *that*?[21]

Rabbi Yaakov Menken was even dodgier in his attack on Derfner's articles, which he called "needlessly inflammatory"—a criticism he did *not* extend to rabbis who labeled a legitimate criminal charge a "blood libel" and orchestrated physical assaults on police. Apart from that curious double standard, Menken's main contribution to the story was falsification. According to him, Yisrael Valis confessed "under duress"—a claim never established in court— and there were no physical signs of child abuse on Valis' dead son (as already noted, evidence showed that there were). Meanwhile, in Menken's analysis, to suggest that Orthodox leadership had anything to do with stealing Malka Sitner's body, despite abundant proof of their long-standing approval of such acts, was "a calumny bereft of the least note of underlying reason."[22]

The obvious question missing from these Orthodox apologetics, and others like them, was why so much pious outrage was mustered to protect parents accused of causing their children's deaths, while no one in the Orthodox rabbinate showed a similar concern about the ill-fated children themselves. That, of course, is the reason these stories matter so much. They are among the clearest possible illustrations of where children really stand in the power structure of Orthodox Jewish society. Is a child's right to live at least as important as the public image of those who would extenuate its death? If the Orthodox community's answer is "yes"—as it certainly should be—then why were Rafael Valis and Malka Sitner reduced to nonpersons in Orthodox public discourse, while our rabbis incited their flocks against those few who sought justice for them? And if the answer is "no," is it any surprise that our community tolerates cover-ups when children are merely sexually abused?

* * *

Perhaps, one might argue, the Valis and Sitner cases were departures from the Orthodox norm, incidents that could only happen under the peculiar conditions of Israeli secular/religious politics. It is true that ultra–Orthodox mobs have not attacked morgues in the United States; it is also true that the special culture of state-supported insularity for the *haredim*—in which a large proportion of adults are not even gainfully employed, so that their lives revolve entirely around religious teachings and institutions—is notably an Israeli phenomenon.

But I'm afraid the priorities dramatized by the Valis and Sitner stories are far from uncommon. Consider the case of *m'tzitzah b'peh*—that is, the oral suction of an incision traditionally used in Jewish circumcision. When this practice triggered reasonable concern from New York health officials, Orthodox leadership never wavered: exactly as in the Valis and Sitner cases, it took sides against vulnerable children and in favor of those who endangered them.

The issue had simmered in New York City since late 2004, when Rabbi Yitzchok Fischer, a *mohel*—that is, a rabbi who surgically circumcises newborn Jewish boys in the ancient ritual Jews know as the *b'ris milah* (or simply *b'ris*)— reportedly infected a series of infants with herpes simplex through the traditional use of *m'tzitzah b'peh*. In this part of the procedure the *mohel*, after cutting off the foreskin, sucks some blood from the baby's penis, his mouth in direct contact with the wound. Ironically, this practice was originally prescribed by the Talmud in order to protect the child from infection or sickness as a result of the incision: Galen, the reigning medical expert of the early Middle Ages, regarded such bleeding as a sovereign remedy. We know today, of course, that this oral suction not only doesn't protect children from infection but can actually promote it. Wise religions adapt: for more than a century, most Orthodox Jewish *mohalim* have used a sterile glass tube for this part of the ritual, avoiding any direct contact with the wound.

However, the ancient practice has persisted in many Hasidic communities and, increasingly in recent times, under the auspices of fundamentalist-minded Orthodox rabbis for whom the Talmud is still the last word on all subjects.[23] Today these more fundamentalist communities have come to dominate contemporary Orthodox practice wherever their numbers are concentrated, with predictable consequences for *m'tzitzah b'peh*. According to Rabbi Chaim David Zwiebel, a leading official of one of America's largest Orthodox Jewish organizations, oral suction is now used in about 2,000 circumcisions every year in New York City alone, accounting for about two-thirds of all ritual circumcisions among Orthodox Jews there.[24] Rabbi Fischer preferred to perform the ritual the old-fashioned way—and, as we will see, preferred not to acknowledge the medical danger of placing one's mouth on a newborn baby's bleeding genitals.

There may be some legitimate difference of opinion about the statistical level of risk posed by *m'tzitzah b'peh* in general. But when the *mohel* is infected with the chronic virus herpes simplex—and Fischer's record certainly suggested that he was among the many infected adults—the picture is ominously clear. Herpes, which causes cold sores, is rarely more than a nuisance to adults, but it can be fatal when conveyed into the bloodstream of a newborn. Rabbi Moshe Tendler, an independent-minded Orthodox professor of Talmud at Yeshiva University and also a microbiologist, has emphasized that the proper focus under such conditions should be on the danger to children: "The rule that's above all rules in the Torah," he says, "is that you cannot expose or accept a risk to health unless there is true justification for it.... Now there have been several cases of herpes [in circumcised infants] in the metro [New York] area.... All we're talking about now is presumptive evidence, and on that alone it would be improper according to Jewish law to do oral suction."[25] In Fischer's case, the presumptive evidence looked serious indeed: by late 2004 there were three known cases in which babies he had circumcised had contracted the virus, and one of the three had died as a result.

New York City's health commissioner ordered Fischer to undergo blood tests for herpes, and to stop using oral suction until the issue was resolved. But, according to court papers filed by the health department, he went right on using oral suction on bleeding babies. In December 2004, the city sought a court order to stop him, warning that "the possible transmission of herpes simplex in infants is continuing as a result of the ... practice of Metzizah bi peh."[26]

At that point, the story hit the local press, though I learned about it only the following Saturday, as did many other Orthodox Jews all over the United States. I'm not a keen reader of tabloids and had only barely heard that week some talk about the connection between circumcision and herpes. But when the time came for the rabbi to deliver his sermon in the elegant main sanctuary of Passaic, New Jersey's largest Orthodox synagogue, I was surprised to hear him depart from his usual practice of commenting on the weekly Torah passage and instead pronounce angrily on the Fischer case. What he had to say was worse than surprising: he insisted it was absolutely forbidden for any religious Jew to believe a word against such a well-known rabbi and *mohel* simply because charges had been stated in "a secular newspaper." He didn't mention the infant death, the undisputed infections or the legal papers filed under penalty of perjury by health department attorneys, all of which were publicly available by then. Conveying what turned out to be a widely-distributed rabbinic statement prepared on Rabbi Fischer's behalf, he went on to say that he could assure us all "for a fact" that Rabbi Fischer didn't even have herpes: he had already taken a blood test under the auspices of a prominent university hospital, and it was negative.

Pronounced solemnly between the polished wooden walls and stained glass of a large sanctuary to a silent congregation, the declaration sounded almost credible; I began to wonder if, after all, New York City officials might be acting hastily. But the "fact" turned out be a fabrication. The promised medical report from Fischer never materialized. Through his lawyer, Mark J. Kurzmann, Fischer claimed publicly to be "cooperating" with the city's orders to undergo a blood test, but no evidence of such a test was ever presented to authorities.[27] Without any evidence clearing the rabbi, New York state health officials barred him from performing oral suction, but soon withdrew the ban on the strength of an assurance that "the [Hasidic] community was instituting its own self-policing procedures." Alas, that assurance proved as untrue as Fischer's earlier claims: in 2007, "after Rabbi Fischer was linked to another case of neonatal herpes ... he was prohibited ... by the state Department of Health from performing metzitzah b'peh 'in and throughout the state of New York,'" and further "prohibited from engaging in any other practice in which he '[allows his] mouth or oral fluids to come in direct contact with an infant's genitals.'"

The ban didn't stop the rabbi, however. He went on performing oral suction on bleeding penises, meanwhile claiming, in defiance of the well-known facts, that the act had had no consequences. In March 2012, nearly five years after the putative "self-policing" arrangement, the *New York Jewish Week*'s Hella Winston reported a tape-recorded conversation in which Fischer scheduled a circumcision, including *metzitzah b'peh*. On tape, Fischer assured the parent of a newborn boy that the procedure is "perfectly OK," insisting that a recently reported death of yet another infant the previous September from a herpes simplex infection was "mistakenly reported to the public as being the result of metzitzah b'peh" when in fact the infection "had nothing to do with the mohel." False again, at least according to the director of public affairs for the chief medical examiner of New York City.[28] And still Fischer went on defying health authorities, risking a potentially lethal infection in every baby he circumcised.

With the infant death toll mounting and facing a well-publicized scofflaw, New York City Mayor Michael Bloomberg finally seemed to have had enough. "There is probably nobody in public life who fights harder for the separation of church and state than I do," he told reporters, "but I just wanted to remind everybody: religious liberty does not simply extend to injuring others or putting children at risk."[29]

Now it was the turn of the Orthodox rabbinate to act. To rational minds, there could seem little doubt as to the correct move. Every consideration militated in favor of cooperating with the government's position. Medical evidence pointed up the risk posed to newborns by *m'tzitzah b'peh*, at least when the *mohel* was infected with herpes (as are a great many adults). Jewish law had originally sanctioned the practice only under the mistaken belief that it *protected* children; and even the Talmud required only suction, not necessarily the *oral* suction that placed children at risk. Orthodox Jewish authorities had allowed a safe alternative for well over a hundred years, and some contemporary Orthodox scholars (like Rabbi Moshe Tendler, quoted earlier) actually *preferred* the use of a sterile tube. The Health Department was not demanding a ban on oral suction, only the use of an "informed consent" waiver to be signed by parents before their son's circumcision. Finally, Talmudic tradition has always accepted the authority of governing secular law so long as it does not require a Jew to violate a religious imperative, which was certainly not the case here.

If the safety of children really were a priority of the Orthodox rabbinate, then, the rabbis' acquiescence to health authorities in this case should have been a foregone conclusion.

Yet the rabbis did the exact opposite.

Instead of accepting the twin dictates of medical reality and ethical priority, the Orthodox leadership went to war. Two hundred ultra–Orthodox rabbis promptly signed a joint statement accusing the Health Department of "lies and mischaracterizations" in support of its "evil decrees," forbidding all Orthodox Jews "to participate in the evil plans of the New York City Health Department" even to the extent of signing a form acknowledging the possible risk of *m'tzitzah b'peh*. The city government's real goal, the rabbis falsely claimed, was to outlaw circumcision altogether.[30] Rabbi David Niederman, head of the influential United Jewish Organizations of Williamsburg, even told the *New York Post* that "no one will comply with the law" if it even minimally reduced rabbinic authority to require oral suction.[31] He was not alone: in Israel, an Orthodox rabbi told the press that "haredim will continue to uphold the tradition without any change," regardless of government action.[32]

"Going to Battle," screamed the cover of the Orthodox weekly *Ami Magazine*, which in a single August 2012 issue ran three separate articles on the subject.[33] Not long afterward, *Yated Ne'eman*, an English-language mainstay of the right wing of American Orthodoxy, called the Health Department's warnings about *m'tzitzah b'peh* a "libel," insisted—per the already established rabbinic party line—that the proposed measure was the beginning of a worldwide campaign against Jewish circumcision, and accused the government of "callousness to the Jewish community," or worse.[34] Rabbi Yisrael Belsky, head of Yeshiva Torah Vodaas in Brooklyn and one of the United States' most influential Orthodox rabbis, was still recuperating that summer from a medical crisis that had kept him hospitalized for some three months earlier in the year, but there was no sign of frailty in his determination to fight any attempt to impose sanitary standards on *mohalim*. To *Ami*'s editor in chief, Belsky denounced the application of health regulations to the use of oral suction in terms most readers would associate more readily with Taliban mullahs than with someone in twenty-first century New York City.

"Where do these people come in and tell *mohalim* what to do?" he demanded. "They don't have any understanding of this field."[35] (I'm reminded of the quick-tempered Israeli driver of a crowded bus I was riding into Monsey, New York many years ago. When asked to put out the cigarette he was smoking in defiance of local law and to the annoyance of several passengers, he stuck out his thickly-bearded jaw and snapped, "I don't tell you how to do your jobs; don't tell me how to drive my bus.") As for the goal of protecting children from a dangerous infection, Belsky could hardly contain his contempt for the medical data involved, which showed that over an eleven-year period eleven newborns in New York City alone had contracted herpes after the procedure, resulting in ten hospitalizations, two infant deaths and two cases of brain damage.

"What do they know?" he exclaimed to the interviewer. "They don't know anything! ... Mathematically, the number of kids getting infected from *metzitzah* is so low that it doesn't even weigh in as a percentage. It's not even on the chart of percentages. When the numbers are that low it is impossible to determine the true cause of herpes." Having thus dismissed statistics, epidemiology and microbiology in one breath, Belsky offered his own version of medical "science" to prove that sucking blood directly from a child's penis is actually safer than using a sterile tube: "I know that when I make a *metzitzah* my mouth gets some liquid in it and I spit it out.... [The sterile glass tube] doesn't do that. The suction is not effective. The scientific method is to use proofs. The proof is that this method works."[36]

Head-in-the-sand fundamentalism would be bad enough when served up by a single, if influential, Orthodox rabbi. But *Ami Magazine*'s reporting unwittingly revealed that the same attitude infected even the most exalted levels of the Orthodox rabbinate. Rabbi Moshe Feinstein, Russian-born but later transplanted to the Lower East Side of New York City, was probably the single most revered Orthodox authority in American history. Stories abound of his kindness and compassion, as well as the wisdom with which he applied his vast Talmudic knowledge to modern conditions. (A virtual hagiography full of such tales was published shortly after his death in 1986.)[37] Yet according to *Ami*, Feinstein had vehemently insisted on *m'tzitzah b'peh* even in the early 1980s, when the New York Orthodox community was in a state of near hysteria over the newly-discovered AIDS virus. (I can remember someone wrongly suspected of having the disease in New York's Lower East Side, where I was living, being barred from the local ritual bath.) A *mohel* infected with AIDS can certainly pass the deadly virus to an infant through oral suction of a wound, and rabbinic law, as already mentioned, makes a threat to human life the highest of priorities. But Feinstein refused to consider the lethal risk to children; instead, he relied on the superstition that no harm could possibly arise from the performance of a divine commandment.[38] That so prestigious an authority was willing to put young lives at risk on such flimsy grounds ought be a sobering reflection for Orthodox Jews; but Feinstein's pious fantasizing was all right with *Ami*, which approvingly quoted a contemporary rabbi as saying that a child could only be infected during oral suction if the *mohel* has eaten non-*kosher* food.[39] Belsky tossed a little more nonsense onto the heap, commenting that he wasn't worried about passing herpes to a newborn because he always washed out his mouth with Listerine before sucking blood from the penis.[40]

Even that was not all. *Ami* also interviewed Rabbi Aaron Glatt, affiliated with the relatively modern wing of Orthodoxy, who was prepared to allow that one *might* avoid oral suction to "err on the side of caution." But Rabbi Glatt was emphatic that oral suction during circumcision should be considered an unconditional civil right of every religious Jew—or rather, of every *mohel*. "I would hope that everybody in the Jewish community would be advocating for the total ability for every Jewish person to practice their religion," he insisted. "No one is forcing anyone to do *metzitzah b'peh mamesh* [really].... [But] it's not something that should be in the newspapers or regulated by the Department of Health."[41] Rabbi Avraham ("Romi") Cohn made this rights-based appeal even more explicit:

> We have a Constitution that gives us freedom of religion. We must openly declare that the mayor has no right to regulate [circumcision] or any other aspect of religion.... I came to this country only because the Constitution grants religious freedom. Now that freedom is being threatened.[42]

This was not mere talk: the rabbis were prepared to act as well. In October, several Orthodox rabbinic organizations—including Agudath Israel of America—filed a federal lawsuit against New York City's Department of Health, claiming that even the modest requirement that parents be informed of the possible medical risk of the procedure amounted to a denial of religious freedom. Although legal experts generally dismissed the suit's claims as worthless, that didn't deter the rabbis from kicking off a public campaign to raise money and political support for their legal maneuvers against what is arguably the most Orthodox-friendly city government in the world.[43] Not one Orthodox periodical noted the irony that the same rabbinic organizations scrambling into federal court to protect their version of religious freedom have for years adamantly resisted any resort to the secular justice system on behalf of Jewish victims of sex abuse.

Apart from hypocrisy, the most disturbing thing about the rabbinate's position—and the main reason I have told the story in such detail—is its erasure of children from an issue in which they should have figured centrally. The outrage is especially acute because it characterizes a declaration, by the Orthodox leadership, of what were clearly meant to sound like civil rights. In Rabbi Cohn's encomium the libertarian vocabulary is perfectly deployed: *right, freedom, Constitution, practice of religion, religious freedom*. But something crucial is missing. In all this talk of "rights" there isn't a word about the rights of newborn children, the ones who by all accounts are the most threatened by oral suction.

Frank Schaeffer, criticizing the use of First Amendment language by other religious fundamentalists, got it right when he said, "Religious freedom means freedom to worship in the church of your choosing and—after you're eighteen—to believe anything you want. Before you're eighteen, society should protect you."[44] The idea seems almost too obvious to need writing down. But when it comes to circumcision, what "rights" and what protection will children enjoy if the Orthodox rabbinate has its way? No one will be asking eight-day-old babies whether or not they want to have the mouth of a man carrying a virus pressed to their bleeding genitals; no one will be asking their consent before exposing them to a possibly lethal infection. And "freedom?" Their only freedom will be the freedom to be treated however Orthodox rabbis see fit.

The rabbinate's obstinate stand on *m'tzitzah b'peh* and its historical tendency to side with Orthodox Jews accused of child sex abuse, taken together, reflect a remarkably consistent synopsis of the stages of denial: you can practically tick them off on your fingers. First, the mere possibility that the problem may exist is dismissed out of hand: traditional circumcision—as Rabbi Feinstein insisted—*can't* be dangerous; and Orthodox Jews simply aren't capable of something as repellent as child sexual abuse. Second, as disturbing evidence accumulates, the facts are ignored or ridiculed. Medical authorities who connect *m'tzitzah b'peh* to herpes infections are dismissed as fools by the likes of Rabbi Belsky, just as, years earlier, psychologists who confirmed the sexual abuse of Orthodox Jewish children were called radical feminists, anti-religious activists, and so on. Third, rabbis angrily reject attempts to protect children with regulation from without, whether by "informed consent" waivers for oral suction or mandated background checks for teachers in Orthodox schools.[45] Finally, when evasions fail and the battle is really joined, the rabbinate writes children out of the topic altogether: *m'tzitzah b'peh* is solely about the rights of rabbis and *mohalim*; the child sex abuse issue is really about Orthodoxy (that is, Orthodox rabbis and adult men) under attack from a hostile media.

If the mechanics of denial are predictable, so are the depressing effects on the ideals of Orthodox Judaism itself, which in this rendering seems little more than a party line—an ideology in which all that matters is what the rabbinate demands; in which truth is a tool; in which children are essentially expendable, and hurting them (if need be), holy.

*　*　*

In the preceding pages, I have examined controversies addressed by contemporary Orthodox Jewish leadership with a view to illustrating the consistently low priority assigned to children. If my analysis seems one-sided—if you cannot reconcile it with the popular image of traditional Jewish families as fiercely protective of their offspring—consider how even writing about children in the Orthodox Jewish press tends to betray the same half-hidden contempt, the same habit of letting children disappear behind the priorities of their elders' religious politics. Let me give one particularly poignant example. In December 2012, a lone gunman, possibly suffering from mental illness, killed twenty young children—as well as six adults—at an elementary school in Newtown, Connecticut. The dead had scarcely been buried when the *Jewish Press*, the world's largest English-language Orthodox Jewish weekly, published a column by one Nonie Darwish arguing that the children's deaths had been caused by liberal "indoctrination" and that the killer, not the children, was the true victim:

> The American epidemic of mass gun shootings by young men could be a cry for help by several generations of American kids who have suffered under decades of experimentation and indoctrination in our public schools. It could also be a cry for help by American single mothers, who are told they can take the role of both men and women in the family including the difficult task of raising young boys to adulthood alone.... [K]ids need fathers as much as they need mothers.... It is time for America to end the self-righteous pressure on our kids to change America.

In this bizarre screed, the dead in Newtown became the casualties of feminism, single mothers (the killer had been raised by a single mother), and an emasculating indoctrination of little boys that had secretly ripened via "decades of experimentation." (According to Darwish, "the environmental agenda, the feminist agenda, the gay agenda, the Islamist agenda, the class-envy agenda, the racial-divide agendas, the animal-rights agenda" are all somehow being forced on children in American kindergartens.) Next to so much intellectual violence, the actual mass murder at Newtown was a mere "cry for help."

Maybe you think the exploitation of dead children for such vulgar tubthumping was too much even for ultra–Orthodox readers? Well, not if one judges by the responses posted to the newspaper's on-line version: out of six published comments, not one found anything to criticize in Darwish's ravings.[46] In fact, an Orthodox rabbi would later circulate similar sentiments, linking the mass murder of schoolchildren in Newtown to a "father-detached child" and "the growing sense of entitlement" among the poor.[47] Yet when a few Palestinian youths were videoed merrily throwing snow at two young ultra–Orthodox Jews a few weeks after Darwish's column, the same newspaper and its readers could hardly contain their outrage at the "Arab thugs" and "hooligans" whose "patent savagery" and "disgusting … antisemitic attack juxtaposed with Jewish helplessness" caused one reader's "stomach to turn." Columnist Yori Yanover even compared the giggling kids with snowballs to the perpetrators of the Kishinev pogroms![48]

Clearly, Orthodox Jews can get angry when they want to—or when their leadership wants them to. The trouble is that their emotions have so little to do with the actual needs of real children, or the dangers those children face in the real world. Certainly today's kids are going to have plenty to worry about as they mature, but no one who thinks of children seriously—that is, as the human creatures they really are—would list animal rights activists or snowball-wielding Palestinians among the troubles looming over their future. That is the work of people for whom children are empty quantities to be manipulated for their elders' political ends—and it should not escape our notice that to write about children in this way is itself a kind of violence. In effect, such writing robs children of their most basic right: the right to *be*, to exist of themselves and for themselves, and to be valued in the same way. To reduce them, as Darwish and Yanover both do, to figures in an elaborate paranoid fantasy is one short moral step from using children to fulfill an adult's sexual fantasies. Both represent a form of child exploitation, and neither can easily take root in a mind that conceptualizes children as human beings with human needs and corresponding human rights.

And since very few in the Orthodox rabbinate seem to object to the Darwish-Yanover line, I return to a paraphrase of the question with which I opened this section of the book: Whom do such leaders really protect? Over a century ago, Samuel Butler noted the paradox that clergymen, who are expected to instruct the young in religious subjects, have a vested interest in what they teach—a fact that might invalidate them as teachers of anything else.[49] But Orthodox rabbis clearly have vested interests that go beyond theological propositions. Their power over their religious followers depends on the insularity they preach to their communities. Their near-monopoly on political control among the faithful requires the inculcation of fear and hostility toward non–Jewish authorities. Even their prestige in religious matters depends, at least partly, on the reluctance of Orthodox Jews to check their statements against secular sciences—a reluctance nourished, in turn, by the teachings and edicts of the Orthodox rabbinate.

These facts point to a political dimension in the question of rabbinic attitudes toward children. I introduced this chapter with a quotation from a book published in 1968, criticizing American policy in South Vietnam—a topic apparently remote from these issues. But the point made in the epigraph is depressingly relevant. Just as you cannot expect landlords to fight for rent reduction, you cannot look to Orthodox rabbis to labor in a cause that is bound to undermine their own authority. As I have tried to show, the scale of priorities the rabbis vigorously maintain relegates children to a low position; challenging that placement, by giving child sexual abuse the priority it deserves, threatens to shake the whole system. Given those basic realities, how can we expect men whose authority depends on keeping the status quo to prioritize an issue that could only embarrass the powers that be?

6

Truth and Consequences

A civilization that proves incapable of solving the problems it creates is a decadent civilization.

A civilization that chooses to close its eyes to its most crucial problems is a sick civilization.

—Aimé Césaire[1]

To begin this chapter, I ask the reader's indulgence in advance: I am going to take us on a brief excursion back in time.

It's 1850, and Isaac Mayer Wise, rabbi of a synagogue in Albany, New York, has been asked publicly whether he believes in the coming of the Messiah and in bodily resurrection of the dead. He answers in the negative. His statement is hardly surprising, given his liberal theological tendencies, but it is offensive to some—as it would be to a great many Orthodox Jews in the 21st century.

Autumn arrives. With the fall season comes Rosh ha–Shana—one of the holiest days in Judaism's calendar. Somber religious services commence, but before long, thanks to simmering unrest caused by his earlier remarks, Rabbi Wise is "removed bodily and forcibly from his pulpit," as Professor Joseph Blau records, by some of Albany's more traditionally-minded congregants.[2]

Now let's return to the present and pose the obvious, melancholy question: Why is it we cannot write that at some time during that same century and a half, at least *one* Orthodox rabbi—somewhere, any time at all—was bodily ejected from his synagogue for covering up cases of child abuse? Alas, nothing of the kind can be found in the annals of modern Jewish history, though I could easily name quite a few rabbis who have been implicated in such offenses. In our own time, just think of the rabbinic luminaries who defended Rabbi Yehuda Kolko, who later pleaded guilty to endangering the welfare of a minor. Or the rabbis who sing the praises of Rabbi Israel Weingarten, the convicted rapist of his own daughter.

Maybe, you'll say, one case of violence against a rabbi over a century and a half ago is too remote to employ as a standard in such matters? But consider the sharply differing reactions of Orthodox Jewish leadership to two quite recent incidents, occurring almost simultaneously. In December 2006, the leaders of Neturei Karta—a fringe group of ultra-religious and virulently anti–Zionist Jews—met with the president of Iran, Mahmoud Ahmadinejad, offending a political consensus among Jewish leadership that sought to isolate Ahmadinejad as a result of his statements denouncing Israel and expressing skepticism about the Nazi holocaust. Less than a week before that meeting, Rabbi Kolko was arrested on charges of child sexual abuse that allegedly spanned nearly four decades and reportedly involved dozens of the rabbi's students. Officials of Agudath Israel of America issued statements about both events. But the prominent Orthodox organization's vigorous expressions of contempt for the anti–Zionists ("disgrace to the Jewish people," "do not represent anyone but themselves," "do grave harm to Jews")[3] rendered its spokesman's deadpan evasiveness over the arrest of the alleged sexual predator almost laughable by contrast:

> Why would we have comment about the arrest of an individual? Because he was an employee, more than 30 years ago, of one of the camps we run (that have had thousands of employees over the years)? I don't think that requires comment on our part.[4]

I am reasonably sure that the members of Neturei Karta who met Ahmadinejad were never employees of Agudath Israel, but that did not shield them from the organization's obloquy. I also think that, in the eyes of most reasonable people, groping a child's genitals can cause at least as much "grave harm" as shaking the hand of the Iranian president. (Neturei Karta's representatives made it clear that they did not share Ahmadinejad's doubts about the Holocaust and agreed only with his political opposition to Zionism.) Still more important, as noted in Chapter 1, Kolko's alleged victims accused Orthodox Jewish leadership of covering up for the rabbi for over three decades, a searing allegation without a parallel in the Neturei Karta episode. Why, then, was Rabbi Kolko's arrest so easy for Agudath Israel to dismiss, if not because rabbinic leadership is still more exercised over threats to its traditional authority than over the alleged violation of the bodies of its community's children— even when rabbinic complicity is charged as well?

I want to devote some pages here to exploring this dichotomy. I do this not simply to illustrate a double standard—in itself, an interesting but not especially fruitful sort of inquiry—but because I think one can infer, from the vastly different practical consequences, the kind of principles Orthodox leadership actually brings to bear on different sorts of misbehavior. The question is this: What actually happens to those who, by exposing cases of child sexual abuse within the religious community, effectively challenge the rabbinic leadership—whose policy, as we have seen, discourages such exposure—and how does their treatment differ from the consequences suffered by rabbis or prominent lay figures caught in public scandal involving crime, fraud or sexual misconduct? The answer to that question says a good deal about the real values of Orthodox leadership—more, I would argue, than a hundred sermons, official statements or articulations of organizational policy.

As a matter of fact, the question can be answered with reasonable finality. And what it reveals is not encouraging.

Consider, first, what happens to Orthodox Jews who disclose unwelcome facts about child sex abuse among their coreligionists. On this question the evidence is overwhelming. Steven Resnicoff's recent study (cited in Chapter 1) is only one of many reports describing the viciousness with which the Orthodox community punishes its truth-tellers. Professor Resnicoff notes that "many ... important Orthodox authorities ... have feebly permitted, and in at least some cases possibly encouraged, reprisals against those who have reported abuse, including its victims and their families."[5] Here are a few examples of such rabbinically-approved "reprisals":

> [A] therapist ... said that he had received threats because of his activities concerning child abuse in the Orthodox community.... His children were threatened, he said, with not being accepted into yeshivot [religious schools] or for shidduchim [i.e., for arranged dates that might lead to marriage], and he was threatened with financial ruin....
>
> In 2007, Rabbi Nuchem Rosenberg established a telephone hot-line for abuse victims in Williamsburg, New York. The result, he says, is that he was ostracized by members of the Orthodox community. He allegedly received death threats and suffered a forehead injury from some projectile....[6]
>
> In 2006, a mother reported to secular authorities that her fifteen-year-old daughter had been raped by a thirty-five-year old man. Local rabbinic authorities were reportedly "furious" that she went to secular authorities rather than to a rabbinic court.... This pattern seems to have persisted for years....
>
> The law of Mesirah, or informing, is extraordinary within Jewish law.... If someone adamantly announces that he is going to violate the rule and inform on another Jew to Gentiles (including Gentile governmental authorities), then every Jew has the obligation to use force, even deadly force if necessary, to prevent the informant from fulfilling his purpose.[7]

However appalling, these details are old hat to anyone familiar with Orthodox Jewish life. More than a decade before Resnicoff's article, Rabbi Dr. Mordechai Glick, a prominent Orthodox psychologist, offered similar complaints in a letter to the *Jewish Press*: "If the police do get involved [in a child sex abuse case], a massive cover-up and pressure campaign usually ensures that the case will either not get to trial or if it does, will be dropped because potential witnesses are pressured (code for threatened) to refuse to testify or outright lie."[8]

In fact, in the rare cases in which victims actually do manage to press criminal charges all the way to trial, the backlash tactics are, if anything, more intense than those described by Glick. When Rabbi Nechemya Weberman of the Satmar Hasidic sect went on trial in Brooklyn for repeatedly abusing a girl sent to him for counseling, several of Weberman's fellow Hasidim were caught illegally photographing the victim as she testified—a ploy clearly intended to warn other sex abuse victims that pressing charges will mean at least a loss of privacy, quite possibly physical danger.[9] After Weberman's conviction, the victim's family suffered systematic reprisals from the Hasidic community.[10]

One would like to treat such outrages as the work of extremists, or as a recent departure from the Orthodox norm. But they are neither. Threats and intimidation have long been among the methods for silencing critics in traditional Jewish communities. Moses Leib Lilienblum wrote in 1876 of being persecuted, in a deeply religious Jewish town within the Russian Pale, merely for owning secular books and for advocating a few modest religious reforms. The results of even this mild a break with rabbinic Orthodoxy were quick, extreme—and typical:

> The town elders tried, on false charges, to have me banished to Siberia. The kinder ones were ready to contribute fifty rubles for my children's welfare if I would disappear. They incited street urchins against me.... Some people informed government officials against me. Some said I issued false receipts, while others said I was teaching deceit to the young. Some Hasidim even tried to poison me.[11]

Lilienblum's experience as a dissident was unusual only in the fact that it was described in print, as was the expulsion of the future Yiddish playwright S. Ansky from his Orthodox Jewish community when rabbis suspected him of "modern" influences.[12] Given such precedents, open defiance of prevailing norms has been understandably rare among Orthodox Jews; nor do we even hear of an Orthodox Jewish adult being accused of child abuse until modern times.[13]

Alongside such practices, Orthodox leadership still sanctions, at least in some cases, the suppression of inconvenient facts in the name of faith. Two recent illustrations will suffice. When an Orthodox rabbi named Natan Slifkin (educated in right-wing Orthodox *yeshivos*) published children's books that included cautious references to evolutionary theory, he was bitterly assailed by leading ultra–Orthodox authorities because his work was perceived as a threat to reigning rabbinic norms. His work was denounced as heretical, he was publicly accused of "ridicul[ing] the foundations of our emunah [faith]," and his (Orthodox) publishers were pressured into rejecting any further manuscripts from him, even those that were clearly uncontroversial. And all this despite the fact that the views expressed in his books were directly drawn from the writings of such pillars of Orthodoxy as Maimonides and Rabbi Samson Raphael Hirsch![14]

The second example is even more pertinent, since it deals directly with child abuse cover-ups. After hearing that the prominent Rabbi Mattisyahu Salomon, in an address to a large Orthodox Jewish convention in 2006, had spoken approvingly of hiding child sex abuse charges "under the carpet," I learned that a transcript of his speech had been posted on an Orthodox-run blog. I promptly checked for the text, only to discover that the blog had been closed by the administrator, and that the transcript I wanted was no longer available. In response to my email messages, the administrator admitted that he had a transcript but flatly refused to share it with me. By way of explanation, he commented that "the last guy who asked for it was a journalist." When I suggested to him that there was an obvious value in knowing what such an influential Orthodox rabbi had said about a subject of public concern, he scoffed that the "argument of 'truth should not be suppressed' is one originating from the non–Jewish world." Q.E.D.[15]

*   *   *

What I have offered above as a summary of the treatment of Orthodox Jews who repeat unpopular truths about their communities—particularly where sex abuse is in question—could be greatly expanded, but the significant facts would remain the same. Now let us compare this ominous record with the experience of prominent Orthodox figures who have been embroiled in public scandals of a different description.

It is no secret that financial misconduct has plagued Orthodox Judaism in recent decades. At times, even Orthodox rabbis have joined in the chorus of dismay stirred by the news of yet another corrupt Orthodox rabbi/businessman, as did Rabbi Josh Yuter in 2011 in connection with a sampling of high-level fiscal shenanigans among his coreligionists:

> In July 2009, forty-four people were arrested in Operation Big Rig 3 including prominent Jewish leaders in the Syrian community for crimes including money laundering, political corruption, and organ trafficking.... In 1986, [Rabbi] Dovid Feinstein's yeshiva Mesivtha Tifereth Jerusalem was involved in its own money laundering scandal....[16]

What Rabbi Yuter described was the tip of an iceberg. Harry Maryles, another Orthodox rabbi, has since lamented the frequency of "criminal activity" among his fellow Orthodox clergymen, noting that far too many rabbis with impeccable ultra–Orthodox educational credentials have been caught committing theft, fraud or other financial misdeeds; he concludes, sensibly enough, that "the fact that so many prominent—and not so prominent—Rabbis that have been caught doing things like this [fraud and bribery] have also had this kind of education can't be ignored."[17]

The fact is, the chronic recurrence of such misconduct among Orthodox Jews hardly seems surprising when we consider the religious leadership's reaction to typical cases. Rabbi Leib Pinter furnishes us with an excellent example. A prominent rabbi and popular inspirational writer, whose book *Don't Give Up* boasted glowing approbations from several Orthodox authorities, Pinter was once sufficiently influential to allegedly play a significant role in the slander campaign that wrecked the publishing career of Rabbi Natan Slifkin.[18] The innocent reader might expect, however, some lessening of Pinter's moral stature after he pleaded guilty in 2008 to stealing $44 million in federal funds in a mortgage fraud scheme, for which he was sentenced to eight years in prison.[19] Yet the rabbinate's reaction to Pinter's fall was remarkably muted. Unlike the writings of Rabbi Slifkin—deemed objectionable largely because of their early endorsement by an Orthodox rabbi the inquisitors did not like[20]—a book by a proven fraud has never been the subject of a rabbinic ban; so far as I know, none of the Orthodox rabbis who endorsed Pinter's treacly tome has withdrawn his approbation since Pinter's exposure as a thief and a liar. Nor have the rabbis who publicly stigmatized Slifkin, on the strength of the false charges Pinter allegedly hatched against him, apologized for their attacks or repudiated their source. They haven't even suggested that, in light of Pinter's shattered credibility, the Slifkin case might deserve reexamination.

Maybe this isn't really surprising: even fraud in religious matters has little effect on the Orthodox rabbinate, so long as the specific form it takes doesn't ruffle any conventional pieties. Rabbi Reuven Schmeltzer was another of the hatchet men who pursued Slifkin for his "heretical" analysis of Talmudic creation stories. Yet in a book of his own, purporting to prove that every word contained in Talmudic texts must be accepted as literally true by Jewish believers, Rabbi Schmeltzer went to the breath-bereaving extreme of falsifying traditional sources to better fit his thesis.[21] By the standards he and his rabbinic cohorts used to condemn Slifkin, Schmeltzer's book was actually worse than anything Slifkin wrote, both in its treatment of authoritative texts—which Schmeltzer flagrantly misrepresented—and in the contemptuous attitude toward Jewish tradition demonstrated by an author willing to distort it for his own ends. Yet the phalanx of Orthodox rabbis who publicly endorsed Schmeltzer's book has never abandoned him. In fact, a popular spokesman for right-wing Orthodoxy, Rabbi Dovid Kornreich—who once encouraged homosexuals to commit suicide if they cannot be "cured"[22]—publicly described Schmeltzer's book as "a very useful handbook of important source material which enjoys a very solid consensus of support"[23]—long after proof of the book's spurious scholarship had been widely circulated via Internet.

Rabbi Hertz Frankel's case further demonstrates how lightly fraud can weigh on the Orthodox leadership's moral scale. Frankel, for years the principal of a Hasidic girls' school in Brooklyn, pleaded guilty in 1999 to the theft of millions of dollars in public school funds. In a contemporaneous official statement to his coreligionists, he confessed manfully that he was "the victim of a great injustice" and elaborated, to the *New York Times*, that "the end justifies the means"—after all, the scheme had benefited members of his religious community at the expense of underpaid teachers and non–Jewish children.[24] Did other Orthodox rabbis take a more principled line on Frankel's offenses? If so, the effects have been hard to discern. Before his guilty plea, Frankel, in addition to his scholastic duties, had been "administrator and spokesman for the Satmar Chasidim for four decades."[25] After his guilty plea, he remained a highly-placed Satmar spokesman, and he continued to serve as principal of his community's largest girls' school.[26] In recent years he has even published a weekly guest column in the Orthodox *Ami Magazine*, packed with reminiscences about the revered former leader of the Satmar sect, the late Rabbi Yoel Teitelbaum.[27] It does not seem to have occurred to *Ami*'s editors that their paeans to Teitelbaum might have been more convincing if offered by someone other than an unrepentant felon.

Even these cases pale next to the rabbinate's boisterous propaganda campaign on behalf of Rabbi Sholom Rubashkin, a *kosher* meat mogul convicted on 86 counts of bank fraud involving tens of millions of dollars. Despite his crimes and the overwhelming evidence establishing them,[28] Rubashkin was vigorously supported by a wide array of prominent Orthodox rabbis and institutions, who raised hundreds of thousands of dollars for his legal defense fund with fire-and-brimstone appeals to the Orthodox "street." (The fundraising continued even after Rubashkin lost his final appellate challenge in October 2012, when the U.S. Supreme Court rejected his petition for review.)[29]

Before his trial had even commenced, Rabbi Pinchos Lipschutz, editor and publisher of the influential Orthodox newspaper *Yated Ne'eman*, was already calling Rubashkin the victim of "lynch mobs" whose "real" goal was to outlaw *kosher* slaughter, and, *en passant*, to stigmatize all Orthodox Jews as "dirty, unkempt, vile Neanderthals." For good measure, Lipschutz even took a swipe at the "liberal media and the unions who have contributed to the losses of millions of American jobs." Where the rabbi got his information about these "facts" is anyone's guess; the only evidence of Rubashkin's innocence he shared with his readers was that the Orthodox Jews near Rubashkin's plant in Postville, Iowa all "get along."[30] (Naturally, Rabbi Lipschutz did not describe how Rubashkin "got along" with the illegal aliens he employed, including children as young as thirteen; according to local union organizers, their working conditions at Rubashkin's plant were "a nightmare," including "extraordinarily low" wages, lack of "basic worker safety and protection," and systematic abuse by supervisors.)[31]

After a jury found Rubashkin guilty of massive bank fraud, the rabbinic campaign in his support escalated from passionate to hysterical. A Miami *yeshiva* dedicated a community benefit to the convicted felon, "an honor reserved for respected members of the community." Fundraising rallies and prayer meetings for Rubashkin were convened by the faithful in cities dotting the United States. (Both of my children got the word from their respective parochial schools in northern New Jersey.) The Rubashkin cause was so popular that it even united Lubavitch and Satmar Hasidim, despite enduring quarrels between the two sects. And all this notwithstanding graphic evidence that besides bank fraud and labor law violations, Rubashkin had sanctioned slaughterhouse methods so cruel that animals were left "writhing in pain as they bled to death," contravening Jewish law that requires a quick and humane end to each animal's life.[32] Evidently, there was some truth to the pro–Rubashkin claim that his cause had helped "bring together" Orthodox Jewish groups: the same Orthodox rabbis who could never agree to denounce the swindling of non–Jews, to discourage extreme inhumanity to animals, or even to protect Jewish law—ostensibly the rabbinate's highest priority—could at least join in barnstorming for an unapologetic criminal.[33]

The moral atmosphere around Rubashkin grew so perverse that anyone willing to join the campaign enjoyed instant absolution for all previous sins. For instance, the Orthodox Jewish press was full of praise for Brett Tolman, a Christian lawyer and former politician whose claim on history, before he took to flacking for Rubashkin, was that he sneaked a clause into the renewed Patriot Act (at the behest of the Bush administration) that expanded presidential powers to appoint U.S. Attorneys without Senate approval.[34] Tolman's legislative sleight of hand—a mere staffer at the time, he had no authority to change the text of a bill—was overwhelmingly rejected by lawmakers once Tolman's fakery was discovered,[35] but meanwhile the Bush White House had rewarded the ambitious young aide with a 2006 appointment as the new U.S. Attorney for Utah.[36] As far as Orthodox leadership was concerned, all that sleazy background was erased from history once Tolman spoke at a fundraising rally for Rubashkin in December 2010 (which I heard via telephone hookup). He earned even more rabbinic praise for co-authoring an article for the *National Law Journal* insisting that Rubashkin was a victim of civil rights violations and—believe it or not—anti–Semitism.[37]

Ah, but don't Orthodox rabbis caught in *sexual* misconduct, at least, pay a price for their sins? Let's look at a couple of such cases and see how the punishment has compared with the offense. In July 2012, *Israel Hayom* reported that a "sex scandal is about to shake the haredi (ultra–Orthodox) world" after a prominent Hasidic rabbi was accidentally spotted by one of his followers alone with a much younger, naked woman who was not his wife. But although the newspaper called the revelation "the tip of the iceberg" and promised "more details ... in the coming days,"[38] further facts were slow to emerge in the press. The Orthodox world did not shake. The rabbi, eventually identified as Eliezer Berland, though accused of multiple illicit affairs and child sexual abuse, simply migrated out of the country with many of his followers—a far cry from the fate of, say, the parents of the alleged young victim of Solomon Hafner, who for pressing abuse charges against the rabbi were publicly vilified and driven from their religious community.[39] The equally sensational story of Rabbi Leib Tropper's sexual escapades with a prospective female convert—a story supported by tape-recorded telephone conversations between the young woman and the influential, married rabbi—did lead to Tropper's resignation as head of Eternal Jewish Family, the conversion consortium-cum-fundraising gimmick he had helped found and, for years, manipulated for the ideological bullying of new converts, as well as allegedly for his own personal gain.[40] But Eternal Jewish Family, under new leadership, neither repudiated Tropper nor altered the abusive course he had set for it. In fact, there was no shortage of Orthodox propaganda in Tropper's defense even after the story broke.[41] It is also worth noting that even if Tropper's former rabbinic allies do treat him henceforth with suspicion (a possibility supported by no publicly-available evidence), this "punishment" will amount to less than the outright institutional ban recently decreed by two of Orthodox Judaism's leading right-wing rabbis against *the entire families* of all Orthodox Jews with Internet access.[42] So even if Tropper's ostracism from Orthodox institutions should turn out to be real— unlike the phony version applied to indicted child abuser Avrohom Mondrowitz, who remains to this day a popular member of an Orthodox synagogue[43]—Tropper can at least look forward to plenty of company in exile.

All in all, apart from accurately reporting child abuse to police, the only "scandals" that really seem to draw down the wrath of the Orthodox community imply moral standards so ludicrous as to be scarcely worth mentioning. Thus Pearl Perry Reich, a formerly Hasidic woman, was roundly denounced among Orthodox Jews when she appeared on television to describe the campaign being waged against her on behalf of her ultra–Orthodox husband, who—while refusing to grant her a religious divorce—was demanding sole custody of their four children. But the same authorities whose mouthpieces accused Reich of being "out to deliberately stir hatred"[44] apparently had no problem with the hate speech of Pamela Geller, an Islamophobe whose ravings are so outlandish that even the director of the Anti-Defamation League Center on Extremism (an organization that has done its own share of Muslim-bashing) has accused her of "xenophobia."[45] Geller was invited in 2013 to speak at a synagogue run by Hasidim of Lubavitch[46]—one of the largest and most influential Hasidic groups in the world—despite her notoriety for many years' worth of on-line rants including claims that President Barack Obama is the illegitimate son of Malcolm X, was "involved with a crack whore in his youth," and has secretly used the White House as a base for Muslim "jihad."[47] And Geller isn't even Orthodox. But who's counting? The policy that allowed Orthodox spokespeople to condemn Reich, while embracing the likes of Geller, extended even to double standards about personal details. One common element in the Orthodox case against Reich concerned her work as a model, which was said to involve "flaunting [her] body"; yet Geller, with no professional justification whatsoever, recorded a video of one of her delusional screeds while wearing only a bikini.[48]

* * *

As we compare two kinds of "truth and consequences" within the Orthodox community—the results of truth-telling about abused children against the effects of scandalous exposure—it is enlightening to examine cases that implicate both sets of concerns. Few people would deny that the use of underage religious school students as couriers for illegal drugs constitutes a form of child exploitation, morally if not legally. The exposure of such conduct twice within eight years in two separate Hasidic *yeshivos*, one in the United States and one in Israel, also involved "scandal"—that is, it presented the Orthodox community in an unpleasant public light, one that promised only to grow harsher if the story could not be quickly contained and minimized in the public media.

For this reason, the story's treatment by Orthodox leadership offers something akin to a controlled experiment vis-à-vis rabbinic priorities. Viewed as a story about the mistreatment of children, the facts called for a thorough examination of the institutions and individuals that might have been involved, to ensure the protection of other children from a similar fate. On the other hand, seen merely as a "scandal" about Orthodox Jews facing personal difficulties in sight of a non–Jewish public, the story deserved only suppression or spin-doctoring. In the event, Orthodox leadership's handling of the disturbing facts revealed no interest at all in investigating the problem; instead, the story was ignored at first and, when that became impossible, was imaginatively recast as a tale of Orthodox victimization. Unmistakable evidence of exploitation of Orthodox children by Orthodox Jews was shunted aside. The wrong questions were investigated. The wrong evils were assailed.

In early 2000—at roughly the same time a Bobover Hasid, Rabbi Solomon Hafner, was getting a pass from the Brooklyn D.A. on charges of first-degree child sex abuse (see Chapter 3)—young Brooklyn students from the same sect were going to prison after being caught in a drug-smuggling ring orchestrated, in large part, by one of the sect's former members, a 19-year-old named Shimon Levita.

It was an ugly story of startling proportions. Police believed the ring, which had been operating for years, had managed to bring over a million Ecstasy pills into New York City in just *one three-month period*, providing "much of the Ecstasy that ha[d] been flooding the city's nightclubs and rave dances."[49] Apart from the sheer quantity of illegal drugs at issue, the scheme's most alarming feature was its exploitation of minors. Dozens of Bobov Hasidim, many of whom were underage, had been recruited as couriers to bring illegal, brain-damaging drugs into the United States, where they were sold at enormous profit. For two years, Levita handed out $1,500 bribes and promises of free trips to Europe, inducing teenagers to carry large sums of money to various overseas locations and to bring back with them unopened bags containing what some of them apparently thought were diamonds. The actual cargo in each instance consisted of Ecstasy pills by the thousands or tens of thousands, manufactured in Amsterdam and intended ultimately for sale at New York nightclubs at $25 to $30 a pop—a fact of which the Hasidic couriers were not entirely innocent, according to prosecutors, who stated at the time of Levita's indictment that "although there were warning signs along the way that the couriers were smuggling drugs, they generally closed their eyes to these facts."[50]

The eyes-wide-shut posture was true *a fortiori* of the couriers' elders. Many of the drug-runners were teenagers attending *yeshivos* in an insular and highly centralized religious society. They could hardly have taken frequent trips back and forth to Europe without attracting the attention of rabbis, teachers and school administrators, to say nothing of their parents and other family members. Yet there is no evidence that anyone in the Bobov community ever asked any questions about where these kids were going, why they were missing school or what on earth they were doing as they repeatedly traveled overseas.

It remained for the federal judge who sentenced Levita to raise what seemed to be a surprising question to the seventy-odd Bobov Hasidim crammed into his courtroom, all bent on "seeking leniency" for the ex–Hasid:

> Where was the community when all of this was going on? ... Where was the family when 18-year-old boys were traveling from Paris to Amsterdam, Montreal, New York and Atlanta?
> They were gone for long periods of time.... They were traveling around Europe. They applied for passports. Where were the teachers? Who was keeping tabs on these boys who were bringing drugs back and taking money there?...
> As young yeshiva boy after young yeshiva boy stands before me accused of smug-

gling drugs, I think there should be some very serious thought given to what is going on here.

In what the *New York Times* called a "scathing lecture," Judge I. Leo Glasser went on to "upbraid" the Hasidim, in a "quavering" voice, for "allowing an international drug smuggling ring to flourish in their midst." But for all the reaction his words provoked, he might have been talking to statues. Neither Levita's entanglement of Hasidic youngsters in the world of organized crime, nor the resulting prison sentences that shamed many a Hasidic family, seemed to trouble anyone in the Bobov community; in fact, Judge Glasser received no fewer than thirty letters from Bobov Hasidim urging clemency for a man who had not only forsaken his community's religion—usually considered a serious sin in those circles—but had cruelly deceived and exploited many of its children.[51] Where was the community, indeed? Judge Glasser's "scathing lecture" implied that the Bobovers had no idea what was going on under their noses. But even assuming an entire community, administrators and all, could really have been ignorant of so blatant a scheme, the Hasidic leadership's indifference to Levita's crimes even after they were exposed—indifference varied only by the community's eagerness to *defend* the abuser of its children—suggested complicity on a scale beyond that of mere negligence.

Orthodox Jewish media dutifully followed Bobov's lead. The entire story went virtually unreported in Orthodox newspapers. The *Jewish Press*—the largest English-language Orthodox Jewish periodical in the United States—has never mentioned it, as far as I can determine,[52] though the facts were reported in the secular press, the non–Orthodox *Jewish Daily Forward* and the mainstream Jewish magazine *Moment*. *Moment* even suggested that the "truly global" Ecstasy trade had already "infiltrate[d] yeshivas and rabbinical seminaries" not only in the Bobov enclave, but in "the insular Orthodox communities of Williamsburg ... and Monsey, north of New York City," where "recruiters found gullible youngsters who thought they would be smuggling diamonds, not narcotics."[53] That would seem to indicate that the threat to Orthodox Jewish children ran beyond a single outbreak of drug-dealing in one Hasidic neighborhood—especially since, at nearly the same time and in a separate case, it was learned that bank accounts belonging to Bobov's main *yeshiva* had been "used to launder $1.75 million of what turned out to be Colombian cocaine money."[54] But none of this raised a ripple of concern among Orthodox Jewish publicists. No one in the Orthodox rabbinate or Orthodox media stepped forward to suggest that vigilance at other *yeshivos* might be in order.

If the rabbinate's silence about Levita's case betokened indifference to the evidence of institutionalized child exploitation in its religious schools, its collective voice—when it did address the same subject eight years later—suggested an attitude even more culpable. I will examine the facts of the story, as presented largely in the Orthodox press, and with those facts in mind I will attempt to analyze the response of Orthodox leadership.

On April 6, 2008, three young Hasidim of the Satmar sect—one under eighteen, all three students at a *yeshiva* in B'nei B'rak, Israel near Tel Aviv—were arrested at Tokyo's Narita International Airport after 90,000 Ecstasy pills were found under false bottoms in their suitcases.[55] The drugs—which the young Hasidim had picked up in Amsterdam—were worth more than three and a half million dollars at street value.[56]

I can only speculate about why the same Orthodox leadership that kept mum throughout the Brooklyn drug-running scandal in 2000 intervened loudly in this more recent case. Perhaps it was feared that with no significant Jewish community in Japan, Japanese prosecutors would be politically free to pursue a far-ranging inquiry. Or maybe the facts connected with the arrest threatened to make the story public knowledge, regardless of what Orthodox actors did. What is clear is that once the rabbinate and its publicists decided to intervene—and they did so immediately—they were strictly in damage-control mode. No Orthodox rabbi suggested any connection between the arrests in Tokyo and the *yeshiva*-based drug ring that had unraveled in Brooklyn eight years earlier, despite credible evidence at the time that the Ecstasy trade was infiltrating Orthodox schools in several locales. No one asked whether these couriers, too, might represent only part of a larger criminal enterprise. Instead, the leadership focused entirely on the plight of the young men under arrest, while "raising funds to hire the best legal team possible in Japan."[57] Investigating the way drug dealers had once again penetrated the Orthodox community was never on the agenda.

The immediate choice of Lubavitch Hasid Mordechai Tzivin as lead attorney for the young couriers gave a good indication of the kind of support the rabbinate was mobilizing. The high-profile Tzivin listed among his clients not only large-scale drug traffickers but such sinister thugs as Yair Klein, an Israeli colonel who equipped and trained right-wing death squads in Latin America, and outfitted the Lebanese Phalangist militia that massacred hundreds of Palestinian civilians during Israel's 1982 invasion.[58] Tzivin's religious values were on display, incidentally, when he chided the Israeli government's lack of "Jewish DNA" for failing to fight Klein's extradition from Russia to Colombia to stand trial for the bloody trail he'd left behind there; Klein, whom Tzivin called "a combat hero," was a Jew, and that should have been enough to shield him from punishment. Later the same year, Tzivin would show similar priorities when he publicly urged Israel to bribe Thai officials on behalf of another of his Jewish clients, who faced a death penalty for drug smuggling in that country.[59]

While Tzivin and his associates filled the Orthodox media with appeals to "Jewish DNA," the Orthodox press played along by assuming that the attempted delivery of millions of dollars' worth of Ecstasy to Tokyo by Hasidic students was an isolated event. On the day of their arrest, Tzivin told an on-line Orthodox news outlet that his clients had "fallen victim" to the "con maneuver" of an unnamed man who had asked them to transport antique religious books from Amsterdam to Tokyo.[60] The unnamed recruiter turned out to be a 31-year-old Orthodox Jew named Bentzion Miller, who hailed from the same Hasidic sect as the couriers.[61] But what was Miller's connection with the Ecstasy trade, and who had recruited *him* to prey on *yeshiva* students? Those obvious questions were never posed in the Orthodox press. What is more, the relevant facts were consistently fudged: Miller was described as a "businessman," or a casual "friend"[62]—that is, someone the couriers just happened to meet in synagogue.

But the truth was that Miller was "a personal aide and confidante to the Satmar Rebbe of Kiryas Yoel," meaning that he was closely linked to the highest authority in one of the world's largest and most centralized Hasidic communities.[63] (Not only that—some accounts claimed he was responsible for coordinating charitable activities at the *yeshiva* where the young men studied.)[64] That should have led honest reporters to ask how much the Rebbe or those around him might have known about the scheme orchestrated by Miller. This was particularly true given reports that he had not been working alone: another Satmar Hasid, Haim Roter, was suspected of involvement in the plot. (Roter reportedly fled to Europe to escape arrest,[65] after which his name completely disappeared from Jewish coverage of the story.)

And there was more. According to officials cited in Israel's premier newspaper, *Ha'aretz*, Miller had been acting as liaison to Avraham Malachi, described by Israeli police as a "leading foot soldier of the Abergil clan, an Israeli crime family involved in international drug-running operations."[66] (In fact, at the same time Malachi was routing Ecstasy through Hasidic youths, he was also using Argentine retirees as mules for cocaine and hashish.)[67] Could a 31-year-old Hasid have found his way to the upper echelons of one of Israel's biggest crime families all on his own? And would a gangster of Malachi's experience entrust a single delivery of three and a half million dollars' worth of Ecstasy to an untested novice? Surely it was more likely that the Abergil family and Satmar had a broader and longer acquaintance than the single transaction police had foiled at Narita Airport. But this issue was never broached in any Orthodox publication.

In fact, where Orthodox media couldn't ignore evidence of a criminal enterprise at work, they often just falsified it. Spokesmen for the suspects in Japan argued that, thanks to their "background and education," they were "not even aware of what illegal drugs were."[68] Even assuming the truth of that claim—for which no evidence was provided—the young men, just like the Bobovers recruited in Brooklyn years earlier, clearly *did* know they were breaking the law. Early press reports, based on information from the couriers' own legal team, noted that they were "told they were smuggling antiques so as to avoid paying taxes"[69]—which gives the lie to the Orthodox press's extravagant protestations about the "innocent background" of the three, including their attorney's flatly false claim that "the facts show that the boys are completely innocent."[70] (It also sheds an interesting light on the pious homilies that one of the three, Yaakov Yosef Greenwald, wrote from his prison cell in Japan, which were then reverently circulated by the faithful as part of the fundraising campaign on the couriers' behalf. Not a word of Greenwald's religious musings expressed remorse for the fact that he was consciously committing a crime when arrested—even if it wasn't the crime for which he was actually charged. No Orthodox commentator on that text, so far as I know, ever mentioned this omission.)[71] Only when it was clearly expedient to blame the whole plot on Miller, while omitting all references to his close connection to the leader of the Hasidic sect, did Orthodox opinion-makers insist that Miller had "assured [the couriers] that everything was legal."[72] Had that been true, the couriers surely would have said so from the beginning—which they did not.

Worse, Orthodox spokesmen gave implausible and even contradictory accounts about the details of the crime. According to one story, the "boys" thought they were delivering the "antiques" to an art fair being held in Tokyo "in a few weeks."[73] But the only art fair around that time in Tokyo ended April 6, before the couriers even arrived in Tokyo (they reached the airport that night); what is more, the fair was for "contemporary art," so that "antiques" or old Judaica would not have been included.[74] A second cover story had it that the couriers thought they were carrying rare objects to Lubavitch Hasidim in Japan.[75] Alas, the premise that *yeshiva* students from Satmar would have done such a favor for their Lubavitch arch-rivals is difficult to credit.

There was also an intriguing omission in all of the public accounts of the couriers' actions. The timing of the arrest at Tokyo's Narita Airport (on Sunday evening) means that the couriers almost certainly spent the previous Jewish Sabbath in Amsterdam before leaving for Tokyo Saturday night.[76] But since cooking, traveling, handling money, the adjustment of electric appliances, etc. are all strictly forbidden to Orthodox Jews on the Sabbath—from sundown Friday until after dark on Saturday night—the couriers could not have spent that period on their own; they must have had Orthodox Jewish hosts in Amsterdam, over the Sabbath, before they flew away on Saturday night. *This means that other people (knowingly or not) were likely involved in the drug-trading scheme*—since all arrangements were made by Miller in advance. Such people, if identified and questioned, might well have been able to name other Orthodox couriers who had spent nights or Sabbaths with them on other shadowy errands. But not one of the articles in the Orthodox press ever mentioned this crucial fact—a pretty strong indication that no one in charge wanted to pursue information about how large or how deeply-rooted this drug ring might turn out to be. Another was Orthodox leadership's failure to protest when the couriers' lead attorney publicly denounced the Jewish press for satisfying readers' "curiosity" about the case; the lawyer thought it "low and destructive" for Orthodox Jews to "know what is happening," even, apparently, if the purpose of that knowledge was to protect youngsters from international drug-smuggling.[77] These comments were prominently circulated in Orthodox media—and never denounced or refuted. "Jewish DNA," I suppose.

In the end, as far as Orthodox Jewish discourse was concerned, the story closed as it had begun: a description of a *yeshiva*-based drug-trading ring that managed to avoid any inquiry into who was running the ring, how it had infiltrated the *yeshiva*, or how many Orthodox Jews (including children) had been snared by the scheme. One can only wonder at the mental discipline required to ignore these obvious questions during several years of "reporting" the story. Orthodox correspondents managed instead to emote on cue: cheering when one of the couriers was acquitted,[78] and when another, Yosef Banda (the youngest) was transferred to an Israeli prison and released after serving less than two years of his sentence[79]; grieving when the third "boy" (who was not underage) was sentenced to six years at hard labor and a $50,000 fine.[80] Never raising inconvenient questions about the scope of the *yeshiva*-based racket, Orthodox reporters kept the story on the level of "human interest," which of course discouraged any serious discussion about the issues the case raised.

This distorted focus was equally in evidence in Orthodox coverage of the one suspect the reporters did not overtly try to protect. When Bentzion Miller went on trial in Israel for having recruited the young *yeshiva* students, the Orthodox press did not hesitate to report that the families of the couriers testified against him[81]—a remarkable exception to the usual Hasidic code of silence—but never asked why these witnesses put all the blame on Miller, while no one else connected with Satmar was so much as mentioned in connection with drug-dealing during the trial. Other selective silences in the Orthodox press were equally suggestive. It was reported that after being sentenced to just three years, Miller was released for "good behavior" after spending a mere eight months in prison—a fact that should have stimulated reporters to ask about possible string-pulling in the case, ultra–Orthodox political influence being notorious in Israel.[82] But the question was never raised.

Once freed, Miller disappeared from public discourse; apart from a smattering of short articles about his release, the Orthodox press has never even mentioned his name, let alone asked any questions about how this close associate of a Grand Rabbi of one of the world's largest ultra–Orthodox sects was so easily able to use religious students for high-stakes drug trading. This silence is particularly remarkable considering trial testimony that Miller had attempted to persuade other Orthodox students to serve as couriers to distant locations, including Brazil and Singapore.[83] Why assume that none of those other students ever went on the proffered missions? Why not try tracing the movements of students accosted by Miller to see if other Jewish schools were involved in similar drug deals?

In fact, the leadership did more than ignore these questions. It did its level best to prevent other Orthodox Jews from asking them. To deflect the attention of the rank and file from the obvious problem—the penetration of Orthodox community institutions by drug smugglers—rabbis circulated appeals for vast sums to pay the couriers' lawyers who, among other things, ensured that the couriers rarely spoke to the press. Along the way, Orthodox reporters shamelessly exaggerated the suffering the "boys" endured from the rigors of Japanese prisons: "drastically diminished physical and mental capabilities"; catastrophic weight loss[84]; "indescribable" treatment, including "tortures," that put their "lives ... in the utmost danger,"[85] and so on. The *Jewish Press* even cited unnamed "experts" who claimed that the three "would not survive even one year of prison without permanent damage."[86] (The plain truth, as the Orthodox sources themselves had noted earlier, was that the three were "being treated well," and that their "religious needs" were "respected."[87])

Yet even such hysterical propaganda was not enough for some rabbis, who resorted to libeling the entire Japanese people. The leader of the Rachmastrivka Hasidim claimed in March 2011 that "the recent tsunami in Japan, which has left thousands of people dead, was the result of the arrest" of the *yeshiva* students in Tokyo three years earlier. (Although the Rachmastrivka sect "is one of the biggest and most famous" of the world's Hasidic communities,[88] and even though this unconscionable comment of its leader was widely reported, I do not know of a single prominent Orthodox rabbi who publicly repudiated it. Yet imagine the Jewish community's reaction if a Muslim cleric were to claim that a natural disaster in Israel amounted to divine punishment for the arrests of three Palestinian criminals in that country!)

Compare, finally, the rabbinate's advocacy for young drug couriers against the same rabbinate's consistent coldness toward young sex abuse victims. Without hesitation, Orthodox rabbis treated the three *yeshiva*-based mules as innocent victims, even though the couriers knew they were breaking the law, and—judging from the conflicting and incredible stories they told—were probably conscious of smuggling something more serious than *objets d'art*. Yet the same Orthodox authorities hold victims of child sexual abuse to the severest scrutiny, as when Agudath Israel spokesman Rabbi Avi Shafran belittled the credibility of the accusers of Rabbi Kolko on the grounds that some of them were no longer religiously observant.[89] It bears emphasis that *only* sex abuse victims are held to such a standard. A renegade former Hasid, no longer religious, who confessed to recruiting Hasidic children as drug traffickers enjoyed overwhelming Orthodox community support at his trial.[90] But the teenager who reported multiple acts of sexual abuse by Rabbi Nechemya Weberman was publicly compared to a "whore" by the chief rabbi of her Hasidic community, because—though she is apparently still religious—she no longer belongs to that particular sect.[91] Not a single member of *her* community wrote to the judge on her behalf—as did more than thirty Hasidim in support of Shimon Levita—seeking strict justice for her rapist or deploring the harassment and intimidation she suffered throughout the trial. And to date no Orthodox publication has bothered to notice this intolerable irony.

* * *

The rabbinate's treatment of sex abuse victims—which stands in such harsh contrast to its coddling of actual criminals—has extended even to the supposedly sacred sphere of religious law. Bear in mind that abuse victims are routinely castigated by rabbis when they report their assailants to secular authorities. Disclosing a crime, as Professor Resnicoff notes, is considered a violation of Jewish law so grave that "every Jew has the obligation to use force, even deadly force if necessary, to prevent the informant [even the crime victim] from fulfilling his purpose."[92] Yet, as we have seen, rabbinic authorities had no objection to denouncing people like Lilienblum or Ansky to non–Jewish police, even on false charges—which involves a vastly more serious violation of Jewish law—whenever the rabbis entertained the merest suspicion about the Orthodoxy of their targets. Ansky reports that when the rabbis sent a messenger to him with the order to leave town, the emissary threatened that if he didn't move away at once, he would be "marched out by the police." He explained "quietly, with a smile, 'Can't you understand? You're not a child. Two pounds of tea to the police commissioner, and tomorrow you march out with the prisoners.'"[93]

It is hard to see how anyone aware of such conduct—which traditional Jewish leadership has never really condemned[94]—could take seriously the rabbis' current strictures on reporting sex abuse to secular authorities. Which leads me to a final observation about the opinion-makers of official Orthodoxy. When they cannot completely ignore rabbinic inconsistency, the spokesmen for the status quo sometimes resort to a curious strain of doublethink, allowing the pious Jew to simultaneously believe and disbelieve a given rabbinic principle, depending on whether or not the rabbis themselves choose to apply it.

Case in point: Rabbi Jonathan Rosenblum. A vocal defender of Orthodox rabbinic policy, Rosenblum has also produced a splendid example of the now-you-see-it, now-you-don't approach to religious law. In a 1993 book, Rosenblum lauded the famous *yeshiva* of Slabodka by insisting that its founder stressed "individuality" to such an extent that his students were free to "develop[] their own approach"; in fact, according to Rosenblum, "he never said, 'I demand this,' or 'I insist on this.'" Yet Rosenblum's book also reported, without a single editorial comment, how this same open-minded rabbi had one of his favorite students' letters intercepted and censored—a direct violation of Jewish law—to make sure the youth's older sister, a religiously observant professor of mathematics, "did not lure him to university and out of the yeshiva."[95] I suppose someone could produce a credible defense of the rabbi's actions, but it is clearly impossible to reconcile his surreptitious thought control with the liberal values Rosenblum attributed to him. And I don't believe the inconsistency resulted from carelessness. Quite the contrary: forcing on his readers a self-contradictory exposition of rabbinic values was Rosenblum's way of protecting the rabbis' authority from their own double standards. The rabbis must always mean what they say—even when their actions prove the opposite.

And the same goes for rabbinic restraints on sex abuse victims. The victims must believe at all costs that reporting to police is a heinous sin, because the rabbis say it is; that the rabbis violate their own law at will cannot be acknowledged, let alone seriously considered. What's at stake for the rabbis is more than the inconvenient publicity of sex abuse: it's the threat that the faithful might escape their control, that words like "truth" or "sin" or "crime" might come to take on real meaning and impose real consequences.

True, as an approach to reality, this one fails every moral test. But Orwell would have understood it perfectly.

7

Courting Disaster:
How Rabbinic Courts
Can Control a Sex Abuse Case

One witness named Dunne ... partly from fright at the threats and
maledictions of the Chief Justice, entirely lost his head, and at last
stood silent. "Oh how hard the truth is," said Jeffreys, "to come out of
a lying Presbyterian knave." The witness, after a pause of some minutes,
stammered a few unmeaning words. "Was there ever," exclaimed the
judge, with an oath, "was there ever such a villain on the face of the
earth?.... Of all the witnesses that I ever met with I never saw thy fellow."

—Thomas Macaulay, *The History of England*[1]

Rottenberg himself [one of the judges on the rabbinic court] ...
boasted to the authors that he "cornered" one of the social workers
who supported the boy [the alleged victim of abuse], by confronting
him [during his testimony] with the boy's claim that Rabbi Hafner
had pulled his pubic hairs: "I said to him ... 'How stupid could you
be?'" he remembered afterward. "A boy that age, either he doesn't have,
or it's not big enough [to pull]." But Dr. Grimm told the authors that
a physical examination showed the boy did indeed have pubic hair....

—from *Tempest in the Temple*[2]

In April 2002, Rabbi Tzvi Hersh Weinreb, executive vice president of
the Orthodox Union, candidly admitted to the Associated Press that any
Orthodox Jew who suspects that a child has been sexually abused ought to go
straight to the police, not to a panel of rabbis. "If there's a fire," he explained
to reporter Karen Matthews, "you call the fire department, you don't go to the
rabbinical court.... We're obligated to go to the authorities."[3]

It sounds simple.

If only it were.

The "rabbinical court" dismissed so lightly in Rabbi Weinreb's public

129

rhetoric is, in fact, one of the most powerful and stubbornly persistent institutions in traditional Jewish society. For victims of child sex abuse, it is also one of the most dangerous.

In previous chapters I have tried to illustrate the low priority the Orthodox rabbinate appears to assign to the protection of children—a fact betrayed by the rabbis' actions or inaction on a variety of issues affecting children's welfare. What remains is to analyze the institutions by means of which rabbinic priorities take tangible form. The most central of these is the rabbinic court—called *beth din* in Hebrew—which, according to traditional Jewish law, has the exclusive authority to resolve disputes between Jews in a given community. We cannot understand how child sex abuse cases are handled by Orthodox rabbis, let alone articulate any meaningful reforms, until we understand what happens to these cases in the context of Orthodoxy's rabbinic court system. Yet the sobering lessons an analysis of the *beth din* can provide have so far received less than adequate public attention.

It must be observed at once that the rabbinic court's role for Orthodox Jews is no mere analog of what secular judicial systems do within the communities they serve—and I mean by that considerably more than the obvious fact, to which I will return, that rabbinic tribunals lack the practical enforcement powers of secular courts. People raised outside the traditions of Judaism may find it difficult to comprehend the power exerted over the Orthodox Jewish mind by the concept of the *beth din*. The authority of a rabbinic court, as expressed in normative Jewish texts, transcends anything with which the modern West is familiar. According to Moses Hadas, early rabbinic Judaism absorbed the Platonic ideal of a society governed at every level and in every detail by an all-powerful tribunal of sages. For Plato this was a philosophical fiction, but the founders of rabbinic Judaism, Hadas suggests, really meant to fashion a society that matched Plato's description of the perfect relation between individuals and government:

> The principal thing is that no one, man or woman, should ever be without an officer set over him, and that none should get the mental habit of taking any step, whether in earnest or in jest, on his individual responsibility. In peace as in war he must live always with his eyes on his superior officer.... In a word, we must train the mind not even to consider acting as an individual or how to do it.[4]

Rabbinic Judaism gave shape to this idea in the sweeping and intrusive powers granted to the rabbinic court, an institution specifically intended (according to Maimonides) to enforce every aspect of Jewish law upon every individual under its sway, no matter how private or personal the issue might be.[5] What is more, the rabbinic court was meant to be the *only* such authority, for resort to a non–Jewish tribunal to resolve any dispute between Jews was absolutely forbidden by Jewish law ("Anyone who does this is completely wicked").[6] The implications are clear: no Jew raised in the rabbinic tradition was to be allowed "even to consider acting as an individual," as Plato had put it, in any matter whatsoever; and what Jewish tradition substituted for individual conscience and will was the *beth din*. For the traditional Jew, the rabbinic court was to be the equivalent of God on earth, or at least the nearest possible approach to it.

In keeping with such a role, Talmudic descriptions of rabbinic courts often refer to the awesome responsibilities that devolve upon the judges who compose them. But it would be an error to confuse the ideal implied in such passages with the actual history of *batei din*. While in theory a system of justice governed by divine principles might be expected to enforce the most humane standards—and Talmudic dicta, to their credit, point to the need for strict rules of proof and a horror of excessive severity—the accounts we have of traditionally-imposed Jewish justice are not encouraging. The maverick Jewish historian Israel Shahak reports that throughout the Middle Ages rabbinic courts commonly imposed—for any deviation from any article of religious law—punishments that included flogging, imprisonment or expulsion; "in many countries—Spain and Poland are notable examples—even capital punishment could be and was inflicted, sometimes using particularly cruel methods such as flogging to death." When they could, rabbinic judges administered death sentences well into the modern period, and for reasons that scarcely inspire confidence in the rabbis' judicial temperament. In 1848, for instance, the Orthodox leadership of the Galician city of Lemberg is said to have poisoned the liberal rabbi the town's tiny non–Orthodox contingent had imported from Germany.[7]

One would like to think of such actions as corruptions of the Talmudic ideal, but in fact the Talmud speaks with more than one voice on the subject: it advocates lofty-sounding standards and rigorous rules for judges, but the few actual trials it describes vary so widely from its own precepts that historian Paul Johnson cannot be faulted for concluding that "all seem irregular." Like Shahak, Johnson also acknowledges that rabbinic authority, as it ripened in the formative period of the early Diaspora, manifested itself in a highly restrictive and autocratic rule:

> Jewish society was authoritarian and often oppressive.... [The poor] might petition against a rabbi; but no notice was taken if his family background was right. On the contrary: many local ordinances punished all those "who gossip and jest about the deeds of the town notables." ... In short, there was an excessive amount of subordination in the ghetto.[8]

Significantly, it was Moses Mendelssohn—whose proposals for moderate reform make him a hated figure among Orthodox rabbis to this day[9]—who first argued against separate Jewish jurisdiction in the late 1700s, at a time when Jewish leadership demanded (and liberal non–Jews were still prepared to grant) continued state backing of Jewish courts.[10] The rabbis understood perfectly that the "excessive subordination in the ghetto" could only be maintained through the coercive power of *batei din*.

Against that history—and given the fact that rabbinic courts still figure as a lynchpin of rabbinic control in any traditional Jewish community—the protestations of official spokesmen like the Orthodox Union's Rabbi Weinreb ring a bit hollow. Whatever they may say in public, few leading Orthodox rabbis actively encourage their flocks to take criminal complaints directly to the police. In most communities, the reverse is true: in particular, Orthodox victims of sexual abuse are routinely pressured to accuse Jewish assailants only before a *beth din*, and are bullied still more intensely if they turn to secular prosecutors instead. As *Newsday* reported in 2003:

> Intense pressure is often brought to bear on complainants who bypass rabbinical courts—the community's preferred method of settling disputes—and instead go to secular authorities. Witnesses, who are often young, become fearful and wavering. And prosecutors face pressure from a community that votes as a cohesive block. One woman, whose son was called to testify about an alleged instance of abuse, said that extraordinary pressure was placed both on her family and on the family of the alleged victim.
>
> "I had rabbis coming by. They threatened we'll have curses in our family. It might sound silly to you, but it was very frightening," said the woman.[11]

Having devoted much of my professional life to child abuse cases, I know all too well how hard it can be for child victims, and the adults who support them, to seek justice in the first place. Mothers whose children have suffered sexual abuse often report that "the very system that is designed to protect them and their children actually victimizes them"; according to experts who have interviewed them, "Most of the women perceived the procedures of the criminal justice system as punitive toward them and their children. Multiple interrogations and appearances in police stations and court ... were confusing, tiresome, and stressful."[12] Facing that kind of stress on top of the trauma caused by the abuse itself, those victims brave enough to press their cases—if they belong to religious communities—have naturally tended to look to their clergy for support. For Orthodox Jewish victims, that hope has usually been illusory: the procedures and attitudes of rabbinic courts are, if anything, more intimidating to victims than those of the clumsiest secular prosecutors. Thus we find Rabbi Chaim Rottenberg, one of the rabbis who claimed to have cleared Solomon Hafner of child abuse charges in 2000, boasting of having "cornered" a social worker, one of the witnesses who supported the alleged victim's story, with the (false) claim that a boy his age couldn't possibly have pubic hair, which Hafner had allegedly pulled. "How stupid could you be?" he later remembered bullyragging the witness. Nor was Rottenberg any more delicate when it came to informing the alleged victim, a twelve-year-old boy, of the rabbis' decision. Dismissing his account of months of sadistic abuse, Rottenberg told the child, "Are you aware that we can't buy this?"

The bullying tactics so often suffered by abuse victims in *batei din* cannot, I think, be blamed on the idiosyncrasies of particular rabbinic judges. They stem from the nature of the system itself, which is anchored in the principle of rabbinic supremacy and which, for practical reasons, can only assert its authority by harnessing fear: the "curses" offered against the abuse victim's mother quoted by *Newsday*, or the threat of social ostracism. In 2013, Israel's Supreme Court accepted for review the petition of an Orthodox woman who says that because she successfully complained to a civil court about a neighbor who illegally built a balcony above the porch of her own apartment, "she can barely leave the house for fear of being spat on and verbally abused," her "daughter was denied a place in high school," and "she can no longer go to synagogue because of the stigma and social ostracism." "To all intents and purposes," alleges the organization that filed the petition on her behalf, the woman has "been banished from communal life in the city and will not be able to continue living there." All this, according to the *Jerusalem Post*—which also reported the possibility that there are hundreds of similar cases each year in Israel alone—was her punishment from the local rabbinic court for having resorted to secular authorities. "The phenomenon of such decrees is in part tied to a desire by independent [that is, not state-supported] rabbinical courts of haredi communities to preserve the autonomy and standing of their Jewish legal institutions," the *Post* stressed; the rabbis on those courts must resort to such tactics because they "have no authority to issue binding legal injunctions of any kind."[13] Just so. Without the use of emotional terrorism, the rabbinic courts would likely lose much of their influence.

Thus habituated to bullying as an institutional *sine qua non*, rabbis on *batei din* adopt all too naturally the sort of smug, status-based prejudices that undermine any fair hearing of a child abuse case.[14] A youngster accusing a rabbi of a serious crime is likely to be dismissed out of hand as impertinent, and therefore incredible. So it is unsurprising—if morally jarring—to learn that one of the rabbinic judges who questioned Rabbi Hafner's young accuser saw only narcissism in the boy's hearing disability. "Because he's hearing impaired," Rabbi Moshe Farkas casually suggested, "he always wants to get attention." Rabbi Rottenberg similarly sneered that during his testimony about months of alleged abuse, the boy "was bragging on and on ... just eating the attention with such appetite"—never considering the possibility that the boy, whose complaints had been slighted for years, simply needed to be heard. Hafner's judges could be just as coarse in their dismissal of an adult witness. According to Rottenberg, the rabbis felt justified in barring the testimony of the boy's speech therapist on the grounds that she was "low" and "hate[d] Jews"—because she had supported the alleged victim's allegations in a televised interview.[15]

Although the Hafner case is one of very few in which details about the rabbis' conduct during trial can be documented, there is no reason to regard the record of this proceeding as eccentric. Experienced observers of *beth din* cases describe them in terms that generally conform to the Hafner model. Typical testimony comes from Amy Neustein, an Orthodox rabbi's daughter who has studied child sex abuse both inside and outside the Orthodox Jewish community since the late 1980s. Interviewed on a Canadian television documentary, Dr. Neustein offered a harsh indictment of the role rabbis too often play: "Rabbis ... systematically intimidate and threaten abuse victims, their advocates, their supporters, and their therapists." In *beth din* proceedings, according to Dr. Neustein, the rabbinic judges are likely to "work on breaking the victim down. The victim is hauled before the rabbinic panel, and the victim is told that he or she is a liar."

Even if the rabbis genuinely meant well, their good intentions would be virtually beside the point. Speaking on the same documentary, Daniel Sosnowik, an Orthodox Jew who is also a captain in the New York Police Department, flatly denied that "there's any *beth din* that has any of the credentials necessary to listen to [child] witnesses, to interview actual crime victims." New Jersey prosecutor Marlene Lynch Ford—whose jurisdiction includes the large Orthodox community in Lakewood, New Jersey—elaborated the same point: "The rabbinic tribunal does not have the same investigative tools that are available to us. They don't have the authority, subpoena power and so forth, that is available to us under the law, and they don't, frankly, have the history and the tradition" that would enable them to "prosecute these types of cases."[16] In other words, there is no such thing as a "good" rabbinic inquiry into an allegation of child sex abuse. Even where the rabbis don't intervene for the specific purpose of suppressing the truth, they simply aren't equipped to uncover it. Which means that their only proper role—if their true aim is the pursuit of justice—is to bow out.

But bowing out is precisely what Orthodox rabbis have by and large refused to do, with predictably disastrous results for sex abuse victims. Consider the *batei din* (no fewer than three separate tribunals, according to the molester himself) that protected Rabbi Israel Weingarten—protection that worked for years, until Weingarten was finally convicted in a federal court of repeatedly raping his minor daughter. Though none of the rabbis who exonerated Weingarten played any role in the Hafner case, their behavior was tragically similar to the derelictions that marred that proceeding. All three rabbinic panels that supposedly investigated Rabbi Weingarten heard evidence of his sexual abuse. But the rabbis not only consistently refused to believe the victim; they actively aided Weingarten's crimes, while publicly maligning the innocent.

Readers will recall from my account in Chapter 1 that, apart from the hideous record of child rape, abuse and systematic deceit that unfolded during Rabbi Weingarten's federal trial in 2009, what particularly shocked reporters about the case were Weingarten's attempts to humiliate his former victim even in the courtroom. Weingarten's callousness culminated in his insistence on personally cross-examining his daughter about her life as his "sex slave"—to borrow the words of Judge John Gleeson, who, like the journalists, was disgusted by Weingarten's attempt to "to own [his victim] once again" even as she fought to overcome her fear of her father and to testify to the ugly truth.[17]

What readers of these press reports didn't know was that the victim had been through all this before—but with appallingly different results. When Weingarten and his wife divorced in 2001–2002, the couple, in accordance with traditional Jewish law, had attempted to litigate their differences before a *beth din*. But unlike the federal tribunal that affirmed Weingarten's guilt, the rabbinic court awarded the rabbi sole custody of all six of his minor children, including the daughter he had repeatedly abused. In fact, Weingarten would later claim in legal papers that rabbinic courts in the United States, Belgium and Israel had all "thoroughly investigated [the victimized daughter's] allegations and found them to be without merit."[18] As in the Hafner case, the rabbis had their way with the local secular system, too: the award of custody was confirmed by a Rockland County judge. Even Child Protective Services, in two New York counties, meekly accepted Weingarten's claim (echoed by rabbinic supporters) that he was the victim of a slander concocted by a vindictive ex-wife.[19]

We do not have a contemporary record of Weingarten's rabbinic trial, but there is plenty of evidence of the cruel price paid by Weingarten's accusers for telling the truth. Even after his conviction some eight years later, Weingarten could still inundate the presiding federal judge with statements and affidavits from fellow Hasidim, including rabbis, claiming that his ex-wife, who testified to the rabbis about his abuse, was mentally ill, a criminal, a child abuser and a pathological liar. Weingarten's rabbinic fan club didn't shrink from accusing the young victim herself of a long history of promiscuity, lying and sexual misconduct, the latter supposedly carried out with her siblings— including an infant brother—a neighbor, and a maternal aunt.[20]

Even those smears weren't enough for the rabbis entrusted with the Weingarten family's fate. The handful of Orthodox Jews who backed the girl's case came in for calumniation as well. Rabbi Uziel Frankel, lauding the rabbinic kangaroo court that gave a child rapist exclusive control over his victim, insisted in a written statement, submitted after Weingarten's federal conviction, that the real villains were a cabal of angry Orthodox women and the shadowy advocates they had managed to find among their coreligionists:

> In my experiences with so many messy divorce/custody situations within the community, these horrendous allegations do not come to me in any way as a shock. Shamefully, many scorned wives and dysfunctional children will seek to hang an innocent husband/father with a noose made from fictitious molestation allegations. In nearly every case similar to the above that I have experienced, there was a rabbi or were rabbis and/or other community activist [sic] behind the wife *(nearly always from the same related pool)* assisting he[r] in the false allegations.[21]

The more witnesses there were against the accused, the more innocent he must have been; the backing of an abuse charge by professionals or even by sympathetic rabbis only deepened the proof of conspiratorial fraud (as "in nearly every case"). And of course, the "scorned wife" and her "dysfunctional children" were behind it all. Small wonder Weingarten's victim would later say, "I didn't think the day would come when there would be justice."[22] Had she stayed in front of rabbinic judges with minds like Rabbi Frankel's, that day would probably never have dawned.

Apart from its disgraceful record of blaming the victim, the Weingarten case also underscores the double standard dictated by rabbinic judges' horror of unflattering publicity. I've already mentioned Weingarten's boast of having been cleared by three rabbinic courts. That claim is set in its proper perspective, however, by the affidavit of a prominent Hasidic rabbi who sat on one such panel. According to him, the Satmar *beth din* in Belgium—of which he was chief judge—ruled that the victim, then a minor whose parents were still married, "should be separated from her father" due to the nature of her charges; the rabbi went on to claim that "we did not make findings as to the truthfulness or credibility of [her] allegations."[23] It isn't hard to grasp the import of those two statements. Evidently, the rabbis were willing to offer some protection to the victim as long as the story of Weingarten's rapes remained "private"; these Hasidic judges would scarcely have ordered a young girl's separation from her rabbi-father had they regarded her allegations as fraudulent. But when Weingarten was accused in a divorce proceeding, where the allegations were likely to spill over into family court, and still more when he was publicly charged with sex crimes, those same rabbis rushed to Weingarten's defense. Their nimble reversal of right and wrong the moment the case's setting shifted toward a broader public exemplifies the logic of a system whose highest priority is "what's good for the Jews"—that is, the rabbinic elites. Justice for the victim is secondary to the leadership's right to keep its dirty linen out of open view.

Equally revealing along these lines was the conduct of a Rabbi G.A. Royde, who ran a Hasidic school in Manchester to which Weingarten's daughter was apparently sent in an effort to keep her away from her father's abuse. In 1997, while the teenaged girl was staying with Royde, Weingarten—having traveled all the way from Israel—physically attacked Royde in an effort to abduct the girl. When police arrived at the house, the victim told them why she was being protected by Royde and what her father had done to her.[24] All this is stated in documents that are part of the court record. Yet the same Rabbi Royde wrote a letter after Weingarten's federal trial in which he defended the man who had allegedly assaulted him, insisting that he himself "did not believe the story" the victim told.[25] It's no surprise that sexually abusive rabbis lie. But it seems healthy ones, too, can turn reality upside down—even a rabbi whose conduct shows he was well informed about Weingarten's abusive history, who apparently heard his daughter describe her victimization to police, who even suffered Weingarten's blows in the girl's defense. Even such a rabbi stood ready to protect the abuser, not his victim, once non–Jewish authorities were part of the story. What does *that* say about the integrity of a court system run by such men?

And not only ultra–Orthodox rabbis are guilty of priorities like these. Forum Takanah, a "modern Orthodox" tribunal established in 2003 to deal with sexual harassment, was aware of sex abuse allegations against the prominent Rabbi Mordechai Elon as early as 2005, but sat on the charges for years in exchange for Elon's promise to keep away from students. With what result? Elon predictably broke Takanah's rules, allegedly abusing another student even as Takanah was dealing with the first case. In most people's moral accounting, that would seem to make Takanah at least partly responsible for whatever abuse Elon committed after 2005, when a prompt public report might well have broken the cycle of misconduct. Yet when the story finally went public, as Rabbi Yoseif Bloch angrily noted in a column published in the *Times of Israel*, "*people applauded Takanah's 'bravery' in going to the media five years later!*" I cannot improve on Bloch's conclusions:

> It's not OK to create an organization to stand between sexual-abuse victims and the professionals who are trained and ready to help them....
>
> It's not OK to convene ad hoc rabbinic tribunals in order to devise guidelines unfounded in science, law or religion to "solve" the problem....
>
> There is only one reason not to go to the authorities, and that is to protect the abusers.[26]

*   *   *

Bloch's trenchant observations—particularly the final sentence—deserve emphasis. We cannot treat a demand for taking child abuse charges to a *beth din* as morally neutral, even if mistaken. The truth is that those who insist on rabbinic courts for decisions in such matters can have only one real motive, and that is to protect the guilty. I will argue below that, even in theory, there can be no legitimate role for a rabbinic court in any sex abuse investigation. As it turns out, however, theoretical proof is hardly necessary. The facts behind the guilty plea, and the attempted rabbinic cover-up, in one typical case— that of Rabbi Yosef Kolko—is enough to prove Bloch's point: the intervention of a *beth din* is inevitably part of an obstruction of justice.

Let us quickly review the facts. Kolko was a religious school teacher and summer camp counselor in the heavily Orthodox enclave of Lakewood, New Jersey. In 2009, a young Lakewood boy reported that Kolko had repeatedly molested him, both at school and at camp, beginning in August 2008—over a period when the boy was eleven and twelve years old. The victim's father, a respected rabbi, apparently took the Rabbi Weinrebs of the Orthodox community at their word: he approached local prosecutors, who charged Rabbi Kolko with multiple counts of child sexual abuse. In May 2013, Kolko pleaded guilty to aggravated sexual assault and additional crimes, as other alleged victims began making their own abuse reports to prosecutors.[27]

Kolko's confession came too late to save his original victim from further abuse—this time at the hands of his own religious community. Although, to their great credit, some of Lakewood's Orthodox rabbis supported the boy and his father, the community's Orthodox leadership pulled out the stops on a savage propaganda campaign against the victim almost the moment the charges were known. "Many distinguished people, among them rabbis, rabbinic judges and the top rabbis of [Lakewood's premier *yeshiva*] Bais Medrash Govoha contacted [the victim's father]" in an attempt to persuade him to drop the charges against Kolko, wrote Lakewood's rabbinic leaders in an unsigned letter circulated throughout the community in the summer of 2010. When the first wave of pressure failed, the Lakewood rabbis turned to Rabbi Chaim Kanievsky, an outstanding ultra–Orthodox authority who, as noted in earlier chapters, has vouched for the innocence of at least two other perpetrators of severe child abuse in his native Israel (both of whom were eventually convicted). Kanievsky did not pass up the opportunity to extend his record: according to the Lakewood rabbis' letter, he promptly took Kolko's side.[28] Predictably, the weight of prestigious rabbinic opinion took its toll. Although the victim did not recant the charges against Kolko, he and his family were soon forced out of Lakewood altogether, and were living in a distant state when Kolko entered his guilty plea in a New Jersey courtroom.[29]

Let us not forget that, according to Weinreb's dictum, none of this should have happened. "If there's a fire, you call the fire department," Weinreb had said in 2002. In a sex abuse case, "[y]ou don't go to the rabbinical court."[30]

But where was Weinreb, and other rabbis who supposedly shared his position, when even Rabbi Yisrael Belsky, one of the leading authorities at the Orthodox Union where Weinreb was executive vice president, lent his prestige to the slander campaign against Kolko's accusers? Belsky's attack, the venomous details of which I will address shortly, was made in writing and was freely circulated in Lakewood, so it is unlikely that rabbis like Weinreb were unaware of it. Weinreb's failure to respond was particularly hard to fathom given Belsky's implied denunciation of him as either deceitful or ignorant. Weinreb had publicly urged sex abuse victims to bypass "the rabbinical court" as a matter of Jewish law. But Belsky condemned any such position out of hand. Whenever someone "inform[s] upon a fellow Jew to the hands of the secular authorities" instead of a *beth din*, Belsky wrote, "the [Jewish] law is *undisputed* that one who commits such an act has no share in the world to come." Period. Never mind that such a position was directly contrary to New Jersey law, which of course was binding upon all the Lakewood residents to whom his letter was addressed.[31] The prohibition against taking a sex abuse charge to prosecutors was "undisputed," in Belsky's view—meaning that there was no such person as Rabbi Weinreb, or else that his position simply didn't count among those in the know. If that wasn't really the view of Orthodox leadership, why didn't its rabbis respond openly to such a claim?

For our purposes, what is particularly significant about Belsky's letter is that it went beyond the procedural demand that a sex abuse victim report to a rabbinic court rather than to secular authorities. Though nothing like a trial had taken place when his letter was written, Belsky did not hesitate to pronounce his own verdict: "After conducting a thorough investigation I am absolutely certain that [Rabbi Kolko] ... is perfectly innocent of any wrongdoing of any nature whatsoever." Nor did he stop there. "All these allegations," he insisted, were "fabrications" invented by the victim's family. According to Belsky, *they* were the ones guilty of child abuse:

> All the reports made to the secular authorities were only for the express purpose of casting blame for their [the victim's family] own shameful and accursed existence on others. And the truth is that the allegations they make against others are crimes they themselves are in fact guilty of and they seek to cleanse their reputation by blaming an innocent man for their own deeds.[32]

Shades of Israel Weingarten! Not only was the parent who tried to protect the victim a liar and a slanderer, he was a child molester too. And it wasn't only Belsky who was prepared to make that claim. The anonymous Lakewood rabbis implied no less in their own letter (cited above):

> Besides the overwhelming lack of proof by the [accusers] against the [accused], the household of the [accusers] suffers from many issues relating to the environment

necessary for raising healthy and normal children. If we were to write what we know, you would be torn between crying & vomiting.

They also endorsed Belsky's accusation—the same one made in Weingarten's defense by Rabbi Uziel Frankel—that those Orthodox rabbis who supported the victim were evil people who "for reasons of status and power" were "violating the Torah." And in all this, sadly enough, Belsky and the others had plenty of rabbinic support. "It is a self-evident matter that no one in the world has the power to assert a charge against anyone," ran a Hebrew statement signed by nine prominent Orthodox rabbis and circulated in Lakewood in 2010, "unless the two of them have gone to an accepted rabbinic court which will hear [the dispute] between them.... And even more so ... if he raises the matters before the secular authorities ... [without] a clear, written rabbinic ruling regarding this act ... from an expert rabbinic court."[33]

Now all this rabbinic chest-beating to support a child abuser and to defame the innocent is bad enough. It is doubly shocking when we realize that none of the rabbis who openly maligned the victim's family in such terms has made a public apology since Kolko pleaded guilty in May 2013—particularly in light of the Lakewood rabbis' crocodile tears over the suffering of the *perpetrator* and *his* family three years earlier. ("He is destitute. His parents are heartbroken. His family suffers terrible pain and anguish.") But we should not lose sight of the fact that the rabbis' written claims—unopposed, as I have stressed, even by Orthodox leaders whose prior statements should have put them squarely on the victim's side—reveal the true agenda behind their insistence on the exclusive jurisdiction of rabbinic courts. Never for a moment did Belsky or the Lakewood rabbis distinguish between their demand for a rabbinic court and their insistence on the abuser's innocence, or for that matter on the supposed wickedness and hypocrisy of the brave few who told the truth. Belsky, as we have seen, was ready to acquit Kolko before any rabbinic trial had begun. And the Lakewood rabbis were singing Kolko's praises and lamenting his misfortune without even pretending to have heard a scrap of evidence.

If the rabbis had had their way, the man who ultimately "admitted committing a variety of sexual acts on a boy" he, as a teacher and camp counselor, "had a legal responsibility to care for"[34] would have walked away scot-free. That was the true meaning behind all the pious calls for adjudication of a child's charges by a rabbinic court—and, equally, the true meaning behind the silence of the Rabbi Weinrebs of the Orthodox Jewish world when their pleasant propaganda was exposed for what it was.

*   *   *

The rabbinic intervention in the Kolko case teaches a sobering lesson about the role a *beth din* really plays in child abuse investigations. But its example should not surprise us. Rudimentary logic rules out *any* serious role for Jewish courts in *any* child sex abuse case—unless, of course, their true function is to suppress reports altogether, a position that Orthodox rabbis still heatedly deny they hold, though the evidence of actual cases, as we have seen, tells against them.

First of all, it is obvious that Jewish courts cannot "try" accused sex offenders, let alone punish them if convicted. Even if they had access to the sort of expert testimony that is often indispensable in such cases—and of course they rarely do—rabbinic courts are clearly unequal to the job of conducting any case dealing with a criminal assault. They lack a police force to gather information; they have no power to compel witnesses to testify; they cannot issue search warrants to seize hidden evidence; they cannot detain suspects before trial; and they cannot impose a sentence on the guilty party.

The system's spokesmen do not actually deny any of this. When they allude at all to the role of a *beth din* in a case of alleged abuse, they generally describe the court as a sort of gatekeeper between the Orthodox accuser and the police. Go first to a rabbinic court, they say, and let the rabbis determine whether the case should be passed on to secular authorities. That was clearly the message of a panel of Orthodox rabbis speaking at a May 2011 conference under the auspices of Agudath Israel of America, one of the most influential Orthodox organizations in the world.

Rabbi Shlomo Gottesman, heading a conference panel that specifically addressed the issue of reporting sexual abuse, insisted that only Orthodox rabbis can determine what constitutes "reasonable suspicion"; therefore, he declared, no one may report a case of child sex abuse to authorities without first receiving rabbinic permission. The innocent reader might suppose that claiming a rabbinic monopoly on what is "reasonable" must represent a fringe position even among Orthodox rabbis—as it certainly ought to—but Agudath Israel of America's executive vice president, Rabbi Chaim David Zwiebel, actually went Gottesman one better. The mere "claim" of sexual abuse by an individual witness is not enough to take the matter to secular authorities, he told the *Jewish Daily Forward*: there must also be "some circumstantial evidence or something that would appear to bolster the claim." In fact, Zwiebel insisted on this formula even where the witness is a "mandated reporter"—that is, someone legally required to report suspicions of child abuse to secular officials.

Agudath Israel's position was promptly described as a likely violation of New Jersey law by a Lakewood prosecutor—a claim of real significance, in light of the rabbinic cover-up of the Kolko case that was under way in Lakewood at that very moment. What is more, Rabbi Yosef Blau, one of those unusual Orthodox rabbis who have publicly challenged the official consensus, told the *Forward* flatly that "there is no decent justification why anybody in their right mind should think rabbis are qualified to make that judgment"—that is, whether a child sex abuse claim is "reasonable" in the first place. Zwiebel's counter was to blame the trouble not on the rabbinate but on the Orthodox rank and file. "At the end of the day," he pontificated, "as a community that feels itself bound by Torah, it still is the case that we [rabbis] have to think about questions like *mesirah* [informing to secular authorities] and about the relevance of Halacha in determining these kinds of issues."[35] What a burden the rabbis must shoulder to help along the benighted Orthodox masses.

Of course, the Gottesman-Zwiebel position is nothing but double-talk. True, not every suspicion is a reasonable one. In fact, in some cases, a witness may herself be in doubt as to the significance of what she knows—for instance, if she has overheard a very young child make an ambiguous statement that might or might not point to sexual abuse. But in a case like that, a mental health professional with experience in child abuse is much more likely than a panel of rabbis to help the witness resolve her uncertainty. And what other sort of case can pit a witness's judgment of what is "reasonable" evidence against the rabbis'? The only possible example is one in which the witness is in no doubt at all, but in which the rabbis intend to countermand the witness's intention to report a suspected crime to the police, substituting their own judgment for hers. Apart from the fact that such a ruling, if obeyed, would almost certainly violate the law whenever the witness is a mandated reporter, a *beth din*'s attempt to suppress a witness's sex abuse report makes no moral or logical sense. Again, there may be cases in which the witness thinks her suspicion amounts to more than it really does. But the only reasonable way to test such a suspicion is to report it. If the police think the information is suitable to act upon, the witness cannot be faulted for thinking they should have done so; and if they do not, the matter ends there. In other words, the only child sex abuse cases that could conceivably come before a *beth din*, even according to the system's staunchest advocates, fall into one of three groups: those in which the rabbis are incompetent to judge because they lack the needed expertise; those in which the rabbis' actions will be nugatory, either because they allow a report that would have been made without their intervention, or because they resist a report that would have had no effect in any case; and those in which the rabbis' actions necessarily frustrate the proper functioning of the criminal justice system. Either the rabbis of the *beth din* accomplish nothing at all or else they obstruct justice. There is no third alternative.

So one can only concur in Rabbi Blau's emphatic rejection of the whole *beth din* process in such matters. No doubt this is why the system's paladins repeatedly shift their ground, sometimes claiming that a *beth din* is only a step toward proper law enforcement, then effectively conceding (under the slightest pressure) that the real function of the *beth din* is to protect the accused. As we have seen, the rabbis' actions in Yosef Kolko's case illustrate the same pattern. His defenders did not stop with the demand that the accusers take their charges to a *beth din*. Both Rabbi Belsky and the anonymous Lakewood rabbis crammed their letters with baseless conclusions as well. According to them, Kolko's family was in "anguish" because "no one comes to their aid"; in contrast, the victim's father was an "informer," "a two-bit rav [rabbi]," a "guilty part[y]" and an enemy of the entire community whose mistreatment of his own children left the anonymous authors "torn between crying & vomiting." Belsky, too, went well beyond defending the guilty: he accused the victim's family of "casting blame for their own shameful and cursed existence on others." And all these conclusions were reached before anything like a rabbinic trial had taken place.

The rabbinic screeds in the Kolko case are unusual to the extent that they were published; their contents are not only typical but utterly predictable. Defenders of the *beth din* system have literally nothing to offer, and no demands of any significance to make on religious Jews, if rabbinic courts are to be nothing but way stations on the road to the public prosecutor. If the *beth din* is to have a meaningful role at all, the only function it can assume without absurdity is that of advocate for the accused. Naturally, there will be occasions when even *a priori* support for the accused child abuser will coincide with the appropriate legal result, just as the hands of a stopped clock will sometimes coincide with the correct time of day. But this no more amounts to justice than motionless clocks can be said to tell the time.

* * *

Rabbinic defenders of the status quo sometimes offer additional excuses for using *batei din* to deflect child sex abuse cases from the secular justice system. Not one of them inspires any real conviction.

Rabbis sometimes argue, for instance, that Orthodox victims don't really benefit from the police and criminal courts, since recourse to such a public process inevitably compromises their privacy. In Chapter 4, I quoted Rabbi Jonathan Rosenblum's insistence that rabbis suppress child sex abuse charges out of concern for what is "best for victims, their families and the community," since "the knowledge that incidents will be publicized can keep victims or their parents from coming forward."[36] Except to the extent Rosenblum's coy reference to "the community" is understood to mean "the rabbis," his logic boils down to the idea that Orthodox sex abuse victims would rather let their attackers go free than risk their own public exposure. No doubt this is true in some cases; but what on earth gives rabbis the right to make that decision for each and every victim, which is what the argument supports? Besides, in many cases the opposite is true: victims often find that only a public criminal trial against their abusers gives them the vindication they need. "Victims of abuse need to speak out.... And the community needs to speak out in order to hold the perpetrators responsible and in order to protect other innocents from potential harm," writes Mark Dratch,[37] another Orthodox rabbi who, as founder of the Jewish Institute Supporting an Abuse-Free Environment (JSAFE), has been sharply challenging the status quo among Orthodox leadership. Several of my own clients have told me that they could not feel whole without seeing the man who abused them publicly face justice. Obviously there can be no single, *a priori* rule for all sex abuse victims. Rosenblum's "rabbis know best" nostrum is patronizing nonsense.

Similarly, it is claimed that an alternative to the criminal justice system, one that works quietly with offenders and keeps the issue within the confines of the Orthodox community, is less threatening to Orthodox victims and does as much good as the criminal courts. That was the theory behind the sex offenders' program established by the Orthodox-run Ohel Children's Home and Family Services agency, which for several years allegedly worked with the Brooklyn District Attorney to address sex abuse charges inside the local Orthodox community. The record of Ohel's shadowy system, about which the agency has released only the sketchiest information, illustrates just about everything that is wrong with the theory of rabbinic "alternatives" to the secular courts. We do not know how many offenders were supposedly treated in the program; we do not know how their behavior was monitored while they were in treatment, or indeed whether they were monitored at all. What little we know about the protective value of the system can be gleaned from the case of Stefan Colmer, who was allowed to leave the program in 2002, "simply because he had decided to get married and didn't want to inform his new wife that he was a pedophile. During the following years, he sexually abused at least two thirteen-year-old boys"—while the Ohel agency did nothing.[38]

According to Hella Winston of the *New York Jewish Week*, Ohel's silence after Colmer walked out of its offenders' program—a program that was supposed to protect the Orthodox community better than police and prosecutors could—"raises several thorny questions," such as, "Should Ohel have agreed to treat Colmer, knowing that he had never been reported to the police?"[39] Amy Neustein and I added some questions of our own:

> Why didn't Ohel have a fixed policy that would have triggered some sort of action in the event Colmer refused to complete an agreed-upon therapy program as an offender? ... Couldn't a program whose ostensible purpose was to protect the community have included a provision, agreed to in advance by the offender, that violation of Ohel's rules would result in, say, a report to the police or (assuming no

crime had yet been committed) appropriate notification to protect potential victims?[40]

Needless to say, Ohel has never answered any of those questions. Nor have Orthodox rabbis demanded a better response.

Without such basic safeguards in place, no program like Ohel's could ever qualify as a way of dealing with child sex abuse. According to published experts in the field, the notion of a treatment program for offenders in lieu of criminal prosecution is a pipe dream; such treatment only works *as part of* the justice system, "as a condition of a suspended sentence or as part of a work release program." Actual therapeutic experience with sex offenders has shown that "being held accountable by the criminal justice system was essential.... [T]herapy was not possible for these offenders unless or until the cases were reported to the police."[41] And cooperation with law enforcement is equally essential to ensure the safety of potential victims if the offender drops out of the treatment program, as Colmer did. The rabbinic defenders of "alternative" handling of sex abusers either don't know these basic facts—or refuse to tell the truth about them.

Finally, some rabbis argue that *batei din* can deal with "the internal problems of our community"—that is, with Orthodox cases of child sex abuse—at least as well as the "cumbersome, insensitive, and largely incompetent government apparatus." Such is the argument of Rabbi William Handler in a column published by the *Jewish Press* in May 2013.[42] Even that Orthodox newspaper's chief editor questioned Handler's argument "in light of the colossal failure of our religious leaders to respond, much less supervise and try, in one abuse case after another"—much to the editor's credit, in my view.[43] In any case, Handler's argument is both false and irrelevant. It is false, because the Handlers of the Orthodox world assume that secular officials are automatically unfair to Orthodox Jews (a position that says more about them than about the justice system), and because their complaints about police, courts and the child welfare bureaucracy are no truer of those institutions than of any others that could even theoretically deal with child abuse suspicions. It is irrelevant, because even if it were true, it would not justify Handler's conclusion—namely, that all child abuse cases "must be referred to our top Torah leadership"—a "cure" that, as we have seen, would be far worse than the disease. Would anyone who really cared about justice in child sex abuse cases endorse the tactics of the rabbis who gave an alleged victim's mother "a statement from a psychologist who had never examined her son, saying he was not fit to testify"? Where, if not in a *beth din*, would judges be likely to ask the alleged victim's "family to sign a document saying the boy was crazy so that they could get the criminal case thrown out"?[44] Such practices, well known to Orthodox leadership, have never elicited public criticism from the powers that be; nor are they ever mentioned by the likes of Rabbi Handler as they sing their paeans to rabbinic superiority.

*　*　*

The injustices wrought by the *beth din* system in sex abuse cases are so breathtaking, and so well attested in the available record, that the most astonishing detail of all is the refusal of Orthodox leadership to acknowledge them. Nowhere in the public statements of powerful Orthodox rabbis can one find a confession that rabbinic courts have failed sex abuse victims—not the *beth din* that falsified evidence in the Hafner case, not the one that "cleared" Yosef Kolko, not the three separate rabbinic courts that turned their backs on Rabbi Israel Weingarten's massive record of incest and rape. As far as Orthodox leadership is concerned, these things (though far from secret) never happened. And the meaning of such silence is no less obvious when Orthodox rabbis do offer comments on some aspects of the rabbinic court system, while ignoring the failures that matter most.

Such an event occurred in the days immediately preceding Kolko's guilty plea on multiple counts of child sexual abuse—a confession that blew to smithereens the pretenses of the rabbis who had condemned his victims, while demanding the exclusive jurisdiction of rabbinic courts over the case. By the most unsettling of coincidences, that same week saw the publication of a long article addressing the imperfections of *batei din* in America by Rabbi Yitzchok Frankfurter, editor in chief of the popular Orthodox weekly *Ami Magazine*.

But Frankfurter's criticisms had nothing to do with protecting abused children or taking excessive power out of the hands of vindictive rabbis. Taking his cue from Israeli rabbis he called "saintly personages," Frankfurter instead insisted that "the *batei din* in America need a *chizzuk* [strengthening]."[45] He argued that reforms devised for the parallel *beth din* system in Israel, if imported to the United States, could achieve a similar improvement in American rabbinic courts. But the procedures described in his article all related to disputes over money. Not a word of his analysis addressed the intervention of rabbinic courts in criminal matters, let alone in cases of child sex abuse, in which (as he must have known) their role is especially improper and the results especially pernicious. For Frankfurter, that crucial issue appeared not to have arisen at all.

Or maybe it did—if only in an oblique way. Rabbi Yehuda Silman told Frankfurter that his own rabbinic court in Israel never writes down the reasons for its rulings. "There's a legal reason not to do it," Silman counseled, according to Frankfurter's article. "Our power to issue a [ruling] comes from ... the laws of arbitration. The civil court won't usually set aside the ruling of a *beis din*; it happens only under extraordinary circumstances. But if we wrote the reasoning down, they would begin to analyze it and somehow find a way to claim that the decision wasn't reasonable."[46] An interesting pair of assumptions is visible between these lines, both of them grimly resonant for sex abuse victims. First, rabbis should regard secular courts as their natural enemies. Second, for the rabbis, asserting their power—that is, having their rulings enforced—is more important than making their reasoning clear, as a responsible tribunal should be eager to do. As a matter of fact, Silman's advice was adopted proleptically by the rabbinic judges of Solomon Hafner, who stopped tape-recording their court sessions midway through the proceedings "because they [D.A. officials] were going to subpoena it," as one rabbinic judge candidly put it, and the rabbis did not want the details of their investigation to be heard by secular authorities.[47] Some years earlier, the rabbinic tribunal that whitewashed Rabbi Baruch Lanner had similarly sealed its record so that the public would not know the more damaging details of its findings.[48] In each such case, rabbinic authority was protected; but the only other beneficiaries were those accused of child abuse. Frankfurter may not have been thinking along those lines, but the reasoning of Silman, approvingly quoted in his article, fits like a glove.

A final note struck by Frankfurter was even more disturbing, precisely because it was clearly not meant to be. Toward the end of his article, he quoted an Israeli rabbi who lionized the *beth din* in Lakewood, New Jersey: presumably the same one whose rabbinic sponsors had denounced the parents of an 11-year-old child, repeatedly molested by Yosef Kolko, as "guilty parties" and "informers" for reporting him to police; the same rabbis who, after Frankfurter's article appeared, showed so little regard for the truth that they would not even apologize for having abandoned a victim of sexual abuse, nor for having publicly championed a criminal.

No problem. Lakewood's rabbinic court system didn't need reforms at all, insisted the Israeli rabbi (and, apparently, Rabbi Frankfurter, too). "In Lakewood there is already a good *beis din*," he said.[49]

8

Self-Policing or
Thought-Policing?

After I landed at Ben Gurion Airport in late October 2000, the young female Israeli immigration officer cheerfully asked me to remember that Israel was "a small country threatened by people from outside who want to take it." I suggested that the Palestinians had been living in "Palestine"—or modern-day Israel—for generations, that they were not "outside" (save those who had been expelled from their lands by Israel) and that UN Security Council Resolution 242 might, in the end, bring real peace. "What is 242?" she wanted to know.

—Robert Fisk[1]

In the ultra–Orthodox world of Borough Park, friend and stranger were simple words to define. A friend was anyone who looked like us, religious Jews who wore traditional Orthodox garb, had beards and covered their heads with large black *kippas*. A stranger was anyone who did not.... If you wore the garb you were right, if you did not you were wrong....

When I first tried to write about abuse in our community, to use the words needed to describe what was happening to so many children, I was firmly told not to. Some subjects are better left in silence, the rabbis said. Orthodox Jews did not need such words. Those were words for gentiles. We had built walls and had built them high; the outside world could never enter.

—Judy Brown[2]

One early afternoon in November 2010, a 15-year-old African American named Corey Ausby was walking toward a bus stop in the Park Heights neighborhood of Baltimore. He was supposed to meet his mother; the two of them were heading afterwards to a doctor's appointment.

As he walked, a burgundy convertible swished up the road from behind him, then slowed down as it drew abreast. There were two young men in the front seats, strangers to Ausby. They were both wearing *yarmulkes*.

Ausby didn't know it, but the two were brothers—Eliyahu and Avi Werdesheim—and Eliyahu, the elder of the two, was a member of the Baltimore Shomrim, a neighborhood patrol set up by the Orthodox Jewish community in 2005, ostensibly to work with local police. The brothers had spotted Ausby as he walked down Fallstaff Avenue, and immediately identified him for what he was: an outsider on Orthodox Jewish turf. Once alongside Ausby, the brothers kept their convertible close to the curb, matching speed with the boy, leaning out to taunt him.

"You don't belong in this neighborhood," the two shouted, according to one witness who would later testify at the Werdesheims' trial.

"He was scared," the witness, a former Navy SEAL, said of young Ausby. "He was petrified. It looked like he wanted to disappear and not be there."[3]

But Ausby didn't disappear, so the Werdesheims stopped the convertible, jumped out, and—perhaps with the aid of Orthodox patrol members from other cars nearby—slammed Ausby to the ground and beat his skull with the butt of a two-way radio.

Eliyahu Werdesheim, who did the bulk of the damage to Ausby, would later claim he was acting in self-defense: the black kid had threatened him with a nail-studded board. He didn't mention that Ausby only picked up the board from a construction site along the road after the two brothers had started harassing and threatening him.[4] In the end, the elder Werdesheim was sentenced to three years of probation—no jail time—while his brother was cleared on all charges.[5] And the Orthodox Jewish patrol, like so many others of its kind, went along on its racially divisive way.[6]

The assault on Ausby was not the first incident of its kind to receive public attention. In April 2008, 20-year-old Andrew Charles—an African American sophomore at Kingsborough Community College and the son of a New York police officer—reported being attacked by several members of a Hasidic patrol in Crown Heights, Brooklyn. As rendered by journalist Matthew Shaer in a book on the Crown Heights Shomrim—"guards" in Hebrew—here is Charles' account of what happened:

> [H]e'd been walking with a friend near Albany Avenue, on the fringes of the Lubavitch [Hasidic] settlement. It was late afternoon, the weather cooperating, the sky overhead smudged a black-blue. Up toward Eastern Parkway ... Charles had been approached by two men. Both men were wearing yarmulkes. There had been a stare-down. Maybe an exchange of a few choice words. One of the Jews had apparently pulled a canister of Mace from his pocket and blasted Charles in the face. Charles felt the spray searing the soft skin under his eyelids, and he collapsed to the pavement.
>
> Before he could haul himself up again, a black GMC Envoy SUV barreled down

Albany, and a third kid hopped out, this one allegedly wielding a nightstick. Charles said he took several blows around the back. He had limped down to Kings County Hospital, registered a report with the police....

The Hasid who allegedly beat Charles was a member of a Crown Heights Jewish patrol named Yitzhak Shuchat. Tipped off that police might be on his trail, Shuchat promptly fled to Israel, where he remained for years—apparently unsought by the Brooklyn authorities—until a member of a rival patrol pressed prosecutors to seek his extradition, which was finally ordered by Israel's Supreme Court in December 2012.[7] As of this writing, no one has been tried, let alone convicted, for the assault—a fact that has not appeased the Orthodox Jewish community, which has vigorously resisted all efforts to bring the attackers to justice, even accusing the Brooklyn District Attorney of anti–Semitism for belatedly seeking Shuchat's extradition.[8]

In the previous chapter, I stressed how rabbinic courts can keep Orthodox Jewish abuse victims away from prosecutors and police. But many of the larger Orthodox Jewish communities don't merely want to evade the secular police; they would prefer to replace them. This is the mostly-overlooked point lying behind the proliferation, since the 1980s, of private patrols—or Shomrim, as they are more often called—in the Orthodox Jewish communities dominating several areas of Brooklyn, Miami, Baltimore and a few other cities.

The press's focus on interracial attacks by Shomrim members is understandable—they *are* important, and they help to illustrate the darker side of what are often portrayed as nothing more than helpful "neighborhood watches." But the emphasis on Shomrim's violence against non–Jews has tended to blur the internal function these patrols are mainly intended to perform. I will argue that Shomrim are meant not only to intimidate outsiders but, more importantly, to enforce the rabbinic elites' control over the members of the Orthodox communities they ostensibly serve. As long as that elite seeks to control the reporting of sex abuse to secular authorities, Shomrim patrols are bound to play an important part in abuse cover-ups—as indeed they do.

The first order of business is to disentangle fact from legend. The traditional account of the parturition of Shomrim runs something like this: By the late 1960s, Orthodox Jews in Brooklyn, rapidly multiplying but abandoned by the Jewish parvenus who were hastening to the suburbs, found themselves sharing neighborhoods with poor black and Latino populations. Crime ran rampant, some of it violent, much of it openly anti–Semitic; the police were unable or unwilling to protect the Jews. Had it not been for Shomrim, Orthodox women and children would have been at the mercy of roving gangs of hoodlums.

That is the popular story among Orthodox Jews, and there is at least a grain of truth in it (notwithstanding its racist overtones). It is a matter of record, at any rate, that a great many Orthodox Jews in the late 1960s *believed* that their Brooklyn neighborhoods were unsafe. In fact, distress in Brooklyn's Jewish communities at the time was so acute that it gave rise to a fledging self-defense movement. After a raucous public debate in 1968, a previously obscure firebrand named Rabbi Meir Kahane declared that "never again" would Jews tolerate violence quietly—instead, he insisted, they would take matters into their own hands. Thus was born the notorious Jewish Defense League, whose first official objective was to escort elderly Jews safely to and from Brooklyn markets. (Kahane and his acolytes would later graduate to acts of terrorism, first against a New York impresario who worked with a Soviet ballet company, later against Palestinians in Israel and the West Bank.)[9]

But the facts behind the popular narrative, far from linking the birth of Shomrim to nascent dangers faced by Orthodox Jews, actually prove the opposite. Shomrim could not have been formed to counter a growing criminal menace to Orthodox communities, because by all accounts that menace had reached crisis levels by 1968—when Kahane established the JDL—while the first real Shomrim in Brooklyn did not appear until at least *ten years later*, with most Shomrim groups dating from a period still more recent.[10] Virtually all of these groups were founded by rabbinic leadership during a period— roughly the 1980s and 1990s—when Orthodox communities, by virtue of their rapidly growing numbers, centralized organization and voting discipline, were either already politically dominant in their respective areas or soon would be. In other words, Shomrim patrols were never products of Jewish vulnerability; they were, and are, creatures of Jewish power.

This point emerges still more clearly once key facts about the Shomrim patrols are juxtaposed against those of the earlier Jewish Defense League. Kahane, the JDL's founder, was a marginal figure shunned by the rabbinic leadership and local politicians. Shomrim groups, in contrast, were established with the explicit approval of the leading rabbis of the neighborhoods they served and (in keeping with rabbinic pressure) have always enjoyed extraordinary political support.[11] In fact, among the fruits of their influence both inside and outside the Orthodox communities, Shomrim today boast "fairly sophisticated equipment, including police-style mobile-command center trucks," not to mention lavish cash handouts from the public till (thanks to obliging city officials).[12] Clearly the Shomrim, products of politically powerful enclaves, did not merely replicate the protection-oriented goals of Kahane's fringe group—something Orthodox leadership could have attempted at the same time as Kahane, had it wished to. The rabbis who backed Shomrim must have had a different function in mind.[13]

Equally unpersuasive is the rationale that Shomrim patrols are an answer to their communities' putative fear of the official police. "A lot of people in the community are a little apprehensive of the police," a Brooklyn Shomrim member told the *Christian Science Monitor*. "They don't want to interact with the police unless they absolutely have to." Why not? The *Monitor* attributed their reluctance to the Jewish experience in "Eastern European and Russian shtetls where, more often than not it was the authorities who were behind their persecution."[14] Borough Park Shomrim spokesman Simcha Bernath pursued this version of Jewish history to even darker extremes: "We have a major elderly population, and many of them are Nazi concentration camp survivors, and even though they love the United States, they still have that scaredness with the police."[15]

No one denies that ultra–Orthodox Jews tend to shy away from secular police. But when rabbinic apologists start to people the landscape of 21st-century Brooklyn with jackbooted gendarmes and concentration camps, it's high time for some skepticism. First, concentration camp survivors make up, at most, a small fraction of Borough Park's total Jewish population—not nearly enough to explain a whole community's post-traumatic associations with policemen.[16] Second, the implication that any man or woman in official uniform automatically reminds every elderly Jew of an SS officer is patently absurd. (Do Orthodox Jews run from mailmen? Hotel porters? Traffic cops?) Third, notwithstanding what the apologists told the *Christian Science Monitor* and the paper naively repeated, it is simply false that Polish and Russian police were "more often than not" persecutors of Jews. True, the Russian government instigated pogroms as it lost its grip on power in the waning years of the 19th century. But such atrocities were seldom led by the official police force, which in Eastern Europe, as a rule, either left the Jewish communities under the control of their rabbis or, as the Enlightenment touched even Russia after 1795, generally acted to enforce the law when it acted (independently) at all. Significantly, some of the sharpest criticism of the 19th-century police to be found in traditional Jewish accounts focuses on the secular authorities' growing refusal to take bribes from Jews or to tolerate the murder of Jewish heretics on their rabbis' orders.[17]

In short, the familiar tales of Jewish victimhood cannot explain why the size and power of Shomrim groups mushroomed precisely as Orthodox vulnerability disappeared behind unprecedented wealth and political influence—circumstances that would have had the opposite effect on any group formed for self-defense. "In the diaspora Jewish life has never been so free, so prosperous, so unthreatened," observed the *Economist* in a major 2012 survey of Orthodox Jewish life subtitled, appropriately enough, "Alive and well." And nowhere is this truer than in the United States, the survey found,[18] where Orthodox Jews, conservatively estimated today at 20 percent of the Jewish population, stand at the very center of today's Jewish success story. If American ultra–

Orthodox patrols were born of fear—whether of outsiders or the police—why would they remain indispensable to communities that enjoy such unprecedented tranquility?

Once we dispose of the smokescreens, the real reason for the growth of Shomrim patrols is not hard to discern. The simple fact is that Orthodox rabbis prefer their communities to be governed by a police force answerable to rabbinic rather than municipal authority. That's why the patrols had little rabbinic support when ultra–Orthodox communities were not yet powerful enough to interfere with ordinary systems of political control: their relative weakness meant that the patrols, by default, were sure to fall under the authority of the police and would be subject to city and state laws. Once Orthodox leadership had sufficient clout to run its communities' institutions as it saw fit, Shomrim emerged as one of the rabbis' priorities.

Correctly understood, the history of the patrols helps to illustrate their function, which in simple terms is to extend rabbinic power over Orthodox Jewish communities. Matthew Shaer, though painting a generally favorable picture of the Shomrim in his recent book, concedes that even New York City's famed police department is forced to yield to the Hasidic patrols on their own turf. "[E]veryone understood that the Shomrim and the Shmira were basically untouchable," writes Shaer of two such groups. "Catch them doing something, and maybe you could lock them up. Until then, you know, work out any way you can. Bide your time, stiff upper lip, keep calm and carry on, look the other way, grin and bear it."[19] "In Brooklyn, it almost seemed like there were two penal codes," retired police Captain William Plackenmeyer similarly told *Newsday* in 2003, "one for the Hasidic community and one for everyone else."[20]

Unsurprisingly, the Orthodox communities' non–Jewish neighbors have been among the first to feel Shomrim's effects. In Crown Heights, Brooklyn, for instance, black residents have "complained—not at all unreasonably—that they were targeted, harassed and beaten by the 'Jew police.'" As early as April 1987, the patrols had made enough trouble to spark a large public protest before the home of the community's chief rabbi, with speakers noting that while New York City authorities largely ignored the problems of the area's black neighborhoods, the growing power of the Shomrim had made matters even worse. Their offenses included a vicious attack on a black teenager in July 1986, which led to assault convictions for four Hasidim. Apart from that, a black woman's house had been firebombed, apparently by Hasidim; blacks who wouldn't move out of housing coveted by the Jewish community were allegedly harassed or threatened. Several men complained of being grabbed and shoved into the back of a squad car, just for being black. "Sometimes I feel like we are living in an apartheid state where a tiny minority is controlling our state," one woman told the *New York Times*.[21]

But while these abuses tell an important part of the story, the Orthodox rabbinate particularly prizes Shomrim for the power the patrols give the rabbis over the Orthodox Jews themselves. "When it comes to Jew-on-Jew crime ... Shomrim will always consult a rabbi before involving the police," the *Christian Science Monitor* correctly reports.[22] Given the deference of the secular authorities, this means in effect that rabbis decide when and how the law is to be enforced among Orthodox Jews. And as anyone who has read this far can easily guess, rabbinic power of this sort has profound implications for Orthodox sex abuse victims.

That Orthodox rabbis covet such authority should come as no surprise. However recent a phenomenon in the modern United States, rabbinic control over intra-community law enforcement for Orthodox Jews is not at all unprecedented. Until the rising tide of Jewish emancipation swept through Europe in the 19th century, Orthodox rabbis generally governed every aspect of their communities' lives with exacting rigor, and often with a heavy hand. Severe penalties were imposed for deviations from rabbinic orders—and these could even be enforced by non-Jewish civil authorities. As late as the early 1800s, the famous Rabbi Moshe Sofer, in a *responsum* addressed to the Jewish community in Vienna, lamented that recent liberal legislation in that city had weakened the strictness of religious observance. By way of contrast, he boasted that in his native Pressburg (now Bratislava), "when I am told that a Jewish shopkeeper dared to open his shop during the Lesser Holidays, I immediately send a policeman to imprison him."[23]

That was written less than two hundred years ago; if you think the ambition of Orthodox rabbis to impose their rule on Jewish communities died with the advent of modernity, think again. Halfway through the 20th century, Israel's Chief Rabbi, Isaac Herzog, declared that his rabbinate's "aim" was "to bring about a state law which will make the law of the Torah [that is, rabbinic law] binding."[24] Bear in mind that Israel's Orthodox rabbis, who still fight for this goal, do so even though Israel is officially a secular state, and even though most Israeli Jews are not Orthodox; they do it simply because Israeli politics enables them to pursue the kind of power they've enjoyed during most of Jewish history since the Middle Ages. And not only in Israel. With the passage of time, analogous opportunities have opened for the rabbinate in heavily Orthodox enclaves within the United States as well. *Voila*—Shomrim!

Seen in this light, there is something eerily prophetic about the story of how, in December 1947, a representative of the ultra–Orthodox Agudath Israel welcomed Ben-Gurion's plan for violent attacks on the Palestinian inhabitants of what was to be the Jewish State: "We were told that the army had the ability of destroying a whole [Arab] village and taking out all its inhabitants; indeed, let's do it!"[25] Remember that Agudath Israel was not pro–Zionist—in fact, for many years it had sought a *rapprochement* with Palestine's non–Jewish population.[26] Yet no moral considerations seem to have constrained this pious Orthodox party when its leaders believed a sufficiently strong Jewish force could create, though violence, the sort of community its rabbis preferred. Today, Agudath Israel of America supports Shomrim for similar reasons. In the wake of recent, high-profile reports detailing "intimidation of ultra–Orthodox Jews in Brooklyn by their own communities to keep them from bypassing rabbinic authorities and reporting abuse," Agudath Israel's executive vice president, Rabbi Chaim David Zwiebel, insisted that his organization would continue to place "the weight of rabbinic authority" above the law; he brushed off suggestions that this might damage relations with "a government leader."[27] Zwiebel's position is easy to understand once we ask the obvious: How is a "government leader" to know that a rabbi has forbidden an abuse case from going to the police, if Shomrim can successfully threaten the witnesses into silence?

* * *

It should go without saying that much of what Shomrim patrols actually do amounts to reasonable, even beneficial community service. But to understand Shomrim's special impact on sex abuse cases, we need to be clear about two things. First, we must understand the policy that Shomrim (on rabbinic instructions) apply to the reporting of a sex crime committed by an Orthodox Jew. Second, we need to know what Shomrim patrols are prepared to do, or at least to threaten, in order to enforce the rabbis' will against abuse victims who seek to defy it.

The first question is easily answered. In July 2011, I published a column in one of New York's popular tabloids that repeated much of what was already known about the seamy side of Brooklyn's Shomrim patrols:

> New York police have criticized Shomrim groups for failing to notify them of some of the calls their operators received; in fact, it has been widely reported that the Jewish patrols regularly withhold information on suspected child molesters if they are Jewish.

I reminded readers that at the very moment Shomrim were conducting a much-touted search for a missing Hasidic boy named Leiby Kletzky, Shmuel Kamenetsky, one of America's most respected Orthodox rabbis, had "emphasized at a conference that child sexual abuse allegedly committed by a Jew must be reported first to a rabbi, who then decides whether police should be contacted." In many cases, I pointed out, following Kamenetsky's directives would violate New York law, but no leaders or spokesmen from Shomrim patrols had repudiated his position. (They still haven't.)[28]

Once my column appeared, I waited in vain for Orthodox rabbis or Shomrim leaders to deny, or at least to qualify, these damning accusations. Not one did. Oh, there was criticism, of course. Some Orthodox Jews called me a traitor; even a comparison with Hitler surfaced in one of the angrier emails. But not a single critic disputed the truth of what I had written about Shomrim's rabbinically-driven policy of protecting child molesters. In fact, revealingly enough, the whole question was sidelined as the Orthodox writers castigated me precisely for *telling the truth*. I was told I was not really Jewish, or at least not Orthodox, since I had revealed an unflattering secret about Jewish leadership; I was said to be "blaming" the "community" because of a "sick and evil child abuse agenda." Whatever my critics thought of the column, one thing that clearly *didn't* trouble them was that powerful institutions in their communities were abetting crimes against children.

It's always risky to generalize public opinion from a bunch of irate emails, but my critics' blame-the-messenger position was not really eccentric. In fact, it had a respectable Jewish pedigree. Current scholarship shows that in their public writings running back as far as the 17th century—by public, I mean accounts certain to reach non–Jewish audiences—Jews have deliberately minimized the violence carried out by members of their communities.[29] The consequences have been unsurprising. After centuries of practice, public dissimulation has gradually become so familiar to traditional Jews that nowadays they hardly notice their dishonesty until it's highlighted by another Jew's candor, a shock that prompts them to blame the truth-teller for exposing them instead of the pious lie in which they have become entangled. Thus *Washington Jewish Week* editor Phil Jacobs trivialized a Shomrim member's bigoted assault on young Corey Ausby as "an embarrassing incident," a mere "mistake." To Jacobs, who is an Orthodox Jew, the real villains in that story were those who saw in the incident "some sort of racial imbroglio"—as if attacking a black kid after shouting "You don't belong in this neighborhood" had no racial implications from the start. Jacobs even argued that Shomrim deserve special dispensations because their members "have given up many a Shabbos to get in the car and track down a missing person"[30]—never mentioning that the altruistic Shomrim are unlikely to perform such services for anyone but Jews.[31] (And yet Jewish publicists have lauded Jacobs as a "hero" for "protecting children and humanity" by exposing sexual abuse within Orthodox Jewish communities.)[32]

In any case, there is really no dispute about Shomrim's deliberate role in suppressing sex abuse reports—there's only a bit of controversy about how much one should write about it. And Shomrim are only part of the picture. "Modesty patrols," though less visible to the non–Jewish public, are devoted specifically to sexual issues within some of the largest ultra–Orthodox communities, and these have played a notorious part in the intimidation of child victims. For instance, during the rape trial of Rabbi Nechemya Weberman, a Satmar Hasid who repeatedly molested a girl sent to him for "therapy," a woman testified that "masked men from the religious modesty committee, based in Monroe, New York, had come into her bedroom at night when she was 15 or 16 years old to take away a cellphone that she was not permitted to have." Significantly, "the same committee ... regularly referred young boys and girls" to Rabbi Weberman for "counseling."[33] As one outspoken critic put it, rabbinic leadership

> was in effect, extorting money for Weberman. I strongly suspect they kept some of it. Given widespread rumors about his sexual misconduct, Satmar [Weberman's Hasidic community] was in effect pimping the girls to Weberman, adding insult to injury by making the victim pay to be victimized.

Strong words, but evidence presented at Weberman's trial showed that members of the community who ended up on the wrong side of the "modesty committee" were required to pay large sums to Weberman and other hand-picked Hasidic "therapists" (Weberman had no professional credentials) or face public condemnation and ruin.[34] Why would the patrols coerce vulnerable people into the care of an unlicensed and overpriced therapist, one with a lecherous reputation to boot—unless there was money to be made in looking the other way?

Their indirect participation in actual sex abuse remains a controversial claim, but there is no doubt that the modesty patrols, at least as much as Shomrim, function like a secret police, the purpose of which is to

> conduct surveillance on those who are thought to be transgressing. Examples include local businesses that may be featuring immodest window displays or creating an atmosphere conducive to mixed-sex socializing. Young people who are spending time with members of the opposite sex or leaving the community to attend movies or go to bars or clubs are also targets, as are those who are having affairs.
>
> Armed with their "evidence," Vaad members then approach their subjects and, according to [Joel] Engelman, attempt to persuade them to pay for therapy—with "therapists" they select—or risk public exposure....
>
> Engelman recalls one situation where he was present in which a community member ... was told he had to put his "at risk" daughter in therapy ... or face her expulsion from school.
>
> ..."He was crying. 'How am I going to get $225?' And they said basically, 'This is the situation, sorry, can't help you, this is what you need to do.'"

Engelman had reason to know. He was a driver and personal assistant for one of the unlicensed "therapists" used by the Satmar Vaad (or "modesty committee"), and his own case of alleged abuse at the hands of Rabbi Avrohom

Reichman was covered up by the Vaad when Engelman and his parents made an issue of it.[35]

So much for Orthodox patrol policy. As for the second question—what are the vigilantes prepared to do in order to enforce rabbinic strictures against reporting a Jewish offender to the police?—here, too, there isn't much doubt about the relevant facts. While hardly typical, Mafioso-style tactics are not unheard of against community members who seriously test rabbinic authority. For example, when a younger relative of the Lubavitcher Rebbe, one of the most prominent Hasidic leaders of the latter 20th century, publicly criticized the direction being taken by the movement, he found himself facing a web of threats and physical violence: a car tried to run his daughter off the road; his mother was seriously assaulted by unknown thugs.[36]

"Modesty patrols," too, have their menacing side, as Vered Daniel, among many others, can testify. A young Israeli mother, Daniel had stopped in the religious town of Beit Shemesh to buy a stroller, and was standing next to the open trunk of her car when she and her seven-month-old daughter found themselves under a fusillade of stones, hurled by men who disliked her modern clothing. (Relatively modern, that is: she was wearing a long, loose-fitting black dress.) "I was terrified," she told reporters afterward. "I had my baby with me.... I was helpless." Two Orthodox women helped Daniel take cover inside the store, but ten minutes later, when Daniel tried to drive away, the patrol attacked again, this time smashing her windshield. "These were massive rocks," Daniel recalled. "I held my hands up, I indicated that I was leaving, but they wouldn't stop."[37]

And when such things happen, don't expect any public rebuke from ultra–Orthodox leadership. After press reports in Israel and the United States exposed a rash of ultra–Orthodox violence, including daily harassment of eight-year-old "modern Orthodox" schoolgirls,[38] Rabbi Daniel Eidensohn posted an on-line description of a meeting with Rabbi Moshe Sternbuch—one of the most respected leaders of ultra–Orthodox Jews in Israel—at which Rabbi Sternbuch insisted that the actions of the attackers were not his community's responsibility. As Eidensohn recalled Rabbi Sternbuch's remarks:

> He dismissed the issue as being the result of the newspapers looking for a story. He noted that the actual number of victims has been very small—including 1 case of a girl being spat upon—and that the perpetrators were a small number of fringe elements that do not have the approval or encouragement of the chareidi community. He did not see a need for a public comment for something which is obviously wrong and for which there is no justification for blaming the community.[39]

No need for comment? The same Rabbi Sternbuch thought differently when he learned that some Orthodox Jews were prepared to accept the "heresy" that the universe is older than 6,000 years. That drew from him a furious five-page, single-spaced disquisition in which he denounced, among other things, "the ridiculous and nonsensical idea that man developed from the apes" and insisted that "scientists"—who, he wrote, "live like animals to satisfy their lusts"—were responsible for the outbreak of AIDS. Rabbi Sternbuch even ordered his followers to rid their homes of all scientific books.[40] Next to a public polemic like that, it's not easy to see why ultra–Orthodox Jews who assault young girls don't even merit a tepid comment from the rabbi—except, of course, that attacking defenseless people doesn't threaten ultra–Orthodox rabbinic authority, while challenging Talmudic errors does.

It seems worthwhile to add here that Rabbi Eidensohn, an ardent admirer of Sternbuch who has published a volume on Jewish law pertaining to child abuse,[41] has quoted the elder sage as saying that child sex abuse should not be reported to police until a rabbi is consulted; nor should it be reported at all if the abuse only "took place once and will not be repeated." (How any rabbi is to determine whether an abuser will or won't repeat the offense remains a mystery.) Eidensohn justifies the implication that a single act of sex abuse is not really criminal by noting that "police and mental health workers are not always sensitive to religious values" and are "condescending" to Orthodox men accused of sex crimes.[42] Once again, for Orthodox leadership and the patrols they direct, it's solely the perpetrator's perspective that defines the relevant "religious values": that a child was criminally violated doesn't matter if a rabbi decides the abuse "will not be repeated"; after all, we mustn't let the "condescending" police or irreligious social workers think less of an Orthodox Jew who, like Captain Aardvark in *Catch–22*, "only raped her once."[43]

* * *

I have already suggested that the real purpose of Shomrim patrols, and their effect on victims of child abuse, can only be properly understood against the background of the history of rabbinic control over traditional Jewish communities. Officers "equipped with club and whip," obedient to rabbinic judges, are to "circulate in the marketplaces and streets, and around the shops ... to strike all [Jews] who misbehave," wrote Maimonides in his great 12th-century compendium.[44] Maimonides' frank association of rabbinic law with coercive power is typical of Jewish tradition. I want to devote a bit more space to this point, because many people are still misled by a popular view according to which Jews (at least Orthodox Jews) are trained to be studious, gentle scholars who know nothing of physical force, let alone violence. Until we exchange that stereotype for the considerably more complicated truth, we will not be able to see the Shomrim as their victims do.

The first thing to understand is that Jews in traditional diaspora communities have seldom been averse to physical violence to protect what they perceive as their communal authority. One case well known to historians will serve to illustrate the point. In 1621, a Christian miller whose partner's horse had knocked over a Jew in the Roman ghetto reported that "a number of Jews ... hurled themselves upon my companion and they were punching him and kicking him and had even taken his whip and were beating him with it," while, according to another witness, the Jew who had been knocked down "began to abuse us, calling us insolent cuckolds and using many injurious words."[45] The Roman ghetto was far from unique in this respect. In early 17th-century Ukraine, Paul Johnson reports, Jews "put their trust in cannon ... synagogues were built with embrasures and had guns mounted on the roof."[46] For that matter, organized Jewish violence—for instance, against Christian missionaries—was not unusual in Jewish neighborhoods in Brooklyn as recently as the late 19th century.[47]

It is worth stressing that this is not simply a matter of hot-headed people ignoring their religious teaching. Contrary to its conventional image, classical Judaism has seldom raised a moral objection to violence as long as its use is sanctioned by rabbinic authority—which in many cases it is. Only when a Jewish community is sufficiently weak to fear retaliation does Jewish law proscribe protecting a Jew who has murdered a gentile, for example, or "removing a ladder after [a non–Jew] had fallen into a crevice," leaving the unfortunate victim to die.[48] This is probably why in modern times—when their communities are stronger than ever before—Orthodox Jews are showing fewer qualms about the use of violence to further what they perceive as Jewish interests.

Proof of this comes quite easily to hand. Human rights organizations have amassed overwhelming evidence of abuses by the Israel Defense Forces; during the second *intifada* alone—beginning in September 2000—these included "punitive rocket attacks where there was no imminent danger to life," use of "helicopter gunships to carry out extrajudicial executions and to fire at targets that resulted in the killing of civilians, including children," "repeated ... use of excessive lethal force ... in situations where demonstrators were unarmed," "deliberate target[ing]" of civilian victims and Palestinian ambulances, indiscriminate torture of Palestinian detainees, the systematic destruction of civilian homes, and so on.[49] Yet, as documented by Professor Stuart A. Cohen of Bar-Ilan University, the only "concern with the moral dimensions of some combat missions" expressed during that period by Orthodox Jewish soldiers was whether their orders were brutal *enough*: "Why should they abide by the standard rules of military engagement if their enemies do not observe the accepted distinctions between formal combatants and civilian bystanders?" Note that Hitler made a similar comment on the eve of Germany's invasion of Russia, where "the Judeo-Bolsheviks represented a fanatical ideology": "It must not be expected that the enemy will act in accordance with the principles of humanity or international law," so "any attitude of consideration or regard for international law in respect of these persons is an error."[50]

Orthodox rabbis have had nothing to say against the crude cynicism of punishing the victims of the Israeli occupation for the desperate acts of some Palestinian fighters (to say nothing of the idea's Nazi precedent)—and not because the rabbis never soil their hands with military matters. On the contrary, Professor Cohen notes that "a formidable array of [Orthodox] rabbinic figures in the national-religious community" has "explicitly counseled their student-soldiers *against* conscientious objection" to military service. What's more, the only issue apparently troubling the rabbis in the first place was the possibility of having to dismantle an illegal Jewish settlement in occupied territory.[51] Systematic torture, targeting civilians, killing children, destruction of homes—these issues don't seem to have posed a moral problem for the rabbinate. Even its "modern" wing, represented by Yeshiva University President Rabbi Norman Lamm, has recently stressed that "the idea of refraining from harming civilian non-combatants" has "no explicit origin in Torah" and that "there has been some recent revisionist thinking on this subject" so as to favor "Israeli [Jewish] troops" over "enemy Arab civilians."[52] The main point to notice in all this discussion is that the question is *never* whether the use of violence is immoral, even when used against defenseless victims.

Of particular importance, for our purposes, is the fact that many Orthodox rabbis directly endorse the use of violence against Jewish "informers"— as abuse victims who go to the police are still called by the most influential Orthodox authorities. One recent example is especially interesting because it comes from a book written under rabbinic auspices, and with the stated purpose of lionizing the Hasidic rabbis it describes. This book relates, with no editorial comment at all, how a Jew who was merely suspected of passing information to the Soviet NKVD was threatened with death in order to protect other Hasidim from military service during World War II. For Orthodox Jewish children who have been abused (and for those who support them), bits of lore like this one achieve urgent focus when read in conjunction with the following declaration, signed by fifty prominent rabbis and circulated shortly after the child abuse charges against Solomon Hafner were dropped under rabbinic pressure (as described in Chapter 3):

> A Jewish man or woman who informs [to non–Jewish authorities], saying, "I shall go and inform upon another Jew," with respect to either his property or person, and [such person] was warned not to inform and he demurs and insists, "I shall inform!"—regarding him, it is a *mitzvah* [divine commandment] to kill him and whoever has the first opportunity to kill him is entitled to do so...."[53]

As this statement shows, death threats by Orthodox rabbis are not relics of the past: they are alive and well and are pointedly directed at victims of sex abuse who talk to the police. And while I don't know of a case in which such threats have actually been carried out, I do not think these bloody formulations can be dismissed as empty gestures. Today's Orthodox rabbis—the same ones who provide guidance to Shomrim—have shown no compunction about endorsing even deadly violence, so long as no political price is exacted for their association with killers. Just after more than 1,400 Gazans, overwhelmingly civilians, perished under Israeli assault between December 2008 and January 2009, an on-line weekly published by one of the largest Orthodox Jewish organizations in the United States boasted that, with the rabbis' help, Israel's attack was "bring[ing] soldiers closer to their Judaism." The journal described Orthodox clergymen handing out phylacteries and similar ritual objects to soldiers about to join the carnage, while Rabbi Rafael Even-Danan extolled the violent effects of religiously-based patriotism: "The minute you're attached to a country you are automatically a better fighter." Rounding out the moral atmosphere, Rabbi Avi Berman, Israel Director General for the Orthodox Union, suggested that the role of Jewish clergy was to help ensure that Israeli soldiers obeyed their officers' orders, no matter how repellent:

> When you're a pilot or a tank commander and you have to push that button, it's not easy to do; you don't get over it. But what gives you strength and gets you through it is belief in the Almighty and the land that He gave us.... We're trying to help these soldiers develop that relationship with the Almighty and build a sense of comfort around that.[54]

The article containing these edifying reflections never mentioned that some 300 of the civilians slain in Gaza were children.[55] But then, if Orthodox rabbis expect to be obeyed when they command witnesses of child abuse to shut up and stay out of the way of the rabbi or paterfamilias doing the violating—and if they expect to be taken seriously when they threaten to have dissenters murdered—why shouldn't they build "a sense of comfort" around killing children, too?

* * *

An especially disturbing fact about Jewish aggression, past and present—and one relevant to the Orthodox patrols' record of concealing child sex abuse cases—is the extent to which Jewish scholars and publicists have been at pains to gloss over the truth. In fact, the more relevant the subject of Jewish violence becomes, the less Jewish intellectuals seem prepared to discuss it. "Even-handed assessments of the reciprocal role of violence in Jewish-Christian relations were to become increasingly rare in post–Holocaust Jewish historiography, both in the land of Israel and in the Diaspora," notes contemporary scholar Elliott Horowitz. As an example, Horowitz describes how the well-documented Jewish massacre of Christians that accompanied the Persian conquest of

Jerusalem in 614, along with many similar atrocities, was gradually effaced from Jewish history books from the late 1940s onwards—that is, beginning at precisely the time Jews took over power in Palestine (now Israel) and were, as a result, able to employ violence much more freely than at any time in recent Jewish history.[56]

Since this book focuses on cover-ups—and "cover-up" is the only appropriate name for the deliberate evasion of a highly topical reality—I must add, sadly, that few in Orthodoxy have broken this code of silence; in fact, the liberal figures in its ranks have dissembled about Jewish violence as readily as the religious right wing. I have found nothing on the subject from the pen of Rabbi Joseph B. Soloveitchik, a prolific essayist and a leading "modern Orthodox" authority until his death in 1993. Shmuel Hugo Bergman, one of the founders of the left-leaning Brit Shalom movement and a traditionally observant Jew, did lament in 1967 over the increasingly violent attitudes toward Arabs—who, he noted with dismay, were likened to Nazis—taught in respectable Israeli religious schools.[57] But in the early years of World War I Bergman himself reportedly advocated the expulsion of Palestine's entire Arab population to Iraq, a fact that prompted Israel Shahak to pillory him among those "'dovish' ... gentle persons who ... seemed incapable of hurting a fly," and whose "deceptions" were all the more dangerous for that very reason.[58] Could Shomrim patrols ever have stooped to obstruction of justice if even a few influential Orthodox rabbis, particularly those in the "liberal" camp, had put their humanitarian principles into practice?

The cover-up policy extends beyond the rabbis. Rank-and-file Orthodox Jews contribute to the poisoning of the atmosphere by promoting what the *Economist* has aptly called "a curious amalgam of victimhood and intolerance" that is "the prevailing political sentiment in Jewry today."[59] After Shomrim member Eliyahu Werdesheim's conviction for assaulting 15-year-old Corey Ausby, posters to on-line Orthodox news blogs angrily charged that the Jewish community was being sacrificed to protect the "white judge" from violent attacks by Baltimore's black population.[60] Meanwhile an obliging press, instead of exposing such racism in the terms it deserves, has been working overtime to soften the edges for easier public consumption. Thus, journalist Matthew Shaer describes an alleged assault on a black youth by a (different) Shomrim member in language that shifts the blame to the victim:

> He [the alleged victim] knew how to talk to the media, how to rile up a crowd. "Every day I attempt to function normally [but] it's impossible because there is so much confusion as a result of this incident," he told a gaggle of demonstrators in May.... Even his mother, Wendy Craigg, got into the act. "I can't even function," Ms. Craigg said. "My child's life was almost taken from him. Where are the police now?"

This young man reported that one Jew sprayed mace into his eyes, after which another Jew clubbed him with a truncheon—and the Shomrim's only defense was that, allegedly, a black kid nearby had lobbed stones at some Jews. Yet the victim's every word gets a snide twist in Shaer's retelling. His natural distress over the attack is a ploy "to rile up a crowd"; his mother's appeal for justice is an "act." Shaer even refers derisively to the victim having given the "requisite interviews to the tabloids, taking pains to note that his attackers were Jewish"—as if reporting a crime to the newspapers were somehow proof of anti-Semitism.[61] And all this is in striking contrast to Shaer's soft-pedaling of the bigotry lying just behind the surface of the Shomrim record. True, he admits that "the primary mission of the Jewish anticrime organizations has always been to serve the Jewish community. Everything else was ancillary." But he fails to draw the obvious inference that the patrols discriminate along racial lines. He even ignores the documentary evidence of the fundamental religious text that, as he himself acknowledges, governs every aspect of the spiritual life of the Crown Heights Shomrim members.[62] Although English translations of this book—popularly known as *Tanya*—are widely available, Shaer never once tells his readers about the contents of this deeply racist work, according to which all non–Jews are inferior beings "in whom there is absolutely nothing good," whereas "all of creation was created solely for the sake of the Jews."[63] Would journalists show similar reticence about linking the violent acts of the Ku Klux Klan, say, to *their* racist ideology?

Jewish media have sometimes gone even farther. During the trial that led to Eliyahu Werdesheim's conviction, a former reporter for the *Baltimore Jewish Times* admitted on the witness stand that he had allowed Werdesheim to edit an article his paper published two weeks after the Shomrim member's attack on Corey Ausby, featuring an exclusive interview with Werdesheim and his brother—who was also charged—so as to leave out "several facts about the incident."[64] As far as I know, this evidence of Jewish media complicity in a criminal cover-up has scarcely been mentioned in the Jewish press—not even in articles that appeared shortly after the reporter's testimony.[65] (To his credit, the reporter did alert prosecutors to the omissions in his original article, but only months later, after both Werdesheims had already been charged.)[66]

Passive complicity in such matters is bad enough. But to protect its Shomrim, Orthodox leadership seems prepared to go farther still. Three and a half years after he allegedly clubbed an innocent man, a group of "top rabbis, community heads, and [Orthodox] Assemblyman Dov Hikind" inscribed their support for Shmira member Yitzhak Shuchat on a web site that accused the Brooklyn D.A. of anti–Semitism. With amazing effrontery, Orthodox apologists showcased the alleged attacker as a victim of ethnic discrimination, ignoring the evidence that Shuchat and his fellow Orthodox pseudo-cops had singled out a black man for assault.

"Yitzhak Shuchat is being targeted by the D.A. because he is a Jew," claimed the "Free Yitzi" web site endorsed by all those Orthodox heavy hitters.[67] "[T]he incident lacks any indication of even the slightest racial motivation," insisted self-described "civil rights activist" Eliyahu Federman, who also claimed the whole affair was no big deal to begin with: "Charles [the victim] did not break any bones or suffer permanent injury."[68] Even after Shuchat's extradition was finally ordered by Israel's Supreme Court in December 2012, Assemblyman Hikind frantically pressed Israeli officials to refuse to return Shuchat to strand trial[69]; other apologists turned up the shrillness as well as the racism in their appeals, with Shuchat's Israeli lawyer claiming, for instance, that "details of his event [sic] will be made known to black prisoners and prison guards and there is no doubt that they will try to hurt him."[70]

*   *   *

Writing about Shomrim has prompted me to explore, at the same time, the twin blemishes on the patrols' record: their discrimination against non–Jews, and their interference with child sex abuse investigations within their own communities. I have discussed both here (though the latter merges more obviously with the focus of this book) because it seems to me that Shomrim's two characteristic sins—racism and the protection of Orthodox child abusers—are in certain ways fundamentally related. Both are expressions of fear: the fear typically cherished by the powerful when they think their power may be threatened by those they have victimized.

For this reason, I wasn't surprised when Rabbi Herschel Schachter, one of "modern" Orthodoxy's leading scholars, recently fused both prejudices into one combustible whole. In a revealing public statement, Schachter warned that child abuse accusations must be carefully "screened" by "experts in Jewish law," and never accepted at face value, because a child's report might cause a rabbi or Orthodox teacher to be sent to prison where "they can put you in a cell together with a *shvartze* [African American], with a ... black Muslim who wants to kill all the Jews."[71] Some Orthodox Jews I know have tried to dismiss these comments as aberrational. They aren't. They honestly reflect the prejudices of rabbis whose fear of sacrificing Jewish superiority over non–Jews[72] is matched by their fear of losing control over abused children. After all, those children's complaints, if believed, would wreak havoc on the hierarchies of traditional Jewish society—leveling children with adults, students with teachers, lay people with rabbis. The prospect of a child taking down an abusive clergyman is terrifying to defenders of the status quo; that's why it summons the specter of phantom enemies—those "black Muslims" who yearn "to kill all the Jews"—into the imagination of a rabbi for whom every allegedly abused child is a threat to be fended off.

And that brings us, finally, to the intellectual or psychological aspect of the Shomrim problem. At bottom, the power Orthodox rabbis have given their private patrols is less about physical coercion (though that obviously plays its part) than about thought control directed at the Orthodox community. Shomrim serve, most of all, to symbolize and to embody a dominant idea of Judaism that is tribal rather than moral, coercive rather than compassionate, centered less on the fulfillment of spiritual ideals than on protecting and strengthening the Jewish community's power structure.

I call this "thought control" because, to persuade Jews to accept this sort of social organization, its proponents must make them overlook the moral dangers of imposing an unjust order—a product of current Jewish power—in the name of bygone vulnerabilities. Orthodox leadership realizes that its fear and suspicion of sex abuse victims cannot be named openly; such things must be hidden behind a set of values that can rationalize the suppression of truth and the denial of justice as necessary measures to protect a beleaguered Jewish minority. But this, in turn, requires the Orthodox community to twist its own putative moral values inside out: to fend off the imagined threat, the community must adopt the very methods that have figured most prominently in Jewish characterizations of the Jews' historic oppressors—violence, bigotry, power politics—even as the leadership invokes the memory of that oppression to justify the new regime. In other words, the power manifested by Shomrim gives implicit rabbinic sanction to a moral role reversal by which Jews draw on a history of victimization in order to become better victimizers themselves. Reform Rabbi Drorah Setel puts the point neatly:

> Jews have a history arising out of our own oppression and we have the capacity to respond to that history by being outraged and angry and sensitive to injustice done to ourselves and others. But the flip side of our history of oppression, a side we don't like to talk about is that the experience of suffering also teaches us how to inflict suffering. The experience of injustice teaches us how to be unjust.[73]

Reflecting on atrocities committed by Zionist forces in 1948, the respected Zionist official Yosef Nahmani wrote in his diary: "Where did they come by such a measure of cruelty, like Nazis? *They had learnt from them* [*i.e.,* the Nazis]. One officer told me that those who had 'excelled' had come from [the concentration] camps."[74] It's understandable that victims may, given the opportunity, unleash on others some of the torments they themselves have suffered—history is replete with examples of this. What is more troubling is the adoption by elements of Jewish leadership of a mindset that in the past characterized the oppressors of Jews, with the effect of sanitizing oppressive acts aimed at a new group of victims. Here is the Reverend A.E. Patton, for instance, denouncing "the Jewish hordes" reaching America in the early 20th century, people he saw as

> stealthy and furtive in manner, too lazy to enter into real labor, too cowardly to face frontier life, too lazy to work as every American farmer has to work, too filthy to adopt ideals of cleanliness from the start, too bigoted to surrender any racial traditions or to absorb any true Americanism....[75]

All of the minister's pejoratives imply the incompatibility of Jews with what are assumed to be the Western norms of civilization and progress. Now turn to this description of Arabs—Palestinians in particular—offered by a distinguished Israeli Jew and printed in one of his country's leading newspapers in 1955:

> The danger [to "us"] stems ... from the lack of logic, the easily inflamed brains, the boasting, and above all: the blasphemous disregard for all that is sacred to the civilized world.... They are all emotional, unbalanced, instantaneous, senseless.... By discussing with them on the basis of Western concepts, we dress savages in a European robe of justice.[76]

Thirty years earlier, the author of these racist taunts might well have been the butt of the same insults in the Reverend Patton's society. Now, as a representative of Jewish power, he turns the old equation on its head, claiming the sanction of "the civilized world" for the repression of an Arab underclass and deploying the stereotypes formerly used against Jews: bigotry, irrationality, "disregard" for the "sacred" Western values. When rabbis use Shomrim patrols to enforce their hierarchies—Jews over non–Jews, rabbis over laymen, adults over children—they are, consciously or not, acting out a similar reversal, aping an oppressive arrangement of values whose evil they know all too well but cannot admit without relaxing their grip on power.

Of course, it is much harder to face the pain of abused children than to dismiss them as simply one segment of an array of threats to rabbinic authority, as Schachter (like too many other rabbis) evidently perceives them. But the challenge cannot be shirked. If Orthodox Judaism is to be a religion and not a political party, complete with bosses and enforcers, it will have to rethink the message its reliance on Shomrim sends loud and clear to abuse victims: Your right to justice depends on whether it's good for the rabbinate. That's a principle that obviously defies any real notion of justice, and to that extent the principle is abusive in itself. (Hence my juxtaposition of epigraphs at the beginning of this chapter, the first concerning the Israeli equation of Palestinian resistance with anti–Semitism—conveniently, "from outside" the comfort of the Jewish state—the second describing the Orthodox community's insistence that "words for gentiles" about child abuse have no place in "our" world.)

The question I posed for this section of the book was "Who guards the guardians?" And I think by now my answer should be self-evident. In a very real sense, though, the question misses the point. As I have tried to show, the very concept of safety the rabbinic leadership has constructed for Orthodox communities is fundamentally false; in fact, the "protection" the rabbis offer—whether by means of rabbinic courts or Shomrim patrols—exposes many of the most vulnerable among us to more danger, not less. And that is the real point of departure for a better future. We will begin to answer the question "Who guards the guardians?" only when we understand that our communities' "guardians" were never really protecting us in the first place.

PART III

The Culture of Denial

[Rabbis] Sheftel Neuberger and Berel Weisbord came to New York to "thank us" for giving them information about our abuse, but made it clear that they were not going to apologize, nor did they feel any need to help us with our requests. The number one request was to publicize the danger that this hypocritical "talmid chochom" [Torah scholar] represents to young men and boys everywhere....

Rabbi Hopfer told me he was concerned that if it became public knowledge, that all of the people [Rabbi] Eisemann had "made frum" [religious] would be disillusioned.... Rabbi Ahron Feldman ... told my friend that for victims to publicize his abuse, it would be just as abusive as what he had done....

This attitude fits in very well with the [Agudath Israel's] approach of covering up and protecting molesters at all costs.
—Dr. Asher Lipner, blog posting, June 12, 2012

9

A History of Silence

Why are the victims in the position of not being able to speak about what happened to them in those days; why is it still dreadfully difficult for them, even twenty or thirty years later, to tell what they experienced as children? And why is it so important that these things be discussed? I am of the opinion that these two questions are closely related. For something one cannot talk about also cannot be buried, finds no resting place. If one doesn't refer to it, the wounds continue to fester from generation to generation.

—Bruno Bettelheim[1]

One of the most unsettling truths articulated by Judy Brown, author of *Hush* and challenger of the Orthodox status quo on sexual abuse, is that silence about abuse does more than ignore or evade; carefully enforced, it exerts a contaminating power over reality itself.

"In the ultra–Orthodox world ... words are important: what you can use and what you cannot," Brown told a conference of Orthodox mental health professionals in 2011. In her own childhood, Brown said, she learned that "sexual abuse was not a word. If there was no such word, then there were no such children. And truly, by a miracle, somehow for decades there were none. Nobody was allowed to see them. They did not really dare exist."[2]

Which, I think, sums up the matter perfectly. During the long years when Orthodox rabbis steadfastly refused to discuss sexual abuse, abused children in a very real sense did not "exist"—not because no children were being abused, but because as victims of abuse they could not *dare* to exist, not without a discourse against which their experience could be measured or understood. I take Bruno Bettelheim to have been aiming at the same thing when he wrote (in words I quoted above) that "something one cannot talk about" is something that "finds no resting place." Human categories are not only expressed by language; they exist in language, which means that the withdrawal of language from certain kinds of experience is a form of psychological violence, particularly against those people for whom such experiences are inseparable from self-knowledge.

So when we trace the history of the Orthodox Jewish community's collective silence about child sex abuse, we're engaged in much more than an academic exercise. It is important to analyze what is not said about child abuse, and why it is not said, as carefully as we analyze the abuse itself—and ultimately for the same reason. Thus we note, as I mentioned in Chapter 3, how Judaism's traditional law codes proscribed the beating of young students only during three weeks out of the year. And we record, sadly, that the silence of these texts about the use of physical violence against children at other times has elicited no comment from within Orthodox Jewish circles, not even from the most modern authorities. Is this because beating schoolchildren is considered normal today? I doubt that—but then, why the continuing silence? Is the issue too trivial to be worth mentioning? Or have we just become accustomed to averting our eyes from cruelty to children, particularly when paying attention would force us to apply to it the right words, and therefore to assess its real moral significance?

Where taboos are, the use of the wrong words can easily crowd out the right (but forbidden) ones—thus coating deadly silence with a diversionary noise. Janet Heimlich, author of a recent book on religious child maltreatment, has noted in a blog posting that some of her findings were challenged on the strength of a phrase. "In Judaism," she was told, "children are viewed as 'gifts from God.'" So how could Judaism be reconciled with child abuse? For a reply, Heimlich turned to alleged abuse survivor Joel Engelman, who grew up in a Brooklyn Hasidic community. Yes, wrote Engelman, phraseology like "gifts of God" is "thrown around" by religious Jews when talking about children.

> But what does that mean? Does it mean that children are protected from child abuse? It is obvious to me that this is not the case, as the rabbis who beat me on a regular basis would use that against us, and say, "This is why I'm beating you every day, because you are so special and pure in the eyes of God, that you especially need your soul cleansed of impure thoughts and wrong actions."[3]

Here is a strange noise indeed. Yet the seemingly disparate elements—child beating, a horror of sexuality, sentimental rhetoric about children—are closely related. The notion of children as "gifts" to their parents—that is, in more prosaic language, as a species of property—not only doesn't protect children raised in the Jewish tradition but actually places Orthodoxy smack in the middle of an abusive system of thought, as explained by Alice Miller:

> The advice regularly given in the old pedagogical manuals was to "break" the child's will at as early an age as possible, to combat his "obstinacy," and always to impart to him the feeling that he is guilty and bad; they stressed that one should never allow the impression to arise that an adult might be wrong or make a mistake, should never give the child an opportunity to discover adult limitations, but that

the adult should, on the contrary, conceal his or her weaknesses from the child and pretend to divine authority.[4]

As Engelman's experience shows, this cruel doctrine has always been the real meaning behind the sentimental pretense of juvenile "purity." Children are "pure" because adults project onto them our own fear of sexuality; they are "gifts" because their "purity" gives us, their elders, a religiously sanctioned way of scapegoating our own contamination ("This is why I'm beating you every day"). And, of course, whatever we do to consummate the scapegoating can't be called "abuse"—especially not by its victims. Meanwhile, behind all these untruths and self-centered rationalizations, it's easy to miss what is *not* being asked. For if we really thought of our children as "gifts from God," wouldn't we want to shield them from harm, including sexual exploitation? Again, Engelman has the unhappy answer:

> Do parents protect their children because their kids are "gifts from God"? All indicators in the orthodox community seem to be saying NO. The rabbi who sexually abused me as a child is still teaching children every day, despite very public accusations from several victims, and this scenario is sadly, not uncommon at all.[5]

Examples could be multiplied almost endlessly. But I find one recent case particularly poignant, because it highlights the radical isolation of abuse victims identified by Judy Brown, and the roots of that isolation in the victims' erasure from the public discourse the rabbis are (so far) willing to permit. In December 2012, when a Hasidic rabbi and unlicensed psychotherapist was convicted of repeatedly raping a young girl, the community's punishment of the victim—for going to police after she turned eighteen—included the expulsion of her young nieces from local religious schools. At the same time, community members circulated a text message—asking each recipient to forward the message "to at least 10 people"—that justified ostracism of the victim by pointing to the rapist's "five kids [who] are home without a father."[6] Calling this hypocritical doesn't really do justice to the offense. It's bad enough to claim that a community's punishment of children for the crime of being related to an abuse victim proceeds from that community's tender regard for its little ones—and to prove the point with public support for the children of a convicted rapist. But these Hasidim did more than that. In effect, they simply wrote off the children who suffered because of abuse: *those* children no longer existed; one didn't even have to compare them to the children of the abuser, let alone justify their punishment for telling the truth—or for being the nieces of someone who did. Which is why, when the same Hasidim launched a massive fundraising project to pay for the convicted rabbi's legal appeal, they could fill two pages in the Yiddish newspaper *Der Yid* with the declaration that "[t]he entire community is sitting on that defendant's bench God forbid."[7]

"The *entire* community": a totality from which the rapist's victim and all who supported her had magically disappeared.

And it isn't only Hasidim who play that game. "Modern" Orthodox leadership restricts the permitted vocabulary in similar ways, and for similar reasons. In early 2013, a student at an Orthodox college-level women's *yeshiva* posted a few words on her Facebook page stating, without any details, that she was "a survivor of sexual abuse." She added:

> Are you going to change your opinion of me just because three evil people took advantage of me?
> Are you embarrassed of me? Are you willing to share our story?
> Let's see who my real friends are.

She found out soon enough. Just a few hours after her posting, she received a stern email from Esther Shkop, a dean at her school. Headed "Breaking all Boundaries," Shkop's message accused the student not only of violating school policy but of demeaning herself—and all fellow students—by telling the truth:

> [Y]ou have chosen to identify yourself by your pathology. You no longer appear as a full human—but rather as "case study" of a young woman warped by her childhood experiences, and is thus identified wholly by that past.... You seem too intent on wallowing in the past, and drawing sick attention to yourself for all of the wrong reasons.
> At the same [time], you identify yourself as a student of Hebrew Theological College, and by association besmirch your peers as well as yourself.
> This misuse of social media is definitely a violation of the HTC Personal Conduct Policy....[8]

Although Shkop later apologized for her "insensitive and harsh email," she apologized only for its tone, and for her failure to offer the victim sympathy or opportunities for psychological counseling. She did not retract anything that really mattered: not her accusation that telling the truth "besmirched" her school and all its students; not her trivialization of sexual abuse as a "pathology" carried by the victim alone; and certainly not her implication that only a "sick" person would want to tell the truth about sexual abuse among religious Jews. In fact, even in her "apology" Shkop continued to insist that publicly identifying oneself as a victim of sex abuse was "immodest" and therefore inappropriate for an Orthodox Jew.[9] Shkop seems not to have realized that in blaming the victim she was not only taking the abusers' side but carrying on the abusers' work. The vocabulary she employed implicitly rules out a legitimate place for the experience of abuse—to mention it is to "no longer appear as a full human"—thus leaving the victim's perspective literally no place among "full humans" save as a guilty secret known only to survivors, and not discussed even among them. In other words, Shkop's approach amounts to a particularly

cruel and re-victimizing species of denial, and (not coincidentally) a strategy
for prioritizing the community's public image over traumatizing realities. Israel
Weingarten would surely approve.[10]

Like the cruelties perpetrated by *batei din* on survivors of abuse, I do not
think such attitudes represent individual failings alone. Their roots run deep
in traditional Jewish literature. The Hebrew Bible contains the following searing passages in which God himself metes out sexual abuse as punishment for
misbehavior:

> I shall expose her nakedness before the eyes of her lovers; no man can save her
> from me.[11]
>
> I shall gather all your lovers to whom you have pledged yourself, those whom
> you loved together with those whom you hated, I shall gather them all against you
> round about, and I shall expose your private parts to them and they shall see your
> nakedness.... They shall strip you of your clothes and take your valuable things,
> and leave you nude and naked.[12]

Layers of Talmudic tradition have done nothing to cushion the graphic impact
of these lines, which attribute rape, or something approaching it, to the God
of justice, while foreclosing the victim's perspective from any serious attention.
The rabbis seem to have accepted the premise that so long as the victim belongs
to the abuser (as the wife does to the husband, as the Children of Israel do to
God), the victim's sexual violation is not a crime. And of course, where there's
no crime there's no reason for an apology, let alone a punishment.

These ideas didn't die with the Middle Ages. They echo in the work of
Samson Raphael Hirsch, a famous 19th-century modernizer of Orthodox
Judaism. Even the "progressive" Rabbi Hirsch could conceptualize rape as a
victimless act, as is evident from his comment on the traditional Jewish interpretation of Deuteronomy 21:11[13]—which according to most opinions sanctions the rape of a woman taken captive in battle—to the effect that criminal
penalties are suspended because "in the first heat of the conquest [the soldier]
has already yielded once to his passion."[14] Note the passivity attributed to the
rapist who "yields" to his passion, and the equally ominous blurring of the line
between appetite and object, so that the rape victim is reduced to mere
impulse-stimulant, not a human being with a right to justice in terms of her
own experience. In this respect, Hirsch echoed Maimonides (in his time,
another liberal), who prescribed the death penalty for any non–Jewish woman
with whom a Jewish man has had illicit sexual intercourse—*even if she was the
victim of rape*—his logic being that, by her very existence, the victim represents
an indirect moral threat, a reminder of sin.[15] In this view, victims of sexual
assault are not victims at all; they exist (if that is the right word) merely as
temptations, as "impure thoughts" better off forgotten—or dead. Religious
descriptions of sexual violence that preclude any reference to the victims invite

Nietzsche's acid remark that "a religious person thinks only of himself"[16]—and, of course, they add one more sturdy pillar to the edifice of denial.

* * *

What are the grounds traditionally invoked in support of Orthodox Judaism's see-no-evil, speak-no-evil policy on child sexual abuse? As one would expect, Orthodox rabbis generally rely on arguments rooted in Jewish law to rationalize the suppression of evidence in sex abuse cases, or to condemn Orthodox Jews who refuse to toe that line. But the most remarkable fact about this aspect of rabbinic policy is that the arguments are untenable—and I base this judgment on solid rabbinic authority. In the arguments that follow I rely largely on the published writing of Rabbi Mark Dratch, chairman of the (Orthodox) Rabbinic Council of America's Task Force on Rabbinic Improprieties, and founder of the Jewish Institute Supporting an Abuse-Free Environment (JSAFE). The careful analysis undertaken by Dratch and others convincingly debunks the cover-up rationales offered in reliance on Orthodox rabbinic leadership. But the leadership's arguments are advanced so often that public refutation remains an important task.

First, Orthodox rabbis often claim that to publicly accuse another Orthodox Jew of a crime—indeed, to say anything derogatory about him—constitutes the sin of *lashon ha-ra* or "evil speech," unless the charge has already been proved. Judaism quite rightly stigmatizes slander and gossip, but classing accusations of a criminal assault with forbidden tale-bearing automatically rules out virtually any report of an incident of child sex abuse; after all, the charge cannot be proved without a victim's report, and according to this logic a victim cannot make a report until the charge is proved. Fortunately, the argument founders not only on logical grounds but according to the traditional law applicable to *lashon ha-ra* itself. "When a person's intent in sharing truthful but negative information is for a constructive and beneficial purpose," writes Dratch, "the prohibition against *lashon ha-ra* does not apply."[17] In fact, as Dratch shows, the 19th-century author of the "epic work on the laws of derogatory speech" actually *required* a victim to speak out publicly for certain legitimate purposes. These include protecting others from harm, shaming the perpetrator into repentance, clearing one's own reputation, and furthering one's psychological health by airing the truth.[18] Every one of these legitimate motives applies to cases of sexual abuse.

It is true, as Dratch is quick to remind his readers, that an unfounded criminal charge or similar accusation "can be a tool of abuse" when used to defame the innocent. (For that matter, defenders of Orthodox sex abuse victims know this all too well; we are often subjected to slanderous attacks from some of our coreligionists.) But Dratch stresses that it is no less a form of abuse "when warnings to refrain from derogatory speech are used to silence victims of abuse who cry out for help." And he concludes:

> Victims of abuse need to speak out, for all kinds of personal reasons, in order to help themselves. Their supporters need to speak out in order to help them. And the community needs to speak out in order to hold the perpetrators responsible and in order to protect other innocents from potential harm.

It is hard to see how any well-intentioned person could quarrel with that. But, as we shall see in the following chapter, *lashon ha-ra* is more than a matter of traditional Jewish law; it is also a potent political weapon, used to keep criticism and dissent under the control of the rabbinic elite. The rabbinate is reluctant to let go of that sort of power.

Another claim, related to but not identical with the first, is that shaming the Jewish community with a child sex abuse accusation constitutes a forbidden *hillul Hashem*, or "desecration of [God's] name." This is because, in Dratch's words, "traditional Jewish law deems an act committed by a religious Jew that arouses public disgust (particularly on the part of non–Jewish observers) a 'desecration,' in effect, of God Himself, since in the eyes of the Talmud Jews are identified with God through the responsibility of observing His law." The fear that the penalty for this grave sin will be inflicted on the Jewish community "if child abuse charges are publicized is used as a tool to enforce the victim's silence."[19]

Such logic, to no one's surprise, runs parallel to a common threat used by child molesters themselves: "If you tell, bad things will happen, *and that will be your fault.*" Children may well be bullied into believing threats of this description. But it is surely no credit to the rabbinate to have borrowed such a cynical maneuver from the abusers, let alone to have granted it a religious cover. Is there anything but cruelty in the claim that the victim who tells, not the criminal, is responsible for the embarrassment of the community that results when the criminal is exposed? What is more, the argument, if it can be called that, is actually alien to Jewish law. Again I quote Rabbi Dratch:

> First, it is the unethical behavior in and of itself—not merely discussing it—that constitutes a desecration of God's name. The abuser, not the abused, has committed *hillul Hashem*. To silence victims who have a right to speak, to oppose those who seek justice and the protection of innocent victims, is also the kind of conduct that desecrates God's name.
> Second, when efforts to deny or suppress the truth about a crime are exposed, the scandal is much greater than the exposure of the crime alone....
> Third, there is ample precedent not only for allowing exposure of such matters, but also for actually requiring it....
> Finally, the essence of *hillul Hashem* is that it creates a godless vacuum in the world and in people's lives. This perfectly describes the effects of child sexual

abuse—particularly when the abuse is concealed and denied. When that happens, victims of abuse are doubly exploited, first by their attackers and then by the reaction of the family and community they thought would help them. In many cases, these victims lose faith in themselves, in their religious community, and in God.... This is exactly the sort of "desecration" the laws of *hillul Hashem* are meant to prevent.[20]

I am not aware of any scholarly rebuttal of the arguments summarized by Dratch—nor can I easily imagine one. Common as it is, the threat that abuse victims will be responsible for unleashing the anger of the gentiles—and of God—on the Jewish community if they dare to tell the truth has nothing to do with Jewish law. It is a cold-hearted ploy that not only makes rabbis accomplices to child abuse but implicates them in some of the abusers' most disgusting tactics.[21]

The most common rabbinic argument against reporting child sex abuse charges to police is based on the Talmudic notion of *m'sirah*,[22] a term usually translated as "informing," though strictly speaking the Talmudic context delimits the prohibition as the betrayal of one's fellow Jew to robbers or extortionists—not to law enforcement officers. True, there are references to non–Jewish government authorities—such as tax collectors—in the relevant Talmudic texts, but according to many influential commentators these reflect nothing more than the early Diaspora reality of predatory officials who often harassed vulnerable Jewish communities and were, in fact, hardly better than common thugs. A typical commentary from the late 19th century explains the laws against "informing" in just these terms:

> It is known to all readers of history that in ancient times, in distant countries, a person had no security, in person or property, thanks to raiders and robbers, *including those who took upon themselves the name of "official,"* as is well known even today in some countries of Africa—[where] the raider and thug act as functionaries of the government.... *And from these circumstances proceed all of the laws regarding the "traducer" and "informer" found in the Talmud and legal decisors....*[23]

This view has been specifically upheld by Rabbi Eliezer Waldenberg, a contemporary Orthodox authority of unquestioned prestige.[24] Under this approach, the Talmudic laws related to "informing" have no application at all in a generally just legal system; in today's United States, for instance, there would be no justification for protecting a suspected criminal from the police. Even Orthodox rabbis reluctant to endorse this approach, including the highly respected ultra–Orthodox Yosef Shalom Elyashiv, have nonetheless authorized reporting suspected child molesters to secular authorities on the grounds that the public threat they pose cannot be countered in any other way.[25] This view, too, has a long pedigree in Jewish tradition: Rabbi Dratch reports that as early as the Middle Ages, when "rabbinic courts lacked the authority to enforce their rulings," they "often granted permission to Jewish litigants to turn to the general courts for adjudication and for enforcement of their legal rights.... In such cases, there is no violation of traditional Jewish law."[26] Dratch also cites more recent rabbinic rationales that support abuse victims' reporting even without a rabbinic court's authorization.[27]

None of this, however, seems to outweigh the Orthodox leadership's deeply ingrained prejudice in favor of deflecting, if at all possible, the scandal likely to attend a public accusation of a sex crime. In view of the sources outlined above, this seems to be less a matter of religious law than of Orthodox culture—but that only makes the prejudice harder to uproot. Rabbi Yosef Blau put his finger on the issue in an extraordinary *j'accuse* against his fellow Orthodox rabbis some years ago:

> Anyone in contact with survivors of abuse is aware that they rarely get any support when they complain to rabbis. How many teachers have been fired from one school only to be hired by another. The true reason that they were let go was not revealed because the fellow needs to make a living and the scandal will hurt his family.... [W]here is the concern for new victims and their families?.... The true losers are all of us as we allow the existing chillul hashem [desecration of God's name] to continue.[28]

In other words, child abuse victims must expect to pay a heavy price when their abuse is reported to the police, since this will inevitably fuel unpleasant publicity. Note that what we encounter here amounts to a reversal of the moral relationship of abuser to victim—in this view, the victim's accurate report is worse than the original crime! Yet so far as I know, Blau's accusation that "scandal" threatened against the abuser and his family commands more compassion from Orthodox Jewish leadership than the devastation of actual child sexual abuse—to past and future victims, to *their* families, and to the community itself—has never been denied.

To make matters worse, notwithstanding the traditional consensus I have just outlined, Orthodox rabbinic opinion is far from unanimous in its approach to the practical aspects of reporting an Orthodox Jew's criminal act to secular authorities. Rabbi Moshe Feinstein, for example—probably the single most revered Orthodox rabbi in the United States until his death in 1986—published only one ruling on the parameters of *m'sirah*. But what he wrote has ominous implications for abuse victims,[29] especially because his prestige lends lasting authority to an extraordinarily unsympathetic position.

The *responsum* in question was written in 1960, to answer a query about the permissibility of reporting a Jewish criminal—in this case, a shopkeeper who knowingly sold non-*kosher* meat—to secular authorities. In his ruling, Feinstein sternly prohibits accusing any Jew to police or prosecutors, regardless of the circumstances, except on one condition: namely, that the victim must secure the prior approval of a rabbinic court which, in its judgment, cannot otherwise ensure the accused's good future conduct and determines that prosecution in secular courts is likely to do a better job.

Feinstein gives two separate reasons for this ruling. Readers will note that neither of his reasons takes into account any of the liberal rabbinic opinions—that is, those supportive of victims—I have already discussed.

First, Feinstein argues that since Orthodox Jews are enjoined to take their disputes to rabbinic courts for adjudication in the first instance, they may not accuse a Jewish criminal to secular police. This argument, I think, overlooks the difference between a private dispute and the public danger posed by a criminal act, a point clearly understood by the authors of more sympathetic rulings on criminal reporting. In fact, I do not know of another contemporary Orthodox rabbi who has treated *m'sirah* within the general context of an obligation to give rabbinic courts preference over secular ones.[30] The significance of such an approach is far from theoretical. It means that a panel of Orthodox rabbis will always make the initial decision about whether a report of a crime within the Orthodox community can ever see the light of day. I explained in Chapter 7 why such a position necessarily invites an obstruction of justice. Yet Feinstein, it seems, was willing to cling to a minority view of Jewish law to achieve exactly that result.

Worse, Feinstein maintains that the criminal courts are always off-limits to Orthodox Jews, except where the accuser can be sure that the accused—if he is Jewish—will not face a penalty in excess of whatever is prescribed by the Torah for the same offense. (Feinstein does not explain how we are to compare, say, the severity of incarceration with that of a rabbinically-mandated flogging, nor does he tell us how the victim is to anticipate, when he makes his report, the gravity of the sentence the accused will receive in the end.) The impact of this reasoning (Feinstein's second argument against reporting to police) is profound, since it will apply to almost all cases—unless, again, a rabbinic court has given a victim the go-ahead, something Feinstein's logic actually gives the rabbis strong grounds not to do.

Yet the most disturbing part of Feinstein's ruling comes at the end. After outlining the two objections already listed, he writes:

> Apart from this, it is possible [if an offender is taken to court] that he will deny [the charge] and swear [to the denial] before the secular court, and [thus] this [reporting to authorities] will cause him to swear a false oath, [in which case] *there is also punishment, God forbid, for the one who adjures*.... And therefore it seems, in my humble opinion, that first he must be judged before the rabbinic synod, [whose members should enforce their ruling] to the extent they are able ... and if they cannot succeed, then he may be brought before secular authorities.[31]

Part of Feinstein's discussion is given over to a technical interpretation of a particular Talmudic passage. But technicalities aside, this reasoning is astounding for its successful inversion of the roles of victim and perpetrator. According to Feinstein, by truthfully accusing the wrongdoer, the victim actually becomes the offender: by "forcing" the guilty party to perjure himself in an effort to escape justice, the victim becomes responsible for the perpetrator's false oath. Once again, a representative of Orthodox leadership can't seem to help playing a blame game with those least responsible for their own abuse.

It is only fair to note that Feinstein's ruling was not made in a case of alleged child abuse; we cannot be sure whether he would have resorted to similar reasoning had such a problem been directly presented to him by another rabbi. But nothing in his text precludes violent offenders from seizing this line of defense, and I find it hard to believe that he was unaware of such crimes when he added these cautionary words to his *responsum*. During the many decades in which he served as America's leading decisor of Talmudic legal questions, he must surely have dealt with queries from victims of rape, molestation, physical abuse and similar offenses by Orthodox Jews. We have no written record of his answers to them.[32] But his implied response to their cries for justice—in the only published *responsum* we do have—sets a disturbing precedent. Yes, a rabbinic court *might* grant the victim permission to pursue the charge in a secular forum, notwithstanding the possibility of the assailant's false oath. (Presumably, the rabbinic judges would have to accept moral responsibility for "forcing" the defendant to make it.) But that decision would always be up to the rabbis, who would have a pious alibi any time they preferred to suppress an abuse case altogether. What is more, the excuse offered by Feinstein's logic would have nothing at all to do with the severity of the crime or the credibility of the accusation.

In other words, the reasoning of one of America's most influential Orthodox rabbis celebrates as righteous conduct what, in plain terms, should be called an obstruction of justice. At any rate, I have no doubt "obstruction of justice" is the phrase Orthodox rabbis themselves would use to describe this logic—if a German court, say, were to bar accusations against Nazi war criminals on the grounds that the accused might end up making a false oath to exculpate himself. How depressing, then, to note that as far as I know there hasn't been any protest about this ruling from within the Orthodox rabbinic establishment.

*   *   *

It takes more than one set of influences to shape a religious culture. In the case of Orthodox Judaism, some influences that affect the topic at hand— child sexual abuse—may not even be specific to Orthodoxy. After all, experts who have examined the dynamics of sexual abuse by clergymen of other religions have noted that "absolute respect for all church leaders and officials can be manipulated to prevent defiance, disclosures, and escape" by victims of abuse[33]—a description that tallies closely with the conduct of Orthodox rabbis who have used their clerical positions to intimidate the children they molest, though the comment was not written with the rabbinate in mind.

Still, I cannot discuss traditional Judaism's silence about child abuse without inquiring into the possible impact of a formidable religious *oeuvre* on the way today's Orthodox Jewish parents treat their children. Consider first the Talmud, which specifically warns that a man who fails to fulfill a vow may be punished by the death of his children, since they are considered his "handiwork"—that is, his property.[34] This already suggests the depressingly familiar theme of children existing to fulfill their elders' destinies, not their own. And I am far from comfortable with the description of childrearing offered in one of the classic texts of the Jewish ethical canon, the 10th-century *Duties of the Heart* by Rabbi Bahya ibn Paquda:

> [During a child's infancy,] *God inspires the parents' hearts* with kindness, love and compassion for their offspring, *so that rearing it is not a burden to them.... All the labor and trouble involved in bringing it up,* bathing and dressing it, gently leading it, and warding off everything harmful, even against its will, is of little account in their sight.
>
> The offspring passes from infancy to childhood. *His parents do not tire of him nor become angry at his multitudinous wants and slight recognition of the burden* which they bear in caring and providing for him.[35]

I have italicized some phrases to underscore the implication that raising children is a hateful thing, a burden no one would accept were it not for supernatural intervention—and which, significantly, is not appreciated by the children who are its beneficiaries. Why so? A wife or husband may impose "burdens" as well—for that matter, fathers and mothers do, too—but I have never seen it argued in Jewish texts that tolerating them is offensive to nature. (On the contrary, Jewish law enjoins honoring parents as a sacred duty, and encourages married love as well.) Only love and respect for children is assumed to exist by virtue of a miracle. What does this say about our sense of obligation to *them*—the most vulnerable members of our families?

Turn from this to the way the tradition shows its heroes treating *their* children, and one's discomfort often intensifies. Is it really necessary for today's Orthodox press to apotheosize Rabbi Yisroel Meir Kagan, author of one of the most authoritative 20th-century compendia of Jewish law, for having said at his son's funeral that it was best to give all of one's love to God, rather than to divide it between God and one's own child?[36] For that matter, is it helpful to remind readers that the same sage publicly rebuked one of his sons at the boy's *bar mitzvah*, admonishing the thirteen-year-old in front of every-one with the words, "I see that you will never become a great scholar"?[37] Are these really the prime lessons in childrearing our rabbis should want to per-petuate?

Along with such attitudes toward children comes another assumption no less dangerous to Jewish victims of sex abuse. This is the notion that Ortho-dox Jews are so much better behaved than other people that abuse, where it exists at all, must be relatively rare in our communities. Thus Rabbi Yakov Horowitz, genuinely disturbed about the prevalence of child sex abuse among Orthodox Jews,[38] nevertheless insists that "by virtue of the moral compass of our Torah and the nature of our sheltered society, we have a lower percentage of these issues than the general population."[39] There isn't any evidence to sup-port such a claim; on the contrary, the embryonic research data we have "sug-gest that prevalence rates of sexual abuse in that [Orthodox Jewish] community parallel the rates of abuse in the larger society." In fact, early research figures "indicate[] that sexual abuse experiences among [Orthodox] women are more common than obesity (20 percent of the population)," a statistic two recent experts found "staggering."[40] Horowitz himself acknowledges one (1) Ortho-dox Jewish pyschologist having told him of receiving no fewer than *five calls each week* from parents whose children were abused, or from adults who were abused as children. And he admits that this represents only a fraction of the problem.[41] So why set the standard of proof higher for Orthodox Jewish vic-tims by implying that the crimes they allege are less likely to have occurred simply because the perpetrators are Orthodox? And why burden victims with the added assumption that the community that stands, by and large, on the side of their assailants is inherently more ethical than the "larger society" in which they have at least a chance of finding support?

I repeat: the insistence that the practices of Orthodox Judaism necessarily reduce child abuse is factually baseless, and spreading this claim can only hurt Orthodox abuse victims. But it is closely linked to the notion of an innate Jewish superiority over non–Jews, and this idea, alas, is tolerated over a wide range of Orthodox Jewish opinion. I am not aware of any public remonstrance from Orthodoxy's "modern" wing about the overt racism of one of its iconic figures, Rabbi Avraham Yitzchak Kook—Palestine's Chief Ashkenazic Rabbi from 1921 to 1935—even though Kook was publicly quoted as saying "the dif-ference between the Israelite soul ... and the soul of all non–Jews, at any level, is greater and deeper than the difference between the soul of a human and the soul of an animal."[42] If even "modern" Orthodox Jews are prepared to accept bigotry like that, it really should not surprise us when our rabbis turn the same chauvinism against our children, making them pay the price for a self-image that entails the superiority of Orthodox Jewish adults to other people—superiority that logically includes relative freedom from suspicion in matters touching on child abuse.

Sometimes the link between bigotry and abuse denial is so obvious, in fact, that the most painful observation of all is that it goes unnoticed. Let me give a particularly glaring example. Year after year, systematic abuse has been the fate of thousands of Palestinian children as a consequence of Israel's occupation of the West Bank and Gaza. As the Israeli columnist Gideon Levy wrote in 2004:

> Death is, of course, the most acute danger that confronts a Palestinian child, but it is not the only one. According to data of the Palestinian Ministry of Education, 3,409 schoolchildren have been wounded in the intifada, some of them crippled for life. The childhood of tens of thousands of Palestinian youngsters is being lived from one trauma to the next, from horror to horror. Their homes are demolished, their parents are humiliated in front of their eyes, soldiers storm into their homes brutally in the middle of the night, tanks open fire on their classrooms.[43]

This column appeared in Israel's premier newspaper, *Ha'aretz*, and the facts Levy cites are available from many other sources as well. The Israeli human rights organization B'Tselem reports, for instance, that in the southern Hebron hills "[t]he common method of intimidation [by Jewish settlers] is setting dogs at [Palestinian] children while they are grazing the sheep and goats or on their way to or from school."[44] Yet, when the children of religious Zionists in the Israeli town of Beit Shemesh came under a milder form of harassment from ultra–Orthodox men while on *their* way to school (some were spat at and called "prostitutes"),[45] the indignation of the victims' parents—though certainly justified—contained not the faintest recognition of the parallels between the treatment of their children and the systematic degradation of Palestinian youngsters. Their silence was particularly damning because their religious communities are far from guiltless in the mistreatment of Palestinian children: religious Zionist leadership openly rationalizes the abuse of Palestinians on the grounds that Jews in the Occupied Territories have an inherent right to dominate all non–Jews who live there. In fact, when three children of radical West Bank Jewish settlers were killed (along with their parents) in a relatively rare attack in 2011, a former Chief Rabbi eulogized the dead by comparing Palestinians to Nazis and pledging to continue their oppression ("We will not bend, we will not give up ... and nothing will prevent our faith in the righteousness of our path").[46]

Isn't it obvious that the *haredim* who spat at the young "modern Orthodox" girls, because their community stands in the way of *haredi* neighborhood expansion, took their lesson directly from an Orthodox rabbinate that embraces the torture of Palestinian children because *their* communities stand in the way of religious Zionist ambitions in the West Bank? If we tolerate the teaching that other people's children are legitimate targets, we have no right to be astonished when the same teaching is applied to our own children. Yet the underlying discriminatory principles are seldom even noticed, let alone condemned.

Misreading the nature of child abuse can mar even the best-intentioned efforts. In Chapter 1, I praised Rabbi Ron Yitzchok Eisenman for his outspoken support of Orthodox Jewish sex abuse victims, particularly for his insistence that the crimes committed against them should be promptly reported to police. I stand by that praise. But when Eisenman first made his position public, he paired advocacy for abuse victims with an attack on modern sexuality and gay rights, an approach that particularly disturbs me because it arises from prejudices all too common in the rabbinate.

At "a time when 'alternate life styles' are accepted and embraced," Eisenman said, and the conservative norms of traditional Orthodoxy "are often looked at as old fashioned or archaic," we must resign ourselves to facing evils (namely child sex abuse) that our grandparents "perhaps did not encounter."[47] I want to address a few words to the assumptions at work behind these comments.

Of course, much of what Eisenman said that night—for instance, that "religious" motives should not be invoked to rationalize the protection of child molesters—badly needed to be said. But why frame the issue of child sex abuse as a *new* problem for Orthodox Jews, a "temptation" our grandparents "perhaps did not encounter"? Given everything we know, it is at least as likely that the problem only *seems* new, now that discussing it is no longer taboo; assuming otherwise implies the inherent perfection of Orthodox Jewish society, and thus tends to steer us away from any real communal self-examination. The same tendency only gets stronger when an Orthodox rabbi associates the problem of child abuse, as Eisenman did, with an invasion from *without*, a contagion emanating from the lawless modernity that supposedly governs non–Orthodox America. ("The perverse has become the standard," Rabbi Eisenman lamented toward the beginning of his remarks.) Consciously or not, this sort of thinking effectively equates vigilance against child sex abuse with more, not less, religious paranoia aimed at anyone not quite like ourselves—a posture that does nothing to help abuse victims and can easily hurt other vulnerable people. Even if there were some sort of connection between sexual diversity and criminal abuse (and to assert one is as false as linking the former to any other crime), it's an oxymoron to encourage intolerance as a way of promoting the humane treatment of children, or anyone else.

Besides, trying to read child sex abuse out of Jewish history is, frankly, nonsense. There isn't the least evidence that Orthodox Jewish children were never abused before our grandparents' time. As for the corrosive effects of "modernity"—well, blaming Jewish sins on "new" influences is actually one of the hoariest themes of rabbinic sermonizing. Over a century ago, to take one instance, Orthodox rabbis in Russia were blaming an outbreak of pogroms on young men reading Yiddish stories or books on secular subjects penned in Hebrew. We know this from the Yiddish playwright S. Ansky, who also wrote that the rabbi of Liozno, where the young Ansky was teaching at the time, accused Orthodox girls of equal responsibility for anti–Semitic violence because of their licentious behavior, of which the specific sins were showing too much of their arms at weddings and—horrors!—sometimes singing songs *when alone in their rooms*.[48] Scapegoating modern trends—and sexuality, no matter how innocent—seems to be a game for all ages. But if Orthodox rabbis identify different intellectual contaminants at different times as the cause of all evil (while rabbinic sexual paranoia seems to stay fixed at full throttle, generation after generation), how can the doctrines or "influences" of any given moment be said to produce an aberrational dysfunction?

*   *   *

Before I conclude this chapter, let me quickly burn a couple of straw men.

Must we assume that all child sex abuse charges against rabbis, or other Orthodox Jewish adults, are true? Of course not. Do Orthodox leadership's protests about the dangers of "witch hunts," public "hysteria," etc. as a result of public complaints of sex abuse—self-serving as those concerns doubtless are—contain at least a germ of truth? Well, yes. They probably do. Groundless sex abuse charges *do* occur, and such charges *are* profoundly damaging to those affected. But I cannot see that these elementary facts are of any relevance to the discussion I have undertaken in this book. The detection of an unsubstantiated charge doesn't begin to justify the cover-up of a legitimate one. Even if the "bad" charges outnumbered the good—and no one familiar with the issue thinks they even come close, for meritless charges seem to be infrequent at best—cover-ups would remain just as unconscionable.

Sex abuse denial in the Orthodox rabbinate, as elsewhere, is not about preventing "witch hunts." It's about maintaining a power structure that can't endure without exiling the language of truth-telling, as surely as it exiles victims. "I could not write a story for which I had no words," Judy Brown has said, to explain why she couldn't broach the subject of child abuse before writing *Hush*.[49] That formulation is less a confession of impotence than an indictment of communal cruelty. To withhold from the victims of violent crime the kind of words that can describe the nature of their victimization is not merely to compound their suffering. In a very real sense, it is to deny their humanity—to erect a barrier between what is and what matters, to define, through silence, a class of experience that consigns its victims to the inexpressible, the unthinkable, the inadmissible. To carry on the history of such denial is to corrupt everything that ought to be at the heart of a religion.

Which brings me to a final point—and an explanation. I have devoted a good deal of space in this chapter to those Talmudic principles on which Orthodox leadership relies in its efforts to suppress reports of child sex abuse within its communities. I have done this fully conscious that these issues may be of peripheral concern, at best, to many readers. But I wanted to be fair. I wanted to explore the religious underpinnings of the rabbinate's actions, for if the cover-ups deplored in this book were in fact dictated by religious principles—tenets in which Orthodox rabbis sincerely believe, and by which they consider themselves bound—it would only be right to record that fact, which would in some sense mitigate the rabbis' offense.

We have seen, however, that traditional Jewish law affords the rabbinate no alibi. Talmudic law does not require the suppression of child sex abuse reports. A reasonable reading of the traditional Jewish literature, medieval and contemporary, supports doing everything necessary to bring a perpetrator to justice. At the very least, respectable authority for such a position undoubtedly exists; so if Orthodox rabbis choose, instead, to rely on some contrary authority, they are responsible for that choice and answerable for its consequences.

Since that much is clear—and as an Orthodox Jew myself—I must now add a religious observation to my previous strictures against the backlash strategies so commonly employed against Orthodox abuse victims. It is not enough to say that rabbis who use these strategies are using their religion as a cloak for crime. The fact is that they are defying their religion altogether. The same Talmud that allegedly frowns on non–Jewish constables and secular courts is perfectly clear, and ominously emphatic, when it comes to criminal cover-ups committed by religious Jews. "When judgment is delayed, perverted or corrupted," declares the Talmud, "sword and spoil increase"; and as the commentaries explain, "perverting judgment" refers to the intentional causing of an unjust verdict when a crime has been committed or alleged.

In fact, the ancient text threatens not only bloodshed ("the sword") but plunder (presumably at the hands of non–Jews) as a consequence of suppressing the evidence of crime.[50] Recall that precisely this "danger"—the possibility of violence against Jews by gentiles—has been used for years to rationalize suppressing child abuse charges, as if gangs of anti–Semitic hoodlums were just waiting for an Orthodox Jew's arrest on child molestation charges as an excuse to launch a pogrom. That's clearly nonsense. But to the extent the Orthodox rabbinate believes in the Talmud, it must believe that every time Orthodox rabbis, or Orthodox Jews under their sway, intentionally help a Jewish criminal escape justice, they really *are* inviting an outbreak of violence against their religious community. They, not abuse victims, are threats to their coreligionists and fomenters of anti–Semitism. They, not abuse victims, are sinners whose transgressions offend the most precious laws of God. That is what the Talmud says; that is what Orthodox rabbis are duty-bound to believe. To act in violation of that precept exposes them not only as criminal conspirators but as religious hypocrites.

Maybe, for as long as they live, the cover-up crowd will be lucky enough to avoid confronting the victims they have wounded or maligned. One never knows. But the accomplice-rabbis are still mortal, and so, according to their beliefs, are all certain to face God one day. What excuse are they going to give *him*?

10

The Politics of Piety

The "mass man" ... is specified primarily by a moral, and not an intellectual, inadequacy. He wants "salvation"; and in the end will be satisfied only with release from the burden of having to make choices for himself. He is dangerous, not on account of his opinions or desires, for he has none: but on account of his submissiveness.
——Michael Oakeshott[1]

The questions we ask are driven by what we know; and what we know depends on the questions we ask. This chapter represents an attempt to formulate some of the questions that have shaped the analysis undertaken in this book, particularly about the interplay between child sex abuse and religious politics, since I know that for me these questions have been years in the making and even now may be far from obvious to my readers.

To begin with: Why don't more Orthodox rabbis see the survivors the way I see them?—for if they did, they couldn't keep up their investment in the skewed priorities that still frame the issue. They couldn't, for instance, fuss aloud over the ancillae of an abuse accusation before dealing with the effects of the abuse itself—as in the case of a victim I know who, after years of turmoil, was challenged by a rabbi when he was finally ready to speak out against his abuser: "Are you sure you want to do this to his wife and children? After all these years?" "I kept telling this rabbi, '*I'm* not doing anything to his wife and children,'" the young man told me bitterly. "'*He* did it to them.' I don't know if he ever understood me."

Writing primarily of his own religious culture—that of conservative Protestant Christianity—Fred Keene has identified a political aspect in any religious leadership's preoccupation with the victims' "proper attitude" toward their abusers:

It protects the powerful. If a person with more power—whether familial or ecclesiastical or economic—does something harmful to another, it is very convenient to have the dominant religion teach that the person harmed must forgive the wrong. If the person harmed will not do so, then that person can be shamed and blamed for being "unforgiving," and responsibility for the crime can be shifted from the perpetrator to the victim.[2]

As we have seen, Orthodox Jewish communities, no less than the Protestant ones Keene has in mind, are hierarchical by nature: lay people obey rabbis, students defer to teachers, children are taught to submit to their elders. The Talmudic edict denying eternal life to one who insults a scholar (the designation used is the same as the title applied to rabbinic authorities generally)[3] is often quoted to stress the obligation of submission to the rabbinate under any and all conditions. So isn't it time to ask whether this represents the heart of the problem? Don't child sex abuse accusations entail an implicit political threat to the reigning order in a patriarchal society?[4] And if so, should we be surprised by the hostility with which the powers that be counter such threats, whatever their excuses?

Once we pose such questions, we don't have to look very far for answers. Consider how Rabbi Pinchas Stolper, the founding director of the National Council of Synagogue Youth (NCSY), repeatedly brushed off criticism of Rabbi Baruch Lanner (soon to be convicted of sexually abusing students) because of his "good works." Even when the evidence of Lanner's abusive conduct—which included physical assaults as well as sexual abuse—proved impossible to ignore, Stolper still defended him, claiming "He has had such a magnificent impact" on many young people, "despite some obvious sickness that is not sexual but has to do with needing to be in control." And how did this allegedly non-sexual "sickness" manifest itself? As the *Jewish Week* reported:

> Rabbi Lanner's need for control was a dominant theme in numerous interviews and conversations. What emerges is a pattern of an extremely bright, talented and troubled man who created his own universe of adoring teens—a universe in which loyalty to him was paramount.
>
> "Do you love me?" Rabbi Lanner would repeatedly ask teen officers of NCSY during required daily phone calls to him, either early in the morning or late at night. "Tell me you love me," he would demand. "Tell me you love me." And they did.
>
> Dealing with boys, Rabbi Lanner reportedly would use four-letter words and tell crude jokes freely in his private conversations with them, disparage those not in his inner circle, and often greet them with a swift, hard kick in the groin. When they sometimes would crumple to the ground in pain, he would laugh, insisting he was just showing he was one of the guys.[5]

Stolper's implicit insistence that, since Lanner's primary interest was "not sexual" but "needing to be in control," his conduct could not really amount to sexual abuse is a rather desperate species of denial. To begin with, it displays profound ignorance of the dynamics of child sexual abuse. "[S]exual assault," according to an expert whose writing about offenders appears in a basic text on the subject,

> is not motivated primarily by sexual desire. The sexual offender is not committing his crimes to achieve sexual pleasure any more than the alcoholic is drinking to quench a thirst.... [Sexual abuse] is the use of a sexual relationship to express a variety of unresolved problems or unmet needs in the psychology of the offender that have less to do with sensual pleasure and more to do with issues surrounding competency, adequacy, worth, recognition, validation, status, affiliation, and identity. It is the sexual misuse of power.[6]

"In general, perpetrators are likely to be 'me-first' individuals who satisfy many non-sexual needs when they engage a child in sexual behavior," confirm three authors in the same standard work; they even elaborate some of these "non-sexual needs" in language that is uncannily relevant to Lanner:

> Authority and power enable the perpetrator, implicitly or directly, to coerce the child into sexual compliance.... Gratification [for the abuser] may be enhanced by the child's accessibility, naivete, trust, affection, and compliance.... [M]ost [perpetrators] are content to persuade or entice the child into sexual behavior with their own position of power and dominance remaining implicit.... A few perpetrators enjoy the process of forcibly overpowering the victim, terrifying him or her, and inflicting pain.[7]

It's obvious from all this that Stolper's fallback defense of Lanner—that his abuse wasn't really "sexual"—cannot be taken seriously. But what's worse is that his rationalization of Lanner's abuse implicitly vindicates the core of Lanner's offense: the abuse was excusable, in Stolper's final analysis, to the extent Lanner was saving souls; that is, he was using his dominance to establish the dominance of the rabbinate. If I'm right, the problem is not only Stolper's inability to see Lanner's crimes for what they were. It lies in his failure to see that his line of defense justifies an essentially abusive relationship between Orthodox rabbis and other people, a relationship into which an individual rabbi's sexual abuse of his students fits like a hand in a glove.

Stolper was far from alone in this sort of thinking. Even at the time of Lanner's downfall, Orthodox rabbis praised his "charisma" and "dynamism" while deploring his sexual manipulations—never noticing that the good and bad items in his resume were really the same, the former merely cloaked in conventions of respectability. The NCSY report that denounced Lanner regretfully hailed him as "a charismatic leader who could mesmerize an audience and who was extremely effective in motivating teenagers"—praise that could have been given with equal justice to Adolf Hitler—with no comment at all on the close ties between spiritual control and sexual manipulation of young adolescents. (The report even echoed the Orthodox party line that "promiscuity, depression, anxiety and other psychiatric illnesses" are borne into Orthodox communities through exposure to the larger "environment.")[8] It seems to me that to condemn a rabbi's sexual abuse while applauding a seductive teaching technique *a la* Lanner is not just psychologically naïve. Taking this line implicitly validates the most unscrupulous forms of emotional manipulation—embracing, in other words, exactly those aspects of religious authority that are most closely tied to child abuse, and placing *hoi polloi*, in matters of moral choice-making, in the role of children.

The following passage, circulated in 2006 by an Orthodox organization, unwittingly captures the flavor of this attitude *in medias res*:

> Rav Reisman [a prominent American Orthodox rabbi] related that while in Yerushalayim [Jerusalem] this past summer, during the Israel-Terrorist War [in Lebanon], he heard a shiur [lecture] from HaRav Druk, Shlita [may he live long]. HaRav Druk noted that people on the street were blaming the war on many things. *One blamed it on cell phones. A second on lack of tznius [modesty in dress].* A third *on improper use of affluence. A fourth on the irreligious.*[9]

The Israeli army was raining bombs on Lebanon in a pointless and brutal war, as retaliatory missile strikes claimed civilian lives in Israel as well. And in the thick of it, a random sampling of pious Israeli Jews blamed it all on women's hemlines, "the irreligious," even "cell phones." No word from any of these people—apparently none was expected—about the possible effects of bigotry or xenophobia on the senseless carnage, though these are things for which religious Jews might conceivably bear some responsibility. I sense something almost deliberately infantile in all this. Note that three of the four "reasons" for the war cited in this little sermon were tied to one another with the crimson thread of illicit sexuality. What is more, the sexuality suggested in each case was immature and voyeuristic. An uncovered woman's knee or elbow is supposed to lead Orthodox Jews into lubricious fantasy. Orthodox Jews reflexively identify "the irreligious" with a sexual permissiveness tempting by its propinquity. Cell phones are the most recent targets of rabbinic wrath because they can now be used to access the Internet—hence pornography. It is as if the minds shaping these rationales were frozen at the earliest stage of sexual curiosity, unable or unwilling to grow up to the point of making their own sexual judgments. Are religious people so morally and intellectually handicapped really prepared to take on the evil of child sexual abuse, with all its real-life paradoxes?

* * *

One of the survivors I know once mentioned, as we discussed his experiences with Mondrowitz, that he never told his parents what he had told me. When I expressed surprise, he explained: "It would have destroyed their religion. They trusted this rabbi so much. They looked up to him.... Even then, I understood that they couldn't face the betrayal. I had to face it. But I couldn't make them do it."

That is the brave statement of a brave man, but it doesn't give the rest of us any right to force abuse victims into a similar quandary. Why should the survivor of abuse have to choose between sharing his pain and protecting his parents' piety? It seems to me we should be asking ourselves why religious faith, or at least the sort of faith our leadership teaches us, cannot survive facts—not even honesty between parents and children. Similarly, we should be challenging the reasoning of official spokesmen who minimize the problem of sex abuse by treating it as a mere aberration within an otherwise flawless religious *schema*. Rabbi Avi Shafran, writing for Agudath Israel, exemplified the fallacy when he described abuse as a failure of self-discipline: "To be sure, there will always be observant individuals who sometimes fail the test of self-control.... But that no more indicts Jewish observance than the fact that there are corrupt police or drug-addled doctors renders law enforcement or medicine suspect."[10] Reducing the evil of child sexual abuse to a question of the perpetrators' "self-control" ducks the whole question of a religious culture's involvement in abuse cover-ups. Actually, it does more than that. Its subtle correlative is that abuse victims have nothing to teach the community (what can they tell us about other people's self-control?); the message thus simultaneously reassures Orthodoxy of the perfection of its creed and reminds the victims to hold their peace. In other words, it is itself a rationale for cover-ups—though conveniently dressed in other clothing.

Shafran's complacency about the perfection of Orthodoxy vis-à-vis child sex abuse is particularly galling because the right-wing rabbinate he represents is quite willing to bend its rules if challenged from a different direction. For instance, prominent Israeli rabbis have issued fiats that permit the violation of Sabbath restrictions—generally, the most stringent of all ritual prohibitions in Jewish law—in order "to prevent romantic relationships between Jewish women and [Palestinian] Arab men."[11] Shlomo Aviner, a highly respected Orthodox rabbi, and David Batzri, described in the press as a "prominent kabbalist [rabbinic mystic]," have both ruled that the Sabbath may be desecrated so long as the violator intends to harass Jewish women entering the resort city of Eilat through a "security checkpoint" in the company of "Arab partners." According to Aviner, breaking the Sabbath is "permitted due to the potential physical danger a relationship with Arab men poses to Jewish women," while Batzri decreed that "as religious officials we must protect the Jewish people from assimilation and annihilation."[12]

Underneath this smelly stew of racism and patriarchal sex envy (note that no one quoted in the article expressed any concern about Jewish men in relationships with Palestinian women) lurks a revealing double standard. When an adult Jewish woman freely chooses a romantic weekend with a gentile, rabbinic horror knows no limits; talk of "annihilation" scents the air like brimstone, and the profoundest of religious prohibitions can dwindle to nothing. But when Jewish children are raped by adult Jews, they face a very different rabbinic reaction. No stringencies are waived for *them* when they seek justice, and if they dare to "inform" on their attackers they are scorned and denounced for their alleged violations of Jewish law (wrongly, as I showed in the previous chapter). I can see only one way to explain such a lopsided arrangement of dispensations. Clearly, it isn't the trauma of sexual violation that stirs the rabbinate's feelings; it's only whether the rabbis have the desired level of control over "our" women. And "our" children, too.

There is a larger and no less political point behind all this. What are the highest priorities encouraged by our religious leadership? A sense of compassion for the weak, standing alone, does not seem to be one of them. "For less religious people, the strength of their emotional connection to another person is critical to whether they will help that person or not," comments the co-author of a rather depressing study on the relation between religion and compassion conducted at Berkeley, the conclusions of which were published in *Social Psychological and Personality Science* in 2012. "The more religious, on the other hand, may ground their generosity less in emotion, and more in other factors such as doctrine, a communal identity, or reputational concerns."[13] We may find fault with the pliability of ethical imperatives under the influence of personal emotions, even if we take compassion to be such an "emotion." But it is hardly encouraging to be told that the good deeds of "more religious" people are predominantly motivated by prejudice, religious doctrine, or keeping up with the neighbors.

In my own religious circles, I suppose some of this can be explained away in terms of Jews' long history of persecution. Rabbi Dr. Jeremy Rosen has written, "The more closed and defensive a society, the more protectionist it is…. The more a religion sees itself as being under siege, the more controlling it becomes."[14] But if such considerations mitigate our judgment of the rabbinate's historical behavior, they must simultaneously lead us to challenge the values of the religion it preaches. Discriminatory principles are deeply engraved in traditional Jewish theory and practice. Orthodox Jews still pray only for the Children of Israel; our liturgy quite clearly neglects non–Jews in the blessings we seek in our thrice-daily prayers,[15] just as Talmudic law openly discriminates against gentiles, for instance in their right to recover damages from a Jew who causes them financial loss.[16]

Rosen's defense of the "protectionist" priorities in traditional Jewish culture looks even weaker when we consider that Orthodox Judaism does not face persecution today. Orthodox communities in our time are thriving in New York and Chicago, Jerusalem and Tel Aviv, Toronto and Montreal, Houston and Los Angeles, Paris and Mexico City—to name only a few such places—under the most liberal conditions Jews have ever known. Yet nowhere has this caused Orthodoxy to rethink its exceptionalism. On the contrary, we find a prominent Orthodox rabbi in Brooklyn reportedly proposing tax evasion on the grounds that government officials are predominantly non–Jews,[17] while a Chief Rabbi of Israel justifies stealing food from Palestinians because "the fruit from the trees planted by Gentiles" in the biblical Land of Israel "does not belong to the Gentiles."[18] Can we expect the same people who espouse such principles to suddenly turn egalitarian when dealing with the complaints of abused children?

* * *

Some readers may think I'm making too much of arguments drawn from abusive practices that target adults—at least, in a book about child abuse. But a society's approach to its children is seldom unrelated to its overall power dynamics. Those who wield the broadest authority are freest to give flesh to their fantasies. The penetrating eye of James Cameron caught even Albert Schweitzer indulging in a bit of power play as the famous physician offered medical treatment to impoverished Africans at his hospital in Lambarene: "The Hospital existed for him rather than he for it. It was deliberately archaic and primitive, deliberately part of the jungle around it, a background of his own creation which clearly meant a great deal more philosophically than it did medically."[19]

"A background of his own creation"—that hits the nail on the head. Schweitzer had every right to create as he saw fit, but with what materials? However lofty his intentions, white Europeans would not have been available to the good doctor (nor to any number of less principled men) as a backdrop for his version of the *mission civilisatrice*. The point is not to condemn Schweitzer, of course, but to call attention to a culturally-sanctioned relation between the powerful and the weak, by which the latter may be reduced to the level of possessions, even in the formulation of a genuinely humanitarian project, without stirring any objections from the guardians of conventional morality.

What is true of "natives" is true *a fortiori* of children. They are the most readily available raw material or "background" for the enactment of larger patterns of control. We can see this most clearly in extreme cases—for instance, the uprooting of hundreds of children whose parents were held in Argentine torture centers in the 1970s, whose pasts were then erased so that the state could give them entirely new identities. As Naomi Klein points out, "The baby thefts were not individual excesses but part of an organized state operation," the purpose of which was to cast the children in more conservative (and therefore more acceptable) molds than their real parents would likely have done.[20] We can see similar principles operating uncomfortably close to home— whether in American family courts[21] or in the patriarchal politics of conservative child-rearing activists, one of whom typically warned readers of an Orthodox Jewish web site that because American women "are taking over a number of previously male-dominated professions," their sons will soon be "stripped of masculine virtue."[22] The point I want to stress here is that in such settings, children are effectively the pawns of power politics, with the representatives of the patriarchy imposing their priorities, quite literally, one child at a time.

Traditional Jewish society is no stranger to this dynamic. Joel Engelman, whose story I related briefly in Chapter 2, has described a peculiarly Orthodox Jewish way of manipulating children for political purposes: using them as weapons to punish their parents' nonconformity. "There's a mold," he says,

> and everybody needs to fit that mold. If anybody steps out of line, they automatically lose their chance of a marriage prospect. So if you speak out on anything, on any given issue ... these yeshivas have enormous power in saying, "We'll kick your kid out of school. And then everybody is going to look and say, 'Oh, this kid got kicked out of school. What's going on?'"[23]

Engelman's experience is anything but unprecedented. Consider, just for instance, the report of Moses Leib Lilienblum that when his 19th-century Orthodox neighbors began to clash with him, they immediately targeted his children: "They called my children offspring of unclean parents, and the other children bullied them."[24] Small wonder, where children can be co-opted for such uses, that they can also be exploited in more direct and physical ways. And, conversely, to deny adults the power to decide a child's fate—sexually or otherwise—is to threaten a whole network of social control in which children represent an indispensable resource.

Only against such a background can I understand this comment from Martin Buber, in justification of God's apparent demand for the killing of Isaac:

> It is part of the basic character of this God that he claims the entirety of the one he has chosen [that is, Abraham]; he takes complete possession of the one to whom he addresses himself.... Such taking away is part of his character in many respects. He promises Abraham a son, gives him and demands him back in order to make a gift of him afresh....[25]

Remember how author Janet Heimlich was challenged to prove that Jews who treasure their children as the "gifts of God" could possibly hurt them? Buber's interpretation makes Isaac's status as a divine gift the very reason he can be sacrificed! And consider this anecdote, taken from the memoir of Israel's Chief Ashkenazic Rabbi, Israel Meir Lau.[26] Rabbi Lau approvingly describes how General Moshe Dayan launched an assault on three Palestinian gunmen holding 110 hostages, mostly teenagers, at the Israeli town of Ma'alot in 1974. Dayan decided to attack in force instead of discussing the captors' demand for the release of prisoners in the occupied territories—despite knowing that the use of violence would condemn many of the children to death. Lau expresses no qualms about this decision; he even approves Dayan's annoyance at the young hostages—Dayan referred to them as "klutzes"—because, although they were "youths in the [Israeli] premilitary program" and many of them "knew how to handle weapons," they "left their rifles in the truck cabins instead of taking them with them into the school."

"Tonight I understand the Holocaust," Dayan continued darkly, according to Rabbi Lau:

> People always talk about "sheep to the slaughter." Here, terrorists are holding hostage 110 young Israelis.... They are not within enemy territory, nor are they in a threatening or alien location. They're in their home. They know that underneath the school windows, our people are waiting with outstretched tarpaulins so that they can jump—but still, hardly any of them make a move.[27]

This blame-the-victims tirade—quoted by the rabbi without a hint of criticism—clarifies in an unexpected way the bloody raid that followed. It wasn't only to prove that "Israel will not negotiate with terrorists," as the government claimed afterward. Another crucial reason for the attack was that the officer who led it held the children responsible, at least in part, for their own kidnapping so long as they didn't "make a move" to retaliate or resist. That left the children vaguely at fault for whatever happened to them ("sheep to the slaughter"), thus whitewashing the army after its assault caused dozens of their deaths. We are left to suppose that to Dayan, the value of these children's lives depended on how well they had absorbed the lessons of their Zionist elders— otherwise they, like Isaac, could be sacrificed where "principle" was at stake. Depressingly enough, the same attitude was apparently shared by the Orthodox rabbi (and concentration camp survivor) who would later be entrusted with the religious leadership of all Israeli Jews of European extraction. It's a pattern with which Orthodox Jewish child abuse victims have become wincingly familiar.

*   *   *

Maybe my analysis of the politics behind certain religious doctrines seems like too narrow a fit? But what I have said conforms quite well to a large body of public claims that purport to explain the divine will. And here you needn't rely on my word. God's faithful messengers have had plenty to say about his rulings of late, and a sampling of these taken over the last decade or so, while hardly scientific, is nonetheless illuminating. Leave aside the claims that seem driven by pure mental illness, and what do we find?

Among God's more eventful recent commands were two to President George W. Bush: one to launch a military strike in Afghanistan, another to invade Iraq.[28] (Whether the source of these orders ought to shield him from prosecution as a war criminal, however unlikely that may be in the first place, is an interesting question.) During the same period, God was also telling at least two separate people to kill homosexuals.[29] For those who find murder rather an extreme approach to suppressing gay rights, there's no need to worry: God hedged his bets on this issue, commanding then-state senator Michele Bachmann to introduce a constitutional amendment to prohibit gay marriage in Minnesota.[30] God also took time out to protect the honor of Sarah Palin, who was ordered to sue media outlets over the way they reported her resignation as governor of Alaska.[31] And on it goes.

True, these reports (and dozens like them) all issued from lay people. Ministers and priests might be entrusted, I suppose, with more urgent tasks from on high. So, what has the Almighty been telling *them*?

A representative sampling might begin with the case of a fundamentalist pastor who, at the age of 58 and shortly after his wife's death, was instructed by God to marry a 20-year-old virgin named Greer—and who then related the divine commandment in a published sermon.[32] Some such commands have had darker consequences. Pastor Sherman Allen, according to the *Dallas Observer*, was allegedly told by God to beat women with a wooden paddle, and to sexually abuse some of them.[33]

None of the divine commands in this brief survey is supposed to have been given to an Orthodox Jew. But in keeping with the character of the religious culture I have been describing, we may note that all of God's instructions, as described by the faithful, tend toward violence and repression, and not infrequently toward abusive sexuality (especially, it seems, where the clergy is involved). Perhaps more to the point, I have not been able to find any recent examples of people instructed by God to show kindness, gentleness, tenderness, mercy or compassion. Nor have I found anyone on whom God recently imposed a duty to protect children—or any other vulnerable people, for that matter.

Anecdotal evidence? Of course. But there is more. Consider the divine priorities asserted in a PBS television documentary dealing with the execution of a convicted murderer, Robert Lee Willie, on December 27, 1984.[34] Although Willie was accompanied at the time by a nun—a religious woman deeply involved in his case, who stayed with him right up the moment of his death—

God allegedly chose to address not her but Mike Varnado, the deputy sheriff who had helped capture the condemned man. Here is Varnado's account of what he and God had to say to each other:

> I had never seen anyone go from completely living to totally dead and I was concerned how I was going to feel about doing that.
>
> I was praying, I mean, the whole time. I did more praying, I'm sure, than anybody in this building. I asked God numerous times if there was anything that I did in this investigation that I should bring to light, any problems I've got, any way, that I should immediately tell the prosecutors so this thing could be stopped. And it could have been.
>
> And my conversation with God was probably the deepest and the closest I've ever been able to communicate with him. I actually really felt like I was communicating.... And the message I was getting is, "There's no problem here. This is— this is my will and this is going to be done."

Like the other prophets I've cited in this chapter, Varnado is not an Orthodox Jew, but to me that only renders more intriguing the parallels between his comments and the themes I am developing here about expressions of traditional Jewish piety. First, there is the matter of perspective. Note that Varnado's initial concern was not about the justice or decency of putting a man to death, but about how *he* "was going to feel," given his part in the killing. Second, his modest story of surrendering to God's will veered readily into the complacency of self-absorption: *he* was praying more than anyone in the building; *he* certainly reached God's ears; on a practical level, had he wished, he could even have stopped the execution single-handed. As we have already seen, when leading Orthodox rabbis think about child abuse, they rarely ask how the divine will might look from the perspective of the helpless, unless they are suggesting that God wants the victim of abuse to learn to accept his or her lot, advice apparently still given to some battered wives.[35] The victims' point of view is seldom considered at all.

Perhaps Varnado's most revealing remarks were those in which he claimed the role not only of prophet but of divine judge:

> I don't think Robert Willie was redeemed. I saw him stand at this podium right here and he looked at us and he said, "If you all think killing's wrong, what do you think you're doing to me?" And I saw him look at Faith's Mama and Daddy and say, "I hope you're getting some satisfaction out of this," and this is the tone.

Of course, there are big differences in setting and subject matter, but when I read these self-satisfied words I can't help thinking about how the Orthodox rabbis who persuaded the Brooklyn D.A. to drop sex abuse charges against Rabbi Solomon Hafner accused his alleged young victim of "bragging," of "eating the attention" the rabbis begrudgingly gave him. How comforting it must be to know that someone you intend to hurt—whether by frying him with electric current or by letting his accused attacker walk free—cannot possibly have anything to say to you, even when (or especially when) his words strike uncomfortably close to the truth. The alleged child victim "begged" the rabbis to hear his account of a traumatic violation, but that could only have illustrated his conceit.[36] A man about to be put to death asked his killers how they justified their action, but that only proved his lack of penitence. In both cases, God shielded his followers from any serious examination of their principles in the face of someone else's suffering.

Are these stories exceptional? I would like to think so, but I doubt it. Orthodox rabbis do sometimes undertake a moral examination of their own theology. But the usual result is only a more sophisticated version of Varnado's musings. The questions they pose, though apparently genuine, seem designed to arraign the questioners themselves; at best, the rabbis try to rationalize their unwillingness to carry out a purpose they themselves see as abusive, though religiously mandated. Take for instance the Biblical commandment to annihilate the tribe of Amalek, an imperative found in all contemporary compendia of Jewish law, and at least theoretically applicable to the present day (although, as a practical matter, identification of this tribe remains elusive).[37] Aharon Lichtenstein, a prominent rabbi associated with the Orthodox "modern" wing, and well known for his wide reading in Western philosophy, has written about this genocidal injunction only to indict himself for doubting it:

> At one point, during my late teens, I was troubled by certain ethical questions concerning Amalek etc. I then recalled having recently read that Rabbi Chaim Brisker would awaken nightly to see if someone hadn't placed a foundling at his doorstep. I knew that I slept quite soundly, and I concluded that if such a paragon of kindness coped with these laws, evidently the source of my anxiety did not lie in my greater sensitivity but in my weaker faith. And I set myself to enhancing it.[38]

I find this *mea culpa* uncomfortably naïve. To begin with, no one in post–Freudian times should be so quick to attribute a nightly insomniac search for a nonexistent "foundling" to "kindness" alone. (Rabbi Chaim was famous for his Talmudic learning, but one can't tell from this anecdote how the sage treated actual people he encountered in real life.) Still less tenable is Lichtenstein's use of personal scrupulosity as a measure of a compassionate worldview. We are all well aware that even mass murder—precisely the "ethical question" that used to bother the rabbi—has been condoned for centuries by many of the most scrupulous of saints. An uncannily precise assessment of such men was offered by the English historian Hugh Trevor-Roper as long ago as 1947:

> The Grand Inquisitors of history were not cruel or self-indulgent men. They were often painfully conscientious and austere in their personal lives. They were often scrupulously kind to animals.... But for men who, having opportunities of wor-

shipping aright, chose wrong, no remedy was too drastic. So the faggots were piled
and lit, and the misbelievers and their books were burned, and those gentle old
bishops went home to sup on whitefish and inexpensive vegetables ... while their
chaplains sat down in their studies to compose their biographies and explain to
posterity the saintly lives, the observances and austerities, the almsgivings and sim-
plicity, of these exemplary pastors....[39]

Couldn't a European-born scholar like Rabbi Lichtenstein, writing just a few
decades after the Nazi genocide, draw the obvious moral from the failure of
so many "exemplary pastors" to frame an objection to earlier bloody projects
(think of the Inquisition, think of the Crusades)—instead of idolizing a Jewish
representative of the breed because he used to check his doorstep for a
foundling who never appeared? Nobody with Lichtenstein's historical experience ought to be so trusting in the kindness of "saints."

I'm also uneasy about his assumption of the moral foreground in his
account of the issue, a rhetorical maneuver implying that his struggle with the
Biblical text was itself a test of virtue. Having at first been "troubled" by it,
having later resigned himself to the conviction that his "weaker faith" was the
real problem, the rabbi can now present himself as "sensitive" without actually
repudiating the ethic of genocide.

Does this raise the rabbi's troubles to a moral high ground? Not at all.
For even Heinrich Himmler and Auschwitz commandant Rudolf Hoess, to
name two particularly outrageous examples, claimed to have endured personal
struggles over what their "work" required of them. The redoubtable scholar
Norman Finkelstein, quoting German sources, points out that these war criminals' protestations allowed them to sanitize evil through spiritual self-
dramatization, making them the "victims" of their own inhuman acts:

[W]hat were the Nazis' cloying public displays of angst if not duplicitous exercises
in self-extenuation and self-exculpation? [Historian Hans] Hoehne excoriates the
"spurious self-pity" and "ineradicable ... philistine self-righteousness" of the Nazi
executioners that "prevented them [from] regarding themselves as murderers,"
indeed "enabled them seriously to believe that in fact they were tragic figures." ...
Recalling Hoess's avowal in his memoir that he "never grew indifferent to human
suffering ... I have always seen it and felt for it," [historian Joachim] Fest scathingly
comments that "what he believed to be sympathy for his victims was nothing but
sentimental pity for himself, who was ordered to carry out such inhuman acts."
"Thus," Fest further notes, "he was able to claim merit for a completely self-centered
sentimentality, which placed him under no obligation to take any action, and to
credit himself with the mendacious self-pity of the 'sorrowful murderer' as evidence
of his humanitarianism."[40]

I am not trying to place Rabbi Lichtenstein in the dock alongside Nazi war
criminals. But given such awful precedents, one could wish he hadn't pointed
to his *angst*, rather than to genocide itself, as the problem to be solved. For

such "sentimentality," as Fest aptly formulates it, serves only to place an oppressor "under no obligation to take any action"—a convenient but morally untenable position for a troubled rabbi who would be rocking the boat if he spoke out against Biblically-endorsed cruelty.

Or child abuse cover-ups.

It seems to me that rationalizations like these effectively cancel the whole enterprise of religious ethics. For "if the individual can no longer be held responsible, either because he is no longer in a position to decide or else does not understand that he must decide, then we have an alibi for all guilt."[41] And then the protectors of the abusive Rabbi Lanner, the rabbinic accomplices of Yosef Kolko, the derailers of justice in the Hafner case—all must be excused, since they too "have an alibi for all guilt." That would leave religion itself as the supreme alibi.

And this is true even for those exceptional rabbis who are willing to express some misgivings. What of the larger number whose piety, to borrow Trevor-Roper's phrasing, "sanctifies" the crimes demanded by their religion—as long as they seem to serve a religious purpose?[42] When, for instance, an Orthodox rabbi advises the killing of civilians during wartime as part of the "'purity of weapons' according to the Halakhah [Jewish law]" which, due to its allegedly divine origin, must be preferred to "the alien conception which is now accepted in the Israeli army"?[43] When the most famous recent authority at the liberal end of Orthodox Jewish opinion, Rabbi Joseph B. Soloveitchik, has insisted that "Yaser Arafat and his company" (presumably, all Palestinians affiliated with nationalist organizations) represent the Biblical "Amalek"—that is, that they should be exterminated on sight?[44] From such religious authorities, are we to expect more delicate feelings for children's bodies than for those of non–Jewish civilians?

While we are on the subject, we should note that one revealing measure of the politics animating the Orthodox rabbinate is today's curious retrofitting of traditional Judaism to the fruits of Zionism, a doctrine that once prided itself on its rejection of Orthodoxy. On a theological level, the differences between the two systems of thought are indeed hard to bridge. For instance, what does it mean to be a Jew? With characteristic candor, Ze'ev Jabotinsky jettisoned the religious definition of Jewishness—obviously one of the underpinnings of Orthodoxy—to make way for something better suited to Zionism's "nationalist" ideology:

> The [Jewish] people's mental structure reflects their physical form even more perfectly and completely than does that of the individual.... It is physically impossible for a Jew descended from several generations of pure, unmixed Jewish blood to adopt the mental state of a German or a Frenchman, just as it is impossible for a Negro to cease to be a Negro.[45]

This overtly racial approach to Jewish identity is at loggerheads with the Orthodox definition, according to which anyone can become Jewish through conversion, just as it ignores the obvious fact that Jews can and do assimilate into other cultures. Yet, as even a quick look through today's Orthodox Jewish publications will confirm, Orthodoxy has achieved something like an ideological symbiosis with even the most racist offshoot of Zionism, Israel's Jewish settlement project in the occupied West Bank. In fact, a recent article in an Israeli on-line newspaper stresses that traditional Orthodox Jews in the occupied territories are now "using the same ideology that motivates the settler enterprise," which in turn is driven by the Zionist goals of colonization and control of the biblical Land of Israel.[46] The reasons for this symbiosis are evidently not theological. In the early days of Zionism, Orthodox rabbis formed the highly influential organization Agudath Israel precisely to oppose the Zionist movement.[47] So if the Orthodox rank and file sympathize with Israeli settlers today, it is less because of religious faith than because Orthodox Jews have been trained to think in hierarchical terms, conditioned to define their relations to others on the basis of fear and prejudice. Precisely the racist tendencies of Zionism, I'm afraid, seem to make its politics attractive within much of today's Orthodoxy.

But doesn't grounding a religion in such primitive appeals sap believers of the moral maturity to stand up to what we all know, or ought to know, is a betrayal of the vulnerable among us—including abused children? In this connection, I have to mention the level of unthinking fear at which Orthodox Jews sometimes pitch their arguments on issues that particularly trouble them. Take for example the way the family of the respected Israeli writer Dov Elbaum—who abandoned *haredi* culture but remains, in his words, "a believer"—greeted the news of his decision to leave Orthodoxy:

> My older brother told me that it would have been better if I were killed in a car accident, because that way, in his view, I would have been killed without having sinned. My father asked Rabbi [Eliezer] Schach what to do, and he told him ... not to sit *shiva* [in mourning for the dead]. But my father didn't speak to me for 10 years. Emissaries were sent to try to get me to change my mind, and the peak was when they brought in Uri Zohar [an Israeli show business personality who became ultra–Orthodox], who spent a whole night trying to scare me with a depiction of hell that was totally superficial.[48]

Interestingly, in Uri Zohar's 1985 book *Waking Up Jewish*,[49] the former actor explained his own conversion to Orthodoxy as the outcome of an unbiased, rational investigation. No doubt new converts aren't likely to be persuaded by threats of hellfire, so reasoned persuasion must suffice for *them*. But nobody within the fold, including Zohar, considered making appeals on an adult level to keep the born–Orthodox Elbaum inside the religious community. Incidentally, Zohar's internalization of ultra–Orthodox sex paranoia helps to explain why he, too, has had nothing to say about the protection of child abusers by the rabbis he now idolizes: for instance, in one of his radio commentaries, Zohar argued that it was better to expose children to the risk of contracting AIDS than to teach them the basics of sexuality. Which offers us one more indication of where children really stand in the Orthodox moral hierarchy.[50]

I don't mean to oversimplify. I am well aware that the rationalizations advanced to justify religious cruelty are not always childish. Sometimes their logic is reasonably sophisticated, as in the writing of Rabbi Lichtenstein, some of which I've quoted. I'm also sure that such arguments are well-intentioned and sincere. The authors want to spare others the moral quandaries they have struggled with themselves, and to defend a creed in which they deeply believe. But I remain largely unimpressed. "[T]he subjective morality of intentions," writes Aldous Huxley, "requires to be supplemented by the objective and utilitarian morality of results. One may mean well; but if one acts in an unrealistic and inappropriate manner, the consequences can only be disastrous."[51] Can there be a more "unrealistic and inappropriate" line of reasoning than one that acknowledges the evil of conduct one is obliged to approve, and then attempts to escape the dilemma by disclaiming responsibility for it?

* * *

As this book was being written, 85-year-old Rabbi Norman Lamm, announcing his retirement as chancellor of Yeshiva University, "acknowledged his failure to respond adequately to allegations of sexual abuse against the university's rabbis in the 1980s."[52] Lamm's retirement—and his belated confession—seemed aimed, in part, at containing the fallout from an earlier article in the *Jewish Daily Forward* quoting alleged victims of two rabbis at Yeshiva University's high school for boys, who said they had been sexually abused in the 1970s and 1980s, and quoting Lamm as saying that he had known about the allegations at the time but had elected to deal with them "privately." "My question," Lamm had told *Forward* months earlier, "was not whether to report to police but to ask the person to leave the job."[53]

Lamm claimed he didn't investigate the abuse complaints back then largely because he was preoccupied with the university's severe financial problems. But that hardly explains his continuing refusal to examine the allegations years later, as former students reportedly pressed for an investigation after the Baruch Lanner story broke in 2000. One of them even claimed he had been warned by Yeshiva University's vice president that any legal action he might commence "would not be good for you."[54] After the passage of another thirteen years without any agreement between the alleged victims and Yeshiva University, nineteen former students finally did decide to file a $380 million lawsuit alleging a "massive cover-up of the sexual abuse of [high school] students ... facilitated, for several decades, by various prominent Y.U. and [high school] administrators, trustees, directors, and other faculty members."[55] Days later, "five more former Yeshiva University High students ... stepped forward to say they were molested by staffers at the prestigious Jewish institution."[56]

One more alleged sex abuse cover-up involving prominent Orthodox rabbis—and only time will tell where the allegations will lead. But it is not too early to note that Lamm's admission of fault, tardy and tepid as it was, was still so unusual as to earn him praise for his "courage and moral stature" from Orthodox Jewish sociologist Samuel Heilman. Heilman stressed—sad to say, truthfully—how far Rabbi Lamm's conduct surpassed that of "his Orthodox peers," one of whom, "a prominent rabbinical dean in Rabbi Lamm's own Yeshiva," "has refused to reveal the name of another dismissed faculty member accused of abuse."[57] Personally, I recoil from the idea of praising an administrator for "courage" after he confesses that he was too busy worrying about his school's finances to report an accused molester of his students to the police. But Heilman has a point. Orthodox rabbis have been so unapologetic, by and large, that one welcomes even a small exception. We have heard no apologies from Rabbi Yisrael Belsky, who publicly slandered the family of the victim of Yosef Kolko; none from Rabbi Herschel Schachter, who warned against prosecuting child molesters lest they be put in the same cells as "*shvarztes*"; none from Rabbi Pinchas Stolper for his stalwart defense of Baruch Lanner. To pose yet another uncomfortable question: Why not?

Again and again throughout this book, I have decried the behavior of the Orthodox rabbinate. And I stand by what I have written. But as the material collected in this chapter makes clear, the ideological evils that beset Orthodox rabbis have their all-too-evident counterpart in the extraordinary tolerance of their behavior by the Orthodox rank and file. The politics of piety involves more than the license enjoyed by the powerful. It would be unworkable without the acceptance of those privileges by the rest of a religious society. Unfortunately, our system is turning out plenty of believers who seem to have been designed for passivity above all. Like the "mass man" deplored by Michael Oakeshott, the product of contemporary Orthodox education seems to exist less as an individual than *en masse*; apparently he fears, at least when it comes to rabbis who condone abuse, "the burden of having to make choices for himself" and, in consequence, is "dangerous ... on account of his submissiveness." Yes, dangerous: because when enough people accept the arbitrary rule of the rabbinate, excesses are inevitable within the privileged caste. At least Rabbi Lichtenstein, giving up the power to make his own moral decisions, believed he was ceding that power to God himself. When the rest of us fail to challenge the exploitative actions of the Belskys among us, we are handing over our consciences to mere human beings—human beings whose record hardly justifies their responsibility for their own consciences, let alone those of other people.

And there is no point pretending that the real meaning of this is anything but political. Take the proscription of *lashon ha'ra*, or "evil speech." I have mentioned already how this religious prohibition is manipulated to stigmatize victims of sex abuse who report their attackers. But the picture is clearer, and uglier, when we see it as a whole. Consider some examples we have encountered already. According to leading Orthodox rabbis, it was "evil speech" to reveal Yosef Kolko's crimes to police. It was not "evil speech" for Rabbi Belsky to denounce the innocent and falsely accuse others of Kolko's abuse. It was "evil speech" for the *Jewish Week* to publicize abuse allegations against Baruch Lanner. It was not "evil speech" for Lanner, or his supporters, to publicly defame his victims. It was "evil speech" when Ben Hirsch correctly criticized both Orthodox leadership and the Brooklyn District Attorney in the *New York Post* for their handling of sex abuse cases. It was not "evil speech" when Rabbi Avi Shafran used the pages of *Ami Magazine* to smear Hirsch as a "hater" and anti–Semite for writing those comments. And so on, and so on. These rabbinic uses of religious doctrine are hypocritical, of course. But what can other religious Jews say for ourselves, if we allow such thinking to hold sway over us?

One final comment seems in order about the interrelation of religious politics and Orthodox Jewish sex abuse cover-ups. That today's Orthodox leadership has made common cause with the most resolutely right-wing elements in mainstream U.S. politics is obvious from the pages of almost any issue of any popular Orthodox periodical. The cover of *Ami Magazine* notoriously depicted the Obama White House draped with swastikas in January 2012. (Its editor later admitted this "may have been a poor choice.")[58] The *Jewish Press* has celebrated the virtues of the extreme right-wing Tea Party ("family values over vulgarity, work ethics over entitlements") while ridiculing Occupy Wall Street protesters as "brain-dead college kids."[59] Even faced with sensational revelations about the extent of government surveillance of innocent citizens—exactly the sort of official overreaching that, in the past, might have alarmed Orthodox leadership about the possible effects on America's Jewish minority—the Orthodox weekly *Mishpacha* could only muse about why Edward Snowden, the story's whistle-blowing source, had decided "to become a turncoat" whose "claims of self-sacrifice don't reflect the entire story."[60] With even more reactionary zeal, Rabbi Jonathan Rosenblum assured *Mishpacha*'s readers that the only fault with the government's "commonsensical" assault on privacy was that it didn't yet extend to snooping on every mosque in America.[61] Glenn Beck could hardly have gone farther.

For the Orthodox rabbinate, the value of this alliance with repressive politics is patent: the rabbis have read the drift of American power and want to be on the safe side of Big Brother. But what will such a partnership mean for the rest of us?

Here we can only speculate. But I do think there is a lesson in the way Brett Tolman, a protégé of the Republican right, joined the campaign to support Sholom Rubashkin after the latter's bank fraud convictions (see Chapter 6). The thuggish Rubashkin's appeal to Tolman and his sponsors can hardly have sprung from religious sympathies alone. More likely, people like Tolman are interested in courting the only large, centralized portion of the American Jewish community that does not vote like most American Jews, three-quarters of whom supported Barack Obama in 2008—as did 70 percent four years later.[62] The Orthodox leadership's message to the Republicans, presumably, is that they can make important inroads into the alliance between their Democratic rivals and a large, affluent ethnic voting group—if they support the Orthodox leadership's cover-up campaigns.

Such deal-making, if it bears fruit, should not surprise us; it would only make the rabbinate's behavior typical of elites among American Jews.[63] But the meaning of the alliance is ominous for anyone on the short end of abuse cover-ups. To the extent Orthodox leadership stakes its political future on its ability to deliver voting blocs to the Right, political-machine fashion, it will have to fight tooth and nail against any attempt from within to challenge its dominance. And that means that, for the foreseeable future, even the half-hearted concessions of a Rabbi Lamm are going to be the exceptions. The Orthodox leadership, as a whole, is much more likely to take up the position toward its communities that, in Alice Miller's analysis, has been used for generations to conceal cruelty toward children: the teaching that an adult "should never give the child an opportunity to discover adult limitations, but ... should, on the contrary, conceal his or her weaknesses from the child and pretend to divine authority."[64] When it comes to the rabbinate's future treatment of child sex abuse charges, it isn't hard to guess where that kind of politics is going to leave us.

11

East of Eden: "Innocence," Sex and Sex Abuse

I sent a message of truth to the theologists:
  Dear Fellow Compulsives:
  To insist you know God when you do not know logic or science is
  hideous. Those who say they know God and yet reject truth, however
  selectively, are playing at *being* God. And those men who play they are
  God, perforce use men as toys. When will you end this dreadful game?
                                                          —Philip Wylie[1]

In April 2008, police and child welfare officials stormed a barricaded ranch outside the west Texas town of Eldorado. The raid's target was an enclave of the Fundamentalist Church of Jesus Christ of Latter-Day Saints, a radical offshoot of the Mormon Church. Unprecedented in scale, the Texas officials' foray into this dauntingly "gated," highly insular community of polygamists under the leadership of its "prophet," Warren Jeffs, resulted in the removal of hundreds of young boys and girls from their homes—the largest number ever taken at one time based on a suspicion of child sex abuse. Although the removal of the children would ultimately be overturned by the Texas courts, the child abuse suspicions turned out to be well founded. Child rape and abuse charges were later filed against several of the sect's leaders; Jeffs himself, having been convicted as an accessory to child rape in a Utah court the previous year,[2] would be sentenced to life in prison on new charges, resulting from the Texas raid, in 2011.[3]

Largely as a result of these notorious events, the secretive and reactionary Fundamentalist Latter Day Saints (FLDS) are known to most Americans as a growth culture for child sexual abuse. Which is fair enough—but far from the whole story.

What I want to explore here is the pivotal role the FLDS's insistence on sexual "innocence" played in making so much of its child abuse possible. And I mean to stress that for all its superficial exoticism, the FLDS approach to sexuality is far from unique. If we can understand why the same religious community that placed such a high value on "protecting" its children from sexuality was the same community that tolerated—even participated in—those children's systematic sexual exploitation, I think we will be that much closer to understanding the toleration of child sexual abuse by other right-wing religious movements—including Orthodox Judaism.

Of course, there are significant differences between FLDS and Orthodoxy. Leaving aside some matters of theology, FLDS is a relatively small sect, whose believers number 30,000 at most, bearing a history that begins with Joseph Smith in approximately 1830. (Smith was killed by a lynch mob in 1844.)[4] Orthodox Jews, in contrast, can be counted by the millions worldwide,[5] and Orthodox Judaism is one of the older surviving religions, with roots in the rabbinic movement that gained ascendancy in Judea/Palestine during the first two centuries of the Common Era. Further, while polygamy remains an important part of FLDS practice, it has virtually disappeared from Orthodox Judaism: the medieval sage Rabbeinu Gershom outlawed it for European Jews a thousand years ago, while even among traditional Jews in Near Eastern countries the practice is now rare. (Not nonexistent, though; what is more, some ultra–Orthodox Jews want to revive it, a point I will return to later.)[6]

But however real, the differences between the two faiths cannot eclipse some worrisome similarities. The unifying factor that particularly interests me is the patent fear of children's natural development in sexual matters, and the inevitable, concomitant horror expressed by the leadership of both religious communities about any possible "contamination" by modern advertising and the mores of contemporary lifestyles. Under the goading of a repressive and fear-based theology, FLDS leadership came to insist upon very early marriage, the enforcement of sexual ignorance, and the promotion of a system by which girls and women became, in essence, the sexual property of the men they married so that they could not pursue their own desires. And if that catalogue is starting to feel like *terra cognita* to the attentive reader of this book—well, read on.

For even Warren Jeffs' revved-up sexual repression was not radically different, in theory, from the sexual attitudes now popular among the more right-wing Orthodox Jews. Joel Engelman was only one of many Orthodox Jewish children who have been beaten regularly to keep "impure thoughts" out of them (see Chapter 9). What's more, Orthodox communities have already seen child abuse scandals emerge around rabbis-cum-cult leaders whose practices in some ways resemble those of Jeffs. One need only recall the case of Rabbi Elior Chen, whose teaching—defended by such leading Orthodox rabbis as Chaim Kanievsky (see Chapter 4)[7]—held that small children can be possessed by evil, and that physical torture serves to make them "righteous."[8] Even after

Chen's criminal conviction for acts of horrifying child abuse, a representative of one of Israel's most influential ultra–Orthodox rabbinic organizations was still firmly on the rabbi's side. "Chen is a naïve and delicate soul," he said. "The evidence proves he did nothing. This is a Dreyfus plot."[9]

It is true that the extremes reached under Jeffs were unprecedented even for FLDS; in fact, it is unclear whether his criminal practices stemmed from religious conviction or were the acts of a power-hungry *poseur* who used religious doctrine as a cover for his own ambitions and appetites.[10] But what strikes me as most significant about that question is how little it really matters: Jeffs' abusive teachings look just as logical when viewed as expressions of religious fanaticism as they do when explained as the machinations of a cynical power-seeker. So perfectly congruent are the dynamics of repressive religion with those of patriarchal totalitarianism that their victims cannot tell them apart—nor should they. The real lessons behind Jeffs' story lie in what FLDS shares with other conservative religions, and in its graphic illustration of what the toxic core of that shared sexual ideology really contains.

Popular author Stephen Singular, in his book-length account of the FLDS scandal, comes close to acknowledging this. Unfortunately, the point is obscured by his crowd-pleasing focus on the one religion it is completely safe to demonize in today's America—namely, Islam. Repeatedly, he claims to detect links between Jeffs and Muslim extremists who "convinc[e] others to strap explosives to their chests and kill themselves in a busy marketplace or fly airplanes into buildings":

> From Jakarta to London, New York to Madrid, they'd been acting out stories and myths hundreds or even thousands of years old while spilling blood for their faith. Like the radical Muslim leaders who promised their suicide bombers scores of virgins in heaven for fulfilling their deadly missions, Warren Jeffs had long ago learned how to exploit the critical connection between erotic impulses and violence.

To lend support to this rather oddly-conceived connection—after all, there is no evidence that Jeffs knew anything about Islam, "radical" or otherwise—Singular is prepared to credit "rumors" that "FLDS men occasionally traveled to the Middle East to learn more about how these ancient societies kept women under control." He even tries to buttress the link through the observations of people who admittedly knew nothing about the motives of church leaders, as in this comment concerning a woman who rebelled against FLDS teaching:

> The more Laura [Barlow] uncovered about the practices of Islam, the more parallels she discovered between that faith and the FLDS. Muslims, for example, were promised scores of virgins in heaven if they were willing to become martyrs for their "jihad," or war against the non–Muslim world. One of Joseph Smith's most controversial revelations regarding plural marriage had read: "*And if he have ten virgins*

given unto him by this law, he cannot commit adultery, for they belong to him, and they are given unto him; therefore is he justified." [11]

In these and similar passages, Singular is clearly catering to popular prejudice—and he is ignoring analogies between FLDS and other American religious groups that would have been considerably more to the point. The common claim that Muslims expect "scores of virgins in heaven" for killing non–Muslims has at most a controversial basis in theological fact,[12] while conveniently overlooking how traditional Christianity and Judaism have both flirted with martyrology at least as extreme as anything found in Islam. (The teaching that "martyrdom was the only sure path to God ... spread like wildfire" among early Christians, and Judaism had produced entire communities of holy warriors before the birth of Jesus, let alone Muhammed.)[13] Nor did Joseph Smith and his followers learn polygamy from the Quran; their source was quite obviously the Hebrew Bible, in which polygamy is the rule rather than the exception.

More important, in his effort to link the sexual repression of the FLDS with religious fanaticism, Singular focuses on political terrorism (associated in American minds predominantly with Islam), and this draws him away from the real target. Since I am dealing with Orthodox Judaism, let me offer a corrective by pointing out some particularly notable analogs between Orthodoxy and FLDS sex paranoia.

A few of these are essentially political. For instance, to enforce the subservience of females, women in FLDS are not allowed to get drivers' licenses.[14] The same thing may be observed in several Hasidic communities in New York State, where women are forbidden to drive. (I myself have given rides to Hasidic women who otherwise would have been unable to bring home shopping bags from a grocery store in Monsey, New York.) Similarly, to keep the community as a whole in thrall to its leaders, FLDS members are told that "every person on the outside of the FLDS community [is] evil."[15] *Mutatis mutandis*, Orthodox Jews are given much the same teaching. I have lost count of the number of times I've heard Orthodox rabbis sermonize about the inherent evil of non–Jews.

Still more disturbing parallels have to do with the systematic efforts of both religious communities to isolate young people from any erotic stimulus. Warren Jeffs, who began his career as a teacher, was notoriously obsessed with keeping even very young boys and girls "segregated from one another" and "safe from the modern influences of the outside world." Though obviously afraid of latent eroticism between the sexes, he and other FLDS leaders reserved their greatest loathing for homosexuality, for which they decreed "death on the spot" as the proper penalty.[16]

And Orthodox Judaism? Segregation of the sexes is the rule in most

Orthodox parochial schools today, even for very young children. Rabbi Avi Shafran of Agudath Israel, attempting to account for sex crimes committed by Orthodox Jews, intoned the same roll call of papier-mâché villains invoked by FLDS: "MTV, R-rated movies, contemporary advertising and uncontrolled Internet usage."[17] (Like FLDS leaders, he and his rabbinic superiors denounce only "modern influences" and seldom mention the sexual content of the Bible—or of the Talmud, though as the Orthodox novelist Herman Wouk has pointed out, the latter is "full of sex ... and to the tell the truth, goddamned explicit.")[18] As for homosexuality, America's single most respected Orthodox authority, Rabbi Moshe Feinstein, stressed as recently as 1975 that it not only merits the death penalty under traditional Jewish law but is, in his words, "the most disgusting and contemptible" of sins.[19] On the whole, a perfect match.

There is more. In FLDS, writes a former member, Flora Jessop, "Children are taught never [to] touch themselves, even while bathing.... Children are taught that fine things and jewelry (worn after age 8) are evil.... Both women and children are not given sex education, even on their wedding day." In fact, "many women, even having as many as fourteen or more children, have never experienced orgasms as it is taught that sex is only for procreation—and procreation is considered a duty of the women."[20] These measures go beyond the restrictions imposed in Orthodox Jewish communities, but not a great deal: young Orthodox Jewish men *are* warned not to touch their genitals[21]; Orthodox Jewish women *are* taught, in many communities, to wear only loose-fitting clothing that covers them from elbows to ankles; many abstain from makeup; and sex education, especially for women, is carefully restricted and of limited scope even when it exists (for instance, just before marriage).[22]

Both FLDS and Orthodox Jewish leadership also employ sweeping clerical controls over their communities in an effort to root out dissent. "Every choice," writes Flora Jessop of FLDS, "in every aspect of life is made for [believers] from birth.... The Priesthood teaches the rules and directives in church and the ideas carry over into school teachings.... The outside world, the Government and its citizens are unwelcome and are considered evil—they are to be ignored or intimidated if they journey into the community's streets."[23] The same jealous control by the clergy of every aspect of one's private life is a feature of Orthodox Judaism as well, as I have shown in previous chapters, and it is buttressed by a virtually identical attitude toward the non–Jewish government and its officers. Nor is this parallel limited to matters of theory. Just as Shomrim groups have enhanced rabbinic power among Orthodox Jews by effectively shifting police functions into Orthodox hands, the FLDS church has filled up the ranks of the police departments in the towns it dominates in order to put physical intimidation behind the decrees of its religious elders. According to another ex-member, Carolyn Jessop, "If a woman tried to escape ... she'd get no help or protection from police," and if a woman reported domestic violence, "the police would always side with the husband." Sound familiar?

The similarities between FLDS and Orthodox Judaism extend even to odd details. Warren Jeffs, for example, banned the wearing of red clothing among the faithful.[24] Many groups of Hasidim have done virtually the same thing: when I lived in Monsey, New York, I found that a large proportion of the Orthodox women believed that wearing red garments of any kind is forbidden by Jewish law, though in fact the proscription is a recent innovation advanced by some Orthodox rabbis.

Most important and ominous of all is the fact that behind this systematized "innocence," ignored by the leadership but grimly persistent, is the large-scale sexual victimization of its children. Jeffs himself allegedly sodomized a five-year-old boy while serving as a teacher and principal. (Note the double violation of Jeffs' own rules, the ban on homosexuality as well as the rigid proscription against all sexual activity among children. We have seen similar patterns in the offenses of many Orthodox Jewish sex abusers.) Child sex abuse in FLDS is so common, according to one former member who described herself as a victim of incest, that by the age of eighteen "she knew twenty girls in her position, just off the top of her head." Such abuse "was normal, so normal that no one ever thought of it as illegal."[25]

Is this pairing of innocence and abuse inevitable because the ideal of "innocence" corresponds to the notion of a radical cleavage between body and soul, and because this makes the child's body, as a counterweight to its putative spiritual purity, seem that much more carnal? Is it because where all sexuality is equated with defilement, the most extreme sort of defilement is also the most sexual, and therefore, for some people at least, the most desirable? Is it just the physical analog of the psychological tyranny the leaders of such communities wield over their followers, the children most of all because they are the most vulnerable? Or all of the above? I don't know how to tease out the separate strands of these poisonous ideas, all of which in any case seem to grow from the same patriarchal roots. I can only see the inevitability of the results.

"We don't have any good statistics on the number of these kids who were sexually molested as children, only stories from those who will talk about it," says an official of Utah's Department of Human Services who has dealt with many young people from FLDS, "but a closed society is more prone to every kind of abuse."[26] Which, as we have seen, is just as true of Orthodox Jewish communities as of the Latter Day Saints.

Even among adults, sexual innocence—at least, what is described as such among religious fundamentalists—is sometimes hard to distinguish from sexist crudity and exploitation. Typical evidence of this is Carolyn Jessop's excruciating description of her own wedding night, at the age of eighteen, to a much older FLDS member at a time when she knew nothing about sex and had "never been that close to a man before and certainly not without my clothes." Jessop's humiliation was intensified by her new husband's conversation the next morning with some male friends of his: he remarked that a new dog was better than a new wife ("they were more loyal"), while one of the men joked in response that marriage was like a bath—"Once you get into it, it's not so hot."[27]

Pretty dreadful, yes? But listen now to the following account—not from an FLDS member but from a young Orthodox Jewish woman, describing the night of her wedding to a very religious *yeshiva* student (whom she later divorced):

> Well, we leave the [wedding] hall, we get into the car. The first thing [my new husband] tells me is, "I want you to know the reason why I chose the Buick Century. The Buick Century is because I measured among other cars and the Buick is higher." And he told me that I have to understand that sometimes boys have urges, that they can't wait until they get home, so the reason why he picked the Buick is that if he ever has an urge, he's able to pull over to the side and just take care of what he needs.[28]

"You can't blame boys for acting that way," one incest victim from FLDS reports being told by one of her stepmothers. "They have a sex drive and that's that."[29] Where sexuality is forced into the Procrustean bed of divided soul-body moralism—temptation versus indulgence, "drives" versus limits—almost any offense looks fairly trivial next to the ubiquitous menace of sexuality itself, which, governed only by a repressive religion's efforts to contain and direct it, is always the real horror as far as the clergy is concerned; exploitation, sexism, incest, abuse, even rape are just a few of its unfortunate but inevitable moltings.

* * *

Behind the ideological parallels between FLDS and Orthodox Judaism lies the irony that the ideal of juvenile "innocence" actually feeds communal indifference toward child sex abuse. Beyond what I have suggested already, one likely reason for this is that "innocence" is coded in patriarchal language as an analog of powerlessness. That point finds particularly obvious expression in the institution of polygamy, in which "innocent" women are required to satisfy the sexual needs of dominant men. It is therefore not surprising to find a rich FLDS father refusing to support his young children after their mother, formerly one of his wives, left him; after all, she and the children were his property, so why should he pay for the kids if they no longer served his needs?[30] But Orthodox Judaism is also no stranger to the patriarchal linkage of carnality with power. The *New York Daily News* reported in 1996, for instance, about a service offering ultra–Orthodox Jewish men the use of Jewish concubines, who, for a fee, would provide sexual gratification in a form sanctioned by the Bible and (so the representatives of the service insisted) by traditional Jewish law as well. The article reported that quite a few Orthodox men, including "lawyers, stockbrokers and diamond merchants," had contacted the service— and some of their recorded comments are worth repeating for what they suggest about the religious teaching these men had evidently absorbed.

"I still don't know what love is," said one caller, "and [my wife and I] never talk about sex because that's how we were raised." "I am a married Hasidic man," said another. "I don't get from my wife what I am supposed to get." Some callers even specified physical details about the concubines they felt they deserved, noting that "they were descended from prominent Hasidic families." It is true that Orthodox rabbis interviewed for the article roundly denounced the idea of a concubine service. But none of them addressed the expressions of status-based sexual entitlement so prominent in the male callers' comments—not to mention in the very idea of concubinage.[31]

Polygamy, likewise frowned on by contemporary rabbinic opinion, is not as far from the Orthodox mainstream as one might prefer to believe. "The rabbis at the Chief Rabbinate receive their salaries from the state," a spokesman for an organization that promotes the revival of polygamy among Orthodox Jews told the *Jerusalem Post*. That, he argued, explained the rabbinate's public opposition to the practice. "But if you ask them behind closed doors, they will say it's allowed." Dov Stein, one Orthodox rabbi who openly supports polygamy, justified it in revealing language. Ideally, a woman should consent to her husband's taking of a second wife. But "[e]ven if a woman doesn't agree," he said, "her husband is not her property, and by law he is not prohibited from having an affair with another woman."[32] Since no Orthodox rabbi would dream of permitting a married woman's affair with another man—Jewish law is extremely severe on that point—Stein's insistence that a married man is not "property" should not be taken as an expression of liberalism. Just the opposite. He takes it for granted that a married woman "belongs" to her husband; and the same thinking, as we have seen, will naturally apply to a man's children as well.

It doesn't take much foresight to predict the consequences of conceptualizing powerless people—women and children—as the property of their men. Flora Jessop—herself an incest victim—argues that the puritanical teachings of FLDS entail a refusal to recognize that children can be abused at all:

> The FLDS polygamist parents don't claim to *discipline* their children; rather, they "encourage to follow God's will" by beatings or deprivation of food, etc. Or adults "reason" with children by confining them to rooms or small spaces for days at a time. Many polygamists do not understand the concept of child abuse. They think they are teaching them.[33]

I have no doubt that Jessop means exactly what she says: these parents "do not understand the concept of child abuse." But how can that be? Ignorance of something so simple, particularly on the part of people who claim to cherish their children's innocence, requires a concomitant denial of the children's humanity. The kids' experience of abuse simply cannot count as human experience—and so abused children are never really abused, no matter what is done to them.

With that in mind, consider the case of Menachem Mendel Levy. A married British Orthodox Jew, Levy went on trial in 2013 for the long-term sexual abuse of a family friend's daughter—abuse that started when the girl was fifteen. Though he admitted his sexual relationship with the girl, Levy was stoutly defended by the prominent Orthodox rabbi Chaim Rapoport, who—ironically enough—was "one of the people [the victim] went to for support when she first decided to reveal the abuse." On the witness stand, Rapoport called Levy the "embodiment of repentance," despite Levy's insistence that he was innocent of any wrongdoing and that his victim had "consented" to an "affair" with him—a married man more than thirteen years her senior.

"When the rabbi was asked what Levy was repenting," reported the *Jewish Chronicle*, "he [Rabbi Rapoport] said it was the breach of trust, and added that in Jewish law: 'The age 15, 16, 16 and a half would be seen as somewhat arbitrary.'"[34] In other words, violating a child is the same as going to bed with a willing adult; it's the perpetrator's perspective that matters, while the child's experience of being abused is "somewhat arbitrary"—which is why, since she must have posed a temptation to her abuser in the first place, the girl cannot really be innocent (and he can't really be guilty). Here a prominent Orthodox rabbi joins the members of FLDS in their inability to "understand the concept of child abuse." But no one is likely to believe that the polished Rapoport was a victim of poor education. His failure to see the obvious stemmed from his refusal to recognize the child victim as someone whose experience deserved even cursory recognition in the context of human rights. And in this respect, an Orthodox rabbi proved to be no better than the acolytes of Warren Jeffs.

Along these lines, I want to comment on an attempt to rationalize the Orthodox rabbinate's indifference to child sexual abuse offered by Dr. Marc Shapiro, Professor of Judaic Studies at the University of Scranton. Shapiro, who is Orthodox, seeks an explanation for "so many cases of covering up and defending child sex abusers" in the idea (suggested to him by a "wise person") that many rabbinic authorities simply don't consider abuse "so terrible" a sin:

> The information they regard as authentic and true ... does not come from modern psychology, but from Torah sources and folk beliefs. If you look only at traditional rabbinic literature, you won't conclude that child sex abuse is as terrible as modern society views it.... How do we know about this trauma? Only from modern psy-

chology and the testimony of the victims. Yet this type of evidence does not have much significance in the insular Hasidic world (unless it is your own child who has been abused). Certainly modern psychology, which is often attacked by figures in the community, is not given much credence....[35]

I have no quarrel with this account, as far as it goes. Modern psychology *is* held up to ridicule in the more insular segments of the Orthodox community, and someone who gets all his childrearing information from the Talmud might not readily recognize the deeper effects of sexual abuse on child victims.

Still, I don't think Shapiro's observations explain much—for two separate reasons. First, the rabbinic indifference to child sex abuse is simply too selective to derive from ignorance alone. For instance, the same rabbis who shrug off questions of child molestation wax hysterical over the idea of Jewish children looking at sexy pictures. A few years ago a *yeshiva* in Passaic, New Jersey (where I live) circulated a video about the dangers of the Internet, in which one of America's foremost Orthodox authorities decried as a "tragedy" the exposure of teenaged children to pornography.[36] The same message was thundered at tens of thousands of Orthodox Jews crammed into New York's Citi Field Stadium in May 2012, where "rabbis ... offered heated exhortations to avoid the 'filth' that can be found on the Internet."[37] An Orthodox email list to which I subscribe has even warned against "inappropriate" pictures lurking on boxes of breakfast cereal. At the annual convention of Agudath Israel of America in 2011, one speaker, Rabbi Avrohom Schorr, fulminated that cell phones with Internet access have "destroyed the [holiness] of [the Jewish people].... They have destroyed families." Awfully strong language over a little skin.[38]

One may well doubt the wisdom of such an obsessive focus on sexuality. But the fact remains that Orthodox rabbis do worry very much about the effects of ordinary pornography on Jewish children. So why not about the effects of sex abuse? If teenagers voluntarily looking at naked pictures is a "tragedy," if it "destroys families" and even "the Jewish people," surely children's sexual violation—in many cases forced on them long before adolescence—must be a terrible crime *a fortiori*. Nor should it require any expertise in psychology to make that connection. Yet the Orthodox rabbinate still refuses to do it: in fact, a brother of the same Rabbi Schorr who anathematized the Internet in 2011, himself a prominent rabbi, has joined other rabbis in support of convicted child rapist Israel Weingarten.[39]

Second, if the rabbinic motive for the cover-ups were rooted in mere ignorance of the harm caused by sex abuse, as Shapiro suggests, rabbinic indifference would not extend to matters affecting children's physical safety. The same rabbis who suppress child sex abuse charges wouldn't look the other way in cases in which the danger to children is beyond any doubt. But, as we have seen in Chapter 5, the Orthodox rabbinate has shown precious little concern about obvious threats to child welfare—as in cases of physical child abuse (even deadly abuse), or the medical danger posed by *m'tzitzah b'peh*—so long as the rabbinate's agenda is advanced and the risk is borne entirely by children. Ignorance alone cannot explain such behavior.

The more reasonable explanation, it seems to me, turns on the refusal to consider the point of view, let alone the needs, of an abused child. That is why the elites in the "modern" wing of Orthodoxy can be as casually cruel as Rabbi Rapoport in their defense of child abusers, even those who don't come from the "insular Hasidic world" Shapiro describes and don't ignore or ridicule psychology. Case in point: the breathtaking smear uttered by Emunah Elon—a woman described in the press as a "journalist and women's rights activist"— after the conviction of her brother-in-law, modern Orthodox Rabbi Mordechai Elon, for sexually assaulting a minor. The Orthodox "women's rights activist" actually blamed the victims for Rabbi Elon's troubles, suggesting that "perhaps there are some children who don't like to be hugged and don't understand what that is." Ms. Elon even chided the court that convicted the rabbi because "it takes it upon itself to read his [Rabbi Elon's] mind and interpret his intentions."

Mind you, this was after testimony that Rabbi Elon had "used force" to pull a young victim onto his lap, where he "continued to touch him suggestively through his clothes and all over his body, while forcibly holding him in place to thwart his resistance," and "then proceeded to rub his penis against [the child's] body ... while forcibly holding him in place by the waist." It seems hardly surprising that the child in question "didn't understand," as Ms. Elon cheerfully put it, that these "hugs were not only not indecent, but highly positive." But of course Ms. Elon knew better than to consider the child's opinion in the first place—and thus aligned herself firmly with the forces of denial and cover-up. As her comments made clear, the only perspective that mattered to her was that of Rabbi Elon; and since a court could not "read his mind," his "intentions" were pure by definition—unlike those of a child, whose experience of being violated was in any case automatically unmentionable.[40] Such an "analysis"—call it "modern," call it whatever you like—doesn't differ an iota from the defenses employed by Israel Weingarten, Nechemya Weberman or Menachem Mendel Levy (who claimed a fifteen-year-old girl "consented" to an "affair" with a married man nearly twice her age). Once the victim's perspective is ruled out of consideration, almost anything goes.

* * *

Psychoanalyst Herbert Strean has observed that his Orthodox Jewish patients display a combination of "arrogance and masochism."[41] According to Flora Jessop, the same combination appears among FLDS believers: "While doctrine taught that they are God's chosen people, they often feel inferior and are afraid of everyone they encounter. On the other hand they also view themselves as being far superior to the rest of the world and consider themselves above man's laws."[42] These findings have an ominous ring to me, because Strean links the arrogance-masochism dyad to the habit of such religious believers to see themselves as children in relation to God:

> The more omnipotent we make God, the more impotent and helpless we become. If God is everything in our minds, *we regard ourselves as next to nothing.* Inasmuch as the Orthodox Jewish God influences and controls every facet of living, the Orthodox Jew feels extremely vulnerable without His or Her protection. Consequently, Orthodox Jews, *like helpless children,* must summon God many times a day in order to feel some safety and security.... [At the same time,] [b]ecause Orthodox Jews ... need God so desperately, they have also assigned themselves the role and status of "God's Chosen People."[43]

Notice that in this analysis the fundamental Orthodox assumption of being "God's Chosen People" entails the result that children, the better to serve as metaphors for the chosen, must be "helpless" and constitute "next to nothing"—particularly as against God, represented for the faithful by an Orthodox rabbi. If it is essential for religious Jews to see themselves as "helpless children" in order to be saved and protected by their God-like rabbis, then their own safety is jeopardized whenever they acknowledge that children should not be "helpless," should mean more than "next to nothing"; recognizing children's fundamental rights, in other words, threatens the basis of the only security promised by their religion. People whose emotional needs depend upon denying children's humanity have a strong incentive to keep on doing just that.

Then, too, from a patriarchal point of view children are inextricably bound up with sexuality, of which they are the product, so that granting children their independence implicitly denies their parents control over their own sexual lives—an intolerable result. We find such ideas haunting the mind of Flaubert, who jotted down these thoughts about the inadequacies of Western men of letters, including himself:

> What we lack is the intrinsic principle, the soul of the thing, the very idea of the subject. We take notes, we make journeys: emptiness! emptiness! ... Where is the heart, the verve, the sap? Where to start from? Where to go? We're good at sucking, we play a lot of tongue-games, we pet for hours: but the real thing! To ejaculate, beget the child![44]

Eroticism without ejaculation is "emptiness," and ejaculation too is ultimately functional: procreation is the ultimate test of "good" sex, which in turn stands for "good" life. We can see how the reversal of this perspective means that children symbolize sexual success. But children cannot stand for that and stand for themselves at the same time.

In light of such ideas, maybe it's inevitable that the same Orthodox Jewish leadership that is profoundly threatened by the rights of abused children is scared silly about sexuality itself. I have already mentioned the extraordinary anti–Internet rally in May 2012, at which some 40,000 Orthodox Jews squeezed into New York's Citi Field Stadium to be harangued by rabbis about the dangers of freely available sexual material—an orgy of shame and fear-mongering during which not a word was uttered about the sexual victimization of children. Orthodox psychologist Michael J. Salamon argued that the real issue behind the rabbinate's assault on the Internet was the preservation of its own authority: "By having a following that will make no decisions on its own, the ruler sets the tone."[45] Doubters of Salamon's interpretation need only note the hysterical tone the rabbis chose to set. An ultra–Orthodox advertising campaign in Israel has blamed the Internet for causing cancer—and as if that weren't enough, the rabbis claimed it brings on droughts as well. In 2009, when the influential Council of Torah Sages condemned web sites specifically designed for Orthodox Jews—with content to match—their propaganda accused even these sanitized sites of spreading "slander, lies, and impurities" and of leading innocent readers to "the vilest of places."[46] Such hyperbole gives away the game: when rabbis blame cancer on the Internet, they're clearly being less than honest about their real worries. And when they identify "slander and lies" (that is, criticism of the rabbinate) with the "impurities" found in "the vilest of places," they're virtually admitting what those worries are. And what they aren't. Where rabbinic supremacy is the *summum bonum*, the rights of children aren't likely to make it onto the agenda.

As, indeed, they seldom do. Judy Brown correctly diagnosed the whopping imbalance between rabbinic anti–Internet theatrics and the Orthodox leadership's silence about child sex abuse as follows:

> The Citifield rally is so important to the community because it is another form of denial, another excuse they can point to. It allows them to avoid confronting the most dangerous enemy of all: themselves. The Internet does not molest, only people do; they always have. But if they [the rabbis] can just persist [in] blaming internal problems on evil outside forces they can continue to remain blind to what they refuse to see: themselves.[47]

Brown had earlier given the same reason for writing her novel *Hush*: "We [in the Orthodox community] forgot [to] look inside, to see that the most dangerous enemy always grows from within."[48] Hence the see-saw relation between talking about abuse on one side, and rabbinic anti–Internet fervor on the other. As long as the community's discourse focuses on "temptations" from without, it enhances rabbinic power. But if, instead, Orthodox Jews start thinking about victims of abuse as the real locus of concern, they will never again be able to regard themselves as "helpless children"—nor their rabbis as larger-than-life saviors. And the old patterns of power may well collapse.

Almost as if to prove Brown's point, rabbinic leadership followed up the Citi Field rally not with expressions of concern about child sex abuse but with full-throated support for "moral purity." A fundraising letter for something called "Guard Your Eyes" declaimed in September 2012: "There's never been a more serious problem in Klal Yisrael's Kedusha [the Jewish people's holiness] than which we have now.... This plague has spared no class of Jews, no one is immune." Plague? Worst ever? No class spared? One might have supposed the authors were addressing something akin to the Nazi genocide of the 1940s. But no. The "global scourge" the eye-guardians had in mind, the "affliction" that was "destroying more people's marriages and Yidishkeit [Judaism] than almost anything else today," was the access offered by the Internet to pictures of attractive women. At least that's what one surmises: the authors couldn't bring themselves to name the "plague," though they confessed it was made available through Internet access.

But what about child sex abuse—mightn't the "guardians" have had a word to say on a subject so serious? Heaven forbid. In fact, the organizers of the Citi Field rally had chosen Rabbi Moshe Green to open the event with a reading from the Book of Psalms. A year earlier, according to child abuse activist Rabbi Nuchem Rosenberg (see Chapter 6), Green had publicly claimed that the murder of a young Hasidic boy in Brooklyn represented divine retribution against those Orthodox rabbis who "informed" on child rapist Israel Weingarten.[49] Not that the choice of Green as spokesman should have surprised anyone: the co-founder of the organization that orchestrated the rally, Rabbi Mattisyahu Salomon,[50] had already praised his fellow Orthodox clergymen for sweeping child sex abuse charges "under the carpet."

An observer who can sit through this theater of the absurd—if he or she cares at all about sex abuse cover-ups among Orthodox Jews—is inevitably struck by the recurring theme behind all these tales, one that unmistakably links sexuality with power and control. Seen from that point of view, I suppose sexuality is bound to frighten the rabbinate, as it does the guardians of every totalitarian orthodoxy, not only for what it is but for the privacy of its pleasures, so free of control from above, so heedless of party disciplines. We owe this insight to George Orwell, who suggested a "direct, intimate connection" between the fear of sex and political repression.[51] Some years ago, a Hasid who spoke with me unwittingly made Orwell's point. He explained why some men in his community, on rabbinic advice, disabled the tuning dials of their wives' radios—so that they could only listen to a pre-approved local station run by Orthodox Jews—commenting that this was important because otherwise the women would listen to "ads for sexy things, or hear people talking about things that would give them ideas." Why the men in his community were presumed to be free from the danger of such "ideas" was not explained. As for what empowered the rabbis to decide which thoughts should be thinkable, or why a married couple's sexuality must be subject to rabbinic controls—these were questions that I'm sure had never occurred to this man. In matters of power, as in those of sexuality, he was "innocent": just as his rabbis had doubtless intended.

*   *   *

I should not end this chapter without commenting on the most popular justifications offered within the Orthodox community for the sexual restrictions I have identified in connection with "innocence," as the leadership calls it. The most important of these is articulated, for instance, by Rabbi Avi Shafran in a column I have already cited, in which he claims that "human inclinations are harnessed and controlled by Torah-life and Torah study," with the result that "a Torah-observant life does not lead to aberrant behavior; it helps to prevent it."[52] The theory, in short, holds that placing sexuality under manifold religious restrictions "helps to prevent" abusive or otherwise harmful sexual behavior.

Unfortunately for the rabbinate, there appears to be no correlation between the complexity or severity of religious prohibitions and lowered rates of sexual misconduct. In fact, "a 1999 study shows that individuals who are extrinsically religious are at greater risk for being perpetrators of child physical abuse than those who are intrinsically religious."[53] Since the "extrinsically religious" are driven mostly by "social or external values and beliefs," while "intrinsically religious persons are deeply committed to religious beliefs and values" they themselves hold,[54] it follows that the kind of religious prescriptions offered by Orthodox Jewish leadership—detailed rules, obedience to (external) instruction, conformity with accepted group norms—are not, in themselves, likely to reduce the number of believers who abuse children.

Another popular idea among Orthodox Jews is that maintaining children's "innocence"—that is, strictly suppressing their knowledge of sexual matters—is the only way to protect them from the increasingly obtrusive prurience of the modern world. "The secular world has become so crass when it comes to images and references related to sexuality," as Debra Nussbaum Cohen puts it, that "the *frum* [Orthodox community] has come to treat anything related to sexuality as 'treyf' [non-*kosher*]." But Nussbaum Cohen herself deftly critiques this view, pointing out that when "bodies are treated as a source of fear or anxiety ... it's no wonder that parents have a hard time educating their children to have positive relationships with their bodies." And she adds: "Of course banning secular publications, television, movies and the internet from haredi homes has done nothing to stanch the corrosive effects of sexually dysfunctional behavior of pedophiles in that community."[55]

I don't think anyone can dispute the accuracy of what she says—and if a theory of sexuality does nothing to protect children from abuse, and is likely instead to poison their sex lives (a crucial part of their "relationships with their bodies"), I do not see how the theory can be defended. Surely a more rational approach would be to encourage the development in children of healthy, independent sexuality as a protection against the predators who are bound to pullulate somewhere in every community. But Orthodoxy shows no signs of moving in that direction. If anything, it is seeking the opposite extreme. In the course of an amusing broadside against ultra–Orthodox Jews, an Israeli writer relates this anecdote: as an ultra–Orthodox mother and her seventeen-year-old son leave a doctor's office, the mother confesses to the boy the doctor's fear that the boy may not be able to have children. "How can the doctor know that?" asks the teenager—after all, "he doesn't know who I'm going to marry.... It's the woman who has the children, not the man." When the mother remarks obliquely, "I thought you knew about these things already—after all, you're a big boy," her son replies—"with tears in his eyes," according to the chronicler—"I don't know what it is I don't know, and I don't want to know!" To which his mother answers, "Good!!"[56]

The *tessitura* of popular debate on this aspect of the issue has so far drowned out what I consider its most important feature. The press has singled out the alleged effects of such repression on abusers—as if their sex drives, blocked in more natural directions, have turned toward children as a more or less inevitable alternative.[57] I remain much more concerned with the impact of repression *on the children exposed to pedophiles.* Is it wise—is it just—to leave children with naturally developing libidos unequipped with a corresponding sexual knowledge? Too many Orthodox children may one day level at their parents the same charge as the eponymous hero of E.M. Forster's *Maurice,* after a well-meaning schoolmaster crams the boy's sex education into one parting lecture on an English beach: "'Liar,' he thought. 'Liar, coward, he's told me nothing.'"[58]

I'm also far from certain that the artificial sexual purity imposed on Orthodox Jewish children is not part of a community-wide obsession with appearances. It has been reported, just for instance, that despite evidence that the rate of eating disorders among young Orthodox Jewish women far exceeds that of the general population, their families rarely seek help for them unless their condition has so far deteriorated that they require hospitalization— because, says one prominent rabbi, women must be "as flawless as possible" to marry "well." An eating disorder "would be a terrible, terrible blemish and people will go to unbelievable lengths to hide it."[59] A young person's sexual "blemish"—that is, any sort of sexual history—would be likely to receive similar treatment in a sex-averse religious society.

It is worth noting, too, that the very idea of childhood innocence is a relatively modern one, and that it arose in the Victorian context of sexual guilt. Its filigreed curtain should not screen us, therefore, from the real attitudes toward children implicit in much religious tradition. Fear, anxiety and resentment are far more often the emotions we can intuit behind what moralists over the centuries have written about children—as in the case of St. Augustine, who in a famous passage indicted even newborn infants for mortal sins:

> Who can recall to me the sins I committed as a baby? For in your [God's] sight no man is free from sin, not even a child who has lived only one day on earth.... So then too I deserved a scolding for what I did [as an infant]; but since I could not have understood the scolding, it would have been unreasonable, and most unusual, to rebuke me. We root out these faults and discard them as we grow up, and this is proof enough that they are faults.... This shows that, if babies are innocent, it is not for lack of will to do harm, but for lack of strength.
>
> I have myself seen jealousy in a baby and know what it means. He was not old enough to talk, but whenever he saw his foster-brother at the breast, he would grow pale with envy.... [S]urely it cannot be called innocence, when the milk flows in such abundance from its source, to object to a rival desperately in need and depending for his life on this one form of nourishment?[60]

We may smile at such an analysis today, ensconced as we are in the framework of a more informed developmental psychology. But it is deeply disturbing to realize how many educated and well-intentioned people once took it seriously, just as it is unnerving to read about the inadvertent infliction of what can only be called sexual abuse on the most pampered child inhabiting the most self-consciously civilized court in Europe just four centuries ago. Here is an account of the early childhood of the prince who—as "the first son born to a King of France in more than eighty years"—was considered so precious that literally nothing was too good for him:

> By the age of three—and perhaps earlier—[the boy] knew very clearly what bastards were and in what manner they were fabricated. The language in which this information was communicated was so consistently coarse that the child was often shocked by it.... [T]he Prince's attendants, male and female, liked to joke obscenely with the child about his father's bastards and his own future wife.... Moreover, the Dauphin's sexual education was not merely verbal. At night the child would often be taken into the beds of his waiting women—beds which they shared (without nightdresses or pajamas) either with other women or their husbands. It seems likely enough that, by the time he was four or five, the little boy knew all the facts of life, and knew them not merely by hearsay, but by inspection.[61]

This tawdry tale describes the upbringing of the most privileged child at the center of one of the 17th century's most advanced societies. While we have no record of Jewish children being subjected to similar treatment during that period, there is no reason to believe that the general assumptions Jews made about the needs of children were radically different from those of their neighbors, royal or otherwise. Nor have those patriarchal assumptions died out over the last few centuries. They have been chastened, yes—but at the same time, they have gained new life under the guise of protecting "purity." For as Joel Engelman's case reminds us, a child's innocence is at best a double-edged theory: it can be used to vilify him for being less than innocent, to justify beating him to keep "impurities" out.[62] And when that child complains of a very real violation of his sexual innocence—molestation by a rabbi, say—the same people who boast of protecting his purity are the ones who ignore or malign him.

* * *

Judy Brown is not alone in saying (in a passage I quoted earlier) that the Orthodox community is willing to "sacrifice" its children to the community's preferred self-image, an act of violence rationalized as religious service. Alas, the imagery of sacrifice in such a connection has a long religious history. Here is Bunyan proclaiming his spiritual escape from "the world":

> I must first pass a sentence of death upon everything that can properly be called a thing of this life, even to reckon myself, my wife, my children ... as dead to me, and myself to them....

It was not easy for Bunyan to write those words. As always, he lived what he wrote, and for him the sacrifice was an agonizing one. But he made it nonetheless:

> The parting with my wife and my poor children hath often been to me as the pulling of my flesh from my bones, especially my poor blind child who lay nearer my heart than all I had besides. Poor child, thought I, what sorrow art thou like to have for thy portion in this world! Thou must be beaten, must beg, suffer hunger, cold, nakedness, and a thousand calamities, though I cannot now endure that the wind should blow upon thee. But yet I must venture you all with God....[63]

There can be no question about Bunyan's sincerity, nor about the intensity of his feelings. One's difficulty with this passage (and hundreds like it) is a moral one. Why should a Godly life entail abandoning one's children to "a thousand calamities?" Why not suppose that God prefers his servant to cherish and protect the human beings who depend on him? Doesn't the dilemma Bunyan posits rest on the equation of one's children (and one's wife) with inanimate "things of this life"—implicitly setting love for them *against* the spirit, instead of assuming the harmony of love with Love?

It is not my business to determine other people's theology for them. But I think that as long as we in the Orthodox Jewish community accept the logic of Bunyan's position, we will have to admit, as he did, that our children are not altogether human to us—that in the final analysis they are mere "things" that a pure soul inevitably leaves behind, as it leaves behind its clothes and its jewels, on the way to God. And I do not see how such an admission can be squared with the sentimental view that a religiously-grounded notion of "innocence" is meant to protect children. On the contrary, it proves that what we demand of our children is intended for *our* religious benefit, not theirs[64]; that their "innocence" is just one component of the suffering we impose on them in order to reap the divine rewards of our "sacrifice." To claim any other meaning for the Orthodox Jewish view of children's "innocence," it seems to me, is sheer hypocrisy.

You needn't take my word for this. Just look at the public claims of Orthodox rabbis and their spokesmen. In 2012, nearly fifty of New York's Orthodox rabbis—including the highly influential Yisrael Belsky—signed a public statement denouncing a candidate for New York State Senate because his support for legalizing same-sex marriage and related gay rights meant "destroying the innocence of ... children from the earliest age." Meanwhile, his opponent—an Orthodox Jew who was obviously the intended beneficiary of the rabbis' attack—proudly championed *m'tzitzah b'peh*, which endangers the lives of infants, as one of "the cultural traditions of my faith."[65] Comment is superfluous.

But I think we owe the most brutal illumination of the true meaning of sexual "innocence" to right-wing flack and Orthodox Jewish publicist Dennis Prager.[66] In a column published in July 2013, Prager took aim at educators who stealthily pursue what he called "an agenda to deprive children of their innocence." Just how do they go about this "innocence killing" (Prager's phrase)? According to him, one of their worst tactics is teaching children *about the danger of sexual harassment and abuse.* Prager was particularly incensed that a child, participating in the Democratic National Convention in 2000, had expressed hope that "when I grow up" children will no longer be "wrongfully touched." In Prager's analysis, aspirations like those mean the "robbing of children's innocence by prematurely sexualizing them."[67]

So there you have it. Abusing children doesn't rob them of their innocence; trying to stop the abuse does. Raping a child doesn't "sexualize" her (after all, her perspective is irrelevant). Teaching her she has a right to control her own body constitutes the crime that child sexual abuse doesn't.

The Pragers of the world may choose to believe that Orthodoxy, like "innocence," is threatened by "liberals," but the real enemy of such teaching is reality itself. Ignorance is not innocence; on the contrary, it goes hand in hand with cruelty and vulgarity, and the rabbis most intent on trying to persuade us otherwise are the living proof of it. I will never forget the story of a teenaged girl who told me about her long years of sexual violation at the hands of a family member—who still lives in one of America's most deeply Orthodox enclaves. Repeatedly molested since early childhood, she had to watch as her abuser was married with the blessings of the town's leading rabbis, including some who knew all about his history but refused to tell the truth, even to his new bride. After all, that would have been indelicate. Meanwhile, the girl told me, when she tried to share her agony with one prominent rabbi, he counseled against reporting the sex crimes she had suffered to the police; and he wanted to know, "Did you enjoy it?"

Whenever I remember that girl's face, her voice, her story—and I think of that respected rabbi's obscene reaction to it all—I know that what Flora Jessop says about FLDS is just as true of the Orthodox rabbis who claim to care so much about the innocence of children. "These children," she says, "are not children, but currency.... If you think your religion gives you a right to rape children, then your religion needs to be burned to the ground."[68]

Out of the Closet

To live in a world where men do not love, where they cheat and are callous, is to sink into a preoccupation with death, and to see the futility of anything except virtue.

—John Howard Griffin[1]

"When a phrase is born," wrote Isaac Babel, "it is both good and bad at the same time. The secret of its success rests in a crux that is barely discernible. One's fingertips must grasp the key, gently warming it. And then the key must be turned once, not twice."[2]

I can grasp the key to some of the darkest rooms of my memory, where good and bad live side by side in nearly identical phrases, by visiting "a tiny village only one mile long," a religious enclave "tucked away in the rural hills of Orange County," as television reporter Tara Rosenblum earnestly described the scene. Buried in that unlikely place—Kiryas Joel, New York—a secret hoard of suffering and survival has been preserved, like a moth in amber, in a news video that Rosenblum narrated in 2010. In less than nine minutes, even through the crude glare of the reporting style, one gets unforgettable glimpses of the worst, and the best, in my Orthodox coreligionists as they face the smoldering trauma of child sexual abuse.[3]

The side-by-side contradictions start with the place itself. Kiryas Joel's uniformly Hasidic society strikes some outsiders as comfortingly old-fashioned, others as grotesque. Even its name is problematic. Rosenblum couldn't manage to pronounce it as the natives do: her version was something like "Keer-yahs Jo-*el*," while the Hasidim, whose English is inflected by their traditional Yiddish, shift the accents and soften all but the first consonant, so that it comes out as "*Kiry*us Yoyl." No short pants are allowed in this holy place, no sleeveless dresses, no bare feet—all this is announced on a large, red-lettered sign visible to anyone entering the village. Other prohibitions are left to the imagination. But what does it all mean? A fence to protect "modesty"— or to conceal a rotten core?

For 36-year-old Shlomo Weiss, who grew up in Kiryas Joel, questions like that are tangled so tightly that it takes all the courage of his honesty to sever truth from falsehood. But he says he will no longer conceal the torment of his childhood, during which he was sexually abused for years by his father, a school bus driver.

Rosenblum's camera unravels the fabric of Weiss's suffering: the rabbis' denial, and then, speaking the same language, wearing the same clothes, a glimpse of light. Yes, says the victim's former teacher—a long-bearded man who gestures like a satrap—yes, he remembers Shlomo's story. But, "You can't just accuse a man just because someone says so." No less infuriating is the complacent smirk on the face of Ari Felberman, Kiryas Joel's public relations director (yes, this holy town has a public relations director) when he tells Rosenblum, "There's no cover-up in this community whatsoever." Felberman claims that Weiss never told a rabbi he had been abused—though of course Weiss's own teacher had already conceded, on camera, that he did. He questions whether a man's memory of his own sexual violation can be trusted after nineteen years. And finally, he says, closing the subject, "There may be an agenda."

Against the pious cowardice of the schoolteacher, against Felberman's smooth deceit, the survivor's words stand out like a welt.

"Any living creature should not suffer one percent that I suffered," he says. Now beyond vengeance or despair, he can only wonder at what he has experienced: "I had no idea if this is something wrong, if this happens to everybody, if I have a right to reject...."

He was seven years old when the abuse started. He describes himself as often crying uncontrollably, imagining that "everybody could see it on my face." Now he knows who was really at fault, but the local rabbis are no more willing to face the truth now than they were in his childhood.

"They have blood on their hands," he tells Rosenblum, but his tone is regretful rather than bitter. He has done his best; he has given the rabbis a chance to atone, and they have shirked it—their problem more than his.

Weiss keeps his dignity even when he confronts his father, outside the house he grew up in and has not seen in nearly two decades. "I just want you to get some help," Weiss tells the stocky, bearded, black-hatted man, from whose lips a cigarette nearly falls to the ground when he realizes what is being said and that a camera is recording him. In Kiryas Joel? The older man flees from the sidewalk to the privacy of his house, slamming the window shut so even the reporter can't reach him. But his son is not angry. He has done what he set out to do. The words cannot be erased now, and neither can he. Judging from his face, Shlomo Weiss is relieved, almost elated.

"I just—I just became human, that's all," he tells Rosenblum.

He looks out through the narrow lenses of his spectacles as if astonished by a familiar world. "It's something I've been looking all my life," he says. "For *all* my life."

*   *   *

Ilan Pappé, the Israeli historian and activist, reminds us that Jewish tradition is not only, or even primarily, a tale of oppressive hierarchies. "The wealth of Jewish thought and interpretation could, and did, produce a more humanist and universalist view of the world," Pappé writes. "Indeed, religion can be, and has been ... the bedrock for cosmopolitanism, socialism and universalism."[4] Just as tragedy and victory in Shlomo Weiss's story are held apart by a few simple words, a consciously humane reading of the same religious tradition that has thrown a shadow over the lives of too many child victims can rain down justice on their abusers. It was Isaiah, not a modern victims' advocate, who championed the powerless in words well known to all observant Jews:

> Bring no more vain offerings;
>> incense is an abomination to me.
> New moon and sabbath and the calling of assemblies—
>> I cannot endure iniquity and solemn assembly.
> Your new moon and your appointed feasts
>> my soul hates;
> they have become a burden to me,
>> I am weary of bearing them.
> When you spread forth your hands,
>> I hide my eyes from you;
> even though you make many prayers,
>> I no longer listen;
>> your hands are full of blood.
> Wash yourselves, make yourselves clean;
>> remove the evil of your doings
>> from before my eyes;
> cease to do evil,
>> learn to do good;
> seek justice,
>> correct oppression;
> defend the fatherless,
>> plead for the widow.[5]

This attack on official religious society, pulsing with fury at its cruel indifference and its empty piety alike, is "traditional" enough to be incorporated into the Orthodox Jewish service for the annual Day of Atonement; and it is radical enough to be embraced by Walter Kaufmann, author of *The Faith of a Heretic*.[6] Here the key need not even be turned—only grasped. And not only here. The passion that animates the Hebrew prophets generated echoes in the Talmud, too, where we learn that the act of dispensing justice is inseparable from divine law. So much so that a student must contradict his teacher if he knows a valid argument that will help a poor man in a dispute with a rich one. Where justice is concerned, favoritism and deference are anathema, hierarchies meaningless.[7]

Given traditions like these, it would be wrongheaded to hold everyone under the sway of Judaism responsible for the sins of its contemporary leadership. Such an approach is not only unfair to those who never had the power to mold the system in the first place; it also stands in the way of needed action. As Hannah Arendt reminds us, "Where all are guilty, no one is; confessions of collective guilt are the best possible safeguard against the discovery of culprits, and the very magnitude of the crime the best excuse for doing nothing."[8]

We can do something. Child sex abuse is not a secret, and there is no mystery about the first steps we can take to better protect children from it, beginning with the consistent prosecution of the culprits. Other steps are equally obvious. Dr. Neustein and I discussed several of these in an earlier essay[9]; I will briefly recapitulate them here. Orthodox laity should take its lead from the Catholic clergy scandal and refuse, as a body, to entrust the problem of child sex abuse to the rabbinate. After all, only when Catholic abuse survivors formed their own organization (Survivors Network of those Abused by Priests), and used it to warn other victims away from Church officials—directing them instead to "therapists, trusted friends and family members," and, of course, to services offered by the survivors' organization itself—did they begin to crack the institutional wall of silence.[10]

Once Orthodox Jewish abuse survivors cross the same hurdle, they will be able to exert political pressure on the secular justice system to do its work properly. Of course, they will be doing this without rabbinic help, but I suspect they will find plenty of support from the rank and file. Many jurisdictions have some version of New York's Executive Law § 642(1), which specifies that a "victim of a violent felony offense," or, if the victim is a minor, "the family of the victim," must "be consulted by the district attorney in order to obtain the view of the victim regarding disposition of the criminal case by dismissal." This provision has been honored more in the breach than the observance by the Brooklyn District Attorney when it comes to Orthodox Jewish sex abuse— which is why the dropping of abuse charges in cases like those of Solomon Hafner and Yehuda Kolko came as shocks to the complainants, and could not receive adequate treatment in the press until after each decision was already a *fait accompli*. When Jewish communities bypass their rabbis to demand the enforcement of the law—including the victims' right to consultation by nervous or reluctant prosecutors—the victims will stand a far better chance of getting the justice they deserve.

Speaking of justice, it isn't enough—as every reader of this book knows—to punish the offenders. Those responsible for the cover-ups can and should be criminally prosecuted, too. Charges may be filed under state law—for obstruction of justice, witness tampering, etc.—or under federal civil rights law, which makes it a crime to conspire to "injure, oppress, threaten, or intimidate any person in any State ... in the free exercise or enjoyment of any right or privilege secured to him by the Constitution or laws of the United States,"[11] and equally a crime to "attempt[] to injure, intimidate or interfere with ... any person because of his race, color, religion or national origin" in that person's attempt to take advantage of a benefit of state law, "by force or threat of force."[12] Since recourse to the criminal justice system is a right guaranteed by the federal Constitution,[13] and the use of state police and prosecutors is among the benefits of state law, these criminal statutes are directly relevant to cover-ups in which Orthodox leaders intimidate victims or witnesses, particularly if their tactics include the threatened use of force. It is true that previous applications of the latter statute have always assumed that the culprit and the victim are of *different* religions or ethnicity. But that assumption is not built into the law, and—as Jewish abuse victims know all too well—they are, in fact, singled out for intimidation by rabbis *because of their religion*: if they were not Jewish, they would not be subject to the law against "informing" on a Jew. It follows logically that they should be entitled to the same legal protection as anyone else who is turned away from the police because of his religion (or race, or whatever). By the same token, states that are supposed to offer protection to crime victims who may be subject to threats or pressure—New York is one of them[14]—ought to offer that protection to people who are likely to be pressured not by gangland enforcers but by Orthodox rabbis, or those loyal to them. Such people need it; and under much-neglected law they have a right to demand it.

All this and more can be done. I prefer not to dwell here on the specifics of possible legal reforms, however, because it should be clear to anyone that the crux of the problem is not to be found in the language of the penal codes. If the members of Orthodox Jewish communities were using their political influence to demand justice for abused children, prosecutors—who, as a rule, are neither foolish nor incompetent—would be adopting the right legal strategies as a matter of course.

The real problem is that in the present state of affairs these officials have nothing to gain, and a good deal to lose, if they pursue Orthodox Jewish child abusers and their protectors to the full extent of the law. And that is because the victims' communities are *not* demanding justice; instead, they are leaving the child sex abuse issue in the hands of a leadership that is demonstrably unable or unwilling to approach the task with even a modicum of honest effort—for reasons I have tried to analyze. Our task, therefore, is to change the political dynamics that have inverted the proper role between the rabbinate and the community it serves. In the process, we will be attacking a set of toxic assumptions that have made Orthodox Jewish neighborhoods among the safest places in the United States to abuse children—something clearly worth fighting over.

To achieve this will not be easy. Political reform seldom is. Further, in this instance we will have to braid together political activism in two distinct segments of the public. A successful campaign will require not only reformist pressure from within, but the harnessing of resistance from people outside the Orthodox Jewish community who are, nevertheless, injured in the general institutional derangement that accompanies the protection of Orthodox criminals. Taxpayers of all religions, for instance, are unwittingly subsidizing Shomrim patrols, which receive money from local government while interfering with the law. Citizens of all religions are affected when an entire community is encouraged to ignore its legal obligations toward society as a whole, which (as I have tried to show) is part of the legacy of a rabbinate that uses discriminatory teaching against non–Jews—and the fear that goes with it—as an excuse for abuse cover-ups. Part of the job of political reform will be learning to address not just the stake of our own community but the shared interest of a broader public in the healthier treatment of child abuse within Orthodox Jewish society.

I do not think I am minimizing the difficulty of the task ahead. On the other hand, I think that in standing up for the rights of children—and for all of us—the religious community will discover that it is stronger than it knew, that it is not doomed to be sacrificed to rabbinic fiats or to patriarchal paranoia, but that its individual members, children included, have rights that can be enforced and value that cannot be eliminated. We can take the point a step further. If it is true, as apologists for the status quo apparently fear, that an end to sex abuse cover-ups will transform Orthodox Jewish society, the fact that the change is seen as a threat is one more reason for demanding it. A social structure can only improve when it coexists with the rights of children. And a social structure whose nature is inconsistent with the rights of children has no moral claim on us to begin with.

*   *   *

Beyond the achievement of institutional reforms lie deeper questions about religion, and about its relation to matters of abuse and victimhood. Here, obviously, I must address myself primarily to religious people; but similar questions are bound to confront anyone who participates in institutions ostensibly dedicated to matters of principle. How do the values we promote actually affect the victims and the perpetrators of sex crimes? To the extent we care about such things, and in light of the problems I have been describing, I think those of us who are committed to traditional Judaism would do well to take a fresh look at Jewish teaching, with a view to reclaiming what is best in it from what is harmful or absurd.

The details of such an analysis are beyond the scope of this book. But a preliminary word may be in order, because defenders of the status quo sometimes try to minimize the problem of sex abuse cover-ups by pointing to the diversity of opinion contained within the religious tradition. I myself have stressed, for instance (in Chapter 9), that teachings solidly within the bounds of traditional Orthodoxy demand an approach to sex abuse reporting that is seriously at odds with the rabbinate's current policy. But the kind of examination I am suggesting here is subtler and more profound than choosing one line of rabbinic thought over another. To illustrate, let us consider one statement of principle issued by one outstanding figure in contemporary Orthodox Judaism—appropriately, a statement pertaining to an ethic of sexuality. The late Rabbi Joseph B. Soloveitchik, known as a doctrinal liberal as well as a brilliant and influential Talmudic scholar, declared it the duty of religious Jews "to influence the non–Jewish world, to redeem it from an orgiastic way of living, from cruelty and insensitivity, to arouse in mankind a sense of justice and fairness." These were doubtless meant to be soaring words—and they do contain the germ of something genuinely revolutionary. But it seems to me that the ideals at issue are tarnished by the vagaries of a moralist who, on the one hand, was prepared to identify all non–Jews with "an orgiastic way living" and, on the other hand, saw no "cruelty and insensitivity" in preaching that homosexuals are sinners, and that the humanity of gay people is asserted today only because "it's quite in vogue to be heretical."[15] I can understand the claim of the traditionally religious person that God's commands take precedence over every other consideration. And I can see how accepting such a claim might allow someone to justify acts of cruelty—on the grounds that they are divinely mandated. But that isn't a way of eliminating or combating cruelty, as Soloveitchik claimed; on the contrary, it guarantees a place for cruelty in a moral universe.

Salvaging the best from the dross in pronouncements like this one requires a critique that is respectful and radical at the same time—no small achievement. But I do not see any other course open to someone who values the claims made by traditional religion. If we devote ourselves to what is supposed to be an ideal law, surely that devotion should spur us to rid the law of cruelty wherever we can. And it seems to me we can do more than that. At its best, a genuine religious consciousness can do much to awaken every level of

Jewish society from what C.S. Lewis called "the slumber of cold vulgarity"[16]—
of which children are all too often the unnoticed victims. As, for instance,
during the so-called Jewish State's recent military assault on Gaza in November
2012—an attack that killed over a hundred Palestinian civilians, thirty of them
children[17]—during which an Israeli government minister said publicly that "a
tear of a Jewish child is worth more than all the suffering of the people of
Gaza."[18] Where is the prophetic fury over that cynical and racist manipulation
of family feeling? To take another example, where are the protests from the
Jewish community about "supermarket aisles lined with pet food while twelve
million children in the United States lack sufficient nutriments to sustain
growth and development"?[19] Where is the outrage of the Jewish public at an
Israeli Justice Minister and a Supreme Court President when a newspaper
reports that the two are "siding" with a judge publicly accused of beating his
own children?[20]

Seeking the best from our religion also means making the right sort of
demands on our religious leadership. If our rabbis are taking sides against children—and they are—our protests against them cannot be occasional and
anonymous; until we are unequivocal about where *we* stand, the same patterns
are likely to continue. In 2013, as this book was being completed, Kelly Myzner
lost custody of her young children to a Hasidic husband credibly accused of
abusing them in the deeply Orthodox enclave of Monsey, New York. The judge
not only penalized Myzner for having left the Hasidic lifestyle but "berated"
her, according to a news report, for having taken pictures of a welt on her
oldest son's genitals, which appeared while the boy was with his father. (He
reportedly said that his father had bitten him there.) But then, the judge was
an elected official in a county "where the Orthodox Jewish community has a
large population that votes as a bloc"; what is more, the judge reportedly raised
nearly $125,000 from the Hasidim in her judicial campaign. "When a parent
leaves the chasidic lifestyle, the community comes together to keep that parent
away from the children, in any way possible," according to Shulem Deen, who
left Hasidism years ago "and is now estranged from his own five children,"
reports the *Jewish Week*.[21] I have heard no organized protest from the Orthodox
Jewish public about its leadership's evident priorities in this or similar cases,
although I do note one hopeful fact: the Myzner story did get reported. As I
described in Chapter 3, an article I wrote for the *Jewish Week* in 1997 about
an Orthodox Jewish custody case with eerily similar facts (though that case
arose in Brooklyn) never saw the light of day.[22]

People who care about their religion must care about the effects of its
teaching. There is evidence that the effects of Orthodox Judaism may be felt
in widening circles of society at large, and in more than one country. We have
seen how rabbinic influence has corrupted the functioning of the secular justice

system in one of the largest cities of the United States. Orthodoxy also plays an important role in the government of the Middle East's most powerful country. Rabbinic influence over matters of Israeli social policy is too well documented to require any elaboration here. Let me mention one other example that received hardly any media attention in this country—most likely for the sort of reasons I discussed at length in Chapter 3. Ehud Olmert, a former prime minister, was forced out of Israeli politics by corruption charges for which he was tried in 2012. But the case against him largely unwound when the government's star witness admitted, during closed testimony, that she had fabricated her story. A major Israeli newspaper then reported that her motive was religious: an Orthodox Jewish woman from New Jersey, who had worked for Olmert after moving to Israel, the witness said she had lied about her former boss because her rabbi—a senior fellow at the right-wing Shalem Center—had instructed her to do it, with a view to aiding Olmert's chief political rival at the time.[23]

To be sure, the rabbi, Joseph I. Lifshitz, denied the story.[24] But six years earlier, Lifshitz had published an essay in which he argued (based on the work of a 13th-century Jewish authority) that neither the rights nor the morality of an individual has any standing against a Jewish communal policy aimed at "national survival and the institution, on earth, of the divine glory"—such policies to be determined solely by its rabbinic leaders, who are empowered to "stratify" the principles behind Jewish ethics "and rank them by employing moral judgment." In Lifshitz's interpretation, rabbis must "rank" these principles—with the rabbis' notions of how to achieve "national survival" ranking at the top—for the very interesting reason that, when taught the priority of "national survival," ordinary Jews will be "more likely to accept communal rules that harm their individual rights."

Translated into practical politics (as his article appears to advise)[25] this would suggest a perfect rationale for Lifshitz's alleged subornation of perjury against Olmert: if the right-wing rabbi believed a change of Israeli government was needed to advance the goals of "divine glory" or "national survival," such as by enhancing Jewish settlement of the West Bank, that principle would "rank" above the presumed desire of his follower to tell the truth in a court of law.

Of course, this doesn't prove that Lifshitz instigated a false criminal charge. Officially, he has not even been accused of such an act. But given the dramatic allegation against him (supported by the reported statements of a woman who appeared to have no ulterior motive for wishing him ill), one might have expected a lively discussion among Orthodox Jews about the relative or absolute ethical value of bearing false witness, or about the proper relation between religion and politics. I have heard none. A poor augury for

Orthodox Judaism's willingness to confront similarly eventful cases of pious fraud.

I know there are many people who see in all this only an argument against religion in general. Such people may point, in addition, to the work of researchers at the University of Illinois at Chicago, who recently found that, from the point of view of a child victimized within a religious context, God is numbered among the perpetrators. "Religious contexts and justifications may add an additional layer of complexity and harm to the experience of child physical abuse," say the authors, in part because the combination of abuse and religion lead the victim to see his violation as "supernaturally sanctioned."[26]

I share the outrage of the critics of religion at the way religious institutions can (and do) poison the spiritual lives of sex abuse victims. But I do not share their confidence that the solution is to abandon religious teaching altogether. It is child's play to prove that the secularization of today's intelligentsia has not rendered it more virtuous or less hypocritical. We know, for instance, that virtually the entire intellectual class of the United States approves the mountain of "Holocaust education" dished out to the American public, supposedly to inoculate it against bigotry and militarism. But has all the talk about the Nazi genocide during World War II led to mass revulsion at the massacres committed by *American* forces during that same war (or later ones)—have Americans even acknowledged that at Hiroshima and Nagasaki the United States unleashed a new form of mass murder that posed, and still poses, a unique threat to civilization itself? The facts about this American crime are certainly no secret.[27] Philip Wylie, the popular author of *Generation of Vipers*— no bleeding heart—had already condemned the Hiroshima bombing ("War against the generations ... Horror and Shame") in 1949,[28] and Arthur Miller unflinchingly compared America's use of the A-bomb to the Nazi atrocities in his 1964 play *After the Fall*.[29] But these were exceptions. As a rule, even describing the slaughter of Japanese civilians as a "holocaust" is still taboo. When Israeli President Shimon Peres made the mistake, he was reprimanded by Elie Wiesel—a Nobel Peace laureate (and ex–Hasid) who styles himself a universal witness to human suffering. From his home in New York, the same icon of secular do-goodism then shamelessly lent his prestige to the cheerleading for America's criminal aggression against Iraq, by invoking—of all things—the Holocaust.[30] So much for "Holocaust education." And so much for the superiority of secular moralizing over its religious counterparts.

It seems to me that with all its faults, religious teaching still has the crucial capacity to puncture complacent assumptions and jingoistic relativism. That is saying a great deal. It is one of the glories of Jewish tradition that, at its best and in the best sense of the word, it is a *dissident* tradition—that is, it is a call for self-criticism, for turning morality inward, examining ourselves before we examine others. The Hebrew prophets did not merely call down anathemas on the enemies of their kings. They measured their own society, its nobles, its priests against the standards set by their own values—and found them wanting. That message still resonates today. Where rabbis like Joseph Lifshitz teach the worship of a clergy-ruled state, the great founders of his religion preached that God cares little for power or for piety. Every Jewish renewal since then has embraced the prophetic emphasis on social justice.

Religion can also be a powerful corrective to popular modern ideas that question the irreducible significance of the individual and appear prepared to sacrifice human beings, like so much raw material, to various ideals: progress, say, or the "free market." "Thought in our time," wrote Albert Schweitzer in 1963, "is still founded in inhumanity. The history of the world in our time is still inhuman through and through, and we accept this as a matter of course."[31] A deeply religious man, Schweitzer was also critical of organized religion, but he knew that its traditions had never been more essential than they are now, when humanity has produced monsters that may actually have the power to consume their creators, and the rest of creation along with them. To accept inhumanity today is not just evil; it invites the suicide of the species.

* * *

As I approach the end of this book, it seems appropriate to examine my own authority, as it were, to criticize some aspects of my religious heritage so closely. My treatment of today's Orthodox Jewish institutions does not imply any claim of personal superiority, though I suppose some readers may take away that impression. Here the words of art critic E.H. Ramsden are so apt that I cannot resist quoting them at length:

> ...[T]he assignment of the critic cannot, in some ways, be regarded as other than invidious, since, however unjustifiably, the imputation of a sense of superiority and a certain arrogance of attitude in his approach seems to be inevitable.... Perhaps this arises from a subconscious recognition that the exercise of the critical faculty and the practice of the theological virtues are not always compatible. It is futile to allow faith to impair or hope to impede the critique of the judgment and useless to invoke charity at the expense of truth.... The task of the critic is therefore essentially rigorous; a task to be performed dispassionately, without prejudice, without partiality and without prevarication.[32]

These observations are at least as true in matters of religion as in other subjects: the "theological virtues" cannot interfere with honest inquiry into questions of principle. On the other hand, the critic ought to be just as honest about himself, and his motives, where these may be relevant to the sort of principles he is examining.

My own record is far from perfect. I made my personal journey into

Orthodoxy in the middle and late 1980s. It was almost another ten years before I was aware of the child abuse cover-ups dissected in this book, and it shames me now to realize how shocked I was by the discovery—even though I had already lived through the years of the *intifada* and the first Gulf War. As a result I knew, or should have known, how brutally Israeli soldiers and settlers had repressed the overwhelmingly young, nonviolent Palestinian protesters[33]; how Israeli forces had massacred defenseless worshipers at the *Haram al–Sharif* in Jerusalem in 1990[34]; how Israel's government had refused to distribute gas masks to Palestinian children during the 1991 war, as it did for Israeli Jewish children.[35] I already knew, in short, about systematic cruelty toward non–Jews, including children, practiced by the Jewish State and—more to the point—enthusiastically endorsed by my own Orthodox Jewish society.

After the Jerusalem massacre, which took place just after prayers had ended at the Western Wall for the Jewish holiday of *Sukkoth*, a rabbi I knew called the incident a "miracle," echoing Israeli propaganda to the effect that the unarmed Arab worshipers were the real aggressors, that they had planned to hurl stones at the Jews in the plaza below, and that the hail of gunfire that killed 18 people and wounded 300 more had prevented something "terrible." When I cast my mind back to that time I am confounded by the ease with which the rabbi, a decent and gentle man, could be made to see a miracle in an atrocity. But what really defies my comprehension is how *I* could have seen and heard all this without drawing the obvious conclusions. Bad enough that I failed to grasp that the same leadership I saw applauding cruelty to non–Jews in a faraway place was just as likely to accept violent abuses closer to home; much worse, it seems to me now, was the sin of my own complacency, which apparently was prepared to ignore victimized children (and others) until they virtually appeared on my doorstep.

My complacency even extended to the smug assumption that child sex abuse was not my community's problem, that it was exclusively linked to poverty and ignorance. I would have been stunned by the finding of a recent study of sexual violence that "Latino and African American youths, and those from low-income families, were less likely to have coerced another person to engage in sex than were whites and those from higher-income families."[36] Today this does not surprise me; I know that sex abuse is not fundamentally the product of poor education or an "orgiastic way of living," in the rabbinic fantasy of Joseph Soloveitchik—that it has little to do with "ethnicity" and everything to do with power and privilege. Realizing that much, as I do now, marks an obvious improvement, but the knowledge has its dark side: it means that as long as I casually accepted the fruits of my own privileges as a white, middle-class American, I was part of the problem without knowing it. And to the extent I participated in Orthodox Jewish life without addressing its leadership's betrayal of its children, I was part of *that* problem, too.

So when I write about the need to reform my religious community's approach to the sexual abuse of children, I am writing as a penitent, a penitent who, moreover, is all too aware of the faults and foolishness that may still impede my vision. As Carolyn Jessop says, "Arbitrary limits are the horizons beyond which we cannot see."[37] Against such limits, the only weapons I know are those of religion itself: hope, devotion, self-improvement and prayer.

* * *

I can point to very few certainties on the path I am trying to illuminate. One is that no one can be whole who participates in or tolerates the maiming of others. Another is that religious progress will never come through the spread of dogmatism, however useful a particular credo may appear at a given time. I mentioned in a note to Chapter 7 the free-wheeling attack launched in 1914 by a prominent Orthodox rabbi, Eliyahu Meir Feivelson, on the long-dead early reformer Moses Mendelssohn—an essay recently reissued in English, in abridged form, by an American *yeshiva*. I want to focus for a moment on the theme of that essay, which is that the use of the mind is dangerous to true piety. Here is a typical extract:

> A true believer in [God] and His Torah ... radiates to his family and his disciples and to all who come in contact with him, his love of Torah.... But an equivocating philosopher, despite his performance of [the commandments], gives off an aura of coldness, of scoffing, of skepticism about all that is holy.[38]

I assume the *yeshiva* that disseminated this writing knew what it was doing. Presumably its administration believed, like Feivelson, that threatening young Jews against thinking too much is the best way to keep them within the religious fold. The same idea appears to be increasingly popular among the Orthodox leadership at large, but it strikes me as dangerously wrong. Albert Schweitzer insisted that, on the contrary, freedom of thought leads to greater religious strength, not less: "The man who thinks stands up freer in the face of traditional religious truth than the man who does not, but the profound and imperishable elements contained in it he assimilates with much more effect than the latter.... The deeper piety is, the humbler are its claims with regard to knowledge of the suprasensible."[39] I suppose that's why the preacher's "loose immodest tone" (in W.H. Auden's phrase) is seldom imitated by the Schweitzers of the world—and also why we are still familiar with people like Schweitzer, by name and teaching, long after their deaths, while we don't give a damn about Auden's preacher even at the moment he is roaring from the pulpit.

So what I have to say is less about theory, let alone theology, than it is about the interrelation of human lives and the infliction of human suffering. I began this chapter in Kiryas Joel, and I may as well end it there too—noting sadly that to leave that place is to leave behind, for the moment at least, some of that emblematic locale's impoverishing secrets. Israel Weingarten once lived in Kiryas Joel with the daughter he raped; to this day, his former community denies his guilt and refuses to forgive the truth-telling of his victim, even though the old rabbi is now serving a thirty-year sentence for his crimes—the one and only Orthodox Jew from Kiryas Joel ever to be convicted of a sexual assault. In 2008, Bentzion Miller, the "personal aide and confidant" of the Satmar Rebbe in Kiryas Joel, arranged a shipment of 90,000 Ecstasy pills that resulted in the arrest of three young Hasidic *yeshiva* students at a Tokyo airport. I do not know where Miller is today. But I'm sure someone in Kiryas Joel does know, and surer still that its leadership doesn't care whether Miller is exploiting more children, so long as he is following the instructions of Orthodox rabbis and contributing to the communal treasury.

Repeating these facts is all I can do. Though I can describe the abscess beneath the pious exterior, I cannot heal it: the real cure must come from within, and for that to happen the walls of denial will have to be pierced, once and for all. Courageous declarations like those of Shlomo Weiss mark heroic steps forward. But they cannot, in themselves, transform a community.

Will anything? When Schweitzer was asked to categorize himself as either an optimist or a pessimist, he answered that his knowledge was pessimistic, while his willing and hoping were optimistic.[40] This might be called the articulation of a religious psychology—one that refuses to accept the finality of what the mind "knows," when such knowledge can't keep pace with the will and hope that nourish a fully experienced human life. I find myself in instinctive agreement with Schweitzer, and this brings me very close to a word with which I have never kept easy company: I mean "faith." In the only dream I can recall in which the topic of religion arose directly, I remember asking an obscure figure, its identity unknown to me, how one can possibly believe in God. "*Live* God," the stranger answered. "Believe in life."

Whether or not we expect success, and if we do how rapid or gradual a success, I do not see how we can continue any sort of religious enterprise without trying to right the wrongs to which I have devoted this book. Again, I am under no illusions about the difficulty we face. Nechemya Weberman's recent conviction, for instance, did not prompt any reflection among his fellow Hasidim about their complicity in child abuse. On the Jewish New Year in 2013—a day supposedly devoted to repentance and self-examination—"[t]he brave Orthodox Jewish teen whose testimony helped convict the prominent Brooklyn counselor who had sexually abused her was driven out of her own synagogue." According to the *New York Post*, the solemn prayers were halted after a man loudly called her a *moser* ("informer")—and did not resume until she left. Meanwhile, three thugs who tried to intimidate the victim and her husband into dropping the case against Weberman "pleaded guilty ... in a deal that gave them no jail time."[41]

But outrages like these only underscore the necessity of a fresh beginning. And I cannot believe that the renewal we need is beyond the reach of the traditions that have brought us this far. The bill of indictment against the current leadership contains serious charges, certainly—but the remedies it seeks, far from threatening the religious community as a whole, can only improve it. The victims' grievances, after all, are neither surprising nor fanatical. Faced honestly and diligently, they will lead to nothing worse than some painful communal confessions and much-needed reforms. But if avoided, misrepresented, scorned, ignored, castigated, sneered at, the survivors' complaints will sink ever more corrosively into the vitals of the culture that tries to reject them. I'm reminded of a comment of Leo Strauss on a species of theorizing he found so blind to reality's urgent needs that he accused it of "fiddl[ing] while Rome burns."

"It is excused," he wrote sardonically, "by two facts: it does not know that it fiddles, and it does not know that Rome burns."[42]

If I were inclined to excuse today's Orthodox rabbinate I could do no better than to repeat Strauss's words. But if such a formula genuinely exonerated the rabbis it would, at the same time, write off traditional Judaism altogether. Better to say that the twin forms of ignorance—blindness to the crisis, denial of its own indifference—spell out the terms of the existing leadership's incapacity to speak on behalf of the religion it claims to represent.

That raises the question of the future of my own religious tradition, but I do not want to belabor the point. No doubt many of my readers are not very interested about whether Orthodox Judaism will thrive or perish in generations to come. I have no quarrel with them. I don't much care myself about the persistence of any particular creed; what I care about is what people *do* with what they believe, how their lives are informed with the values that affirm the best of which human beings are capable. Given the direction in which modern civilization appears to be drifting, it may not be too much to say that to live as a true dissident—to "live God," that is, by whatever name one chooses to call it—is the only thing likely to save us all from disaster. And no amount of bitter experience has destroyed my hope that such a life is within our reach. But to the extent we tolerate the dominion, over what purports to be a religious society, of the same charlatans who have fed us for decades on a diet of lies, cruelty and hypocrisy, we may well sacrifice our best chance for a brighter future—for ourselves, and for the children who must live tomorrow from the seeds we plant today.

Chapter Notes

Introduction

1. Michael Lesher, "Orthodox Cops: Separate and Unequal," *New York Post*, July 31, 2011, pp. 21–22. Some of the specific claims made in the column will be discussed later in this book.

2. See also Amy Neustein and Michael Lesher, "Justice Interrupted: How Rabbis Can Interfere with the Prosecution of Sex Offenders—and Strategies for How to Stop Them," in *Tempest in the Temple: Jewish Communities & Child Sex Scandals* (Amy Neustein, Ed.) (Lebanon, NH: Brandeis University Press, 2009), pp. 197–229.

3. Marcy Oster, "Kamenetsky: Report Child Abuse to Rabbis, not Police," *Jewish Telegraphic Agency (JTA)*, July 21, 2011. In New York, where Rabbi Kamenetsky made these comments (in a Brooklyn speech in July 2011), state law unconditionally requires doctors, social workers, psychologists, family therapists, school officials, teachers and many other professionals to report suspected child abuse to a state-run hotline. (New York Social Services Law § 413.) Obviously, precisely those professionals are among the people most likely to have evidence of possible child abuse, and in fact some were in the audience Rabbi Kamenetsky was addressing. In neighboring New Jersey, where many Orthodox Jews likewise regard Rabbi Kamenetsky's word as law, *anyone* with a reasonable suspicion of child abuse is unconditionally obligated to report to authorities. (New Jersey Statutes § 9:6–8.10.)

4. Robert Kolker, "On the Rabbi's Knee: Do the Orthodox Jews Have a Catholic-Priest Problem?" *New York Magazine*, May 14, 2006.

5. See Hella Winston, "Brooklyn DA Announces New Plan to Urge Reporting of Abuse," *New York Jewish Week*, April 2, 2009.

6. Colleen Long, "Nechemya Weberman, Orthodox Counselor, in Brooklyn, Guilty of Sexual Abuse," *Huffington Post*, December 12, 2012; Sharon Otterman, "Hasidic Therapist Sentenced to 103 Years in Sexual Abuse Case," *New York Times*, January 22, 2013. The sentence was later reduced to 50 years. (Staff, "Nechemya Weberman's 103-Year Sentence Cut in Half," *Jewish Daily Forward*, February 9, 2013.)

7. Charles Hynes, "Brooklyn DA Charles Hynes Calls Weberman Case Landmark vs. Predators," *New York Daily News*, January 19, 2013.

8. Amy Neustein and Michael Lesher, "A Single-Case Study of Rabbinic Sexual Abuse in the Orthodox Jewish Community," in *Understanding the Impact of Clergy Sexual Abuse* (Robert A. McMackin, Terence M. Keane and Paul M. Kline, Eds.) (London, New York: Routledge, 2009), pp. 74–93. The authors received a 2010 Pro Humanitate Award from the North American Resource Center for Child Welfare for this chapter.

9. Ben Hirsch, "A Jewish Civil War," *New York Post*, January 22, 2012.

10. Avi Shafran, "Open Season on Charedim—and Torah," *Ami Magazine*, February 1, 2012, p. 22.

11. *Id.*, p. 24, "Sushi Solution?" (Iran), "Rights Group Really Wrong" (Islamists and Nazis).

12. Shafran's approach was echoed in a January 27, 2012 column in the Yiddish-language Brooklyn newspaper *Der Yid*, titled "A Hateful Op-Ed Article in NY Newspaper Aims to Import Incitement against Haredim to NY." *Der Yid* called Hirsch a "self-hating Jew" and an "agitator," even though—again, like Shafran—the newspaper made no attempt to refute any of Hirsch's arguments.

Part I

1. By an Orthodox Jewish survivor of sexual abuse, posted to *Unorthodox-Jew* (theunorthodoxjew.blogspot.com), October 26, 2007.

Chapter 1

1. Luigi Pirandello, Preface to *Six Characters in Search of an Author* (trans. Eric Bentley), in *Naked Masks* (Eric Bentley, Ed.) (New York: E.P. Dutton, 1952), p. 372.

2. *Public Summary of the Report of the NCSY Special Commission* (authored by Richard Joel (chair), Fred Ehrman, Allen I. Fagin, Matthew J. Maryles, Jules Polonetsky, Dr. Susan Schulman, Prof. Suzanne Last Stone, Rabbi Dr. Abraham J. Twerski, Jacob Yellin), December 21, 2000 (hereafter, "*NCSY Report*").

3. Eric Greenberg, "Rabbi Lanner Guilty," *New York Jewish Week*, June 28, 2002.

4. According to its website, www.ou.org, the OU claims "over 800 synagogues across North America" as members; NCSY, the constituent organization that employed Lanner, "has chapters in 39 U.S. states, in Canada, Israel, Europe and South America, reaching over 35,000 Jewish teens each year."

5. *NCSY Report*, pp. 22–25.

6. Gary Rosenblatt, "Stolen Innocence," *New York Jewish Week*, June 23, 2000.

7. See the posted comments of Rabbi Eliyahu Stern to Virtual Talmud (blog.beliefnet.com/virtualtalmud), June 7, 2006, for an account of his experience (the author was a student at Orthodox-run Yeshiva University at the time the article appeared); see also Felicity Barringer, "MEDIA; Paper Seen as Villain in Abuse Accusations Against Rabbi," *New York Times*, July 10, 2000; *Columbia Journalism Review*, November 2000 ("[T]wo rabbis used their pulpits to castigate the paper; a major advertiser threatened to lead a boycott.")

8. Gary Rosenblatt, "Stolen Innocence." According to the article, Rabbi Blau "came to regret" the rabbinic court's decision over the years that followed, particularly after learning that Lanner had successfully pressured at least one witness into lying on his behalf. But not even Rabbi Blau commented publicly until he was quoted in the *Jewish Week* article, eleven years after he first heard charges against Lanner.

9. Gary Rosenblatt, "Stolen Innocence." Rabbi Blau candidly admitted that "the number of men and women who have been hurt [by the covering up of the accusations against Rabbi Lanner] is incalculable."

10. *NCSY Report*, p. 20.

11. Gary Rosenblatt, "Stolen Innocence."

12. *NCSY Report*, esp. pp. 20–21.

13. *Id.*, p. 14 [emphasis added].

14. Gary Rosenblatt, "Stolen Innocence."

15. *NCSY Report*, pp. 18–19, 3, 20.

16. *Id.*, pp. 25, 26.

17. Gary Rosenblatt, "Stolen Innocence." As noted above, Rabbi Blau had first-hand experience of at least some of the cover-up. Mordechai Willig, an Orthodox rabbi who had prominently attacked Lanner's accusers, eventually apologized for "errors in judgment and procedure that caused unnecessary pain and aggravation" to Lanner's victims. He also acknowledged that both he and the other Orthodox rabbis who sat on the 1989 tribunal that defended Lanner, despite significant evidence against him, suffered at the time from an "inadequate ... understanding of abuse." (Avi Robinson, "Rabbi Willig Apology Stirs Campus," *Commentator*, March 6, 2003.)

18. Elliot N. Dorff, Foreword to *Tempest in the Temple: Jewish Communities & Child Sex Scandals*, p. ix. Rabbi Dorff is not Orthodox, but his education and experience overlap considerably with those of Orthodox rabbis. (See p. xii.)

19. Adam Fifield and Michael Lesher, "A Child's at Stake: A Custody Fight Becomes a Political Nightmare," *Village Voice*, October 1, 1996, pp. 10, 12–13; Michael Lesher, "Speaking with Their Silence: A Troubling Child Sex Abuse Case in Orthodox Community Raises the Question, Where Are Our Leaders?" *New York Jewish Week*, November 1, 1996, p. 28.

20. Holly Rosenkrantz, "Out of COJO's Shadow," *City Limits*, March 1, 1998.

21. Kevin Flynn, Tom Robbins, Marcus Baram and Kimberly Shaye, "Dov Faces Indictment; Feds Set to Charge Hikind with Misuse of Funds," *New York Daily News*, August 4, 1997.

22. Paid Notice (obituary), "Schmidman, Rabbi Morris," *New York Times*, May 10, 2004. (Shmidman's name is sometimes spelled "Schmidman" in the press.)

23. Joyanna Silberg and Stephanie Dallam, "Out of the Jewish Closet: Facing the Hidden

Secrets of Child Sex Abuse—And the Damage Done to Victims," in *Tempest in the Temple*, p. 77, citing *American Journal of Psychiatry*, November 2007 (Yehuda, Friedman, Rosenbaum, Labinky & Schmeidler, 2007).

24. See note 19, above, for book citation.

25. Amy Neustein and Michael Lesher, "Justice Interrupted," pp. 197–229.

26. Eishes Chayil [Judy Brown], *Hush* (New York: Walker Publishing Company, 2010).

27. *Tempest in the Temple*, p. xvii.

28. See Ben Harris, "Extradition decision renews focus on alleged abusers who fled to Israel," *Jewish Telegraphic Agency (JTA)*, November 15, 2007.

29. Found at theunorthodoxjew.blogspot.com.

30. Another such blog is "Failed Messiah" (failedmessiah.typepad.com). This blog, run by Shmarya Rosenberg, provides an invaluable collection of current news often ignored in mainstream Jewish media; it has been a very important resource for much of the news research that went into the writing of this book.

31. Robert Kolker, "On the Rabbi's Knee," pp. 28–33, 102–103.

32. Hella Winston, "No Sex Charge for Kolko; Boys' Parents Foiled by DA," *New York Jewish Week*, April 16, 2008.

33. Hella Winston, "A Suspected Pedophile Eludes the System," *New York Jewish Week*, May 6, 2009. Rabbi Eisenman later distributed the text of his own comments at the large meeting via email.

34. Although sources close to the investigation believed that Colmer sexually abused as many as ten boys he met at the *yeshiva*, the two children named in the actual criminal charges against him apparently came in contact with Colmer by other means. (See Hella Winston, "Colmer Plea Deal Seen Raising Question," *New York Jewish Week*, June 19, 2009.)

35. Hella Winston, "A Suspected Pedophile Eludes the System."

36. A copy of Ohel's Return of Organization Exempt from Income Tax (990) for fiscal year 2009–2010, containing Mandel's salary information, is available on line at http://ag.state.il.us/PDF_IMAGES/Indexes20110822/01058809-2010.pdf.

37. I was among the recipients of Rabbi Eisenman's email. In response to my recent query, he stressed that he did not regard the relocation of an offender as a solution; at a minimum, people in the community to which he moves should be notified. What he meant by the passage I quoted was only that in Passaic itself the immediate "problem" had been removed. Any other implication was unintended.

38. Hella Winston, "A Suspected Pedophile Eludes the System."

39. See Michael Lesher, "The Fugitive and the Forgotten," pp. 146–147.

40. Hella Winston, "Colmer Plea Deal Seen Raising Questions," *New York Jewish Week*, June 19, 2009.

41. They reported this to me personally.

42. Derived from information made available to me in personal communications.

43. As this book was being written, Rabbi Nechemya Weberman, an unlicensed therapist, was convicted on 59 counts of sexually abusing a minor and sentenced (originally) to 103 years in prison—the longest sentence ever handed down in a Brooklyn court to an ultra–Orthodox Jew convicted of child sexual abuse. Though this case, too, counts as a "good" one, once again there was a typical cloud over its just *denouement*: "Prosecutors say they know of more victims [of Rabbi Weberman] who were too afraid to testify." The victim who did come forward faced "harassment and intimidation" from the religious community. (Sharon Otterman, "Hasidic Therapist Sentenced to 103 Years in Sexual Abuse Case," *New York Times*, January 22, 2013.) I will comment further on Weberman's case in Chapter 8.

44. John Marzulli, "Rabbi Israel Weingarten Found Guilty of Molesting Daughter," *New York Daily News*, March 11, 2009. As noted below, the judge, when sentencing Weingarten, stated his belief that Weingarten had insisted on personally cross-examining her—and her mother—precisely in an effort to re-establish control over them both.

45. Transcript (Re-Sentencing) (Document #109), *U.S.A. v. Weingarten*, U.S. District Court, Eastern District of New York, Docket No. 08-CR-571 (S1) (JG), September 12, 2011, p. 18.

46. Letter of Rachel J. Nash (prosecutor) to Judge Gleeson (Document #101), *U.S.A. v. Weingarten*, September 7, 2011, pp. 9–10, 11–13; Transcript (Re-Sentencing), *U.S.A. v. Weingarten*, p. 22. The same fate was visited on the victim's older brother, the one sibling who supported her at trial and whose testimony was damning to Rabbi Weingarten.

47. Transcript (Re-Sentencing), *U.S.A. v. Weingarten*, p. 18.

48. See Donna R. Newman and Jill R. Shellow, Sentencing Memorandum (Document #100), *U.S.A. v. Weingarten*, August 30, 2011, pp. 7–12; Demosthenes Lorandos and Ashish S. Joshi, Defendant's Sentencing Memorandum (Document #75), *U.S.A. v. Weingarten*, April 28, 2009, pp. 1–2.

49. Donna R. Newman and Jill R. Shellow, Sentencing Memorandum, p. 22; Demosthenes Lorandos and Ashish S. Joshi, Defendant's Sentencing Memorandum, p. 13.

50. Donna R. Newman and Jill R. Shellow, Sentencing Memorandum, *U.S.A. v. Weingarten*, p. 12.

51. Transcript (Re-Sentencing), *U.S.A. v. Weingarten*, pp. 22, 19–21.

52. *Id.*, p. 22.

53. John Marzulli, "Rabbi Israel Weingarten's Daughter Claims Mother was Sexual Abuser in Trial," *New York Daily News*, March 9, 2009.

54. John Marzulli, "Rabbi Israel Weingarten Found Guilty of Molesting Daughter."

Chapter 2

1. Aldous Huxley, *Brave New World* (Perennial Classic Edition) (New York: Harper & Row, 1969), p. xii.

2. Relevant details about the case can be found in Michael Lesher, "The Fugitive and the Forgotten: Cracking the Cold Case of Rabbi Avrohom Mondrowitz," in *Tempest in the Temple*, pp. 126–162.

3. Robert Kolker, "On the Rabbi's Knee," pp. 28–33, 102–103.

4. Stephanie Saul, "Tripping Up the Prosecution," *Newsday*, May 28, 2003, p. A6; Michael Lesher, "The Fugitive and the Forgotten," pp. 133–136.

5. See Michael Lesher, "The Fugitive and the Forgotten," pp. 142–143.

6. See Mike McAlary, "Community Coverups again Lead to Tragedy," *New York Post*, November 14, 1990, pp. 5, 25; "Conspiracy of Silence: Child Sex Abuse Case Still Haunts," reported by Cynthia McFadden, *Nightline*, October 11, 2006. (A on-line text version of the program is available at http://abcnews.go.com/Nightline/print?id=2555575.) That a large number of alleged Jewish victims met with police detectives after Mondrowitz fled was con-

firmed to me by a source directly involved in bringing them together.

7. Michael Orbach, "Unmolested," *Tablet*, August 11, 2011 [emphasis added].

8. Nancie L. Katz, "Abuse Victims Hope Healing Begins with Rabbi's Arrest," *New York Daily News*, October 17, 2007.

9. See Aviva Lori, "In the Basement, Behind a Closed Door," *Ha'aretz* (weekend magazine), November 15, 2007; Kristen Lombardi, "Silence of the Lam," *Village Voice*, July 25, 2006, pp. 26–34.

10. Michael Lesher, "The Fugitive and the Forgotten," p. 157, citing Douglas Montero, "Victims Learn Kid–Sex Fiend Served No Time," *New York Post*, September 21, 1999, p. 2–3. Montero's article describes another case in which Ohel allegedly failed to protect children from a sex abuser.

11. See Gitelle Rapoport, "Advisory Council Gives Brooklyn Communities Clout," *New York Jewish Week*, June 8, 1990, p. 7; statement by Jewish Advisory Council of D.A. Charles Hynes, *Jewish Press*, May 25, 1990, p. 18B; Steve K. Walz, "B'klyn D.A. Hynes Makes an Effort to 'Humanize' the Legal Process: Reaching Out to Jews Is Key Element," *Jewish Press*, March 29, 1991, p. 38.

12. See Michael Lesher, "The Fugitive and the Forgotten," p. 133.

13. Roxanna Sherwood, "Child Sex Abuse Case Still Haunts: The Cold Case of Avrohom Mondrowitz and the Silence of a Community," *Nightline*, October 11, 2006. This segment appeared on television under the title "Conspiracy of Silence," reported by Cynthia McFadden.

14. Michael Lesher, "The Fugitive and the Forgotten," p. 135.

15. Interpol Washington memorandum, December 11, 2007. Unless otherwise noted, all such documents were obtained by me from various government agencies by means of requests, administrative appeals and litigation spanning more than ten years.

16. For U.S. coverage, see, *e.g.*, *Nightline*, ABC TV, "Conspiracy of Silence: Child Sex Abuse Case Still Haunts" (reported by Cynthia McFadden), October 11, 2006; Jennifer Friedlin, "Hynes Mum on Mondrowitz," *New York Jewish Week*, October 20, 2006, p. 3; Channel 7 *Eyewitness News* at 11 p.m. (WABC TV New York), "Did an Alleged Sex Abuser Escape Justice?" (reported by Sarah Wallace), Novem-

ber 8, 2006; Tina Kelley, "22 Years Later, a Child Abuse Suspect's Extradition Is Sought," *New York Times*, November 16, 2007, p. B4. For coverage in Israel, see, *e.g.*, Aviva Lori, "In the Basement, Behind a Closed Door"; Matthew Wagner, "US Wants Extradition of Prominent Ger Hassid Accused of Sodomy," *Jerusalem Post*, October 23, 2007.

17. See Matthew Wagner, "US Wants Extradition of Prominent Ger Hassid Accused of Sodomy"; Aviva Lori, "'I Planned to Murder Mondrowitz,'" *Ha'aretz Magazine*, December 6, 2007.

18. Matthew Kalman and Dave Goldiner, "Accused Perv Rabbi Loses Extradition Battle," *New York Daily News*, February 11, 2008, p. 22.

19. Memorandum, "Avrohom Mondrowitz Update," from Rhonnie Jaus and Louise Cohen to District Attorney Charles J. Hynes, January 14, 2010. The official transcript of the oral argument on December 8, 2008 (in Hebrew) is part of the record of *State v. Mondrowitz*, High Court of Justice Docket No. 2144/08.

20. Paras D. Bhayani, "Israeli Judge Speaks to Critical Crowd," *Harvard Crimson*, November 10, 2005. Speaking at Harvard Law School on November 9, Procaccia (according to the article) "portrayed her court as a moderating force in Israeli politics—to vehement criticism from some audience members."

21. *Human Rights Watch World Report 1992* (New York), in Norman G. Finkelstein, *Beyond Chutzpah: On the Misuse of Anti-Semitism and the Abuse of History* (updated edition) (Berkeley, Los Angeles: University of California Press, 2008), p. 169.

22. Mondrowitz's flight from New York at the time of his indictment stopped the "clock" under New York law, so his criminal charges remain timely there. Israeli law has a similar provision.

23. Released to me by the D.A.'s office in 2012, after litigation all the way to New York's highest court. Grammatical and syntactical errors are in the original. (Bear in mind that the memo was written in English by Hebrew-speaking Israeli officials.)

24. See *Matter of Extradition of Ernst*, 1998 WL 30283 (S.D.N.Y., 1998) ("The [retroactivity] argument has been universally rejected in this Circuit in more than 100 years of precedent); *United States ex rel. Oppenheim v. Hecht*, 16 F.2d 955, 956 (2d Cir.1927) ("Extradition

proceedings are not in their nature criminal ... therefore all talk of *ex post facto* legislation ... is quite beside the mark"); *Hilario v. U.S.*, 854 F. Supp. 165, 175–76 (E.D.N.Y.). The Jerusalem District Court had taken the same approach in its ruling that supported Mondrowitz's extradition.

25. As a matter of fact, the extradition of Kenneth Frank (a.k.a. Yonatan Efrat) to the U.S. was upheld by Israel's courts in December 2006, nearly twenty years after his crimes in California were allegedly committed. In that case, the Israeli judges ruled that the statute of limitations could not expire while Frank was being sought outside the country in which he was charged. (See Rebecca A. Stoil, "Runaway Convicted US Rapist Found in Ra'anana," *Jerusalem Post*, December 28, 2006.)

26. On the cover of the Hebrew-language magazine containing Aviva Lori, "In the Basement, Behind a Closed Door."

27. See, *e.g.*, Simon Romero and Marc Lacey, "Fierce Quake Devastates Haitian Capital," *New York Times*, January 12, 2010; Karin Kloosterman, "Israel Rushes to Haiti's Aid," *Israel21c* (israel21c.org), January 14, 2010; Ethan Bronner, "For Israelis, Mixed Feelings on Aid Effort," *New York Times*, January 21, 2010. The Israel Supreme Court decision on Mondrowitz was announced on January 14.

28. Documents confirming the conference call, its participants and its purpose were released to me. However, the only memorandum describing the contents of the call was heavily redacted.

29. Michael Lesher, "The Fugitive and the Forgotten," pp. 158–159.

30. Confirmed in documents disclosed to me; first, describing the conference call between Israeli prosecutors, Brooklyn prosecutors and U.S. Justice Department officials after Israel's Supreme Court ruled against Mondrowitz's extradition; second, summarizing the Jerusalem District Court's decision not to release Mondrowitz on bail.

31. The manipulation of the Brooklyn D.A.'s office to drop charges against accused child sex abuser Rabbi Solomon Hafner will be discussed in the next chapter. A similar history in the case of convicted child rapist Rabbi Israel Weingarten was discussed in Chapter 1.

32. Marcus Tullius Cicero, *Oration for Flaccus 38*, in Shlomo Sand, *The Invention of the*

Jewish People (trans. Yael Lotan) (London, Brooklyn: Verso, 2009), p. 145.

33. Nancie L. Katz, "Abuse Victims Hope Healing Begins with Rabbi's Arrest."

34. The extraordinary indebtedness of D.A. Charles Hynes to Brooklyn's Orthodox Jewish community is a matter of record. See Ray Rivera and Sharon Otterman, "For Ultra-Orthodox in Abuse Cases, Prosecutor Has Different Rules," *New York Times*, May 10, 2012.

35. Karen Winner, *Divorced from Justice: The Abuse of Women and Children by Divorce Lawyers and Judges* (New York: HarperCollins, 1996), p. 131.

36. *Id.*, p. 132; "Judges Sentence Kids to Life of Pain," *USA Today*, November 3, 1995, p. 13A.

37. Adam Fifield and Michael Lesher, "A Child's at Stake: A Custody Fight Becomes a Political Nightmare," p. 10; Michael Lesher, "Speaking with Their Silence," p. 28; Transcript, *Matter of Orbach v. Neustein*, Family Court, Kings County, Docket Nos. V9540/86 and NA8480/86, March 16, 1987. (This and other court documents from the case were provided by Dr. Neustein.) The highly respected Dr. Meltzer was no knee-jerk abuse advocate. For instance, she would later testify on behalf of filmmaker Woody Allen when he was charged with sexually abusing his adopted daughter. (See Peter Marks, "Yale Study About Allen Flawed, Expert Testifies," *New York Times*, April 28, 1993.)

38. Adam Fifield and Michael Lesher, "A Child's at Stake," p. 12.

39. Michael Lesher, "Speaking with Their Silence."

40. Rabbi Moshe Faskowitz, "one of New York's most prominent Jewish rabbinic leaders," according to the *Jewish Press*, told Adam Fifield that helping Orthodox fathers fight their ex-wives was legitimate because Orthodox women "have a history" of vindictiveness. (Michael Lesher, "Speaking with Their Silence.")

41. At Shirley Neustein's request, I did not report this comment at the time. Now that she and the rabbi she named are both dead, it seems appropriate that this part of the story should be told in full.

42. Michael Lesher, "Speaking with Their Silence"; Adam Fifield and Michael Lesher, "A Child's at Stake," pp. 12, 13.

43. *Id.*, p. 12; Susan Rosenbluth, "A 20-

Year-Old Custody Battle Brings Charges of Abuse to the Orthodox Community: In Edgewater, a Mother Waits for Her Daughter to Come Home," *Jewish Voice and Opinion*, March 2005, p. 32.

44. Susan Rosenbluth, "A 20-Year-Old Custody Battle," pp. 31–32; Decision dated July 14, 1988 (Leon Deutsch, J.F.C.), *Matter of Orbach v. Neustein*, pp. 109–110.

45. Adam Fifield and Michael Lesher, "A Child's at Stake," p. 10; see Karen Winner, *Divorced from Justice*, p. 133.

46. David Gold, "New York—Supporting Supporters—and Supportees; Dov Hikind and His Abuse Victims 'Chizuk' Event This Sunday," *VIN News* (VosIzNeias.com), February 27, 2009.

47. Adam Fifield and Michael Lesher, "A Child's at Stake," pp. 13, 10; Susan Rosenbluth, "A 20-Year-Old Custody Battle," p. 31.

48. See amyneustein.com/presentations.htm. This was also made part of the record in her Family Court case. See Decision dated July 14, 1988 (Leon Deutsch, J.F.C.), p. 55.

49. Ray Kerrison, "Incredible Return of Misogynist a Disgrace," *New York Post*, August 31, 1990, p. 2; Amy Neustein and Michael Lesher, *From Madness to Mutiny: Why Mothers Are Running from the Family Courts—and What Can Be Done About It* (Lebanon, NH: Northeastern University Press, 2005), pp. 13–14. Unless otherwise noted, all references to the book are from this (original) edition.

50. In an official affirmation prepared (with my assistance) in 1998, Rachel Anolick, who supervised visits between Amy Neustein and Sherry, reported that Orbach's sister Fran Gutterman, in his presence, "screamed" at Dr. Neustein when she visited Sherry after the latter's hospitalization, "challeng[ing] Amy's right to visit her daughter, claiming that she did not have visitation on that day.... In front of the sick girl, Fran continued her antagonistic attacks against Amy." There is more in a similar vein.

51. Susan Rosenbluth, "A 20-Year-Old Custody Battle," p. 32. The "law guardian" is the child's legal representative appointed by the court.

52. Decision dated July 14, 1988 (Leon Deutsch, J.F.C.), pp. 32, 115–116.

53. Susan Rosenbluth, "A 20-Year-Old Custody Battle," p. 35. Knowing nothing about the case's history, the same doctor also noted

Sherry's sexualized behavior and language when she was admitted for treatment.

54. Adam Fifield and Michael Lesher, "A Child's at Stake," p. 12.

55. Decision dated July 14, 1988 (Leon Deutsch, J.F.C.), p. 25; Susan Rosenbluth, "Waiting for Sherry Part II: Who Doesn't Want *From Madness to Mutiny* Published... And Why?" *Jewish Voice and Opinion*, May 2005, p. 8.

56. Susan Rosenbluth, "A 20-Year-Old Custody Battle," pp. 35–36; Adam Fifield and Michael Lesher, "A Child's at Stake," p. 13.

57. Susan Rosenbluth, "A 20-Year-Old Custody Battle."

58. Susan Rosenbluth, "Waiting for Sherry Part II," pp. 9–10, 12–14. Ironically, the book (based on our research into over a thousand cases), does not name Sherry or her father. I will discuss some of the details of the threats in the next chapter. Not one of the factual claims about the case cited above was rebutted by the critics.

59. Sherry Orbach, "Silent No Longer," *Jewish Press*, May 27, 2005, p. 4.

60. The column claimed that "false allegations" of child sex abuse occur in up to 60 percent of child custody disputes. No source was cited, and the 60 percent figure is completely contradicted by the scholarship on the subject, according to which "even in family courts, false allegations [of sexual abuse] remain rare." (See, *e.g.*, sources cited in Amy Neustein and Michael Lesher, *From Madness to Mutiny*, pp. xviii, 27–28.) Precisely because it was wildly inflated, however, the 60 percent figure for false allegations would have suited people whose real goal was to silence discussion of child sex abuse among Orthodox Jews—which doubtless explained its appearance in the column.

61. These details were confirmed to me by both of Dr. Neustein's parents; see also Decision dated July 14, 1988 (Leon Deutsch, J.F.C.), pp. 4–5, 6–7, 49–50. Sherry may have been at a "summer camp" away from home when the custody papers were actually served, but she returned to Brooklyn soon afterward.

62. No one I interviewed who knew Shirley Neustein ever reported seeing plastic covers on any of her furniture, nor did I when I interviewed her, in her Brooklyn home, in 1996.

63. What they sent included excerpts from email correspondence between me and Sherry. Since I did not provide any of this, I must as- sume the senders were in Sherry's confidence, and that their account of events conforms to Sherry's. As for the timing of Orbach's demand for custody, Orbach tape-recorded his telephone conversations with the Neusteins during the relevant period, and kept detailed records of their timing and content; much of this was later presented in court. Nowhere in the record is there any reference in these conversations to the filing of legal papers until *after* Orbach filed for custody in August 1986. Judge Deutsch, who accepted Orbach's accusations against Dr. Neustein, likewise insisted that "the child sex abuse charges were a contrivance by the grandmother *as a response to the child custody suit commenced by Dr. Orbach* [on August 5, 1986]." (See Decision dated July 14, 1988 (Leon Deutsch, J.F.C.), pp. 53–54 [emphasis added].)

64. Decision dated July 14, 1988 (Leon Deutsch, J.F.C.), pp. 111–112. She also testified as Orbach's witness at the brief custody hearing that followed this decision, at which time Sherry was actually living with Orbach.

65. *Id.*, pp. 32, 71, 77.

66. Alice Miller, *Thou Shalt Not Be Aware: Society's Betrayal of the Child* (trans. Hildegarde and Hunter Hannum) (New York: Farrar Straus Giroux, 1984), p. 162.

67. Douglas Montero, "Victims Learn Kid–Sex Fiend Served No Time," *New York Post*, September 21, 1999, p. 2–3, in Amy Neustein and Michael Lesher, "The Silence of the Jewish Media on Sexual Abuse in the Orthodox Jewish Community," in *Sex, Religion, Media* (Dane S. Claussen, Ed.) (Lanham, MD: Rowman & Littlefield, 2002), p. 81.

68. Amy Neustein and Michael Lesher, "Justice Interrupted," p. 210, citing Stewart Ain, "Sex Abuse Suspect Charged in Fraud Case," *New York Jewish Week*, August 24, 1990, p. 7.

69. Ray Rivera and Sharon Otterman, "For Ultra-Orthodox in Abuse Cases, Prosecutor Has Different Rules."

70. Efrat Forsher and Hadas Shtaif, "Key Witness in Modiin Illit Rape Case: 'I Made It Up,'" *Israel Hayom*, February 7, 2013. The woman also said that she herself had been a victim of sexual assault when she was sixteen, but never received proper treatment.

71. Janet Heimlich, *Breaking Their Will: Shedding Light on Religious Child Maltreatment* (Amherst, NY: Prometheus Books, 2011), pp. 211–212.

72. Sharon Otterman and Ray Rivera, "Ultra-Orthodox Shun Their Own for Reporting Child Sexual Abuse," *New York Times*, May 10, 2012.

73. Janet Heimlich, *Breaking Their Will*, pp. 212–213, 305–306.

Chapter 3

1. Gustav Janouch, *Conversations with Kafka* (2nd ed.) (trans. Goronwy Rees) (New York: New Directions, 1971), pp. 128–129.

2. *Tempest in the Temple*, p. ix.

3. *Id.*, p. xii.

4. Staff Report, "Child Counselor in Brooklyn Is Charged with Abusing Boy," *New York Times*, December 10, 1984.

5. Ray Kerrison, "Another Lisa Steinberg Horror?" *New York Post*, April 5, 1989, p. 2.

6. Irving Greenberg, "Rabbis Can Help by Speaking Out," *Moment*, April 15, 1990, p. 49, in Amy Neustein and Michael Lesher, "The Silence of the Jewish Media," p. 79.

7. For an egregious example, see the comments posted to "A Conversation with Rav Sternbuch About the Recent Reports About Chareidi Extremists" on the blog *Daas Torah—Issues of Jewish Identity* (daattorah.blogspot.com), February 9, 2012. The issue concerned (accurate) news reports about groups of ultra–Orthodox activists who, every day for weeks, harassed eight-year-old girls on their way to and from school—spitting at them, calling them "whores"—because their Orthodoxy was more "modern." (See Isabel Kershner, "Israeli Girl, 8, at Center of Tension Over Religious Extremism," *New York Times*, December 27, 2011.) Yet as the comments show, Rabbi Moshe Sternbuch, one of the world's most revered ultra–Orthodox rabbis, suggested that the news reports were merely the product of hostility toward the Orthodox. And others in his circles agreed with him. One Orthodox Jew who didn't agree noted, for an Israeli newspaper, that the rabbis' position could not be justified rationally: "This is a community where a girl walks down the street in the wrong kind of shirt fabric, and [afterward] there are signs on the wall and proclamations against it. And yet when there were 20 grown men standing here abusing schoolchildren, no one said a word." (Allison Kaplan Sommer, "WATCH: A Visit to Beit Shemesh, 6 Months After the

Harassment of Eight-Year-Old Girls," *Ha'aretz*, July 13, 2012.)

8. See, *e.g.*, Marvin Schick, "Children at Work," on the blog *Marvin Schick* (mschick.blogspot.com), February 10, 2003; Marvin Schick, "A New Low at the Jewish Week," *Cross-Currents* (cross-currents.com), July 27, 2011; Yossi Krausz, "Persecuted by the Press," *Ami Magazine*, June 6, 2012, pp. 49–58. Just how tendentious the argument generally is can be seen from the last of these examples, in which "stories about child abuse in the Jewish community" are dismissed by an Orthodox rabbi as "anti–Semitic" because "[i]t's only kids who were abused in synagogues and yeshivas [the reporters write about]."

9. Yosie Levine, "A Tribute to Past OU President Sheldon Rudoff, a'h," *Orthodox Union* (ou.org), December 19, 2011; Stewart Ain, "Claims Conference Expects to Recover Only 2 Percent of Fraudulent Payments," *New York Jewish Week*, July 20, 2011. With respect to the poor moral pedigree of the Claims Conference, cf. Norman G. Finkelstein, *The Holocaust Industry* (second paperback edition) (London, Brooklyn: Verso, 2003), esp. pp. 84–87, 120–129, 248–249.

10. Sheldon Rudoff, "A Smear of the Orthodox Community," *Jewish Journal*, March 17, 1994, in Amy Neustein and Michael Lesher, "The Silence of the Jewish Media," p. 81.

11. See Neve Gordon, *Israel's Occupation* (Berkeley, Los Angeles: University of California Press, 2008), pp. 106, 140–143.

12. See Melanie Lidman, "J'lem: Police Arrest 3 on Suspicion of Pedophilia," *Jerusalem Post*, January 8, 2012.

13. Yossi Haziz, in JerusalemNet (Hebrew), translated into English on the blog A Mother in Israel (amotherinisrael.com/Knesset-nachlaot-pedophile/), January 4, 2012.

14. The charge that secular media shortchanged the story is also incredible. See, *e.g.*, Melanie Lidman, "J'lem: Police Arrest 3 on Suspicion of Pedophilia"; Yair Ettinger and Nir Hasson, "Breaking Israel's Ultra-Orthodox Taboo on Discussing Sexual Abuse," *Ha'aretz*, February 8, 2013. The accused in this case were marginal figures in the neighborhood rather than rabbis, teachers or influential Orthodox fathers, which may explain the leadership's unusual willingness to publicize the matter.

15. Michael Lesher, "The Fugitive and the Forgotten," pp. 145–146.

16. For the whole story, see Amy Neustein and Michael Lesher, "Justice Interrupted," pp. 197–229.

17. Amy Neustein and Michael Lesher, "The Silence of the Jewish Media," p. 80.

18. Al Guart, "Rabbis' Ruling May Nix Bid to Indict Suspect in Kid-Sex Rap," *New York Post*, March 11, 2000, p. 10.

19. Amy Neustein and Michael Lesher, "Justice Interrupted," p. 212.

20. *Id.*, p. 215.

21. Karen Matthews, "Jewish Court Stymies Reports," *Associated Press*, April 16, 2002.

22. (wwrn.org), April 16, 2002.

23. Amy Neustein and Michael Lesher, "A Single-Case Study of Rabbinic Sexual Abuse in the Orthodox Jewish Community," *Journal of Child Sexual Abuse*, Vol. 17(3–4) (2008), pp. 270–289. The latter article was reprinted in *Understanding the Impact of Clergy Sexual Abuse* (R.A. McMackin, T.M. Keane, and P.M. Kline, Eds.) (London, New York: Routledge, 2009), pp. 74–93.

24. Susan Rosenbluth, "Abuse in the Orthodox Community and the *Beit Din*," *Jewish Voice and Opinion*, July 2006, pp. 11–21.

25. For instance, one of the rabbis' key claims was that the Voydislaver Shul was always crowded with people during the alleged victim's tutoring sessions with Rabbi Hafner. Besides our own observations that showed the building was unused on weekdays, we quoted Rabbi Hafner's wife as saying that the building had been chosen precisely *because* it was unused: "[The boy's family] had asked him [Rabbi Hafner] to learn privately [with the boy] in a very secluded place because he has a hearing aid and his hearing aid will pick up any outside noise, so he must have a quiet place.... There was nobody there..." (Amy Neustein and Michael Lesher, "Justice Interrupted," p. 212.) If we could get this information from the defendant's own wife, plus a simple visit to the site, surely the prosecutors could have learned it too, had they cared enough to check the facts.

26. Samuel Newhouse, "'Tempest in the Temple': A Strange New Book Alleges Corruption & Conspiracy in Brooklyn," *Brooklyn Eagle*, April 7, 2009. Note also the use of the word "conspiracy" in the headline—a word we never used in our chapter about the case—with its obvious implications of paranoia and irrationality. We never used the word "corruption," either.

27. Nor did Dr. Neustein "file for custody" in 1986; she had already had uncontested full custody of the child since 1983; it was her ex-husband who "filed for custody" that year, accusing her of withholding the child from him after an eyewitness—the girl's grandmother—allegedly saw him molesting her. (See Adam Fifield and Michael Lesher, "A Child's at Stake," p. 10, and the detailed discussion of this case in Chapter 2.) In cover-ups, facts are cheap.

28. For "A Single-Case Study of Rabbinic Sexual Abuse in the Orthodox Jewish Community," we received a Pro Humanitate Award from the North American Resource Center for Child Welfare in 2010 for "the intellectual integrity and moral courage required to transcend political and social barriers to champion best practice in the field of child welfare."

29. Amy Neustein and Michael Lesher, "Justice Interrupted," pp. 207–209, 212, 213, 214–215.

30. Karen Matthews, "Jewish Court Stymies Reports."

31. Susan Rosenbluth, "Abuse in the Orthodox Community and the *Beit Din*."

32. Amy Neustein and Michael Lesher, "The Silence of the Jewish Media," p. 84.

33. Adam Fifield and Michael Lesher, "A Child's at Stake," p. 13. Note that Martin Burger has, at various times, spelled his last name "Berger."

34. Susan Rosenbluth, "Waiting for Sherry Part II," p. 9.

35. Amy Neustein and Michael Lesher, *From Madness to Mutiny*.

36. Susan Rosenbluth, "Waiting for Sherry Part II," pp. 8, 10, 13, 12.

37. See Amy Neustein and Michael Lesher, *From Madness to Mutiny: Why Mothers Are Running from the Family Courts—and What Can Be Done About It* (paperback) (Lebanon, NH: Northeastern University Press, 2006), p. 263 n. 10. The first two sentences of this note address the circumstances of Judge Deutsch's early retirement, contradicting nothing whatsoever in the original text of the book.

38. *Id.*, p. 16.

39. Amy Neustein and Michael Lesher, "The Silence of the Jewish Media," p. 81. See Douglas Montero, "Tragic Teens' Life of Hell," *New York Post*, September 21, 1999, pp. 3, 22.

40. Luke Ford, "Gary Rosenblatt" (Profiles), lukeford.net. Though critical of some of

Ford's later blogging about him, Rosenblatt confirmed to me the accuracy of this quotation.

41. *Id.* Rosenblatt confirmed that, in order to placate the Tisches, he wrote them "a private note to apologize" for "having hurt their feelings," though he could not remember the exact wording.

42. Jan Ferris, "Butt Out," *Columbia Journalism Review*, January/February 1994, Vol. 32, No. 5, p. 16. It is only fair to mention that the *New York Times* also rejected the ad, as did some other metropolitan newspapers.

43. Communication of JWB ("Jewish-Whistleblower") to Miriam Shaviv, quoted by Luke Ford, "Gary Rosenblatt" (Profiles), luke ford.net.

44. Amy Neustein and Michael Lesher, "The Silence of the Jewish Media on Sexual Abuse in the Orthodox Jewish Community," p. 81.

45. Hella Winston, *Unchosen: The Hidden Lives of Hasidic Rebels* (Boston: Beacon Press, 2005).

46. Nathaniel Popper, "Victims Press Brooklyn D.A. to Seek Abuse Suspect's Extradition from Israel," *Jewish Daily Forward*, July 28, 2006, pp. 1, 7.

47. Hella Winston and Larry Cohler-Esses, "No Sex Charge for Kolko; Boys' Parents Foiled by DA," *New York Jewish Week*, April 16, 2008.

48. Ray Rivera and Sharon Otterman, "For Ultra-Orthodox in Abuse Cases, Prosecutor Has Different Rules"; Ray Rivera, "Brooklyn Prosecutor's Role in Abuse Case Is Examined," *New York Times*, June 29, 2012. I was one of several people who urged the *Times* to report the same subject (the Mondrowitz case and D.A. Hynes' efforts to dodge it) when new evidence became available in 2003 and again in 2006, when more Mondrowitz victims came forward seeking justice; I was told the story wasn't for the *Times*.

49. Hella Winston, "A Suspected Pedophile Eludes the System." It is doubtless significant that Ohel has considerable clout with Orthodox-run entities that advertise heavily in Jewish media.

50. *Ohel Outlook* for Spring/Summer 2009. The material I refer to appears on page 14.

51. Pamela Mejia, Andrew Cheyne and Lori Dorfman, "News Coverage of Child Sexual Abuse and Prevention, 2007–2009," in *Journal of Child Sexual Abuse* (Robert Geffner, Ed.) (Philadelphia: Taylor & Francis Group, LLC, Vol. 21: No. 4, July-August 2012), p. 481. "Solutions—Including Both Policy Solutions ... and Community Programs Were the Focus of 8% of the Coverage." (*Id.*, p. 474.)

52. *Id.*, p. 480.

53. Wendy McElroy, "Facts or Propaganda? Deconstructing Advocacy," *ifeminists.com* (ifeminists.net), April 29, 2004.

54. Tom Segev, *The Seventh Million: The Israelis and the Holocaust* (New York, 1993), p. 28, in Norman G. Finkelstein, *Beyond Chutzpah*, p. 117. Of course, Ben-Gurion was also instrumental in carrying out serious crimes against Palestine's indigenous Arabs. Western liberals' cavalier disregard of those crimes, at the time and for a long time afterward, is by now a well-known tale. But writing off half of a country's *Jewish* population would normally have had a different result—that is, if it hadn't been only about children.

55. See Ruth Sidel, *Women and Children Last: The Plight of Poor Women in Affluent America* (New York: Penguin Books, 1992), p. 105: "James A. Cook, president of the National Congress for Men ... also ties the problem of economic support to fathers' lack of access to their children.... John A. Rossler of the Equal Rights for Fathers of New York State agrees: 'Many men have had to beg for access to their children.... A man is more than a wallet to his kids.'" Even if significant numbers of divorced men are being wrongly denied "access" to their children (and my own experience in custody litigation suggests otherwise), why is it acceptable to retaliate by starving a child? Implicitly, arguments like these illustrate the persistent notion that children are the property of their fathers—however much these advocates sugar-coat their position in sentimental rhetoric.

56. Alice Miller, *Thou Shalt Not Be Aware*, pp. 38–39.

57. Dorothy K. Kripke, Meyer Levin, Toby K. Kurzband, *God and the Story of Judaism* (New York: Behrman House, Inc., 1962), p. 77.

58. *Shulhan Arukh, Orah Hayyim* 551:18, *Turei Zahab ad loc.* Rashi, at Babylonian Talmud *Makkoth* 8a, "*ha-ab ha-makkeh eth-b'no*," actually appears to say a father has an obligation to strike his son in order to compel the son's obedience to his will, though the implication is softened somewhat by the emendation of *Bayith Hadash ad loc.*

59. Alan J. Borsuk, "Old Fashioned Jew, Old Fashioned Reporter," *Neiman Reports* 51, Fall 1997, pp. 15–18, in Amy Neustein and Michael Lesher, "The Silence of the Jewish Media," p. 82.

60. Amy Neustein and Michael Lesher, "The Silence of the Jewish Media," p. 83.

61. Few of her coreligionists would have. Another Orthodox journalist recently wrote proudly that when publishing in non–Orthodox media, "there were times when I had to turn down the opportunity to report a 'great story' in order to safeguard the image of the *frum* [Orthodox] community." (Yitta Halberstam Mandelbaum, "The Curious Case of Hitler's Jewish Relative," *Ami Magazine*, May 12, 2013, p. 116.) As far as I know, this frank formulation of Orthodox priorities has aroused no controversy within the community.

62. Robert Kolker, "On the Rabbi's Knee."

63. Avi Shafran, "A Matter of Orthodox Abuse," *New York Jewish Week*, June 23, 2006.

64. Margaret Hartmann, "Brooklyn D.A.'s International Hunt for an Alleged Pedophile May Be Slightly Exaggerated," *New York Magazine*, June 29, 2012.

65. Daniel Boyarin, *Unheroic Conduct: The Rise of Heterosexuality and the Invention of the Jewish Man* (Berkeley and Los Angeles: University of California Press, 1997), pp. 154, 163, 167–168.

66. Yair Ettinger and Nir Hasson, "Breaking Israel's Ultra-Orthodox Taboo on Discussing Sexual Abuse."

67. Yakov Horowitz, "What's the Deal with These Protestors?" on rabbihorowitz.com, May 25, 2012.

68. Yossi Krausz, "A conversation with Lisa Twerski," *Ami Living*, June 6, 2012, p. 31.

69. Yitzchok Frankfurter, "Editorial," *Ami Magazine*, April 25, 2012, p. 8.

Chapter 4

1. Charlotte Bronte, *Jane Eyre* (Norton Critical Edition, "Author's Preface") (New York: W.W. Norton, 1971), pp. 1–2.

2. Shahar Ilan, "And the modesty squad kept silent," *Ha'aretz*, February 1, 2000, pp. 1–2, in Amy Neustein and Michael Lesher, "The Silence of the Jewish Media on Sexual Abuse in the Orthodox Jewish Community," in *Sex, Religion, Media*, pp. 79–80.

3. Alice Miller, *Thou Shalt Not Be Aware*, pp. 162, 184.

4. Karen Matthews, "Jewish Court Stymies Reports."

5. Janet Heimlich, *Breaking Their Will*, p. 200.

6. In a statement on a video widely circulated to Orthodox Jewish families; a copy is in my possession.

7. A recording of Rabbi Salomon's comments at the annual convention of Agudath Israel of America, November 23, 2006, was available on the blog Canonist.com, from which I downloaded it.

8. Nancie L. Katz, "Sex-Rap Rabbi Is Busted in Brooklyn," *New York Daily News*, December 8, 2006.

9. Phil Jacobs, "Rabbi, Teacher, Molester—Ephraim Shapiro's Mark on the Baltimore Jewish Community," *Baltimore Jewish Times*, April 13, 2007.

10. Nathan Guttman, "Baltimore Roiled by Abuse Charge Against Late Rabbi," *Jewish Daily Forward*, April 27, 2007.

11. Staff, "Rabbi Chaim Pinchas Scheinberg" [obituary], *Telegraph* (telegraph.co.uk), March 22, 2012.

12. Shmarya Rosenberg, "Exclusive: Letter from Haredi 'Gadol' Rabbi Chaim Pinchos Scheinberg Says Notorious Pedophile Innocent," *Failed Messiah* (failedmessiah.typepad.com), March 21, 2012.

13. Yehuda Heimowitz with Shai Markowitz, *The 6 Constant Mitzvos* (Brooklyn: Mesorah Publications, Ltd., 2009, 2011), p. 14.

14. *Id.*, pp. 73–74. This book renders the rabbi's (Hebrew) surname as "Alon," but most sources spell it "Elon."

15. Yair Ettinger, "Rabbi Elon accused of 'long-term' sexual relationship with student," *Ha-aretz*, February 18, 2010. The following excerpt from the article gives some idea of the tenor of the public charges against Rabbi Elon:

The group [that accused Elon] said that when the first claims of sexual exploitation by the rabbi came to light, they included "the most serious acts that cannot be interpreted any other way." However, the forum's decision to force Elon to retire from public and educational life and impose restrictions on him came after the members realized, a year later, there was "another complaint more severe than the first." The committee dealing with the matter said it was shocked to discover the second complaint was made while it was deliberating the first one.

The committee also presented details of the restrictions imposed on Elon: Immediately after receiving the first complaint, Elon was asked not to be alone with a man. However, "the committee lost faith in statements by the rabbi, who concealed his acts during deliberation on the first complaint," and further restrictions were therefore imposed "that would distance him from the possibility of hurting anyone else in the future." Elon has since been convicted of sexually assaulting a minor; another complainant reportedly refused to testify, for reasons unstated in news reports. (Aviel Magnezi, "Rabbi Elon Found Guilty of Indecent Acts," *Ynet News* [ynetnews.com], August 7, 2013.) Rabbi Elon declined to appeal his conviction. (Aviel Magnezi, "Rabbi Moti Elon Will Not Appeal Sex Offense Conviction," *Ynet News* [ynetnews.com], February 2, 2014.)

16. Esther Wachsman, "His Name Was Nachshon Wachsman," *Orthodox Union* (ou.org), May 9, 2000.

17. Simone Weichselbaum, "Yiddish Posters Up in Williamsburg Asking for Cash for Accused Child Molester Angering Victim's Family," *New York Daily News*, May 14, 2012.

18. Shmarya Rosenberg, "Leading Monsey Rabbis Visit Convicted Child Rapist Rabbi Yisroel Weingarten, Declare His 'Innocence,'" *Failed Messiah* (failedmessiah.typepad.com), January 14, 2011.

19. This was reported to me personally after Rabbi Kanievsky was consulted in the Colmer case.

20. Nir Hasson, "Haredi 'Rabbi' Elior Chen Sentenced to 24 Years in Prison for Child Abuse," *Ha-aretz*, February 28, 2011.

21. Natan Slifkin, "The Gedolim and Leadership," *Rationalist Judaism: Exploring the Legacy of the Rationalist Medieval Torah Scholars* (rationalistjudaism.com), March 23, 2010. Rabbi Elyashiv is now deceased, but Rabbi Kanievsky is very much alive as of this writing.

22. Sarah Pascal, "Reports from the American Aguda Convention Held Over the Weekend November 24–27," *Dei'ah veDibur: Information & Insight* (chareidi.org), December 8, 2011.

23. Ruth Eglash, "Haredi Parents Take on Sexual Abuse of Children," *Jerusalem Post*, June 3, 2009; Tamar Rotem, "Protecting the Pedophiles in Ultra-Orthodox Ramat Beit Shemesh," *Ha-aretz*, June 16, 2009.

24. Jonathan Rosenblum, on *Failed Messiah* (failedmessiah.typepad.com), December 13, 2006.

25. Jonathan Rosenblum, "Think Again: Those Primitive Haredim—Yet Again," *Jerusalem Post*, June 11, 2009.

26. Rosenblum's talent for seeing reality topsy-turvy isn't limited to matters of child sex abuse. Elsewhere in the same column, he referred compassionately to "Jews evicted from their homes in Gaza"—meaning, of course, colonists in occupied Palestinian territory who were finally removed by Israel's government (after much public hand-wringing) in 2005. On the other hand, Rosenblum's column appeared less than six months after an Israeli assault on Gaza killed some 1,400 Palestinians there, 300 of them children, but Rosenblum didn't even mention *them*; in fact, elsewhere he has praised Israel's army for having "performed admirably" in carrying out the slaughter, complaining only that the United States did not veto a Security Council resolution calling for a ceasefire—presumably because the resolution may have encouraged Israel to put a stop to the carnage. (Jonathan Rosenblum, "Operation Cast Lead—Week III," *Cross-Currents* (cross-currents.com), January 14, 2009.) This represents another plank in the hierarchical moral platform for which Rosenblum is an apologist: Jewish dominance trumps non–Jewish life, just as rabbinic power trumps the human rights of child abuse victims.

27. Aldous Huxley, *The Devils of Loudun* (New York: Harper, 1952), p. 322.

28. Barbara Blaine, "My Cross to Bear: How I Challenged the Catholic Church Hierarchy to Atone for Their Sins Against Me and Other Abuse Victims," in *Tempest in the Temple*, p. 174.

29. See, *e.g.,* Jonathan Rosenblum, "Those Primitive Haredim Again," *Jewish Media Resources* (jewishmediaresources.com), June 12, 2009; "Wishing Away Child Abuse: Jonathan Rosenblum Responds," *Tzedek-Tzedek* (tzedek-tzedek.blogspot.com), September 25, 2009. Rosenblum's columns also appear often in such Orthodox publications as the *Jewish Observer*.

30. Tzvi H. Weinreb, "Hush," *Jewish Action*, Summer 2012.

31. Naomi Cohen, "A Lubavitcher's Response to Controversial Book 'Hush,'" *Current Events, Jewish Moms, Motherhood* (jewishmom.com), November 5, 2011.

32. Posted by "A Reader" to "Hush—Book Review," *Frum Satire* (frumsatire.net), November 26, 2010.

33. Posted by "laughing at the easily convinced world" to "Author of Anonymous Book on Haredi Child Sex Abuse Outs Herself," on *Failed Messiah* (failedmessiah.typepad.com), August 2, 2011.

34. Judy Brown, "Orthodox Jewish Child Abuse: Shattering a Traumatic Silence," *Huffington Post* (huffingtonpost.com), August 1, 2011.

35. Avi Shafran, "Hearing Voices," *Cross-Currents* (cross-currents.com), August 2, 2011. According to Shafran, the column had appeared in *Ami Magazine* a week earlier. In response to my query, he wrote me that he "couldn't have had her [Brown] in mind" when he wrote the column, which is certainly true; but he also hasn't written anything to suggest that someone like Brown could actually be well-intentioned in linking Kletzky's death to the larger problem of child abuse.

36. Doug Auer, "Orthodox Cam Plan," *New York Post*, May 26, 2012.

37. Many ultra–Orthodox rabbis have tried to ban the use of the Internet altogether, a position touted, for instance, at a huge public event at Citi Field Stadium in New York in May 2012 (discussed in Chapter 11). However, it is clear that even most "right-wing" Orthodox Jews continue to have Internet access.

38. Zvi Frankel, "Blogs: Transgressing a Major Sin 'In the Name of Heaven,'" *Jewish Observer*, December 10, 2007, pp. 32–33.

39. Avi Shafran, "Blogistan," *Yeshiva World* (theyeshivaworld.com), December 28, 2007.

40. Frankel, "Blogs," p. 33.

41. Asher Meir, "Frum Blogger—*Hayelchu Yachdav?*" *Hirhurim—Musings* (hirhurim.blogspot.com), December 17, 2007.

42. Shafran, "Blogistan."

43. Avi Shafran, responding to Natan Slifkin, "Mapping Blogistan: The Community and Its Critics," Letters, *Ami Magazine*, June 27, 2012, p. 15.

44. Michael Powell, "For Prosecutor in Sexual Abuse Case, Muted Praise from One Corner," *New York Times*, December 18, 2012.

45. Avi Shafran, "Open Season on the Orthodox," *Moment*, February 25, 2000, pp. 47–49; Susan Forrest, "The Comeback of Concubines," *New York Daily News*, December 29, 1996, pp. 18–19. Both are cited in Amy Neustein

and Michael Lesher, "The Silence of the Jewish Media on Sexual Abuse in the Orthodox Jewish Community," p. 85.

46. Sharon Otterman and Ray Rivera, "Ultra-Orthodox Shun Their Own for Reporting Child Sexual Abuse," *New York Times*, May 10, 2012.

47. Meir Soloveichik, "The Virtue of Hate," *First Things* (firstthings.com), February 2003.

48. Sharon Otterman and Ray Rivera, "Ultra-Orthodox Shun Their Own for Reporting Child Sexual Abuse."

49. Steven H. Resnicoff, "Jewish Law and the Tragedy of Sexual Abuse of Children—the Dilemma within the Orthodox Jewish Community," *Rutgers Journal of Law and Religion*, Vol. 13, No. 2, June 2012, pp. 10–11. On this point the article cites, *inter alia*, Nachum Klafter, *The Impact of Child Sexual Abuse*, The Jewish Board of Advocates for Children, September 21, 2008, p. 21; Dale O'Leary, *Gay Teens and Attempted Suicide* (http://www.narth.com/docs/gayteen.html); *Child Abuse May "Mark" Genes in Brains of Suicide Victims*, SCI.DAILY (sciencedaily.com/releases/2008/05/080507084001.htm), May 7, 2008; *Strong Link Between Childhood Sexual Abuse And Suicide Attempts In Women*, MEDICAL NEWS TODAY, June 9, 2009; *Suicide Linked to Sexual Abuse* (personalmd.com/news/a1996061806.shtml). All of my quotations from this article are taken from an advance version that appeared on the Internet in July 2012.

50. Kibbie S. Ruth, "Risk of Abuse in Faith Communities," in *Child Maltreatment: A Clinical Guide and Reference* (3rd ed.) (James A. Monteleone and Armand E. Brodeur, Eds.) (St. Louis: G.W. Medical, 2005), p. 545, quoted in Janet Heimlich, *Breaking Their Will*, p. 174.

51. Judy Brown, "'Ub-u-sive': Spelling Out Abuse After Nechemya Weberman's Conviction," *Jewish Daily Forward (Mobile)*, December 20, 2012.

Chapter 5

1. Benjamin Spock and Mitchell Zimmerman, *Dr. Spock on Vietnam* (New York: Dell Publishing Co., Inc., 1968), p. 44.

2. Judy Brown, "The Importance of Internet Asifa," May 20, 2012.

3. Etgar Lefkovitz, "Man Who Killed Infant Son Gets 6 Years in Jail," *Jerusalem Post*,

November 18, 2008; Staff, "Baby Killer Yisrael Valis Ordered to Begin Jail Term. Court Rejects Appeal to Delay Start of Six-Year Sentence," *Jerusalem Post*, January 5, 2009.

4. Staff, "Rabbis Call for Yisrael Valis' Release," *Jerusalem Post*, April 23, 2006.

5. *Id.*

6. Etgar Lefkovitz, "Man Who Killed Infant Son Gets 6 Years in Jail."

7. Sarah Shapiro, "Yisrael Valis: Two Versions of a Story," *Cross-Currents* (cross-currents.com), June 26, 2006.

8. Etgar Lefkovitz, "Man Who Killed Infant Son Gets 6 Years in Jail."

9. Etgar Lefkovitz, "Alleged Baby-Killer's Trial Opens," *Jerusalem Post*, June 5, 2006.

10. Larry Derfner, "Israel's Ultra-Orthodox Dead Get Proper Burial," *Jewish Journal* (jewishjournal.com), November 22, 2011.

11. *Id.*

12. Larry Derfner, "Rattling the Cage: Community of Collaborators," *Jerusalem Post*, June 8, 2006.

13. Larry Derfner, "More Questions Than Answers," *Jerusalem Post*, June 7, 2006. Derfner's article mentions a *pro forma* statement, attributed to two local rabbis, that they knew nothing about the crime and "opposed any use of violence." But the leading *haredi* rabbi in Ashdod refused to issue any criticism, and not one ultra–Orthodox rabbi was willing to instruct his followers that such criminal violence was forbidden by Jewish law.

14. Jonathan Rosenblum, "Defanging Derfner," *Cross-Currents* (cross-currents.com), June 14, 2006.

15. Jonathan Rosenblum, "Lessons from a Tragedy," *Cross-Currents* (cross-currents.com), June 7, 2006.

16. Larry Derfner, "Rattling the Cage: Community of Collaborators; Staff, "Rabbis Call for Yisrael Valis' Release."

17. *Jerusalem Post*, April 10, 2006, quoted in Sarah Shapiro, "Yisrael Valis: Two Versions of a Story."

18. *Id.*; "Rabbi Elyashiv: Haredi Baby Murderer 'Innocent,' Charges a 'Blood Libel,'" *Failed Messiah* (failedmessiah.typepad.com), April 23, 2006; Larry Derfner, "Rattling the Cage: Community of Collaborators." As noted above, Valis later retracted his confession, but of course that did not alter the physical evidence, which was never questioned by the hospital staff that treated the baby.

19. Staff, "Rabbis Call for Yisrael Valis' Release."

20. Jonathan Rosenblum, "Defanging Derfner."

21. In these and similar cases, Orthodox spokesmen have suggested that their leaders only want to ensure the right of the accused to a fair trial. One can hardly quarrel with that—except that if rabbis endorse massive communal support for the accused criminals merely out of compassion and a sense of justice, they ought in fairness to be equally concerned with the needs of the alleged victims, which they manifestly aren't.

22. Yaakov Menken, "Fisking Larry Derfner, Part I," *Cross-Currents* (cross-currents.com), June 11, 2006.

23. Andy Newman, "City Questions Circumcision Ritual After Baby Dies," *New York Times*, August 26, 2005.

24. *Id.*; Liz Robbins, "Baby's Death Renews Debate Over a Circumcision Ritual," *New York Times*, March 7, 2012.

25. Andy Newman, "City Questions Circumcision Ritual After Baby Dies."

26. Steve Lieberman, "Monsey Rabbi Investigated," *Journal News*, February 3, 2005.

27. *Id.*

28. Hella Winston, "Banned Mohel Still Apparently Performing 'Metzitzah,'" *New York Jewish Week*, March 13, 2012.

29. Liz Robbins, "Baby's Death Renews Debate Over a Circumcision Ritual."

30. Staff, "More Than 200 Rabbonim Declare War on NYC Health Dept Over 'Metzitzah B'peh,'" *Yeshiva World News* (theyeshivaworld.com), August 30, 2012.

31. Kate Briquelet, "Despite Baby Dying After Getting Herpes, Orthodox Rabbis Say They'll Defy Law on Ancient Circumcision Ritual, *New York Post*, September 2, 2012.

32. Moshe Heller, "Mohels Protest Restriction on 'Suction' During Circumcision," *Ynet News* (ynetnews.com), August 10, 2012.

33. Yitzchok Frankfurter, "Between a Battle & a Prayer," *Ami Magazine*, August 29, 2012.

34. Debbie Maimon, "The Battle for Metzitzah," *Yated Ne'eman*, October 26, 2012, pp. 136–137.

35. Yitzchok Frankfurter, "Between a Battle & a Prayer," p. 48.

36. *Id.*, pp. 49, 50. As a further instance of his understanding of "scientific method," Rabbi

Belsky offered a fabricated history of the ban on *kosher* slaughter in Switzerland, according to which Swiss legislators "before the war" decided to prohibit the practice out of disgust at spotting a Jewish lawyer—who had earlier argued in favor of traditional slaughter—eating in a non-*kosher* restaurant. In fact, the ban was inserted in Switzerland's confederal constitution in 1893 (long before "the war") as the result of a country-wide referendum. (See Shlomo Avineri, "What Do Mosque Minarets and Kosher Slaughter Have in Common?" *Ha'aretz*, December 6, 2009.) No Jewish lawyer, no non-*kosher* restaurant; no colorful anecdote for rabbinic sermonizing. But clearly no one at *Ami* was checking Rabbi Belsky's "facts."

37. Shimon Finkelman and Nosson Scherman, *Reb Moshe: The Life and Ideals of Ha-Gaon Rabbi Moshe Feinstein* (New York: Mesorah Publications, 1986).

38. Yossi Krausz, "Fighting Heroic Battles," *Ami Magazine*, August 29, 2012, p. 54. Recall that oral suction is obligatory, if at all, only under rabbinic law; circumcision, as decreed in the Bible, can be performed without it, and (among most Jews) usually is.

39. *Id.*

40. Yitzchok Frankfurter, "Between a Battle & a Prayer," p. 47.

41. Yossi Krausz, "To Be Loud ... or Not to Be Loud," *Ami Magazine*, August 29, 2012, p. 65.

42. Yossi Krausz, "Fighting Heroic Battles," p. 61.

43. Hella Winston, "Metzitzah Arguments Seen Taking Shape," *New York Jewish Week*, September 27, 2012; Debbi Maimon, "The Battle for Metzitzah," p. 136.

44. Frank Schaeffer, "When Freedom Is a Dirty Word," *Huffington Post*, September 22, 2009, in Janet Heimlich, *Breaking Their Will*, p. 320.

45. Amy Neustein and Michael Lesher, "Justice Interrupted," pp. 217–218. As stated there, Elliot Pasik, an Orthodox Jewish lawyer, was instrumental in securing a New York state law "requiring routine background checks of employees of religious schools, including yeshivos.... Pasik's accomplishment ... earned him some harsh attacks in some Orthodox quarters."

46. Nonie Darwish, "Using Children as Weapons," *Gatestone Institute* (gatestoneinsti

tute.org), December 20, 2012, reproduced in *Jewish Press* (jewishpress.com), December 20, 2012 under the title "Stop Messing with Our Children," and comments posted there.

47. Yaakov Rosenblatt, "To Protect and Provide," *Jewish World Review* (jewishworld review.com), February 11, 2013. Rabbi Rosenblatt has also claimed that "secular society weakens the male." (Yaakov Rosenblatt, "Installing My Internet Filter," *Jewish Press* (jew ishpress.com), June 13, 2012.)

48. Yori Yanover, "Arab Antisemites Attack Haredim in Jerusalem," *Jewish Press*, January 13, 2013, and comments posted there.

49. Samuel Butler, *The Way of All Flesh* (New York: Penguin Books, 1947) (originally 1903), pp. 284, 304–305.

Chapter 6

1. Aimé Césaire, *Discourse on Colonialism* (trans. Joan Pinkham) (New York: Monthly Review Press, 1972, 2000), p. 31.

2. Joseph L. Blau, *Modern Varieties of Judaism* (New York, London: Columbia University Press, 1966), pp. 50–51. According to one published version of the story, he was assaulted by the synagogue president; after going home he was arrested, presumably at the latter's instigation, for allegedly disturbing the peace. (Max Raisin, *A History of the Jews in Modern Times* [revised edition] [New York: Hebrew Publishing Company, 1949], p. 255.)

3. Official statement released December 14, 2006.

4. Avi Shafran (Director of Public Affairs, Agudath Israel of America), posted to Canonist.com, December 8, 2006.

5. Steven H. Resnicoff, "Jewish Law and the Tragedy of Sexual Abuse of Children," p. 3.

6. For speaking out about child sex abuse by his fellow Orthodox Jews, Rabbi Rosenberg was later assaulted again: a cup of bleach was thrown in his face, resulting in corneal burns. (Jennifer Bain and Rebecca Harshbarger, "Rabbi Bleach Collar," *New York Post*, December 13, 2012.)

7. Steven H. Resnicoff, "Jewish Law and the Tragedy of Sexual Abuse of Children," pp. 4–6 (note 15), 20.

8. Mordechai Glick, "Dealing with 'Orthodox' Child Molesters: A Response to the Community's Response" [letter to the editor],

Jewish Press, February 4, 2000, pp. 87–88, in Amy Neustein and Michael Lesher, "Justice Interrupted," pp. 198, 226 n. 1.

9. Oren Yaniv, "Judge overseeing sex abuse trial of Orthodox leader Nechemya Weberman gets snippy over courtroom snapshot outing accuser, 4 men detained in connection with illegal photo," *New York Daily News*, November 29, 2012. Rabbi Weberman was eventually convicted on 59 counts of rape and sexual molestation.

10. Simone Weichselbaum and Oren Yaniv, "Satmar Sect's Sick Revenge as Pervert's Posse Bullies Family of Teen Sex-Abuse Victim," *New York Daily News*, December 13, 2012.

11. Moses L. Lilienblum, "The Sins of My Youth," in *The Golden Tradition: Jewish Life and Thought in Eastern Europe* (Lucy S. Dawidowicz, Ed.) (Boston: Beacon Press, 1968), p. 125.

12. S. Ansky, "Between Two Worlds," in *The Golden Tradition*, pp. 308–311.

13. See Mark Dratch, "A Community of Co-enablers: Why Are Jews Ignoring Traditional Jewish Law by Protecting the Abuser?" in *Tempest in the Temple*, pp. 115–116.

14. "The Opinion of the Gedolai Hador Shlita Against the Books of Nosson Slifkin," available on line at http://www.zootorah.com/controversy/pashkevil.jpg; Natan Slifkin, "In Defense of My Opponents," *Zoo Torah* (zootorah.com), October 5, 2008.

15. Exchange of emails between the author and forjerusalem@gmail.com, December 31, 2006—January 1, 2007. I ultimately obtained a recording of the speech, confirming that Rabbi Salomon had spoken in favor of sex abuse cover-ups. With respect to the lack of a "Jewish" basis for the authority of truth, cf. Israel Shahak, *Jewish History, Jewish Religion: The Weight of Three Thousand Years* (London: Pluto Press, 2008), p. 19 ("It turned out to be very easy among the Jews ... to mount a very effective attack against all the notions and ideals of humanism and the rule of law (not to say democracy) as something 'un–Jewish' or 'anti–Jewish'....")

16. Josh Yuter, "The Selective Sanctimony of Orthodox Judaism," on the blog *Yutopia* (joshyuter.com), December 6, 2011.

17. Harry Maryles, "Why Is It Always the Guys with Beards?" on the blog *Emes VeEmunah* (haemtza.blogspot.com), November 30, 2012.

18. Leib Pinter, *Don't Give Up: Rays of Light and Strength for the Hardest Times* (Brooklyn: Mesorah Publications, 2004); Natan Slifkin, "An Account of Events," on the blog *Zoo Torah* (zootorah.org). This account was widely available via Internet since at least June 30, 2005. To the best of my knowledge, Rabbi Pinter has never denied the leading role in the campaign attributed to him by Rabbi Slifkin.

19. Grant McCool, "New York Lender Admits to Fraud of Fannie Mae," *Reuters* (reuters.com), September 11, 2008; Martha Graybow, "NY Man Ordered to Prison for Defrauding Fannie Mae," *Reuters* (reuters.com), March 19, 2009.

20. Natan Slifkin, "An Account of Events."

21. Natan Slifkin, "Rewriting Jewish Intellectual History: A Review of *Sefer Chaim Be-Emunasom*," available via link from "The Complete Review of Chaim Be'Emunasom," on the blog *Rationalist Judaism* (rationalistjudaism.com), September 5, 2009. Some of Rabbi Schmeltzer's alleged written comments on Rabbi Slifkin—"idiot," "animal," "low-life," "sick man," "thoroughly evil person"—are quoted in the post "Puzzled at Passaic," *Rationalist Judaism* (rationalistjudaism.com), November 29, 2010. Again, I am not aware of any denial from Rabbi Schmeltzer.

22. The text of Rabbi Kornreich's long blog posting is available at "Haredi Kiruv Rabbi Advocates *Suicide* for Homosexuals," *Failed Messiah* (failedmessiah.typepad.com), May 14, 2009.

23. Quoted in *The Baruch Pelta vs. Rabbi Dovid Kornreich Debate* (found at http://bpvsfkm.com) under the heading "Dovid Kornreich's Response to Q&A," October 31, 2010.

24. Lawrence Cohler-Esses, "Inside the Satmar School Scandal," *New York Jewish Week*, April 23, 1999; Jacques Steinberg, "After Guilty Plea, Rabbi Explains Actions in a Fund Diversion Scheme," *New York Times*, April 17, 1999.

25. Steve Lipman, "The Trusted Outsider," *New York Jewish Week*, April 23, 1999.

26. See Joseph Berger, "Hasidic Sect Hopes to Buy Huge Armory in Brooklyn," *New York Times*, April 11, 2013; Debra Nussbaum-Cohen, "New York Ultra–Orthodox Discover the Downside of Being Fruitful and Multiplying," *Ha'aretz*, September 24, 2012.

27. See "Rare View: Rabbi Hertz Frankel

Re-writes Satmar History in Ami Magazine," *Dus Iz Nies* (dusiznies.blogspot.com), December 12, 2011 for excerpts and a reproduction of the first page of one such column.

28. See the affirming decision of the United States Court of Appeals for the Eighth Circuit in *United States v. Rubashkin*, Docket Nos. 10–2487/3580, September 16, 2011, especially pp. 2–6, 28–31. This decision is also available in public reports as *U.S. v. Rubashkin*, 655 F.3d 849 (8th Cir., 2011).

29. Staff (from JTA), "Supreme Court Rejects Rubashkin Appeal," *The New York Jewish Week*, October 3, 2012; for continuing fundraising, see "Justice for Sholom" at justiceforsholom.org.

30. Pinchos Lipschutz, "What If?" *Matzav. com* (matzav.com), September 11, 2009.

31. Simone Landon, "Immigration Raid Breaks Up Organizing Drive at Iowa Meat-Packing Plant," *Labornotes* (labornotes.org), August 25, 2008.

32. Jan Lee, "Rabbis Urge Jews to Help Rubashkin as April 28 Sentencing Nears," *Suite 101* (suite101.com), April 26, 2010.

33. See Staff, "Supreme Court Rejects Rubashkin Appeal," *Yeshiva World* (theyeshivaworld.com), October 2, 2012.

34. Karen Tumulty, "Re: The Next Big Problem at the Justice Department?" *Time (Swampland)*, March 9, 2007.

35. Pete Yost and Lara J. Jordan, "Senate OKs limits on Gonzales' authority," *Associated Press*, March 20, 2007.

36. Karen Tumulty, "Re: The Next Big Problem at the Justice Department?"

37. Debbie Maimon, "How the System Failed Sholom Rubashkin," *Shmais News Service* (shmais.com), June 21, 2012. The same article also appeared in *Chabad News*, another Hasidic publication.

38. Yehuda Shlezinger, "Rabbinic Sex Scandal Spawns Crisis Among Faithful," *Israel Hayom* (israelhayom.com), July 18, 2012.

39. In May 2013, it was reported that Rabbi Berland had fled Isreal "several months ago ... after he was accused of sleeping with numerous married women and underage girls." One of the rabbi's accusers told the press, "If I walk in Jerusalem without any protection [his follers] will kill me"—which may help to explain the slow pace of the story. (Shifra Unger, "Woman Tells Police How Rabbi Berland Sexually Abused Her," *Your Jewish News* (yourjewish

news.com), May 2013; see also Yair Ettinger, "Haredi World Divided Over Lastest Sexual Harassment Scandal," *Ha'aretz*, March 22, 2013.) In November 2013 Rabbi Berland was ordered to leave Morocco, where he had been living with his flock. (Staff, "Morocco Expels Fugitive Israel Rabbi," *Ha'aretz*, November 9, 2013.) As of this writing, whether he will ever face justice remains to be seen. Regarding the parents of Rabbi Hafner's alleged victim, see Amy Neustein and Michael Lesher, "Justice Interrupted," pp. 215–216.

40. Shmarya Rosenberg, "Exclusive: The Story Behind the Tropper Scandal," *Failed Messiah* (failedmessiah.typepad.com), December 16, 2009; Staff, "Outreach Rabbi Resigns Amid Cloud of Scandal," *New York Jewish Week*, December 16, 2009. For more about the financial allegations against Tropper, see Baruch Gordon, "Jewish Billionaire Sues Prominent US Rabbi," *Arutz Sheva* (israelnationalnews.com), October 8, 2009.

41. See, *e.g.*, "The Case for Rabbi Tropper's Defense," *Daas Torah—Issues of Jewish Identity* (daattorah.blogspot.com), December 16, 2009.

42. Shmarya Rosenberg, "Leading Haredi Rabbis Call on Schools to Ban Kids Whose Parents Have Internet," on the blog *Failed Messiah* (failedmessiah.typepad.com), December 3, 2012. Some "leniency" is granted to parents who need Internet access for money-making.

43. Confirmed to me by local residents. Rabbinic rulings supposedly isolating Mondrowitz were issued in Brooklyn and Israel around the time of his indictment and were cited seriously to me, over twenty years later, by two prominent Orthodox rabbis.

44. See, *e.g.*, Danielle Blumenthal, "Pearl Perry Reich Doesn't Speak for Me," *Think Brand First* (danielleblumenthal.com), March 3, 2012; Chava Tombosky, "New York—Op-Ed: Debunking Perry Reich, Hasidic Women, and Drawing Inspiration from Struggle," *Vos Iz Neias* (vosizneias.com), March 2, 2012.

45. Jonah Lowenfeld, "Anti-Muslim Activist Barred from Speaking at Jewish Federation Headquarters," *Jewish Journal* (jewishjournal.com), June 25, 2012.

46. Lori Lowenthal Marcus, "One Door Closes, Two Open: Two Shuls Host Geller Talks Sunday," *Jewish Press* (jewishpress.com), April 12, 2013. The article refers specifically to Chava Tombosky, who prominently criticized

Reich (see above). Tombosky is a Lubavitch Hasid. Yet, to the best of my knowledge, she (like Reich's other Orthodox critics) has been silent about Geller's hate speech, even as Geller was embraced by officials of her own sect.

47. See, *e.g.*, Pamela Geller, "CNN Tells, Sells More Lies About Palin—It's Time to Expose the Truth About Obama," *Atlas Shrugs* (atlasshrugs2000.typepad.com), August 1, 2009; Pamela Geller, "How Could Stanley Ann Dunham Have Delivered Barack Hussein Obama, Jr. in August of 1961 in Honolulu, When Official University of Washington Records Show Her 2680 Miles Away in Seattle Attending Classes That Same Month?" *Atlas Shrugs* (atlasshrugs2000.typepad.com), October 24, 2008. I am indebted to the web site *Loonwatch* (loonwatch.com) for collecting the relevant information about Geller under the (fully justified) heading "Pamela Geller: The Looniest Blogger Ever."

48. Danielle Blumenthal, "Pearl Perry Reich Doesn't Speak for Me" (the same charge is repeated in many other comments posted by Orthodox Jews; for Geller's bikini video, see http://www.youtube.com/watch?v=7TG7DT OkU-s.

49. David Lefer, "Ecstasy and the Hasidim Drug Ring Used Youths as Mules in Pill Trade," *New York Daily News*, August 1, 1999.

50. Christopher S. Wren, "7 Charged in Drug Scheme Said to Use Hasidic Couriers," *New York Times*, July 21, 1999.

51. Alan Feuer, "Sentencing a Drug Courier, Judge Rebukes the Hasidim," *New York Times*, March 29, 2000.

52. In response to my query, the newspaper's publisher, Naomi Maurer, emailed me: "Offhand I cannot remember if we carried any articles about this.... But it is possible that if anything there was just a passing mention of this." I have received no other response from the newspaper, nor have I found a trace of any reporting of this story in its pages.

53. Samuel M. Katz, "Israel's Other Export," *Moment*, August 2001, p. 92. The *Times* also reported on the possibly widening involvement of Orthodox institutions in drug trading, though the crucial fact was buried deep in a story on another subject. (Alan Feuer, "In Miami, an Imported Mob Scene," *New York Times*, July 3, 2000.)

54. Joseph Berger, "Holy Hypocrites?" *Moment*, February 2000, p. 52.

55. Yair Ettinger, "Japan Sentences Hasidic Israeli to 8 Years in Jail After Ecstasy Bust," *Ha'aretz*, May 3, 2009; Staff, "Tokyo—2nd Yeshiva Student Imprisoned in Japan Receives Six Years," *Vos Iz Neias* (vosizneias.com), March 24, 2010.

56. Hillel Fendel, "Japanese High Court Rejects Hassidic Appeal," *Arutz Sheva*, May 16, 2011. This would place the drugs' value at about $39 per pill. Apparently the street value of an Ecstasy pill had risen somewhat since 2000, when it was said to be between $25 and $30—or maybe the drug sells at a higher price in Israel than in New York.

57. Staff, "Japan Court: Yoel Zev Found Not Guilty," *Yeshiva World News*, August 29, 2011.

58. DPA, "Israeli Who Trained Colombia Guerrillas Wins Appeal Against Extradition," *Ha'aretz*, April 1, 2010; Yasha Levine, "Yair Klein: Russia's 'Other' Viktor Bout," *Exile*, March 28, 2008; Ben Hartman, "Ex-IDF Officer Said to Have Trained Gunmen Set to Return," *Jerusalem Post*, November 9, 2010.

59. Staff, "Israel—Lawyer in Japan Bocharim Case: State of Israel Ignors [sic] Jews When in Need of Help," *Vos Iz Neias* (vosizneias.com), May 21, 2008; Ha'aretz Service, "Livni Urges Thailand to Commute Israeli Drug Smugglers' Death Sentence," *Ha'aretz*, November 25, 2008.

60. Staff, "Narita, Japan—Israeli Bucherim Arrested for Drug Trafficking," *Vos Iz Neias* (vosizneias.com), April 6, 2008.

61. Hillel Fendel, "Drug-Smuggler Who Enticed Yeshiva Youths Indicted," *Arutz Sheva* (israelnationalnews.com), March 3, 2009.

62. See Staff, "Tokyo—2nd Yeshiva Student Imprisoned in Japan Receives Six Years"; Hillel Fendel, "Japanese High Court Rejects Hassidic Appeal."

63. Staff, "How Organized Crime Families Penetrated the Yeshivahs," *Channel 10 News* (Israel), video and explanatory text (in English) via Vimeo (vimeo.com/3692967), March 16, 2009. (The video is in Hebrew.) At the moment, there are two rival Satmar Rebbes, and the very large Satmar Hasidic community is divided between the two.

64. Malka Heimowitz, "The Nightmare for the Teens Held in Japan Prison," *Jewish Press*, February 11, 2009. Note that the headline describes the couriers as "teens," when in fact two of the three were more than 20 years old.

65. Yair Ettinger, "Japan Sentences Hasidic Israeli to 8 Years in Jail After Ecstasy Bust."

66. *Id.*

67. Yuval Goren, "Four Argentinian Retirees Arrested for Smuggling Drugs for Israeli Ring," *Ha'aretz*, February 19, 2009.

68. Staff, "Court in Japan Absolves Third Yeshiva Student of Drug Charges," HappyJew ishNews.com, August 29, 2011.

69. David Gold, "Jerusalem—How Organized Crime Families Penetrated the Yeshivah's," *Vos Iz Neias* (vosi/neias.com), March 16, 2009. To his credit, Rabbi Jonathan Rosenblum stressed this point in a column that stands virtually alone in the Orthodox press, noting that being "caught smuggling, no matter what they were smuggling," was a violation of religious law far worse than eating non-*kosher* food. (Jonathan Rosenblum, "Chareidim L'Kol Davar," *Cross-Currents* (cross-currents.com), June 5, 2008.) Unfortunately, this important observation soon disappeared from the story as it was reported in Orthodox media.

70. Hillel Fendel, "Drug-Smuggler Who Enticed Yeshiva Youths Indicted."

71. "Inspiring Letter Written by Yaakov Yosef ben Raizel After the Verdict of His Appeal to Klal Yisroel," found on a fundraising site, *Japan Pidyon Shvuyim*, seeking contributions to Orach Chaim Rescue Fund in Lakewood, New Jersey.

72. Staff, "Tokyo—2nd Yeshiva Student Imprisoned in Japan Receives Six Years."

73. Malka Heimowitz, "The Nightmare for the Teens Held in Japan Prison."

74. Kenji Hall, "Contemporary Art Tries Out Tokyo," *Business Week* ("Eye on Asia" blog), April 4, 2008; Kenji Hall, "Tokyo Art Fair Revisited," *Business Week* ("Eye on Asia" blog), April 10, 2008. The dates for the event (Friday, April 4 to Sunday, April 6) can be found on the web site of the sponsoring organization, www.mutualart.com/Organization/101-Tokyo-Contemporary-Art-Fair.

75. Staff, "U.S. Expert Testimony Wins Historic Drug-Smuggling Acquittal in Japanese Court," *PRWeb* (prweb.com), September 9, 2011. The article's reference is to "Chabad," but this is identical to Lubavitch; the former is the name given by Lubavitch Hasidim to their brand of Hasidic religious philosophy.

76. Information available via Internet establishes the following: including the time zone difference, at least seven and half hours elapsed during the couriers' trip from Israel to Amsterdam. The trip from Amsterdam to Tokyo (also including time zone differences) took about 21 hours. The Jewish Sabbath ended no earlier than 7:45 p.m. in Israel on April 5, 2008. Thus, there is simply no realistic way the couriers could have boarded a flight from Ben-Gurion Airport on Saturday night, flown to Amsterdam, met their contacts there at a hotel room, picked up the new suitcases containing the Ecstasy pills, returned to the airport, boarded another flight and flown to Tokyo, retrieved their luggage and taken it to customs, all before midnight Sunday night. It is true that it was 6:30 a.m. on Monday in Tokyo by the time news of their arrest was announced in New York. But by the time of the announcement one of the couriers had already retained a prominent Israeli lawyer, of whom they had no prior knowledge (Mordechai Tzivin), and the lawyer had already made statements to the Israeli press. Given the relevant time differences, that could not have happened by the time the arrest was announced, had the couriers been arrested in the wee hours of Monday morning. Rather, it is virtually certain that they flew from *Amsterdam* (where the Sabbath ended about 9:30 p.m. on Saturday night), reaching Tokyo on Sunday evening, at a time when business offices, banks and newspapers were still open in Israel, six hours earlier—Sunday being a business day in Israel. If so, however, the three must have spent the Sabbath in Amsterdam. This fact is fudged in a report based on Orthodox sources (Staff, "U.S. Expert Wins Historic Drug-Smuggling Acquittal"), and mentioned nowhere else that I can find.

77. Mordechai Tzivin, "Jerusalem—Continuous Erroneous Reports on Charedi Web Sites About the Japan Boys Must Stop," *Vos Iz Neias* (vosi/neias.com), February 7, 2010.

78. Staff, "U.S. Expert Testimony Wins Historic Drug-Smuggling Acquittal."

79. Hillel Fendel, "Japan: Isreali [sic] Bochur Freed from Prison," *CrownHeights.info* (reprinted from *Arutz Sheva*), January 17, 2011.

80. Hillel Fendel, "Japanese High Court Rejects Hassidic Appeal."

81. Staff, "Benzion Miller Sentenced for Involvement in Sending Bochrim to Japan with Drug-Laden Suitcases," *Lakewood View*, September 15, 2010.

82. Noam Amdurski, "Man Who Set Up

Jailed Japan Bochurim Walks Free," Matzavwww, May 26, 2011.

83. *Id.*

84. Malka Heimowitz, "New York—The Nightmare for the Teens Held in Japan Prison."

85. COLlive reporter, "Ladies Rally for Japan Captives," *COLLive* (collive.com), March 15, 2009.

86. Malka Heimowitz, "New York—The Nightmare for the Teens Held in Japan Prison."

87. Staff, "Narita Chiba, Japan—Israeli Bucherim Remain in Prison," *Vos Iz Neias* (vosizneias.com), May 16, 2008.

88. Staff, "Rabbi: Tsunami Result of Haredi Arrests," *Ynet News* (ynetnews.com), March 31, 2011.

89. Avi Shafran, "A Matter of Orthodox Abuse," *New York Jewish Week*, June 23, 2006.

90. Alan Feuer, "Sentencing a Drug Courier, Judge Rebukes the Hasidim."

91. Yerachmiel Lopin, "Supporters of Victims of Weberman to Protest Satmar Rebbe Speech on Tuesday, Dec 4, pm," *Frum Follies* (frumfollies.wordpress.com), December 4, 2012. This blog posting also includes a link to an audio of the actual speech (in Yiddish).

92. Steven H. Resnicoff, "Jewish Law and the Tragedy of Sexual Abuse of Children," pp. 4–6 (note 15), 20; see *Shulhan Arukh, Hoshen ha–Mishpat* 388.

93. S. Ansky, "Between Two Worlds," in *The Golden Tradition*, p. 311.

94. See Israel Shahak, *Jewish History, Jewish Religion*, pp. 20–21.

95. Yonason [Jonathan] Rosenblum, *Reb Yaakov: The Life and Times of HaGaon Rabbi Yaakov Kamenetsky* (Brooklyn: Mesorah Publications, 1993), pp. 52–54, 48, 41–42.

Chapter 7

1. Thomas B. Macaulay, *The History of England* (abridged, Hugh Trevor-Roper, Ed.) (Middlesex, New York: Penguin Books, 1968), p. 120.

2. Amy Neustein and Michael Lesher, "Justice Interrupted," p. 214.

3. Karen Matthews, "Jewish Court Stymies Reports."

4. Plato, *Laws* 942ab; Moses Hadas, *Hellenistic Culture, Fusion and Diffusion* (New York: Columbia University Press, 1959), esp. Chapters 7 and 20, cited in Israel Shahak, *Jewish History, Jewish Religion*, p. 15.

5. Moses Maimonides, Mishneh Torah, Hilkhoth Sanhedrin 1:1.

6. Yosef Caro, Shulhan Arukh, Hoshen ha–Mishpat 26:1.

7. Israel Shahak, Jewish History, Jewish Religion, pp. 18, 21.

8. Paul Johnson, *A History of the Jews* (New York: Harper & Row, 1987), pp. 130, 294–295.

9. See, *e.g.*, the nasty anti–Mendelssohn polemic entitled "Netzach Yisrael" by Rabbi Eliyahu Meir Feivelson (Warsaw, 1914). An abridged version of the essay, in English, was published by Neve Yerushalayim College, a women's *yeshiva*, in 1999. This was the version I read.

10. Paul Johnson, *A History of the Jews*, p. 301.

11. Stephanie Saul, "Tripping Up the Prosecution."

12. Suzanne M. Sgroi and Natalie T. Dana, "Individual and Group Treatment of Mothers of Incest Victims," in *Handbook of Clinical Intervention in Child Sexual Abuse* (Suzanne M. Sgroi, Ed.) (New York: The Free Press, 1982), p. 211. Law enforcement officials have made significant efforts to improve this aspect of the system since these comments were made, but victims still report finding the process stressful and often intimidating.

13. Jeremy Sharon, "Court to Review Rabbinical Court's Social Exclusion Order," *Jerusalem Post*, May 22, 2013. Ironically, the woman went to court for religious reasons: her neighbor's illegal balcony prevented her from using her own porch for a *sukkah*, the ritual hut used by religious Jews during the autumn festival.

14. Cf. Macaulay's description of the development of Judge George Jeffreys into "the most consummate bully ever known in his profession" from an early immersion in the highly stratified criminal justice system of 17th-century London. (Thomas B. Macaulay, *The History of England*, p. 74.) A sample of Jeffreys' judicial behavior introduces the present chapter—along with a thumbnail description of part of a *beth din* proceeding, for easy comparison.

15. Amy Neustein and Michael Lesher, "Justice Interrupted," pp. 213–215.

16. *Sex Scandals in Religion*, Episode 2: "Wall of Silence," Vision TV (Canada), Alan Mendelsohn, director, May 16, 2011.

17. John Marzulli, "Rabbi Israel Wein-

garten Found Guilty of Molesting Daughter," *New York Daily News*, March 11, 2009; Transcript (Re-Sentencing) (Document #109), *U.S.A. v. Weingarten*, Docket No. 08-CR-571 (S1) (JG), September 12, 2011, pp. 18, 19–21, 22.

18. Demosthenes Lorandos and Ashish S. Joshi, Defendant's Sentencing Memorandum (Document #75), *U.S.A. v. Weingarten*, p. 13.

19. Donna R. Newman and Jill R. Shellow, Sentencing Memorandum (for defendant) (Document #100), *U.S.A. v. Weingarten*, pp. 7–11.

20. Demosthenes Lorandos and Ashish S. Joshi, Defendant's Sentencing Memorandum, pp. 10–14.

21. *Id.*, p. 7 [emphasis in original].

22. John Marzulli, "Rabbi Israel Weingarten Found Guilty of Molesting Daughter."

23. Affidavit of Rabbi David Weis, *U.S.A. v. Weingarten*, September 7, 2011, p. 1, para. 1 and p. 4, para. 10 b-d.

24. Letter of (Assistant U.S. Attorney) Rachel J. Nash to Judge Gleeson (Document #101), *U.S.A. v. Weingarten*, p. 11.

25. Demosthenes Lorandos and Ashish S. Joshi, Defendant's Sentencing Memorandum, p. 13; see Letter of Rachel J. Nash to Judge Gleeson, p. 14.

26. Yoseif Bloch, "Sorry, Rabbi, It's Not OK," *Times of Israel*, May 27, 2013 [emphasis in original]; Yair Ettinger, "Rabbi Elon Accused of 'Long-Term' Sexual Relationship with Student," *Ha-aretz*, February 18, 2010.

27. Kathleen Hopkins, "Lakewood Yeshiva Teacher Pleads Guilty to Sex Assault," *Asbury Park Press*, May 13, 2013. Rabbi Kolko was sentenced to "nearly 13 years" in prison after an unsuccessful attempt to retract his guilty plea. (Wayne Parry, "Victim of NJ Yeshiva Teacher: More Should Speak Up," *Associated Press* (on abcnews.go.com), October 17, 2013.)

28. The text of the Lakewood rabbis' letter, in English (with the names of the victim and his family redacted), can be found at the web site for Survivors for Justice (survivorsforjustice.org), under "Law and & Halacha," among the documents listed under the heading "The Yosef Kolko Case" as "Lakewood Kolko flier—redacted."

29. Kathleen Hopkins, "Lakewood Yeshiva Teacher Pleads Guilty to Sex Assault."

30. Karen Matthews, "Jewish Court Stymies Reports."

31. New Jersey Statutes § 9:6–8.10. Under this law, *anyone* with a reasonable suspicion of child abuse is unconditionally obligated to report to authorities.

32. The text of Rabbi Belsky's letter, the original Hebrew and in English translation, is available on the web site of Survivors for Justice (survivorsforjustice.org) under "Law & Halacha," among the documents listed under "The Yosef Kolko Case" as "Rabbi Yisroel Belsky's Letter to the Lakewood Community" [emphasis added].

33. The Hebrew text of this declaration can be found at the web site for Survivors for Justice (survivorsforjustice.org), under "Law and & Halacha," among the documents listed under the heading "The Yosef Kolko Case" as "Lakewood Kolko flier—redacted" (at the end). The translation is mine.

34. Kathleen Hopkins, "Lakewood Yeshiva Teacher Pleads Guilty to Sex Assault."

35. Paul Berger, "Ultra-Orthodox Group Affirms Abuse Cases Go First to Rabbi," *Jewish Daily Forward*, May 25, 2011.

36. Jonathan Rosenblum, "Think Again: Those Primitive Haredim—Yet Again."

37. Mark Dratch, "A Community of Co-enablers," p. 113.

38. Amy Neustein and Michael Lesher, "What Went Wrong at Ohel Children's Home—and What Can Be Done About Its Failure to Protect Jewish Children from Abuse?" in *Sexual Abuse—Breaking the Silence* (Ersi Abacı Kalfoğlu and Rehat Faikoglu, Eds.) (Rijeka, Croatia: InTech [open access], 2012), p. 195.

39. Hella Winston, "A Suspected Pedophile Eludes the System."

40. Amy Neustein and Michael Lesher, "What Went Wrong at Ohel Children's Home," p. 195.

41. Patricia A. Graves and Suzanne M. Sgroi, "Law Enforcement and Child Sexual Abuse," in *Handbook of Clinical Intervention in Child Sexual Abuse*, pp. 310, 331.

42. William Handler, "Molestation Cases Must Be Handled by G'dolim, Not by 'Experts,'" *Jewish Press*, May 26, 2013.

43. *Id.*, "Note from the editor."

44. Stephanie Saul, "Tripping Up the Prosecution," p. A6.

45. Yitzchok Frankfurter, "The Pursuit of Justice," *Ami Magazine*, May 12, 2013, p. 70.

46. *Id.*, p. 72.

47. Amy Neustein and Michael Lesher, "Justice Interrupted," p. 214.

48. See Ana M. Alaya, "Victims: Rabbi Failed to Protect Children," *Star Ledger*, January 31, 2003, p. 38.

49. Yitzchok Frankfurter, "The Pursuit of Justice," p. 77. "*Beis din*" is another rendering of the Hebrew "*beth din*."

Chapter 8

1. Robert Fisk, *The Great War for Civilisation* (New York: Alfred A. Knopf, 2006), p. 448.

2. Eishes Chayil (Judy Brown), "Orthodox Jewish Child Abuse: Shattering a Traumatic Silence," *Huffington Post*, August 1, 2011.

3. Weijia Jiang, "Witness in Neighborhood Watch Trial Says Werdesheims Followed the Victim Before the Beating," *CBS Baltimore* (baltimore.cbslocal.com), April 26, 2012.

4. Hassan Giordano, "Werdesheim Trial Takes Bizarre Twist as Victim Refuses to Testify," *Examiner* (examiner.com), April 26, 2012; Matthew Shaer, "Vigilante Justice and the Jews," *Jewish Daily Forward*, May 13, 2012; Steve Kilar, "Elder Werdesheim Brother Convicted in Assault of Teen," *Baltimore Sun*, May 3, 2012.

5. Alan H. Feiler, "Werdesheim Gets Probation, No Jail Time," *Baltimore Jewish Times*, June 27, 2012.

6. Regarding this group's racially-charged recent history, see Jane Metzner, "NAACP: Shomrim Facebook Posts 'Disgusting,' 'Prejudiced,'" *Pikesville Patch* (pikesvillepatch.com), August 3, 2012.

7 Matthew Shaer, *Among Righteous Men: A Tale of Vigilantes and Vindication in Hasidic Crown Heights* (Hoboken: John Wiley & Sons, 2011), pp. 71–73; Simone Weichselbaum, "Suspect in Beating of Cop's Son Livin' It Up in Israel as Victim's Father Fumes," *New York Daily News*, November 16, 2010.

8. Simone Weichselbaum, "Jewish Leaders Blast Move to Extradite Crown Heights Hasidic Man Yitzhak Shuchat, Charged with Hate Crime," *New York Daily News*, November 30, 2011.

9. See Aaron Rakeffet-Rothkof, "Rabbi Meir Kahane: His Life and Thought" (review of the book by the same title by Libby Kahane), *Jewish Action*, Spring 2009, pp. 84–85; Staff, "Jewish Defense League," *Southern Poverty Law Center* (splcenter.org) under "Intelligence Files." As argued in the latter text, the JDL's founding may also be seen as a response to racial tensions stirred by the New York City teachers' strike in 1968; Kahane himself circulated a good deal of propaganda during the strike claiming that blacks and Hispanics were threatening Jewish communities.

10. See Sean Gardiner and Alison Fox, "Civilian Patrol, Not Police, Was Family's First Call," *Wall Street Journal*, July 15, 2011; Corey Kilgannon, "For Hasidim, First Call for Help Often Isn't to 911," *New York Times*, July 15, 2011; Jordan Heller, "Jewish Street Patrols Curb Crime—and Generate Controversy," *Christian Science Monitor*, February 10, 2009. Aside from the heavily Orthodox neighborhoods in Brooklyn, Shomrim patrols have been formed in Orthodox enclaves in Monsey (New York), Baltimore, Miami, Waterbury (Connecticut) and London, England. All were formed more recently than the 1980s—Baltimore's as recently as 2005.

11. Meir Kahane, *The Story of the Jewish Defense League* (Radnor, PA: Chilton Book Company, 1975), p. 34; Gary Buiso, "Kosher Pork: Jewish Groups Rake It In," *New York Post*, July 30, 2011. Also see following note.

12. Nick Pinto, "The Shomrim: Gotham's Crusaders," *Village Voice*, September 7, 2011; Adam Dickter, "Council Members Defend Shomrim," *New York Jewish Week*, August 9, 2011; Gary Buiso, "Kosher Pork."

13. The only other Orthodox Jewish patrol similar to Kahane's formed in the 1960s, the Crown Heights Maccabees, illustrates the same pattern. Police regarded group members as "untrained vigilantes" and "put steady and unrelenting pressure" on its founder "to shut down the Maccabees," which he eventually did. The Shomrim in Crown Heights arose in the late 1970s, when the Lubavitch community was much more powerful—and, as shown below, *those* patrols, unlike the Maccabees, are largely untouchable by local police. (See Matthew Shaer, "Vigilante Justice and the Jews.")

14. Jordan Heller, "Jewish Street Patrols Curb Crime."

15. Nick Pinto, "The Shomrim: Gotham's Crusaders."

16. As of 1999, responsible high-end estimates of the *total* number of Jewish concentration camp survivors ranged from 14,000 to

18,000 (Norman G. Finkelstein, *The Holocaust Industry*, pp. 125–126 and sources cited there). Certainly, far fewer survive today. Even if fully a quarter of the survivors lived in Borough Park, which is not the case, they would account for less than 8 percent of Borough Park's ultra–Orthodox population, which is conservatively numbered at over 50,000. (Gregory Beyer, "Living In: Borough Park, Brooklyn," *New York Times*, October 8, 2010.) Such a proportion could hardly explain an entire community's "scaredness with the police."

17. Israel Shahak, *Jewish History, Jewish Religion*, pp. 18, 20–21. Russian police did, of course, enforce anti–Semitic legislation and sometimes joined in pograms after 1880, though seldom taking the lead in anti–Jewish violence. (See Paul Johnson, *A History of the Jews*, pp. 360–361, 364–365.)

18. Staff, "Judaism and the Jews: Alive and well," *Economist*, July 28-August 3, 2012, p. 2 of inserted text (between pp. 42 and 43).

19. Matthew Shaer, *Among Righteous Men*, p. 28.

20. Stephanie Saul, "Tripping Up the Prosecution," p. A6.

21. Matthew Shaer, *Among Righteous Men*, pp. 59, 50–52.

22. Jordan Heller, "Jewish Street Patrols Curb Crime"; see Matthew Shaer, "Vigilante Justice and the Jews."

23. Israel Shahak, *Jewish History, Jewish Religion*, p. 18. See also Jacob Neusner, "Rabbis and Community in Third Century Babylonia," in *Religions in Antiquity* (J. Neusner, Ed.) (Leiden: E.J. Brill, 1970), p. 447, describing how rabbis "exerted full and unchallenged authority" over "trade, real estate dealings, torts and damages, marriage and divorce" in Jewish communities even in the 3rd century C.E.

24. Joseph Badi, *Religion in Israel Today: The Relationship between State and Religion* (New York: Bookman Associates, 1959), p. 29, quoting from "Legislation and Law in the Jewish State," *Yavneh* (Jerusalem-Tel Aviv, April/May 1949), p. 9, in Joseph L. Blau, *Modern Varieties of Judaism*, p. 181.

25. Ilan Pappe, *The Ethnic Cleansing of Palestine* (Oxford: Oneworld Publications, 2006), p. 57.

26. See Melvin I. Urofsky, *American Zionism from Herzl to the Holocaust* (New York: Anchor Press/Doubleday, 1976), pp. 38–39.

27. Paul Berger, "Agudath Israel: Abuse Claims Go to Rabbis," *Jewish Daily Forward*, May 23, 2012.

28. Michael Lesher, "Orthodox Cops: Separate and Unequal," pp. 21–22; see Hella Winston, "Tragedy in Borough Park Puts Shomrim Under Scrutiny," *New York Jewish Week*, July 19, 2011 (in which a Shomrim official specifically admits withholding a list of suspected molesters with rabbinic instructions); Josh Nathan-Kazis, "Shomrim Don't Want Police to See Security Video," *Jewish Daily Forward*, August 8, 2012.

29. Elliott Horowitz, *Reckless Rites: Purim and Legacy of Jewish Violence* (Princeton: Princeton University Press, 2006), pp. 189, 196–198.

30. Phil Jacobs, "Learning from an Embarrassing Incident," *Washington Jewish Week*, May 7, 2012.

31. Orthodox Jews are strictly forbidden to violate the Sabbath for the sake of a non–Jew, even—with limited exceptions—if the non–Jew's life is in danger. (See Israel Shahak, *Jewish History, Jewish Religion*, pp. 102–104.) I emailed Jacobs (a former Shomrim member) to ask if he knew whether the Baltimore patrol would, in light of the traditional prohibitions, drive cars to search for missing non–Jews on the Sabbath. He did not respond.

32. Emily Wax, "'Standing Silent' follows uncovering of sexual abuse in Baltimore's Orthodox Jewish community," *Washington Post*, March 19, 2012.

33. Sharon Otterman, "Hasidic Man Denies Abuse of Young Girl He Counseled," *New York Times*, December 5, 2012. Weberman was eventually convicted and sentenced to 103 years in prison.

34. Hella Winston, "Trial Exposes Shadowy Chasidic 'Modesty Committees,'" *New York Jewish Week*, December 6, 2012.

35. *Id.*

36. Matthew Shaer, *Among Righteous Men*, p. 80.

37. Nir Cohen and Noam Dvir, "Beit Shemesh: Woman Attacked for Dressing 'Immodestly,'" *Ynet News* (ynetnews.com), June 20, 2012. See also Aviad Glickman, "Woman Beat, Threatened by 'Modesty Squad,'" *Ynet News* (ynetnews.com), August 14, 2008, describing how a formerly Orthodox woman was bound and seriously beaten by members of a "modesty squad" wanting to know details of her relationships.

38. See Isabel Kershner, "Israeli Girl, 8, at Center of Tension Over Religious Extremism," *New York Times*, December 27, 2011.

39. Daniel Eidensohn, "A Conversation with Rav Sternbuch About the Recent Reports About Chareidi Extremists," *Daas Torah—Issues of Jewish Identity* (daattorah.blogspot.com), February 9, 2012.

40. Moshe Sternbuch, "Relationship of Science to Torah" ("Authorized translation" from the Hebrew by Daniel Eidensohn), found at http://zootorah.com/controversy/RavStern buchEnglish.pdf.

41. Daniel Eidensohn, *Child and Domestic Abuse*, Vol. 1 (Jerusalem, New York: Emunah Press, 2010).

42. Daniel Eidensohn, "Rav Sternbuch, shlita—Guidelines for Calling the Police," *Daas Torah*, June 8, 2008 ("If one knows that someone is being physically abused or will be abused than [sic] it is required to call the police *after consulting a rabbi who agrees he is a future danger* as is common in such cases" [emphasis added]); Daniel Eidensohn, "The Insensitive Condescension of the Secular Press to the Orthodox Community," *Daas Torah*, June 16, 2008. When Rabbi Shlomo Gottesman articulated a position similar to Rabbi Sternbuch's, however—that a rabbi must always decide whether police can be contacted in a child sex abuse case—Rabbi Eidensohn expressed "dismay" about it. (Daniel Eidensohn, "The Distorted Self-Serving View of Halacha at Sunday's Agudah Conference," *Daas Torah*, May 19, 2011.)

43. Joseph Heller, *Catch-22* (New York: Dell, 1961), p. 427.

44. Moses Maimonides, Mishneh Torah, Hilkhoth Sanhedrin 1:1.

45. Elliott Horowitz, *Reckless Rites*, p. 197, and sources cited there.

46. Paul Johnson, *A History of the Jews*, p. 259.

47. Elliott Horowitz, *Reckless Rites*, pp. 202–203.

48. Israel Shahak, *Jewish History, Jewish Religion*, p. 91, and sources cited there.

49. Amnesty International, *Broken Lives—A Year of Intifada* (London, 2001), p. 12; Human Rights Watch, *Investigation into the Unlawful Use of Force in the West Bank, Gaza Strip and Northern Israel* (New York, 2000), p. 1; Amnesty International, *Excessive Use of Lethal Force* (London, 2000), pp. 5–6; B'Tselem (Israeli Information Center for Human Rights in the Occupied Territories), *Trigger Happy: Unjustified Shooting and Violation of the Open-Fire Regulations During the Al-Aqsa Intifada* (Jerusalem, 2002), pp. 11–13 (all of the above are cited in Norman G. Finkelstein, *Beyond Chutzpah*, pp. 100–102); Amnesty International, *Shielded from Scrutiny: IDF Violations in Jenin and Nablus*, November 2002; Jessica Montel, "Operation Defensive Shield: The Propaganda and the Reality," at btselem.org; Human Rights Watch, *Jenin: Military Operations*, May 2002 (all cited in Norman G. Finkelstein, *Image and Reality of the Israel-Palestine Conflict* (second edition) (London, New York: Verso, 2003), pp. xxiii–xxv).

50. Norman G. Finkelstein, *Beyond Chutzpah*, p. liv, citing Helmut Krausnik et al., *Anatomy of the SS State* (New York: Walker, 1965), pp. 356, 318–319, and Horst Boog et al., *Germany and the Second World War*, Vol. 4, *The Attack on the Soviet Union* (Oxford: Clarendon Press, 1998), pp. 497–500, 510, 515.

51. Stuart A. Cohen, "Dilemmas of Military Service in Israel: The Religious Dimension," in *War and Peace in the Jewish Tradition* (Lawrence Schiffman and Joel B. Wolowelsky, Eds.) (New York: Yeshiva University Press, 2007), pp. 326, 328–329 [emphasis added]. Notably, even the "liberal" Rabbi Aharon Lichtenstein belongs to this "formidable array" of rabbinic opinion discouraging Orthodox Jews from citing "conscientious objection" to combat duty in the Occupied Territories. (*Haaretz*, July 19, 2005, pp. B3–B4.) It is unclear how Professor Cohen concludes that West Bank Palestinians, not Israeli soldiers occupying their land, bear sole responsibility for attacks on noncombatants; he cites no sources and adduces no evidence for this claim.

52. Norman Lamm, "Amalek and the Seven Nations," in *War and Peace in the Jewish Tradition*, pp. 228, 238 n. 39.

53. Amy Neustein and Michael Lesher, "Justice Interrupted," pp. 201–202, citing Anonymous, *The Rebbes: The Lubavitcher Rebbe Shlita* (Kfar Chabad, Israel: Chish Printing, 1993), pp. 13–14, and "Severe Prohibition and Serious Warning," *Der Blatt*, June 8, 2000, p. 9 [translation of the latter text from the Hebrew is by the authors of "Justice Interrupted"]. In the case of the suspected NKVD informer, it is worth stressing that according to *The Rebbes* the only danger he posed was of causing other Orthodox Jews to serve in the Red Army.

54. Stephanie Carmon, "War Brings Soldiers Closer to Their Judaism," *Shabbat Shalom* (ou.org), January 22, 2009 [published by the Orthodox Union]. The assault on Gaza also served to illustrate that the Israeli military understands perfectly well how Orthodox rabbis apply religious priorities: although the IDF launched its attack on the Sabbath—killing some 200 people (and wounding 700 others) within minutes—it also blocked aid shipments to Gaza's desperate population in honor of the holy day. (Noam Chomsky, "Exterminate All the Brutes," on chomsky.info, January 19, 2009 (revised June 6, 2009), citing Craig Whitlock, Griff Witte and Reyham Abdel Kareem, "Combat May Escalate in Gaza, Israel Warns; Operation in Densely Packed City, Camps Weighed," *Washington Post*, January 11, 2009.)

55. Amnesty International, *Operation 'Cast Lead': 22 Days of Death and Destruction* (London, 2009), pp. 1, 6–7.

56. Elliott Horowitz, *Reckless Rites*, pp. 236–241, 243–246. For a thorough description of the brutality used to drive Palestinian Arabs out of the new Jewish state in 1948, see generally Ilan Pappe, *The Ethnic Cleansing of Palestine*.

57. Elliott Horowitz, *Reckless Rites*, p. 277.

58. Israel Shahak, Jewish History, Jewish Religion, p. 34.

59. Staff, "Judaism and the Jews: Alive and well," pp. 3–4.

60. From comments posted to Staff, "Baltimore Shomrim Member Found Guilty," *Matzav.com* (matzav.com), May 3, 2012.

61. Matthew Shaer, *Among Righteous Men*, pp. 71–72.

62. *Id.*, pp. 54, 39.

63. Israel Shahak, *Jewish History, Jewish Religion*, p. 32; *Likutei Amarim* ("*Tanya*") (Brooklyn: "Kehot" Publication Society, 1981). To cite one of countless examples, the text states that "all the souls in the world were contained in Adam," and goes on to explain that "his soul was divisible into innumerable sparks—which are the souls of all of Israel from the days of the Patriarchs and the tribes, to, and including the coming of the Messiah." (*Likutei Amarim*, Igeret Hakodesh, Chapter 7, p. 427.) In other words, human souls are distributed exclusively among Jews; non–Jews lack them entirely. This idea is elaborated in many sections of *Tanya*.

64. Weijia Jiang, "Witness in Neighborhood Watch Trial."

65. See, *e.g.*, Matthew Shaer, "Vigilante Justice and the Jews," *Jewish Daily Forward*, May 13, 2012; Alan H. Feiler, "Werdesheim Gets Probation, No Jail Time," *Baltimore Jewish Times*, June 27, 2012; Staff (from JTA), "One Brother Guilty in Baltimore Shomrim Case," *Jewish Daily Forward*, May 4, 2012. The relatively small *Baltimore Jewish Life* reprinted the Weijia Jiang article cited above; I have not found a single major Jewish newspaper that mentioned the story. Jewish readers interested in the truth would find it only by checking *Failed Messiah* (Shmarya Rosenberg, "Shomrim Trial to Go Forward Without a Jury," *Failed Messiah* (failedmessiah.typepad.com), April 25, 2012)—in my opinion, a good policy in any case.

66. Tricia Bishop, "Werdesheim trial to go forward without a jury," *Baltimore Sun*, April 24, 2012.

67. Simone Weichselbaum, "Jewish Leaders Blast Move to Extradite Crown Heights Hasidic Man Yitzhak Shuchat, Charged with Hate Crime."

68. Eliyahu Federman, "Brooklyn DA Trumped Up Hate Crime Charges," *Huffington Post* (huffingtonpost.com).

69. Shmarya Rosenberg, "Dov Hikind Trying to Block Israel's Extradition of Yitzchak Shuchat to Brooklyn," *Failed Messiah* (failedmessiah.typepad.com), December 23, 2012. Hikind acknowledged this himself on his weekly radio show.

70. COLlive reporter, "Man to Be Extradited to U.S.," *COLLIVE Community News Service*, December 6, 2012.

71. Staff, "Schachter, a Top Y.U. Rabbi, Calls for Panels to Screen Abuse Claims," *Jewish Telegraphic Agency (JTA)* (jta.org), March 15, 2013.

72. Cf. Mareesa Nicosia, "East Ramapo Group Buys Kosher in Quest to 'Coexist,'" *Journal News* (lohud.com), June 28, 2013, describing protests by non–Jews in heavily Orthodox Monsey, New York about being barred from shopping at Hasidic stores.

73. Drorah Setel, "Can Justice and Compassion Embrace?" in *Embracing Justice: A Resource Guide for Rabbis on Domestic Abuse* (Diane Gardsbane, Ed.) (New York: Jewish Women International, 2002), pp. 53–54.

74. Benny Morris, *1948 and After* (revised edition) (Oxford: Oxford University Press, 1994), p. 192, quoted in Norman G. Finkelstein, *Image and Reality of the Israel-Palestine*

Conflict, p. 77 [emphasis added]. Finkelstein
also records (p. xxiii), citing Israeli newspaper
accounts, how a "senior Israeli officer" during
the second *intifada* urged the army to "analyze
and internalize the lessons of ... how the German army fought in the Warsaw Ghetto."

75. Melvin I. Urofsky, *American Zionism
from Herzl to the Holocaust*, p. 283, citing Mor-
ton Rosenstock, *Louis Marshall, Defender of
Jewish Rights* (Detroit: Wayne State University
Press, 1965), pp. 217, 205.

76. Edward W. Said, *The Question of Palestine* (New York: Vintage Books, 1992), pp. 89–
90, quoting an article by Dr. A. Carlebach in
Ma'ariv, October 7, 1955. Cf. Israel Shahak,
Jewish History, Jewish Religion, p. 33 ("[W]hile
ostensibly opposing Nazism, [Martin] Buber
glorified a movement holding and actually
teaching doctrines about non–Jews not unlike
the Nazi doctrines about Jews").

Chapter 9

1. Quoted in Alice Miller, *Thou Shalt Not
Be Aware*, p. 183.

2. Judy Brown, speaking at Nefesh (Chicago, IL), November 20, 2011. Video is available at http://www.youtube.com/watch?v=
VVhtrHE6SjE.

3. Janet Heimlich, "Do Orthodox Jews
Hold Children in High Esteem?" Religious
Child Maltreatment (blog) (religiouschildmal-
treatment.com), May 14, 2012.

4. Alice Miller, *Thou Shalt Not Be Aware*,
p. 218.

5. Janet Heimlich, "Do Orthodox Jews
Hold Children in High Esteem?"

6. Simone Weichselbaum and OrenYaniv,
"Satmar sect's sick revenge." Using children as
pawns to punish grownups is nothing new in
Jewish tradition. A dissident from the Orthodoxy of late-nineteenth century Russia wrote
that when he began to question some aspects
of Orthodox ritual, his coreligionists tormented him by attacking his children: "They
called my children offspring of unclean parents, and the other children bullied them."
(Moses L. Lilienblum, "The Sins of My Youth,"
in *The Golden Tradition*, p. 125.)

7. *Id.*

8. Chaim Levin, "Sexual Abuse Victim
Demeaned and Put on Notice for Misconduct
at Hebrew Theological College," on the blog
gotta give 'em hope (gottagivemhope.blogspot.

com), February 28, 2013; reported by Shmarya
Rosenberg on *Failed Messiah* (failedmessiah.
typepad.com), February 28, 2013.

9. Shmarya Rosenberg, "HTC Dean
'Apologizes' for Sex Abuse Remarks; Makes It
Clear the Apology Is All About Her," on *Failed
Messiah* (failedmessiah.typepad.com), March
4, 2013.

10. This is not speculation. Even after his
savage cross-examination of his daughter, who
was also his rape victim, Weingarten claimed,
like Shkop, that he could not discuss child sex
abuse openly because he was "prohibited from
dwelling on lascivious thoughts much less discussing matters pertaining to sexuality with a
woman or girl child." (Donna R. Newman and
Jill R. Shellow, Sentencing Memorandum (for
defendant), p. 20, n. 8.)

11. Hosea 2:12.

12. Ezekiel 16:37–39. The English translations of this passage and the preceding one are
quoted from David Blumenthal, *Facing the
Abusing God* (Louisville: Westminster/John
Knox Press, 1993), p. 241.

13. Samson R. Hirsch, *The Pentateuch*
(trans. Isaac Levy) (Gateshead: Judaica Press,
1999), Vol. 5, p. 409. The verse translates as,
"You will see among those in captivity a woman of beautiful appearance, and you will desire her; you may take her to yourself for a
wife."

14. Though most have followed Hirsch's
line, not all traditional authorities have taken
so crude a view. See Rashi, Babylonian Talmud
Qiddushin 22a, "*shelo yilhatzenah b'milha-
mah*"; Ramban and *Or ha–Hayyim* to Deuteronomy 21:11–14.

15. Moses Maimonides, Mishneh Torah, Is-
surei Bi'ah 12:10 and *Kessef Mishneh, ad loc.*
This view does not appear to have been
adopted by any later authorities; however, I
have not found a traditional text explicitly repudiating it.

16. Friedrich Nietzsche, *The Antichrist*, in
The Portable Nietzsche (trans. Walter Kaufmann, Ed.) (New York: Viking Press, 1954), p.
654.

17. Mark Dratch, "A Community of Co-
enablers," p. 111 and sources cited there.

18. *Id.*, p. 112, and sources cited there.

19. *Id.*, pp. 116–117, and sources cited there.

20. *Id.*, pp. 117–118.

21. The "*hillul Hashem*" threat is often
conflated with a bleak view of the "outside

world" commonly held among Orthodox Jews: victims are warned, in effect, that publicizing the sins of Orthodox Jews will provide a pretext for anti–Semites and thus lead to violence against the community. I addressed this anachronistic idea in the introduction. It is enough to note here that it is not a matter of religious law.

22. See esp. Babylonian Talmud *Baba Qamma* 116b–117a; *Gittin* 7a.

23. *Arukh ha–Shulhan, Hoshen ha–Mishpat* 388:7 [my translation; emphasis added]. The writer's tribute in this passage to "our lord the Czar" as an exemplar of just government was doubtless intended for the censors rather than for Jewish readers; however, his argument in principle for limiting the application of *m'sirah* is clear and convincing. Rabbi Dratch also cites this ruling to support child sex abuse reporting, though he interprets it as waiving the prohibition of *m'sirah* when informing is unlikely to cause "persecution of the entire Jewish community" because "the government is generally fair and nondiscriminatory." (Mark Dratch, "A Community of Co-enablers," pp. 116, 125 n. 73.) In any case, no reasonable interpretation of this passage could bar abuse victims in the United States (or similarly governed countries) from turning to secular authorities.

24. Eliezer Waldenberg, *Tzitz Eliezer* 19:52.

25. Excerpts of a Hebrew pamphlet containing these rulings (*Kunt'ras dam rei'echa*, edited by Tzvi Gertner) are in my possession.

26. Mark Dratch, "A Community of Co-enablers," pp. 114–115.

27. *Id.*, p. 116.

28. Yosef Blau, posted to Canonist.com, September 19, 2006.

29. Moshe Feinstein, *Ig'roth Mosheh, Hoshen ha–Mishpat*, Vol. 1, number 8.

30. The two issues are discussed in completely separate sections of the four-part *Shulhan Arukh*, the compendium that is generally accepted as the basis of practical Jewish law; the use of Jewish courts to resolve private disputes is in section 26, *m'sirah* in section 388, of Part Four (*Hoshen ha–Mishpat*).

31. Moshe Feinstein, *id.* [my translation; emphasis added].

32. At least, not on the question of reporting such crimes to the police. Rabbi Feinstein did take up some questions related to rape in other *responsa*, but these did not discuss communicating with law enforcement officials.

33. Jason M. Fogler, Jillian C. Shipherd, Erin Rowe, Jennifer Jensen and Stephanie Clarke, "A Theoretical Foundation for Understanding Clergy-Perpetrated Sexual Abuse," in *Understanding the Impact of Clergy Sexual Abuse* (Robert A. McMackin, Terence M. Keane and Paul M. Kline, Eds.) (New York: Routledge, 2009), p. 113.

34. Babylonian Talmud, *Shabbath* 32b.

35. Bachya ben Joseph ibn Paquda, *Duties of the Heart* (trans. from Arabic to Hebrew Yehuda ibn Tibbon, trans. from Hebrew to English Moses Hyamson) (Jerusalem/New York: Feldheim, 1962, 1970) Vol. 1, p. 155 [emphasis added].

36. Nosson Scherman and Meir Zlotowitz, *Shir haShirim/Song of Songs* (New York: Mesorah Publications, 1977), p. lii.

37. Louis I. Newman, *Maggidim & Hasidim: Their Wisdom* (New York: Bloch, 1962), p. 243.

38. For example, to his great credit, Rabbi Horowitz urged members of the community via mass emailing to "please, please stand with this victim [the young woman who accused Nechemia Weberman of raping her as a child] … and with the other silent and silenced victims who are watching this case unfold very carefully, and with all survivors of abuse and molestation." (Yakov Horowitz, "What Went Terribly Wrong," mass email from Project YES, September 28, 2012, pp. 3–4.)

39. Yakov Horowitz, "Keeping Our Children Safe," posted on his web site (Rabbi Horowitz.com), December 14, 2006.

40. Joyanna Silberg and Stephanie Dallam, "Out of the Jewish Closet," in *Tempest in the Temple*, p. 77.

41. Yakov Horowitz, "Keeping Our Children Safe."

42. Quoted in Noam Chomsky, *Necessary Illusions: Thought Control in Democratic Societies* (Boston: South End Press, 1989), pp. 214, 390 n. 36, from Eyal Kafkafi, *Davar*, September 26, 1988.

43. Gideon Levy, "Killing Children Is No Longer a Big Deal," *Ha'aretz*, October 17, 2004, quoted in Norman G. Finkelstein, *Beyond Chutzpah*, p. 116. (See also pp. 188–189 for some chilling details.)

44. B'tselem, *Means of Expulsion: Violence, harassment and lawlessness against Palestinians in the southern Hebron hills* (July 2005), p. 23, in Norman G. Finkelstein, *Beyond Chutzpah,*

pp. xxv–xxvi, n. 36. This pattern continues. In 2013, four months after an unarmed 16-year-old Palestinian boy was shot to death by Israeli soldiers as he tried to run away, the army raided his home "in the dead of night, kicking, punching, yanking and destroying," and throwing concussion grenades, injuring more children in what Israeli reporters called "a routine occurrence." (Gideon Levy and Alex Levac, "A Battered House, a Shattered Palestinian Family," *Ha'aretz*, May 31, 2013.) At nearly the same time, Israelis reportedly posted flyers in the West Bank town of Qalqilya with pictures of four children aged 10 to 14 and a caption reading, "We are the army, beware we will catch you if we see you, or we will come to your home." (Staff, "Israel Issues Poster Threatening to Arrest Children," *Ma'an News Agency*, June 1, 2013.) I am not aware of any public criticism of these practices from Orthodox rabbis.

45. Isabel Kershner, "Israeli Girl, 8, at Center of Tension Over Religious Extremism."

46. Ronen Medzini, "20,000 Attend Itamar Massacre Victims' Funeral," *Ynet News* (ynet news.com), March 13, 2011.

47. Rabbi Eisenman's public comments at an event held in his synagogue were later distributed in writing via group email on February 8, 2007.

48. S. Ansky, "Between Two Worlds," pp. 310–311.

49. Judy Brown, speaking at Nefesh, November 20, 2011.

50. Babylonian Talmud, *Shabbath* 33a; see Rashi *ad loc.*

Chapter 10

1. Michael Oakeshott, "The Masses in Representative Democracy," in *American Conservative Thought in the Twentieth Century* (William F. Buckley, Ed.) (Indianapolis & New York: Bobbs-Merrill Company, 1970), p. 121.

2. Fred Keene, "The Politics of Forgiveness: How the Christian Church Guilt-Trips Survivors," *On the Issues*, Fall 1995.

3. Babylonian Talmud *Sanhedrin* 99b.

4. In this connection, cf. Israel Shahak's stinging description of pre-emancipation "classical" Jewish society as "one of the most closed of 'closed societies,' one of the most totalitarian societies in the whole history of mankind..." (Israel Shahak, *Jewish History, Jewish Religion*, p. 19.)

5. Gary Rosenblatt, "Stolen Innocence."

6. A. Nicholas Groth, "The Incest Offender," in *Handbook of Clinical Intervention in Child Sexual Abuse*, pp. 227–228.

7. Suzanne M. Sgroi, Linda Canfield Blick and Frances Sarnacki Porter, "A Conceptual Framework for Child Sexual Abuse," in *Handbook of Clinical Intervention in Child Sexual Abuse*, pp. 9, 27.

8. NCSY Report, pp. 12, 51.

9. Hakhel MIS email distribution, September 14, 2006 [emphasis added].

10. Rabbi Avi Shafran, "A Matter of Orthodox Abuse."

11. Kobi Nahshoni, "Rabbis: Stopping Assimilation Overrides Shabbat," *Ynet News* (ynet news.com), March 4, 2013.

12. Eilat is a popular weekend destination for non-religious Israelis. In order to catch the straying Jewish women before "the point of no return," a pious Jew inquired of these rabbis whether he was permitted to travel from the city to accost them outside the security checkpoint, thus "desecrating the day of rest" according to Orthodox Jewish norms.

13. Yasmin Anwar, "Highly Religious People Are Less Motivated by Compassion Than Are Non-Believers," *Media Relations*, April 30, 2012. The reduced role of compassion among religious believers is particularly disturbing in light of evidence that empathy has roots in inborn neurological reactions. (See, *e.g.*, Abigail Tucker, "Hard-Wired for Art," *Smithsonian Magazine*, November 2012, p. 20: "The researchers found that the image [of a wrist bent back to ward off a blow] excited areas in the primary motor cortex that controlled the observers' own wrists.") If the early findings of studies like this one are borne out by further evidence, this may imply not that traditional religions, including Orthodox Judaism, are failing to inculcate empathy but that they are actually *training it out of* their followers. I do not believe evidence currently available supports such a conclusion, and even if it did, I do not know that such a finding would necessarily "debunk" Orthodoxy's approach to morality. However, if hard evidence along these lines does become available, it may well demand re-examination of some of Orthodoxy's moral assumptions—a subject beyond the scope of this book.

14. Jeremy Rosen in Preface to *Tempest in the Temple*, p. xviii.

15. See, *e.g.*, Avrohom C. Feuer, *Shemoneh Esrei: The Amidah/The Eighteen Blessings* (Brooklyn: Mesorah Publications, 1990). Some typical comments on the main prayers are found on p. 63 ("Our prayers are in the plural to demonstrate that we think not only about ourselves, but that we are concerned for our fellow Jews"); p. 65 ("[A]lthough evil influences may corrupt a Jew and alienate him from his roots, a Jew is never completely lost"); p. 177 ("Informers slander us to the tyrannical gentile governments to curry favor and earn rewards from the rich and the powerful"); and p. 190 ("While we pray for the welfare of the Jewish leaders who are on the top of our social order, we must never forget to respect even the most recent converts to Judaism who are just entering the social structure"). The exclusion of non–Jews from the blessings sought in our prayers is clearly evident in each of these comments.

16. See Moses Maimonides, Mishneh Torah, Hilkhoth N'ziqin 8:5 and Maggid Mishneh, ad loc.

17. Staff, "Ohel's Halachic Advisor: OK to Cheat on Taxes?" *New York Jewish Week*, June 10, 2009.

18. Ze'ev Schiff, "The Army Must Stop the Olive Thieves," *Ha-aretz*, October 30, 2002; Amira Hass, "Will You Just Stand on the Side-Lines?" *Ha-aretz*, November 6, 2002; both of the above are cited in Norman G. Finkelstein, *Image and Reality of the Israel-Palestine Conflict*, p. xxviii.

19. Quoted in Studs Terkel, *Talking to Myself: A Memoir of My Times* (New York: Pantheon Books, 1977), pp. 195–196.

20. Naomi Klein, *The Shock Doctrine* (New York: Henry Holt, 2007), pp. 141–142. In July 2012, an Argentine court sentenced former president Jorge Videla to 50 years in prison for "kidnapping hundreds of babies from leftist activists detained and killed between 1976–1983." (Staff, "Ex-Argentine Ruler Guilty of Stealing Babies," *Al Jazeera English* (aljazeera.com), July 5, 2012.) Interestingly, by contrast, when the United States removed over 14,000 children from Cuba between 1960 and 1962 as part of "Operation Peter Pan"—supposedly to protect them from the new revolutionary government—there was (and continues to be) little domestic criticism of U.S. officials' use of such a tactic, though it was likely based on deliberate deceit and certainly ruptured many

families. (See Luisa Yanez, "Pedro Pan Was Born of Fear, Human Instinct to Protect Children," *Miami Herald*, May 16, 2009; Saul Landau and Nelson P. Valdes, "The CIA, Cuba and Operation Peter Pan," *Counterpunch*, December 16–18, 2011.) Again, power politics trumps the rights of children: Videla could be prosecuted because he fell from power; U.S. officials are not subject to victors' justice and have suffered no consequences for their actions.

21. See generally Amy Neustein and Michael Lesher, *From Madness to Mutiny*.

22. John Rosemond, "Parents, Stop Destroying the American Male," jewishworld review.com, May 9, 2012. I doubt that Rosemond is completely unaware of the practical consequences of such anti-feminist teaching. Dr. Neustein and I have documented many cases in which mothers lose custody of children, even to fathers credibly accused of child abuse, when family court judges and "experts" find the women too uppity. (See Amy Neustein and Michael Lesher, *From Madness to Mutiny*, esp. pp. 7–10, 177–180.)

23. Janet Heimlich, *Breaking Their Will*, p. 211.

24. Moses L. Lilienblum, "The Sins of My Youth," p. 125.

25. Quoted in Harold Bloom (with David Rosenberg), *The Book of J* (New York: Vintage Books, 1990), p. 207. It may be significant that Buber, a Zionist, was unmoved at hearing about the murder of Arabs by Israeli soldiers; he appears to have seen the crime only as a burden carried, afterward, by the *soldiers*. The victims need hardly have existed as human beings, since the Israeli Jews, like Abraham in the Biblical story, were the important figures. (See Edward W. Said, *The Question of Palestine* (New York: Vintage Books, 1992), pp. 113–114.)

26. Because Ashkenazic Orthodox Jews—those from central and eastern Europe—have religious customs distinctly different from those of Sephardic Jews—mostly from northern Africa—Israel has two official chief rabbis, one Ashkenazic, one Sephardic.

27. Israel M. Lau, *Out of the Depths: The Story of a Child of Buchenwald Who Returned Home at Last* (trans. Jessica Setbon and Shira L. Schmidt) (New York: Sterling, 2005), pp. 245–247.

28. Arnon Regular, "'Road Map Is a Life

Saver for Us,' PM Abbas Tells Hamas," *Ha'aretz*, June 24, 2003; Staff, "President Bush Claims God Ordered Invasion of Iraq and Afghanistan," *Insider* (theinsider.org), October 7, 2005.

29. Matthew Williams claimed he had participated in the killing of a gay couple in July 1999 because he was "obeying the law of God." (Staff, "Williams Admits Killing Couple, Says He 'Obeyed God's Law,'" *Gay People's Chronicle*, November 12, 1999.) Ronald Gay, who killed one man and injured six others in September 2000, said he had been told by God to find and kill lesbians and gay men. (Staff, "Murder Charge for Gay-Bar Gunman," *BBC News*, September 25, 2000.)

30. Igor Volsky, "Bachmann: Gold Told Me to Introduce Constitutional Amendment Prohibiting Same-Sex Marriage in MN," *Think Progress* (thinkprogress.org), April 12, 2011.

31. Xeni Jardin, "Sarah Palin, via Twitter: God Told Me to Sue the Internet," posted to boingboing.net, July 5, 2009.

32. Star R. Scott, published on swordof thespirit.org, September 22, 2002. This sermon seems to have been removed from the site; I read it while it was still available.

33. Julie Lyons, "Pentecostal Preacher Sherman Allen Turns Out to Be Reverend Spanky," *Dallas Observer*, February 21, 2008.

34. "Angel on Death Row," *Frontline* (PBS), Show # 1414, April 9, 1996. The transcript is available at www.pbs.org/wgbh/pages/front line/angel/angelscript.html; all quotations that follow are taken from it.

35. See Pinchas Y. Kaganoff, *Yish'm'ru Da'ath* (2nd ed.) (Passaic, NJ: 2012), pp. 219–221 (privately printed). Rabbi Kaganoff stresses that this advice is based on a single opinion that is contradicted by normative rulings stated elsewhere in Jewish law. Still, such advice seems to be given by some Orthodox rabbis.

36. Amy Neustein and Michael Lesher, "Justice Interrupted," p. 213.

37. See Moses Maimonides, Mishneh Torah, Hilkhoth M'lakhim 5:5 and Radbaz, ad loc.

38. Aharon Lichtenstein, "The Source of Faith Is Faith Itself," *Jewish Action Reader, Vol. 1* (New York: Union of Orthodox Jewish Congregations of America, 1996).

39. Hugh R. Trevor-Roper, *The Last Days of Hitler* (New York: Macmillan, 1947), p. 19, quoted in Rolf Hochhuth, "Sidelights on

History," included in *The Deputy* (trans. Richard and Clara Winston) (New York: Grove Press, 1964), pp. 307–308. I would like to add the personal note that I devoured Hochhuth's play, and his historical observations, at the age of fourteen; the experience left a profound impression which time has not eroded.

40. Norman G. Finkelstein, *Image and Reality of the Israel-Palestine Conflict*, pp. 119–120.

41. Rolf Hochhuth, *The Deputy*, p. 352.

42. See Hugh Trevor-Roper, "Sir Thomas More and *Utopia*," in *Renaissance Essays* (Chicago: University of Chicago Press, 1985), p. 52.

43. From an exchange of letters between an Israeli soldier and Rabbi Shimon Weiser, quoted in Israel Shahak, *Jewish History, Jewish Religion*, pp. 93–94. In this published exchange, the rabbi derides the "custom" of "non-Jewish nations" to establish rules that govern warfare. For religious Jews, he insists, war is rather "a vital necessity, and only by this standard must we decide how to wage it." For a sampling of the real meaning of "purity of arms" as practiced by the Israeli army, cf., *e.g.*, Norman G. Finkelstein, *Image and Reality of the Israel-Palestine Conflict*, esp. pp. xxiii–xxxvi, 110–120; Robert Fisk, *The Great War for Civilisation: The Conquest of the Middle East* (New York: Alfred A. Knopf, 2006), pp. 774–778. It is clear from even a brief description that Israel's armed forces exercise little restraint with respect to civilian life. Yet this standard, apparently, wasn't bloody enough for the Orthodox rabbi. As for the views of Orthodox Jews generally, Rabbi Weiser's statements have been well circulated in Israel (and beyond), yet have not prompted any significant public debate among Orthodox Jews, as far as I am aware.

44. David Holzer, *The Rav Thinking Aloud: Transcripts of Personal Conversations with Rabbi Joseph B. Soloveitchik* (Miami Beach: HolzerSeforim, 2009), pp. 164, 166. Note that in this respect the liberal Rabbi Soloveitchik's position was more vicious than most of his Orthodox colleagues, who generally refuse to apply the commandment of genocide to any actually existing people.

45. Ze'ev Jabotinsky, "Letter on Autonomism," in *Selected Writings: Exile and Assimilation* (Tel Aviv: Shlomo Zaltzman, 1936),

quoted in Shlomo Sand, *The Invention of the Jewish People*, p. 261.

46. Associated Press and Israel Hayom Staff, "Israeli Orthodox Jews moving to Arab-Jewish cities, activists say," *Israel Hayom* (israelhayom.com), October 4, 2012.

47. Melvin I. Urofsky, *American Zionism from Herzl to the Holocaust*, pp. 38–39.

48. Tamar Rotem, "Confessions of a religious anarchist in Israel," *Ha-aretz*, May 3, 2012.

49. Uri Zohar, *Waking Up Jewish* (Jerusalem: Hamesorah Publications, 1985).

50. From a post by "Dudi," "Meet Lev L'Achim's Top Missionary Rabbi Uri Zohar," on roshpinaproject.com, April 5, 2010. According to this report, Zohar described Israel's (minimal) sex education program in these words: "The greatest disaster of all is not AIDS, but the teacher who tells about how not to get AIDS. Do you understand what's going on?... Is it possible that the Creator will leave the Jewish people in the hands of so-called ministers of education and female ministers of education and psychologists and Ph.D.s like these and professors like these? Is it possible that the Creator will leave your children in the hands of such soul twisters?" I emailed Rabbi Zohar to confirm the accuracy of this quote. He did not respond.

51. Aldous Huxley, *The Devils of Loudun*, pp. 297–298.

52. Staff (citing JTA), "Norman Lamm Quits Yeshiva Univ., Admits Failure on Sex Abuse," *Jewish Press*, July 1, 2013.

53. Staff (citing JTA), "Y.U. Chancellor Norman Lamm Steps Down After Admitting Failure on Sex Abuse," *Jewish Daily Forward*, July 1, 2013.

54. Paul Berger, "Student Claims of Abuse Not Reported by Yeshiva U.," *Jewish Daily Forward*, December 13, 2012 (print publication December 21, 2012).

55. Paul Berger, "Former Y.U. High School Students File $380M Suit Claiming Sex Abuse Cover-Up," *Jewish Daily Forward*, July 8, 2013.

56. Michael O'Keeffe, "Yeshiva University High Hit by 5 New Sex Abuse Allegations," *New York Daily News*, July 12, 2013. The number of alleged victims has continued to climb. (Paul Berger, "Judge Deals Setback to Ex-Students Suing Yeshiva University for $380M Over Sex Abuse Claims," *Jewish Daily Forward*, August 8, 2013.) In January 2014, the lawsuit

was dismissed by a federal judge due to the applicable statute of limitations. The plaintiff's lawyer reportedly plans to appeal. (Rich Calder, "Judge Tosses 680M Sex Abuse Lawsuit Against Yeshiva U.," *New York Post*, January 30, 2014.)

57. Samuel Heilman, "Better Late Than Never: Rabbi Norman Lamm's Courage Shames His Orthodox Peers," *Ha'aretz*, July 4, 2013.

58. Stewart Ain, "Editor Apologizes for Picture of White House Draped in Nazi Flags," *New York Jewish Week*, January 13, 2012.

59. Sara Lehmann, "A Tale of Two Movements," *Jewish Press*, November 2, 2011.

60. Binyamin Rose, "A Leak in the System," *Mishpacha*, June 19, 2013, p. 49.

61. Yonoson [Jonathan] Rosenblum, "Politically Correct Monitoring?" *Mishpacha*, June 19, 2013, p. 17.

62. See Jeremy Ben-Ami, "America's Jewish Vote," *New York Times*, November 12, 2012.

63. See Norman G. Finkelstein, *The Holocaust Industry*, pp. 23, 149.

64. Alice Miller, *Thou Shalt Not Be Aware*, p. 218.

Chapter 11

1. Philip Wylie, *Opus 21* (New York: Pocket Books, 1949), p. 382.

2. That conviction was later overturned by Utah's Supreme Court. (Staff from Associated Press), "Polygamist Warren Jeffs' Convictions Overturned," *CBS News* (cbsnews.com), July 28, 2010.

3. Stephen Singular, *When Men Become Gods: Mormon Polygamist Warren Jeffs, His Cult of Fear, and the Women Who Fought Back* (New York: St. Martin's, 2009), pp. 293, 297, 301–303; Staff, "Police Raid Compound of Texas Polygamist Sect," *Washington Post*, April 7, 2008; Paul A. Anthony, "More FLDS indictments likely," *GO San Angelo Standard-Times* (gosanangelo.com), July 24, 2008; Leigh Dethman, "Texas Widens FLDS probe," *Deseret News* (deseretnews.com), August 12, 2008; CNN Wire Staff, "Polygamist Leader Warren Jeffs Sentenced to Life in Prison," *CNN Justice* (cnn.com), August 10, 2011.

4. Stephen Singular, *When Men Become Gods*, pp. 3, 7–9.

5. Daniel J. Elazar, "Religion in the Public Square: Jews Among the Nations," *Jewish Political Studies Review* 11:3–4 (Fall 1999).

6. Flora Jessop, "Polygamy 101: A Guide to Helping Practitioners," in *Child Advocacy 101* (Donnalee Sarda, Ed.) (Phoenix: Renaissance Charitable Press, 2008), p. 169; Jonah Mandel, "New Jewish group wants to restore polygamy," *Jerusalem Post*, November 7, 2011.

7. As recently as May 2013, a letter vehemently protesting the innocence of Rabbi Chen, and bearing the names of prominent ultra–Orthodox rabbis, was widely circulated in Israel. (Posted on the *Kikar ha–Shabbath* blog [kikarhashabat.co.il], May 6, 2013 [Hebrew].) Immediately afterward, a counter-claim appeared to the effect that this letter had been written "some years ago, before the [rabbis] were fully aware of the gravity of the crimes committed by Chen," and "apparently reused today without their prior knowledge of permission." (Posted to the blog *Daas Torah—Issues of Jewish Identity* [daattorah.blogspot.com], May 6, 2013.) One would like to believe the latter claim, but none of the rabbis named in the printed letter, as far as I know, has ever publicly disowned it; besides, as noted in Chapter 4, prominent Orthodox rabbis did vigorously support Chen at his trial, and at least one of those—Rabbi Chaim Kanievsky—maintained his position even after a public outcry against it. So the contention that these rabbis now deplore Chen's crimes, but somehow have never managed to say so publicly, notwithstanding their role in championing Chen's cause when it really mattered, is not very credible. Nor is it easy to believe that they only recently learned about the evidence against Chen, which was widely reported while their support for him was at its peak.

8. Aviad Glickman, "Mother Testifies in Abusive 'Rabbi' Case," *Ynet News* (ynetnews.com), April 5, 2009; Aviad Glickman, "4 Elior Chen Followers Guilty of Abuse," *Ynet News* (ynetnew.com), May 12, 2010.

9. Aviad Glickman, "Elior Chen Sentenced to 24 Years in Jail," *Ynet News* (ynet news.com), February 28, 2011.

10. While in prison, Jeffs has accused himself along these lines. (Stephen Singular, *When Men Become Gods*, pp. 242–243.) It is unclear how this message is being received among the faithful. (See Carolyn Jessop [with Laura Palmer], *Escape* [New York: Broadway Books, 2007], pp. 409–410.)

11. Stephen Singular, *When Men Become Gods*, pp. 3–4, 49–50 [emphasis in original].

12. See Nicholas D. Kristof, "Martyrs, Virgins and Grapes," *New York Times*, August 4, 2004; Rebecca Sato, "The Great Koran Controversy: Will Muslim Martyrs Get 72 Raisins Instead of Virgins, and Other Speculations," *Daily Galaxy* (dailygalaxy.com), January 16, 2008. Singular does not adduce any evidence to support his version of Muslim theology.

13. Karen Armstrong, *A History of God: The 4,000-Year Quest of Judaism, Christianity and Islam* (New York: Ballantine Books, 1993), pp. 104–105; Paul Johnson, *A History of the Jews*, pp. 98–99.

14. Stephen Singular, *When Men Become Gods*, p. 31.

15. Carolyn Jessop, *Escape*, p. 283; Stephen Singular, *When Men Become Gods*, p. 23.

16. Stephen Singular, *When Men Become Gods*, p. 26, 27.

17. Avi Shafran, "A Matter of Orthodox Abuse."

18. Herman Wouk, *Inside, Outside* (Boston, Toronto: Little, Brown, 1985), p. 31.

19. Moshe Feinstein, *Ig'roth Mosheh, Orah Hayyim*, Vol. 4, number 115 [my translation].

20. Flora Jessop, "Polygamy 101," pp. 156–157, 161.

21. Even when urinating. According to one of the most influential compendia of Jewish law, such contact may cause "arousal and [sexual] thoughts." (Yisroel M. Kagan, *Mishnah B'rurah*, Vol. 1, 3:14 [26].)

22. See Hella Winston, "So Many Rules, So Little Protection—Sex & Suppression Among Ultra-Orthodox Jews," *Lilith*, Winter 2006/2007; Debra Nussbaum Cohen, "Sexual Dysfunction Is a By-Product of Treating the Body as Treyf," posted to the blog *the sisterhood* on forward.com, May 7, 2010. Cohen reports that many married Orthodox women know nothing at all about their genitalia, let alone about orgasms. Regarding very early marriages (for girls as young as 14) among fringe groups within ultra-Orthodox Judaism, see Hannah Katsman, "Suspected Jewish child abuse cult flees Quebec homes," *Times of Israel* (timesofisrael.com), November 20, 2013.

23. Flora Jessop, "Polygamy 101," pp. 154–155.

24. Carolyn Jessop, *Escape*, p. 217, 216.

25. Stephen Singular, *When Men Become Gods*, pp. 29–30, 33.

26. *Id.*, p. 111.

27. Carolyn Jessop, *Escape*, pp. 80–81.

28. Trial Transcript, Supreme Court of New York, Kings County, September __, 2009, pp. 67–68. I am not identifying the case in order to protect the privacy of those involved.

29. Stephen Singular, *When Men Become Gods*, p. 75.

30. Carolyn Jessop (with Laura Palmer), *Triumph: Life After the Cult—A Survivor's Lessons* (New York: Three Rivers Press, 2010), pp. 240–241.

31. Susan Forrest, "The Comeback of Concubines," *New York Daily News*, December 29, 1996; Amy Neustein and Michael Lesher, "Silence of the Jewish Media," p. 85.

32. Jonah Mandel, "New Jewish Group Wants to Restore Polygamy."

33. Flora Jessop, "Polygamy 101," pp. 153, 167.

34. Anna Sheinman, "She Told the Police She Was Abused. Her Friends Made Her Pay the Price," *Jewish Chronicle* (thejc.com), July 18, 2013.

35. Posted to *Daas Torah—Issues of Jewish Identity* (daattorah.blogspot.com), October 15, 2012.

36. Michael Lesher, "The Fugitive and the Forgotten," p. 159.

37. Michael M. Grynbaum, "Ultra-Orthodox Jews Rally to Discuss Risks of Internet," *New York Times*, May 20, 2012.

38. Sarah Pascal, "Reports from the American Aguda Convention Held Over the Weekend November 24–27."

39. Shmarya Rosenberg, "Leading Monsey Rabbis Visit Convicted Child Rapist Rabbi Yisroel Weingarten, Declare His 'Innocence,'" The declaration of Rabbi Weingarten's "innocence" was a written statement signed by several prominent Orthodox rabbis, personally conveyed to Weingarten by a group of rabbis including Yisroel Simcha Schorr.

40. Edna Adato and Yehuda Shlezinger, "Rabbi Motti Elon Convicted of Indecent Acts Against a Minor," *Israel Hayom* (israelhayom.com), August 8, 2013.

41. Herbert S. Strean, *Psychotherapy with the Orthodox Jew* (Northvale, NJ: J. Aronson, 1994), p. 154.

42. Flora Jessop, "Polygamy 101," p. 157.

43. Herbert S. Strean, *Psychotherapy with the Orthodox Jew*, p. 17 [emphasis added].

44. Francis Steegmuller (translator and editor), *Flaubert in Egypt: A Sensibility on Tour* (Boston: Little, Brown, 1973), pp. 198–199,

quoted in Edward W. Said, *Orientalism* (New York: Vintage Books, 2003), pp. 187–188.

45. Micah Stein, "Rallying Against the Internet," *Tablet* (tabletmag.com), May 17, 2012; Michael J. Salamon, "The Great Internet Asifa," *Times of Israel* (blog) (blogs.timesofisrael.com), May 9, 2012.

46. Micah Stein, "Rallying Against the Internet."

47. Judy Brown, "Ignorance Is Sacred—to Whom," http://dusiznies.blogspot.com/2012/05/author-of-hush-comments-on-asifa.html, May 20, 2012.

48. Eishes Chayil [Judy Brown], "Orthodox Jewish Child Abuse: Shattering a Traumatic Silence," *One Voice* (JFCAdvocacy@yahoogroups.com), August 1, 2011. Brown explained in the column that she had published her book, *Hush*, under a pseudonym "to protect my family and friends from community retribution."

49. Nuchem Rosenberg, posting on his blog (nochemrosenberg.blogspot.com), July 20, 2011.

50. Micah Stein, "Rallying Against the Internet."

51. George Orwell, *1984* (New York: New American Library, 1961) (originally 1949), p. 111.

52. Avi Shafran, "A Matter of Orthodox Abuse."

53. Shelley Jackson et al., "Predicting Abuse-Prone Parental Attitudes and Discipline Practices in a Nationally Representative Sample," *Child Abuse & Neglect*, 1999, (23(1)), pp. 16–17, cited in Janet Heimlich, *Breaking Their Will*, p. 27.

54. B. Hunsberger, "Social-Psychological Causes of Faith; New Findings Offer Compelling Clues," *Free Inquiry*, 1999, (19[3]), pp. 34–38; S.G. McFarland and J.C. Warren, Jr., "Religious Orientations and Selective Exposure Among Fundamentalist Christians," *Journal for the Scientific Study of Religion*, 1992, (31[2]), pp. 169–174.

55. Debra Nussbaum Cohen, "Sexual Dysfunction Is a By-Product of Treating the Body as Treyf."

56. Haim Apelboim, *Shahor 'al gabe labhan*, (Ramat Gan: Moah-Shivuk im Koah, 2000), pp. 91–92 [my translation].

57. I am not aware of any empirical evidence to support this sort of "diverted pressure" argument, though many people tend to

assume its logic. Cf. the observation of Kinsey et al. about the effects on married couples of religious strictures against extra-marital sex:

It is significant to find that frequencies of marital intercourse are lower among religiously active Protestants and higher among inactive Protestants.... The data on the Protestant groups are ... particularly interesting because the restraints which the church has placed upon pre-marital relations, upon extra-marital relations and upon all other types of sexual activity outside of marital intercourse, are justified by the explanation that the whole of one's emotional and overt sexual life should be developed around one lifelong partner in marriage. It would appear, however, that the effect of inhibitions on pre-marital sexual activity are carried over into inhibitions upon coitus with the married partner. Psychologically, this is quite what might have been expected.

The researchers similarly found that nocturnal emissions did not increase in response to abstinence from other forms of "sexual outlet," as had been widely believed by "persons who are interested in moral interpretations in sex education." (Alfred C. Kinsey, Wardell B. Pomeroy and Clyde E. Martin, *Sexual Behavior in the Human Male* (Philadelphia, London: W.B. Saunders, 1948), pp. 569, 571, 476.)

58. E.M. Forster, *Maurice* (New York: New American Library, 1973) (originally 1914), p. 15.

59. Kelli Kennedy, "Eating Disorders a Problem Among Orthodox Jews," *Huffington Post* (huffingtonpost.com), December 10, 2010, cited in Janet Heimlich, *Breaking Their Will*, p. 62.

60. Saint Augustine, *Confessions* (trans. R.S. Pine-Coffin) (London: Penguin Books, 1961), pp. 27–28.

61. Aldous Huxley, *The Devils of Loudun*, pp. 12–13.

62. And not only that case. A former Princeton Seminary professor has suggested that "many religious ideas which children are taught cause them emotional torment and are therefore inherently abusive." (Donald Capps, "Religion and Child Abuse: Perfect Together," *Journal for the Scientific Study of Religion* 31, No. 1 [March 1992], pp. 7–8, in Janet Heimlich, *Breaking Their Will*, p. 25.)

63. Quoted in William James, *The Varieties of Religious Experience* (New York: Mentor Books, 1958), p. 169.

64. Cf. Ben Sorotzkin, "The Denial of History: Clinical Implications of Denying Child Abuse," *Journal of Psychohistory*, Summer 2002: "[W]hile overt abuse is no longer socially acceptable in enlightened societies, the underlying attitudes have not changed nearly as much. Many parents still look at their children as existing for the purpose of fulfilling their own needs, rather than seeing themselves as obligated to help their children fulfill their destiny. The resulting abuse is much less obvious but no less harmful." The observations of Sorotzkin, a psychologist who works primarily with Orthodox Jewish children, are consistently penetrating and humane.

65. Colby Hamilton, "Dozens of Rabbis Come Out Against Councilman Fidler in Senate Special Election," *WNYC* (wnyc.org), February 27, 2012; Colin Campbell, "David Storobin Wades into the Circumcision Debate," *Politicker* (politicker.com), August 23, 2012.

66. For Prager's credentials as a writer on traditional Judaism, see, *e.g.*, Dennis Prager and Joseph Telushkin, *The Nine Questions People Ask about Judaism* (New York: Simon & Schuster, 1975).

67. Dennis Prager, "The Left, Bert and Ernie and Children's Innocence," *Jewish World Review* (jewishworldreview.com), July 2, 2013.

68. Stephen Singular, *When Men Become Gods*, p. 121.

Chapter 12

1. John H. Griffin, *Black Like Me* (Boston: Houghton Mifflin, 1961), p. 94.

2. Isaac Babel, "Guy de Maupassant," taken from *Narrative Magazine* (narrativemagazine.com), Spring 2009.

3. Tara Rosenblum, "Suffering in Silence," *News 12* (New York), September 1, 2010 (available on the website of Survivors for Justice [sfjny.org], under "Audio & Video"). I focus here on the survivor himself, but the comments of Ben Hirsch of Survivors for Justice, also interviewed by Rosenblum, are accurate and incisive.

4. In his Foreword to the 2008 edition of Israel Shahak's *Jewish History, Jewish Religion*, p. xxvii.

5. Quoted in Walter Kaufmann, "Prologue," in Martin Buber, *I and Thou* (trans. Walter Kaufmann) (New York: Simon &

Schuster, 1970), pp. 28–29. The fine translation is Kaufmann's.

6. Walter Kaufmann, *The Faith of a Heretic* (New York: New American Library, 1978).

7. Babylonian Talmud, *B'rakhoth* 6a; *Sanhedrin* 6b.

8. Hannah Arendt, *On Violence* (San Diego, New York, London: Harcourt Brace Jovanovich, 1970), p. 65.

9. "Justice Interrupted," pp. 216–224.

10. See Barbara Blaine, "My Cross to Bear," in *Tempest in the Temple*, pp. 173–174.

11. 18 U.S.C. § 241.

12. 18 U.S.C. § 245(b)(2). These and other legal remedies are discussed more fully in Amy Neustein and Michael Lesher, "Justice Interrupted," pp. 221–224.

13. See *Bounds v. Smith*, 430 U.S. 817, 821, 97 S. Ct. 1491, 1494, 52 L. Ed. 2d 72 (1977); *Bill Johnson's Restaurants, Inc. v. NLRB*, 461 U.S. 731, 741, 103 S. Ct. 2161, 2169, 76 L. Ed. 2d 277 (1983).

14. See Executive Law § 641(2).

15. Menachem Ben-Mordechai, "Rav Soloveitchik's Clear Stand on Homosexuality," *Jewish Press*, May 19, 2013.

16. C.S. Lewis, *The Abolition of Man* (New York: Macmillan, 1955), p. 24.

17. Staff, "Gaza Baby 'Only Knew How to Smile,'" *BBC News*, November 26, 2012.

18. Anshel Pfeffer, "Turning a Child's Tears into War Propaganda," *Ha'aretz*, November 23, 2012.

19. Norman G. Finkelstein and Ruth Bettina Birn, *A Nation on Trial: The Goldhagen Thesis and Historical Truth* (New York: Henry Holt, 1998), p. 82, citing Noam Chomsky, *World Orders Old and New* (New York: Columbia University Press, 1994), p. 142.

20. Revital Hovel, "Livni, Supreme Court President Believed to Be Backing Judge Accused of Child Abuse," *Ha'aretz*, June 19, 2013.

21. Orli Santo, "Satmar Custody Case Hinges on Value of Religious Community," *New York Jewish Week*, June 5, 2013.

22. In that case, too, the young boy complained, among other things, of a nick on his penis that appeared while he was with his father. Yet the boy's court-appointed (Orthodox) lawyer stigmatized the mother because her "unfounded" abuse charges were part of her alleged attempt to "break away from that [Hasidic] community."

23. Ben Caspit, "Kakh q'ras ha-tiq neged

Olmert: Adat ha-sheker sh'risqah ha-praklitot," *Ma'ariv*, July 12, 2012 (Hebrew: summary and excerpts, in English, found in News Nosh: APN's daily news review from Israel (on www.peacenow.org), July 12, 2012). (A new case against Olmert on bribery charges was later prosecuted successfully, without the aid of the Orthodox witness. See Revital Hovel, "Former Israeli Prime Minister Ehud Olmert Sentenced to Six Years in Prison," *Ha-aretz*, May 13, 2014.) On the subject of tacit cover-ups by U.S. news media, it is worth mentioning that although Caspit's article described the "details of this amazing story" as "worthy of a television series or a suspense novel," the allegation that Israeli politics had been dramatically changed via a false charge instigated by an Orthodox rabbi was scarcely noticed in the American press. Imagine the popular reaction here, though, if political consequences of similar scope had been attributed to a false story planted by a Salafi or pro–Iranian Muslim cleric!

24. Isabel Kershner, "Failed Graft Prosecution of Former Israeli Premier Spurs Political Questions," *New York Times*, July 16, 2012. In line with my comment in the previous note, one observes that Kershner's article devotes much space to allegations that the charges against Olmert were "instigated by right-wing political forces in Israel and encouraged by sympathetic American Jews," but only one short line to Caspit's specific claim that the witness's rabbi had "instructed her to lodge a complaint against Olmert," an allegation she attributes entirely to Caspit and never mentions again.

25. Joseph I. Lifshitz, "The Political Theology of Maharam of Rothenburg," *Hebraic Political Studies* (The Shalem Center, Jerusalem), Vol. 1, No. 4 (summer 2006), pp. 411–412.

26. Bette L. Bottoms et al., "In the Name of God: A Profile of Religion-Related Child Abuse," *Journal of Social Issues* 51, No. 2, (1995): pp. 106–107, in Janet Heimlich, *Breaking Their Will*, p. 31.

27. As early as 1946, the United States Strategic Bombing Survey issued an expert government-sponsored report which concluded that "[t]he Hiroshima and Nagasaki atomic bombs did not defeat Japan, nor ... did they persuade Japan to accept unconditional surrender"; that Hirohito and most of the top

Japanese officials "had decided as early as May of 1945 [several months before the bombs were dropped] that the war should be ended even if it meant acceptance of defeat on allied terms"; that the Japanese government was in the process of negotiating a surrender through Russian mediators at the moment the first A-bomb exploded over Hiroshima (a fact well known to the Americans); and that "in all probability prior to 1 November 1945, Japan would have surrendered even if the atomic bombs had not been dropped, even if Russia had not entered the war, and even if no invasion had been planned or contemplated." All of these observations demolished any claim of necessity for the massacre of Japanese civilians which was the clear purpose of the nuclear attacks. (United States Strategic Bombing Survey, *Japan's Struggle to End the War* [Washington, D.C.: 1946], pp. 10–13, quoted at length in *The Truman Administration: A Documentary History* [Barton J. Bernstein and Allen J. Matusow, Eds.] [New York, Evanston and London: Harper Colophon Books, 1966], pp. 43–45.) In light of more recently declassified documents, modern historical research has only strengthened such conclusions. (See Murray Sayle, "Letter from Hiroshima: Did the Bomb End the War?" *New Yorker*, July 31, 1995.)

28. Philip Wylie, *Opus 21*, pp. 325, 331.

29. Arthur Miller, *After the Fall* (New York: Bantam Books, 1964), p. 20.

30. Norman G. Finkelstein, *The Holocaust Industry*, pp. 46, 254.

31. In a preface to Rolf Hochhuth, *The Deputy*.

32. E.H. Ramsden, *'Come, Take This Lute': A Quest for Identities in Italian Renaissance Portraiture* (Bath: Element Books, Ltd., 1983), p. 205.

33. See Neve Gordon, *Israel's Occupation*, pp. 156–157; Noam Chomsky, *Necessary Illusions*, pp. 212–213, quoting Israeli journalist Zvi Gilat: "It is already impossible, it seems, to relate these stories, to ask for an explanation, to seek those responsible. Every other day there is a new story."

34. See Rashid Khalidi, *Palestinian Identity: The Construction of Modern National Consciousness* (New York: Columbia University Press, 2010), pp. 17, 215 n. 22, citing Michael Emery, "New Videotapes Reveal Israeli Cover-up," *Village Voice*, November 13, 1990, pp. 25–29 and Rajah Shehadeh, *The Sealed Room* (London: Quartet, 1992), pp. 24–29.

35. Norman G. Finkelstein, *The Rise and Fall of Palestine: A Personal Account of the Intifada Years* (Minneapolis: University of Minnesota Press, 1996), p. 78.

36. Melissa Healy, "Sexual Violence Common Among Teens. Feeling Responsible Isn't," *Los Angeles Times*, October 7, 2013.

37. Carolyn Jessop, *Triumph*, p. 179.

38. Eliyahu M. Feivelson, "Netzach Yisrael."

39. Albert Schweitzer, *Out of My Life and Thought* (trans. C.T. Campion) (New York: Mentor Books, 1949), pp. 184–185.

40. *Id.*, p. 186.

41. Josh Saul, "Sex Abuse Victim Shamed During Synagogue Prayers," *New York Post*, September 9, 2013. Later, another man who admitted offering the victim a $500,000 bribe not to testify, did receive a four-month jail sentence. (Oren Yaniv, "Man Who Tried to Bribe Sex Assault Victim with $500,000 to Keep Her from Testifying Sentenced to Four-Months in Jail," *New York Daily News*, January 10, 2014.)

42. Leo Strauss, "The New Political Science," in *American Conservative Thought in the Twentieth Century*, p. 427.

Selected Bibliography

Books

Claussen, Dane, Ed. (2002). *Sex, Religion, Media*. Lanham, MD: Rowman & Littlefield.

Eidensohn, Daniel (2010). *Child and Domestic Abuse*, Vol. 1. Jerusalem, New York: Emunah Press.

Eishes Chayil [Brown, Judy] (2010). *Hush*. New York: Walker.

Heimlich, Janet (2011). *Breaking Their Will: Shedding Light on Religious Child Maltreatment*. Amherst, NY: Prometheus Books.

Jessop, Carolyn, with Laura Palmer (2007). *Escape*. New York: Broadway Books.

Hannah, Mo, and Goldstein, Barry, Eds. (2010). *Domestic Violence, Abuse, and Child Custody: Legal Strategies and Policy Issues*. New York: Civic Research Institute.

Kalfoğlu, Ersi, and Faikoglu, Rehat, Eds. (2012). *Sexual Abuse—Breaking the Silence*. Rijeka, Croatia: InTech [open access].

McMackin, Robert, Terence Keane and Paul Kline, Eds. (2009). *Understanding the Impact of Clergy Sexual Abuse*. London, New York: Routledge.

Miller, Alice (1984). *Thou Shalt Not Be Aware: Society's Betrayal of the Child* (trans. Hildegarde and Hunter Hannum). New York: Farrar Straus Giroux.

Neustein, Amy, Ed. (2009). *Tempest in the Temple: Jewish Communities & Child Sex Scandals*. Lebanon, NH: Brandeis University Press, 2009.

Neustein, Amy, and Michael Lesher (2005). *From Madness to Mutiny: Why Mothers Are Running from the Family Courts—and What Can Be Done about It*. Lebanon, NH: Northeastern University Press.

Shaer, Matthew (2011). *Among Righteous Men: A Tale of Vigilantes and Vindication in Hasidic Crown Heights*. Hoboken: John Wiley & Sons.

Sgroi, Suzanne, Ed. (1982). *Handbook of Clinical Intervention in Child Sexual Abuse*. New York: The Free Press.

Singular, Stephen (2009). *When Men Become Gods: Mormon Polygamist Warren Jeffs, His Cult of Fear, and the Women Who Fought Back*. New York: St. Martin's Press.

Winston, Hella (2005). *Unchosen: The Hidden Lives of Hasidic Rebels*. Boston: Beacon Press.

Chapters and Journal Articles

Neustein, Amy, and Michael Lesher (2002). "The Silence of the Jewish Media on Sexual Abuse in the Orthodox Jewish Community," in *Sex, Religion, Media*, pp. 79–87.

Neustein, Amy, and Michael Lesher (2008). "A Single-Case Study of Rabbinic Sexual Abuse in the Orthodox Jewish Community." *Journal of Child Sexual Abuse*, Vol. 17(3–4), pp. 270–289 (reprinted in *Understanding the Impact of Clergy Sexual Abuse*, pp. 74–93).

Neustein, Amy, and Michael Lesher (2012). "What Went Wrong at Ohel Children's Home—and What Can Be Done About Its Failure to Protect Jewish Children from Abuse?" in *Sexual Abuse—Breaking the Silence*, pp. 183–200.

Resnicoff, Steven (2012). "Jewish Law and the Tragedy of Sexual Abuse of Children—the Dilemma within the Orthodox Jewish Community." *Rutgers Journal of Law and Religion*, Vol. 13, No. 2, pp. 10–11.

Ruth, Kibbie (2005). "Risk of Abuse in Faith Communities," in James A. Monteleone and Armand E. Brodeur (Eds.), *Child Maltreatment: A Clinical Guide and Reference* (3rd ed.). St. Louis: G.W. Medical.

Sorotzkin, Ben (2002). "The Denial of History: Clinical Implications of Denying Child Abuse." *Journal of Psychohistory*, Summer 2002.

Periodicals

Eishes Chayil [Brown, Judy] (2011). "Orthodox Jewish Child Abuse: Shattering a Traumatic Silence," *One Voice* (JFCAdvocacy@yahoogroups.com), August 1.

Fifield, Adam, and Michael Lesher (1996). "A Child's at Stake: A Custody Fight Becomes a Political Nightmare," *Village Voice*, October 1, 1996.

Ketcham, Christopher (2013). "The Child-Rape Assembly Line." *Vice Magazine*, November 12.

Kolker, Robert (2006). "On the Rabbi's Knee: Do the Orthodox Jews Have a Catholic-Priest Problem?" *New York Magazine*, May 14.

Lesher, Michael (2011). "Orthodox Cops: Separate and Unequal," *New York Post*, July 31.

Lesher, Michael (1996). "Speaking with Their Silence: A Troubling Child Sex Abuse Case in Orthodox Community Raises the Question, Where Are Our Leaders?" *New York Jewish Week*, November 1.

Matthews, Karen (2002). "Jewish Court Stymies Reports," *Associated Press*, April 16.

Orbach, Michael (2011). "Unmolested," *Tablet*, August 11.

Rivera, Ray, and Sharon Otterman (2012). "For Ultra-Orthodox in Abuse Cases, Prosecutor Has Different Rules," *New York Times*, May 10.

Rosenblatt, Gary (2000). "Stolen Innocence," *New York Jewish Week*, June 23.

Saul, Stephanie (2003). "Tripping Up the Prosecution," *Newsday*, May 28.

Winston, Hella (2009). "A Suspected Pedophile Eludes the System," *New York Jewish Week*, May 6.

Other

Public Summary of the Report of the NCSY Special Commission (2000). Authors: Richard Joel (chair), Fred Ehrman, Allen Fagin, Matthew Maryles, Jules Polonetsky, Susan Schulman, Suzanne Stone, Abraham Twerski, Jacob Yellin. December 21.

Index